Hymns to Śiva

Utpaladeva's Śhivastotrāvalī

WITH ORIGINAL AUDIO

Revealed by

Swami Lakshmanjoo

John Hughes, Editor

Lakshmanjoo Academy

Published by:

Lakshmanjoo Academy

First printing 2014

Printed in the United States of America

For information, address:
Lakshmanjoo Academy
http://www.lakshmanjooacademy.org

ISBN 978-0-9816228-3-5 (paperback)
ISBN 978-0-9816228-6-6 (hardcover)

*This pursuit is dedicated to Swami Lakshmanjoo
to whom we owe everything.*

Contents

Guide to Pronunciation

The following English words exemplify the pronunciation of selected Sanskṛit vowels and consonants. The Romanized Sanskṛit vowel or consonant is first listed and then an English word is given to aid you in its proper pronunciation.

a	as	a in ***A***merica.
ā	as	a in f***a***ther.
i	as	i in f***i***ll, l***i***ly.
ī	as	i in pol***i***ce.
u	as	u in f***u***ll.
ū	as	u in r***u***de.
ṛi	as	ri in mer***ri***ly.
ṛī	as	ri in ma***ri***ne.
e	as	e in pr***e***y.
ai	as	ai in ***ai***sle.
o	as	o in st***o***ne.
au	as	ou in h***ou***se
ś	as	s in ***s***ure.
ṣ	as	sh in ***sh***un, bu***sh***
s	as	s in ***s***aint, ***s***un

Introduction

'All glory be to Thee, O Lord Śiva, who art the only festival in my life!'[1]

"I am mad with the love of Lord Shiva!" With these words, the Kashmiri saint, philosopher and scholar, Swami Lakshmanjoo, greeted two seekers visiting his ashram in the spring of 1988. The seeds of Swami Lakshmanjoo's divine madness can be found many years earlier in the enchanting verses of the *Śivastotrāvalī* (Hymns of Devotion and Praise to Lord Śiva) of Utpaladeva, the medieval Shaiva master and exponent of the Pratyabhijna school of Kashmir Shaivism.

One can just imagine the scene. It is the peaceful moments before dawn, before the sun had shown its face above the mountains to the east of Dal Lake,[2] that most beautiful of lakes, with its peaceful waters and seemingly endless beds of lotus flowers opening for the day. There the young Lakshmana[3] heard his father singing sacred verses during his early morning devotion. The young teen aged boy was enchanted by what he heard and implored his father to explain to him the meaning of those wonderful verses. Where did those beautiful verses come from and what was their meaning?

His father told him the hymns came from a text known as the *Śivastotrāvalī* but pleaded ignorance as to their meaning. He said that he only knew how to chant them and had never learned their meaning. Hearing this the young Lakshmana implored his

1 *Śivastotrāvalī* 14.28.

2 The lake in Srinagar, Kashmir, known as "The Jewel in the Crown of Kashmir" and "Srinagar's Jewel."

3 Swami Lakshmanjoo's name as a boy, chosen for him by Swami Ram with the words: "I am Ram; let him be Lakshmana!"

father to find someone to teach him so he could read these verses and understand their meaning.

At that very moment the search to find the young Lakshmana's spiritual master began and it began at Swami Ram's ashram.

Swami Ram was known to have been a highly accomplished and powerful master of the tradition of Kashmir Shaivism. He had been the family priest of Lakshmana's family but by the time the seeds of the *Śivastotrāvalī* had been planted in Lakshmana's heart and the search for his teacher began he had left this world. Fortunately Swami Ram had left many advanced and worthy disciples from which to choose to school the young seeker in the Shaiva texts. So, when a relative of the family was asked to help in finding a proper teacher he recommended various highly regarded scholarly disciples of Swami Ram. Others, however, did not agree with these recommendations and suggested instead Swami Ram's chief disciple, Swami Mahatabkak, who, although not known as a scholar, was nevertheless very highly regarded for his inner spiritual attainment.[4] Lakshmana indicated his approval of this recommendation, and so enquiries were made as to whether Swami Mahatabkak would accept the boy as his student. When he indicated his agreement arrangements were made for Lakshmana to begin his studies.

With auspicious offerings carefully prepared by his mother, Srimati Arnamali, the young Lakshmana made his way early one morning to Ram Ashram,[5] where, at the feet of Swami Mahatabkak, he began his formal spiritual education in the unbroken oral tradition of Kashmir Shaivism.

And so, in this way, with hearing those magical early morning

---

4 Those searching were apparently oblivious to the fact that Swami Ram had already entrusted the tutelage of the young Lakshmana to Swami Mahatabkak when the boy was only seven years old.

5 The Shri Ram Trika Shaiva Ashram, was gifted to Swami Ram by Swami Lakshmanjoo's father in about 1870. It was here that, over a period of twenty-two years, Swami Ram performed his most intense *sādhana*. The ashram is a mere stone's throw away from Swami Lakshmanjoo's ancestral residence. To this very day, the ashram resounds with the recitation of Shaiva scriptures and the chanting of devotional hymns by devotees.

sounds of Swami Lakshmanjoo's father singing those enchanting verses of Utpaladeva's *Śivastotrāvalī* on the shore of Dal Lake, began the years of spiritual study and discipline of the young boy who was to become one of the preeminent masters of the same Kashmir Shaiva tradition to which Utpaladeva himself had belonged.

Utpaladeva and the *Śivastotrāvalī*

It was on those same waters of Dal Lake that the *Śivastotrāvalī* itself was born. It is said that Utpaladeva would ask his disciples to row him out to the center of the lake in a *shikhara*[6] and once there, inspired no doubt by the wondrous surroundings, would extemporaneously compose those sublime hymns of devotion and praise to Lord Siva. His disciples would write as their master sang ecstatically . . . and a scripture was born that today we know as the *Śivastotrāvalī*![7]. Swami Lakshmanjoo tells us, "I have heard it from my masters that he was situated in a boat on Dal Lake, roaming here and there singing. He was resting; he could not sit because he was mad, and this madness was perfect madness!"[8]

Still today, although its hymns were composed more than a thousand years ago, the *Śivastotrāvalī* is recited daily in Kashmiri Pandit households and by Shaiva devotees worldwide. It has even become the subject of formal study in universities around the world and is considered the greatest example of Kashmiri Shaiva devotional poetry.

Throughout his life, Swami Lakshmanjoo held Utpaladeva, and especially his *Śivastotrāvalī*, in the very highest regard. It is now exactly 50 years since Swami Lakshmanjoo first published in 1964 a word-by-word Hindi translation of the *Śivastotrāvalī*,

---

6 A type of boat unique to Kashmir that is used to navigate the waters of the many lakes in the region, now much favored by tourists visiting Srinagar.

7 Only chapters 13, 14 and 15 were composed as chapters and given their names by Utpaladeva himself. The remaining verses were collated, divided into chapters, and named by his disciples.

8 From the introduction to *Śivastotrāvalī* 13.

along with Kṣemarāja's[9] brief Sanskrit commentary.[10] In subsequent years, Swami Lakshmanjoo recorded a translation of the *Śivastotrāvalī* in the Kashmiri language. Though incomplete, these recordings were made available to the public and have since become very dear to the hearts of his Kashmiri devotees.[11]

Although he was a master of even the most abstruse elements of Kashmir Shaivite philosophy, with an almost photographic memory of the ancient texts and a razor-sharp intellect to interpret their hidden meanings, Swami Lakshmanjoo had a very special place in his heart for the *Śivastotrāvalī*. From the early days, whenever devotees would recite verses from the *Śivastotrāvalī*, or whenever he himself sang those verses or commented upon them, his eyes would well up with tears and his voice would become choked with devotion, unable for the moment to even speak. One can clearly hear examples of this in the recording that accompanies this book.

When commenting on the text, those listening would often ask questions about Shaiva philosophy. Swami Lakshmanjoo would swiftly reply, "Don't always talk of Shaivism. This is a devotional text! In devotion you find two things: the master high, and the devotee in the lower level. The devotee has to weep, the devotee has to cry. When the crying stops, that is Shaivism. We have nothing to do with that here! We want to perceive the master at the stage of his being a master, and we have to imagine ourselves as his slaves."[12]

Clearly Swami Lakshmanjoo had a very profound connection with this particular text and its author, so much so that, once, when questioned about an interpretation that did not coincide

9 The principal disciple of Abhinavagupta, Kṣemarāja, wrote what is considered to be the most important commentary on the *Śivastotrāvalī*. Kṣemarāja was also the author of the *Pratyabhijñā Hṛdāyam*, a collection of twenty sutras containing the essence of the Pratyabhijñā philosophy.

10 *The Śivastotrāvalī of Utpaladevāchārya with the Sanskrit commentary of Kṣemarāja*, edited with Hindi commentary by Rājānaka Lakṣmaṇa (Swami Lakshmanjoo), (Chowkhamba Sanskrit Series 15, Varanasi, 1964).

11 *Shri Utpaladeva's Shivastotravali*, audio recording of selected verses in Kashmiri (Ishwar Ashram Trust, New Delhi, 2009).

12 *Śivastotrāvalī* 13.14, commentary.

with that of Kṣemarāja, he shyly replied, "I have got entry in the heart of Utpaladeva."[13]

Though Swami Lakshmanjoo revered the entire text of the *Śivastotrāvalī*, he had certain hymns that were his special favorites. These are to be found in the thirteenth chapter known as the *Saṁgrahastotra*:[14]

saṁgraheṇa sukhaduḥkhalakṣaṇaṁ
māṁ prati sthitamidaṁ śṛiṇu prabho /
saukhyameṣa bhavatā samāgamaḥ
svāminā virahaḥ eva duḥkhitā / /[15]

O Lord, please listen to the real description of my pleasure and my pain: union with Your nature is my pleasure, and separation from You, my Master, is the cause of my pain.

dāsadhāmni viniyojito'pyahaṁ
svecchayaiva parameśvara tvayā /
darśanena na kimasmi pātritaḥ
pādasaṁvāhanakarmaṇāpi vā / /[16]

O supreme Lord, although it is by Your will that I have been placed in the position of being Your slave, why, even then, have I not been qualified to have Your audience, Your gaze, or even the act of touching Your feet?

śaktipātasamaye vicāraṇaṁ
prāptamīśa na karoṣi karhicit /
adya māṁ prati kiṁāgataṁ yataḥ
svaprakāśanavidhau vilambase / /[17]

O independent Lord, at the time of showering Your grace on me, You should have considered whether I was

13 *Śivastotrāvalī* 13.19, commentary.

14 *Saṁgrahastotra* means, "That hymn that which is the essence of what is to be known."

15 *Śivastotrāvalī* 13.1.

16 *Śivastotrāvalī* 13.10.

17 *Śivastotrāvalī* 13.11.

> qualified for this grace. But You never think in this way. Having received this grace, look at my plight now that You delay in revealing Your nature!

For Swami Lakshmanjoo, as for Utpaladeva, *bhakti*, devotion, or "passion for God consciousness" was everything.[18]

Utpaladeva himself sang in the *Śivastotrāvalī*:

> On this path of Lord Śiva, *śivamārga*, which is away from all delusions, *amāye*, which is absolutely pure and straight, no *yoga*, no penance, and no mode of worship is needed. The only need here is devotion, pure devotion. If they are really attached to You, they will find You. If they are not attached, they may perform *yoga*, they may perform penance, and they may perform *pūjā*, [yet still] they cannot find You. Devotion, *bhakti,* is the only means to find Your nature![19]

And:

> O Lord, You are the nature of everyone and *sarvaś-cātmani rāgavān*, everyone is attached to his own nature, to his own self. So, that self is, in the real sense, Your nature. Therefore, loving You is automatically achieved by everyone because everyone loves themselves. So, Thy devotion is acquired and achieved by everyone. But there is only one difference: *jānañjayejjanaḥ*, that [person] who knows this secret reality, he is glorified, others are not.[20]

Another:

> In this universe there is one shining creeper–that is the creeper of Your devotion. When that creeper of Your devotion has bloomed perfectly, then it bears all kinds of fruits, right from the great yogic powers up to the great power of

18 The word *bhakti*, devotion, appears over 400 times in the hymns of the *Śivastotrāvalī*.

19 *Śivastotrāvalī* 1.7.

20 *Śivastotrāvalī* 1.18

being liberated from repeated births and deaths that is *mokṣa,* liberation.[21]

Finally:

I want to become mad by the intensity of Thy devotion. I want that madness! I don't want to become detached or to be the governor of this universe. I don't want the desire for liberation. I don't want to become Your worshipper. I want to get that madness. I want to be mad by the intensity of my love for You.[22]

Pratyabhijñā

Yet, the sublime hymns of the *Śivastotrāvalī* are not just the out-pourings of an ardent Śiva-*bhakta*, of a poetically-inspired devotee. Even independently of the great fame of his *Śivastotrāvalī*, Utpaladeva is known as one of the greatest exponents of the Pratyabhijñā school of Kashmir Shaivism.

The Pratyabhijñā school flourished at the start of this present age known as Kali Yuga. As time passed, however, it became veiled due to misunderstanding. It was not until the end of the eighth century C.E. that the great Kashmir Shaiva master Somānanda reintroduced the Pratyabhijñā system in Kashmir.[23] Utpaladeva was the principle disciple of that same master, Somānanda. Utpaladeva's disciple, Lakshmanagupta, was, in turn, the master, in the Pratyabhijñā system, of the preeminent master of the Kashmir Shaiva tradition, Abhinavagupta.

Concerning the Pratyabhijñā system Swami Lakshmanjoo tells us, "The word 'Pratyabhijñā' means 'to spontaneously once again recognize and realize your Self. Here, you have only to

---

21 *Śivastotrāvalī* 1.25.

22 *Śivastotrāvalī* 15.4.

23 See *Kashmir Shaivism, The Secret Supreme*, The Schools of Kashmir Shaivism, 19.129-135.

realize; you do not have to practice. There are no *upāyas*[24] (means) in the Pratyabhijñā system. You must simply recognize who you are."

"Wherever you are–whether you are at the level of supreme Being, at the level of *yoga*, or at the level which is disgusting–you can recognize your own nature then and there, without moving anywhere or doing anything."[25]

So astute was Utpaladeva's understanding of the Pratyabhijñā system that he wrote two brief commentaries on *Śivadṛṣṭi*, and later systematized the teachings under the name "Pratyābhijnā" or "Recognition", enticing all with a "new and easy path."[26] Utpaladeva's own *Iśvarapratyabhijñā Kārikā* is considered the most important text on the theory of Pratyabhijñā, but, so lofty were its concepts, that Utpaladeva himself felt the need to write two more commentaries on his own *Kārikā*.[27]

Two generations later, Abhinavagupta sat at the feet of Utpaladeva's disciple, Lakṣmanagupta, to study Pratyabhijñā philosophy. Abhinavagupta himself subsequently wrote two commentaries on Utpaladeva's teachings: the *Iśvarapratyabhijñā Vimarśinī* and the *Iśvarapratyabhijñā Vivṛti Vimarśinī*. At the end of the latter, Abhinavagupta summarized the importance of this system in the following words:

> It may be possible for a person to dive deep into something much more fearful than the upsurging waters of a highly ruffled ocean, made dreadful by the flames of its interior fire named *Vāḍavānala*, kindled immensely by forceful gales of stormy winds at the time of the cosmic dissolution of all solid existence, but it is not at all possible for a thinker to fathom the depths of the philosophy expressed in the *Iśvarapratya-*

---

24 See *Kashmir Shaivism, The Secret Supreme,* The Explanation of the Means (*Upāyas*), 5.33-40.

25 See *Kashmir Shaivism, The Secret Supreme,* 19.130-131.

26 So named by Utpaladeva himself; also referred to as such by Abhinavagupta in his later commentary of the *Iśvarapratyabhijñā*.

27 *Iśvarapratyabhijñā Vṛtti*, a brief commentary on the *Kārikā*, *Iśvarapratyabhijñā Ṭīkā,* a more detailed commentary, which has unfortunately been lost.

> *bhijñā*, which none other than Siva Himself is capable of doing.[28]

In his writings, Abhinavagupta demonstrated that this "new and easy path" of Pratyabhijñā was, in fact, already contained in the ancient *śāstras* but had been hidden. Acknowledging Utpaladeva's genius in revealing these "Tantric secrets," Abhinavagupta again referred to his teachings in his introductory verses to the *Parātrīśikā Laghvṛtti*.

> *sadāgamapravāheṣu bahūdhā vyākṛitaṁ trikam /*
> *śrīmadutpaladevīyaṁ tantrasāraṁ tu varṇyate / /*[29]

> In the flow of the tantras, I have already explained the threefold science of Shaivism in various ways, but here *utpaladevīyam tantrasāram nirūpyate*, I am explaining the essence of all the tantras from Utpaladeva's point of view.

Throughout the *Śivastotrāvalī*, Utpaladeva himself continually emphasizes that the objective world in which we live, with all its highs and lows, is not an obstacle to the realization of God. After all, he says, it is God who has expanded His nature and become the objective world. Hence, We are told in the first verse of the *Śivadṛṣṭi* that even obstacles are "none other than Śiva!"

Utpaladeva tells us again and again that for the true devotee, the trials and tribulations of everyday life can remain unresolved. There is only one thing to be resolved, and that is the revealing of the Lord's nature: "If you reveal Your nature to me," he says, "all those miserable states will vanish by themselves, automatically!"[30]

In reality, for Utpaladeva, there exists only one obstacle to this realization, and that is doubt arising from the impurity of the mind. But doubt of what? The doubt that everything in existence is God:

---

28 *History of Kashmir Shaivism*, Dr. B.N. Pandit (Utpala Publications, Srinagar, Kashmir, 1990).

29 *Parātriśikā Laghuvṛtti with the commentary of Abhinavagupta*, translation and commentary by Swami Lakshmanjoo (original audio recording, USF archives, Los Angeles, 1982), verse 2.

30 *Śivastotrāvalī* 3.16.

kharaniṣedhakhadāmṛtapūra-
occhalitadhautavikalpamalasya me /

dalitadurjayasaṁśayavairiṇa-
stvadavalokanamastu nirantaram[31] / /

There is one desire in me, and that desire is that I would like to clean the impurity of my mind. That impurity, that being away from You, is a terrifying abyss! And, that abyss cannot be filled with ordinary earth; it must be filled with the nectar of God Consciousness. With that flood of the nectar of God consciousness, I would wash the impurity of my mind, and I would be freed from the enemy of doubt, the doubting of Your existence in this universe.

Because we doubt, we always doubt the existence of God consciousness. We say that God exists only in Benares, in Haridwar; God is not here, He is absent here. And if that doubt would vanish, that doubt would be removed from me, then I would perceive You always, in continuity, everywhere, not only in a Varanasi temple!

Abhinavagupta echoes the same understanding in his greatest work, *Tantrāloka*, when, referring to a verse from *Śivastotrāvalī*, he says:

śaṅkayā jāyate glāniḥ śaṅkayā vighnabhājanam /
uvācotpaladevaśca śrīmānasmadgurorguruḥ /
sarvāśaṅkāśaniṁ mārgaṁ numo māheśvaraṁ stuti[32] / /

One's spirituality is destroyed by doubts, and one becomes the victim of obstacles, *śaṅkayā vighna bhājanam*. If you have doubts, you'll become the victim of obstacles, and your

---

31 From the commentary on *Śivastotrāvalī* 18.19.

32 Here the KSTS has *tviti* whereas Swami recites *stuti* (see *Tantrāloka of Abhinavagupta* (*chapters 1 to 18*), translation and commentary by Swami Lakshmanjoo (original audio recording, USF archives, Los Angeles, 1972-1981), 12.24-25.

> spiritual life is altogether destroyed. Our great-grandmaster Utpaladeva has also explained the same thing in his Utpalastotrāvalī.
>
> *sarvāśaṅkāśaniṁ sarvālakṣmīkālānalaṁ tathā /*
> *sarvāmaṅgalyakalpāntaṁ mārgaṁ māheśvaraṁ namaḥ //*[33]
>
> I bow to the path through which Lord Śiva is achieved, sarvā śaṅkāśaniṁ, which is a thunderbolt to destroy all doubts, and where *sarvā alakṣī kālānalaṁ*, all these misfortunes are fired to ashes. So, all doubts are gone, and all misfortunes are over, and *sarvā amaṅgalya kalpāntam*; *amaṅgala*, the absence of joy, is destroyed. I bow to that path of Lord Śiva.

For Utpaladeva in the *Śivastotrāvalī*, that path and its goal are always only one, pure devotion. Thus, in the fifteenth hymn, he concludes:

> In this world, you will find books which will wash away all your three *malas* (impurities)[34]. You will find persons who have mastered all the schools of thought, and you will also find yogis, but peaceful persons you will find only in those who are devoted to You. Those philosophers and all those others are not peaceful. In reality it is all nonsense! *Tvad bhaktāḥ eva kevalā tattvataḥ,* only Your devotees are *svasthā*, peacefully situated, and peacefully appeased.[35]

Conclusion

In this way, using the thread of the highest Pratyabhijñā philosophy, Utpaladeva has woven into the fabric of the *Śivastotrāvalī* the most profound concepts of Pratyābhijña, magically clothing these lofty concepts in the simplest garment of pure devotion.

---

33 *Śivastotrāvalī* 2.28.

34 *Āṇava mala*, *māyīya mala*, and *kārma mala* (see appendix 15, and also: *Kashmir Shaivism, The Secret Supreme* 7.47-49).

35 *Śivastotrāvalī* 15.1.

Utpaladeva makes absolutely clear from the very outset that for the sincere seeker of liberation devotion for God, and devotion alone, is the one indispensable tool.

Utpaladeva has himself composed what would be the perfect epitaph to his life and work when, at the end of the fourteenth chapter, he sings:

I, Utpala, am constantly swinging
in that intoxication of my devotion to Thee!
All glory be to Thee, O Lord Śiva,
who art the only festival in my life!
Glory be the Thee, glory be to Thee,
endless glory be to Thee![36]

36 From *Śivastotrāvalī* 14.23-24.

Acknowledgements

First of all I would like to express my appreciation to those who made the success of this project possible, our team of editors, my son Viresh, my wife Denise and George Barselaar, who meticulously scoured the transcript making additions and corrections and incorporating numerous annotations quoting Swamiji from various sources. I would like to thank Stephen Benson who carefully edited the original transcript and added invaluable suggestions for the audio editing. Also, Michael Van Winkle our audio engineer who employed a number of tricks and techniques to polish, clarify, and enhance the original audio. I am particularly grateful to Claudia Dose for her tireless work in typing the Sanskrit and romanized text, and for the final formatting of the entire text of this book. I would like to thank Mukti Parupudi for preparing the Index for this publication. I would also like to thank my daughter, Shanna for keeping us all on track in meeting the deadlines for this work. They all proved to be invaluable in the preparation of these audios and the accompanying annotated transcript of this *Śivastotrāvalī*.

I would also like to thank Dr. Yajneshwar Shastri and his wife Dr. Sunanda Shastri, both renowned Sanskrit scholars, for their invaluable help in checking the Sanskrit in this document. And finally, my special thanks to Jody Weiss for her inspiration in reconfirming the urgent need to make Swamiji's teachings of Kashmir Shaivism available to all sincere aspirants as soon as possible.

Swami Lakshmanjoo

Swami Lakshmanjoo

The Author

Swami Lakshmanjoo was born in Srinagar, Kashmir on May 9, 1907. He was the most recent and the greatest of the saints and masters of the tradition of Kashmir Shaivism. Having a deep understanding of the philosophy and practices of Kashmir Shaivism, he was like a splendid and shining rare jewel. From early childhood he spent his life studying and practicing the teachings of this unique sacred tradition. Because of his intellectual power and strength of awareness, he realized both spiritually and intellectually the reality of its thought.

Being born with a photographic memory, learning was always easy for him. In addition to complete knowledge of Kashmir Shaivism, he had a vast knowledge of the traditional religious and philosophical schools and texts of India. When translating or teaching he would freely draw on other texts to clarify, expand, and substantiate his teaching. He could recall an entire text by simply remembering the first few words of a verse.

In time, his reputation as a learned philosopher and spiritual adept spread. Spiritual leaders and scholars journeyed from all over the world to receive his blessings and to ask him questions about various aspects of Kashmir Shaiva philosophy. He gained renown as a devotee of Lord Shiva and as a master of the non-dual tradition of Kashmir Shaivism.

Throughout his life, Swamiji taught his disciples and devotees the ways of devotion and awareness. He shunned fame and recognition and did not seek his own glory. He knew Kashmir

Shaivism was the most precious jewel and that, by God's grace, those who desired to understand would be attracted to its teachings. His earnest wish was for Kashmir Shaivism to be preserved and made available to all humankind.

In 1990, in Nepal, during his explanation of the sixth chapter of the Bhagavad Gītā, Swamiji gave a rare glimpse into the fullness and glory of his own experience:

> "I was smoothly going on with my practice and abruptly *śaktipāta* [grace] came and threw all its force in me. It was *tīvra tīvra* (super-supreme) *śaktipāta*. And then it happened and I was newborn. I became so great. I don't mean to boast but this is what happened. I was newly reborn. And, because I had to become Bhairava, I had to experience all of the states of yoga. And it happened, everything happened. I had all experiences; and *cidānanda* also, *jagadānanda*[37] also. Everything happened. You can't imagine the ways of *śaktipāta*.[38]"

On the 27th of September 1991, Swami Lakshmanjoo left his physical body and attained the great liberation.

---

37 *Cidānanda* and *jagadānanda* are the final stages of the seven states of *tūrya*, also known as the seven states of *ānanda* (bliss).
See *Kashmir Shaivism, The Secret Supreme*, 16.113-115.
See also appendix 16.
38 Bhagavad Gītā in the Light Of Kashmir Śhaivism DVD 6.3 (42:01)

Chapter One
The Ecstasy of Devotion
Bhaktivilāsākhyaṁ stotram

SWAMIJI: You already know that this *Śivastotrāvalī* is the collection of songs by Utpaladevācārya, and it is commentated upon by Abhinavagupta's disciple, Kṣemarāja, in Sanskrit, and I have translated it into Hindi.[1]

Utpaladeva was the great grand-guru of Abhinavagupta.[2] He was not only a Shaivite but also he had mystical experience.[3] He became mad after God, sometimes. Sometimes he was reserved because of being a Shaivite but sometimes he turned mad because of being too much attached to Lord Śiva.

And these songs he has sung in a boat in Kashmir. He was carried by his disciples and they were jotting down all that he sung. And these *stotras* (verses) were not [compiled] by Utpaladeva himself. The [compilation] of these *stotras* was done by some other devotee of Utpaladeva. He had sung [them] without any [particular order or division], just in chain form, and those [*stotras*] were [compiled] afterwards by some of his devotees.[4]

Now, this is the first *stotra*, first *śloka*.

---

1 See appendix 1.

2 Utpaladeva's disciple, Lakṣmaṇagupta, was Abhinavagupta's master in the Pratyabhijñā system. Utpaladeva was considered to be the leading exponent of this system, which derived it name from his *Iśvarapratyabhijñākārikā*, considered to be the most important philosophical treatise of this school. Abhinavagupta later wrote two commentaries on Utpaladeva's *Iśvarapratyabhijñākārikā*. [*Editor's note*].

3 On account of Utpaladeva's complete intellectual understanding of Shaivite philosophy, Swamiji nominates him as a "Shaivite". According to Kashmir Shaivism, intellectual knowledge (*bauddha jñāna*) and spiritual knowledge (*pauruṣa jñāna*), viz., "mystical experience", are both requisites for liberation (*mokṣa*). [*Editor's note*]

4 Swamiji said that with the exception of chapters thirteen, fourteen, and fifteen, the devotees of Utpaladeva arranged the verses into chapters and gave these chapters their respective titles.

Chapter 1 (2:09)

न ध्यायतो न जपतः स्वाद्यस्याविधिपूर्वकम् ।
एवमेव शिवाभासस्तं नुमो भक्तिशालिनम् ॥१॥

na dhyāyato na japataḥ svādyasyāvidhipūrvakam /
evameva śivābhāsastaṁ numo bhaktiśālinam //1//

I bow to that devotee who is glorified with the devotion of Lord Śiva and to whom the appearance of Lord Śiva takes place without conducting meditation or recitation of any kind. He does not recite a *mantra* for Lord Śiva and he does not meditate, but even without meditation, without recitation, he attains the state where he feels the oneness of Lord Śiva. I bow to that devotee.

I don't bow to that devotee who meditates and then achieves or who recites and then achieves. That devotee is far away from that devotee who achieves Lord Śiva without doing anything.

Chapter 1 (3:22)

आत्मा मम भवद्भक्तिसुधापानयुवाऽपि सन् ।
लोकयात्रारजोरागात्पलितैरिव धूसरः ॥२॥

ātmā mama bhavadbhaktisudhāpānayuvā'pi san /
lokayātrārajorāgātpalitairiva dhūsaraḥ //2//

In fact, I am always young by adopting the, by tasting the, nectar of Thy devotion. I am always young. But still, in this worldly field, I feel that I am old enough, but internally I am young. Externally, I appear to be old because of too much exertion in these worldly activities, but I am always young because of tasting the nectar of Thy devotion.

Third [*stotra*]:

Chapter 1 (4:28)

लब्धत्वत्संपदां भक्तिमतां त्वत्पुरवासिनाम् ।
सञ्चारो लोकमार्गेऽपि स्यात्तयैव विजृम्भया ॥३॥

labdhatvatsaṁpadāṁ bhaktimatāṁ tvatpuravāsinām /
sañcāro lokamārge'pi syāttayaiva vijṛmbhayā //3//

Although I am old because of being in contact with worldly people and worldly activities–I feel that I am old, I am exhausted–but internally, *labdha tvat saṁpadām*, those who have achieved the wealth of Your devotion[5], and those who are truly devoted to You, and those who are residing in Thine kingdom, for them, activities in these worldly matters become one with that divinity of God consciousness.

Chapter 1 (5:37)

साक्षाद्भवन्मये नाथ
सर्वस्मिन् भुवनान्तरे ।
किं न भक्तिमतां क्षेत्रं
मन्त्रः क्वैषां न सिद्ध्यति ॥४॥

sākṣādbhavanmaye nātha
sarvasmin bhuvanāntare /
kiṁ na bhaktimatāṁ kṣetraṁ
mantraḥ kvaiṣāṁ na siddhyati //4//

Nātha, O Lord, those people for whom this whole universe has become one with Your God consciousness and one with Your presence, for those people who feel Thy presence in each and every part and parcel of this worldly field, those are really Thy devotees.

For them, where is not a shrine? A shrine is also a shrine for them but a bathroom is also a divine shrine for them, a muddy place is also a shrine for them, and a clean place is also a shrine for them. And everywhere there is the possibility to attain God consciousness, for them. They can attain God consciousness in this struggling state of the universe, not only in a temple. In a temple, they attain God consciousness, but in outward worldly

5 Throughout the text, Swamiji often says "Your devotion", which means "devotion to/for You", i.e., devotion to/for God. [*Editor's note*]

states also, they attain God consciousness. For them, there is no difference.

Next:

Chapter 1 (7:16)

जयन्ति भक्तिपीयूषरसासववरोन्मदाः ।
अद्वितीया अपि सदा त्वद्द्वितीया अपि प्रभो ॥५॥

jayanti bhaktipīyūṣarasāsavavaronmadāḥ /
advitīyā api sadā tvaddvitīyā api prabho //5//

Prabho, O Master, *bhaktipīyūṣa rasāsavavaronmadāḥ*, those persons who have become mad by taking the 'nectarized' liquor of Thy devotion . . .

You know the "nectarized liquor of Thy devotion"? It is liquor because it maddens you, but it is 'nectarized' liquor [because] it is filled with the nectar of God consciousness–that liquor.

. . . by tasting that liquor, those devotees are always glorified, they are always divine. Where lies the madness in them? *Advitīyā api sadā*, the madness is . . . in this respect, they are "mad" because *advitīyā*, they always boast that they are the only persons glorified in this universe and they always weep for attaining the nearness of their Master. So, this is madness. Sometimes they say, "I am divine", sometimes they say, "I am nothing". So, this madness they possess. And those mad devotees of Thee are always glorified.

Next:

Chapter 1 (8:59)

अनन्तानन्दसिन्धोस्ते नाथ तत्त्वं विदन्ति ते ।
तादृशा एव ये सान्द्रभक्त्यानन्दरसाप्लुताः ॥६॥

anantānandasindhoste nātha tattvaṁ vidanti te /
tādṛśā eva ye sāndrabhaktyānandarasāplutāḥ //6//

Nātha, O Master, only those people experience the reality of Thy ocean of God consciousness. Those people only experience the reality, experience the position or state, the real state of Thy God consciousness. Those people only, they experience. Who?

Tādṛśā eva ye sāndrabhaktyānandarasāplutāḥ, who are really soaked in the nectar of that universal God consciousness, in the nectar of the ocean of universal God consciousness–those who are soaked in that.

JOHN: What is this "nectar"?

SWAMIJI: *Amṛta* is *ānanda* (bliss), the blissful state of God consciousness. And that blissful state of God consciousness is really an ocean, and in That ocean, those people who are soaked properly, only they can experience the reality of That ocean. Those who are roaming on the shore of That ocean, they don't know the depth and the reality of That ocean. They only experience It superficially.

Next:

Chapter 1 (10:35)

त्वमेवात्मेश सर्वस्य सर्वश्चात्मनि रागवान् ।
इति स्वभावसिद्धां त्वद्भक्तिं जानञ्जयेज्जनः ॥७॥

tvamevātmeśa sarvasya sarvaścātmani rāgavān /
iti svabhāvasiddhāṁ tvadbhaktiṁ jānañjayejjanaḥ //7//

O Lord, You are the nature of everybody. In fact, You are the nature of everybody.

Sarvaścātmani rāgavān. Everybody is attached to his own nature, to his own self.

[For example], you like your self, you want to live, you don't want to be worried in any way, and everybody does the same [thing], individually.

JOHN: Loves himself?

SWAMIJI: Yes.

And that "himself" is, in the real sense, Your nature.

JOHN: God's nature.

SWAMIJI: God's nature.

So, loving You is automatically achieved by everybody. Everybody loves You because they love themselves, so they love You. So, Thy devotion is acquired and achieved by everybody, every individual. But there is only one difference: *jānañjayejjanaḥ*, that [person] who knows this secret reality, he is glorified, others are not.

Chapter 1 (12:06)

नाथ वेद्यक्षये केन न दृश्योऽस्येककः स्थितः ।
वेद्यवेदकसंक्षोभेऽप्यसि भक्तैः सुदर्शनः ॥८॥

nātha vedyakṣaye kena na dṛśyo'syekakaḥ sthitaḥ /
vedyavedakasaṁkṣobhe'pyasi bhaktaiḥ sudarśanaḥ //8//

O my Master, it is a fact that You are achieved when [one] shuns all worldly activities. After shunning each and every worldly activity, You are achieved. This is a fact. You are not achieved till then, unless you shun all of these outward, worldly matters. But, when by shunning these outward worldly matters You are achieved, what greatness is there in achieving [You in] this way? There is no greatness in achieving this way, achieving You this way.

Greatness lies, *vedya* [*vedaka saṁkṣobhe*], in those devotees who achieve You, who experience You, in the very action of the universe. In the very activities of daily life, those who experience You, they really know and experience You in the real sense. *Vedya vedaka saṁkṣobhe*, in the agitation of *vedya* and *vedaka*, in the objective and the subjective world, they experience the nature of God consciousness; and very easily, without adopting any means (*upāyas*). To achieve You after the adoption of means, and *sādhanā*, and meditation, and *yoga*, and everything, it is all humbug. Those who achieve You in the very action of the universe while doing all other works, they achieve You, and very easily, without doing anything.

JOHN: Is this *śāmbhavopāya*?

SWAMIJI: Yes.[6]

Chapter 1 (14:19)

अनन्तानन्दसरसी देवी प्रियतमा यथा ।
अवियुक्तास्ति ते तद्वदेका त्वद्भक्तिरस्तु मे ॥९॥

anantānandasarasī devī priyatamā yathā /
aviyuktāsti te tadvadekā tvadbhaktirastu me //9//

6 See appendix 2 for explanation of *upāyas*.

Now, there is one problem for me.

You have Your *śakti*–Your wife, Pārvatī–You have Pārvatī, and You are fond of Pārvatī because Pārvatī is *ananta ānanda sarasī* (*ananta ānanda sarasī* means "She is glorified with unlimited joy and bliss"), Her nature is glorified with unlimited joy and bliss.

Whose nature?

DEVOTEES: Pārvatī's.

SWAMIJI: And You are fond of that Pārvatī. But, there is a problem in me. *Tadvad ekā tvad bhaktirastu me*, I have adopted one woman for You to possess, and that is devotion. My devotion for You is . . . You should consider that my devotion for You is another lady, i.e., my devotion (*bhakti*). But, my devotion is not accepted by You as much as You accept Pārvatī in nearness. My devotion remains away from Your presence. This is a problem for me.

I want my devotion also–my devotion, this lady–my devotion for You must remain one with You, married to You, i.e., my devotion. So, it means I want to be devoted to You in continuity, without any break, so that You embrace my devotion, You accept my devotion, You will be fond of my devotion. But You have no fondness for my devotion. I devote my time for You but You ignore that. I love You but You don't care. Pārvatī loves You very little and You care for that too much [laughter]! This is the problem.

So, I want that the same condition of [Your] conduct [with Pārvatī] should be adopted with this lady also.

Which lady?

ERNIE: Devotion.

SWAMIJI: My devotion.

Chapter 1 (17:16)

सर्व एव भवल्लाभ-
हेतुर्भक्तिमतां विभो ।
संविन्मार्गोऽयमाह्लाद-
दुःखमोहैस्त्रिधा स्थितः ॥१०॥

sarva eva bhavallābha-
heturbhaktimatāṁ vibho /
saṁvinmārgo'yamāhlāda-
duḥkhamohaistridhā sthitaḥ //10//

This universal path, which is filled in a three-fold way . . .

One is joy, the joyful path, and the path filled with sadness (the opposite to joy), and the path filled with sluggishness, when you want to, *bas*[7], lie down for the whole day and sleep, go to bed. So, this is the triple way of this universe. Sometimes you want to be devoted to the Lord and go to the temple or the church, or anything. That is the path of . . .

DEVOTEE: Joy.

SWAMIJI: . . . joy. And sometimes you want to struggle for constructing a house and repairing your motorcar. This is the path of sadness [because] you [become] tired, exhausted there. Sometimes you want to go to bed and lie down with a heating pad on your chest and *bas*, snore for the whole time. This is the path of *moha* (illusion); this is the path of sluggishness.

. . . this three-fold path, which is existing in this universe, for Thy devotees, all of these three-fold paths direct Your devotees towards God consciousness. It may be sluggishness, it may be sadness, it may be joy. The joyful path carries Thy devotee to that God consciousness, the path with sadness also diverts him towards God consciousness, and the path with sluggishness also [diverts him towards God consciousness].

Chapter 1 (19:44)

भवद्भक्त्यमृतास्वादाद्बोधस्य स्यात्परापि या ।
दशा सा मां प्रति स्वामिन्नासवस्येव शुक्तता ॥११॥

bhavadbhaktyamṛtāsvādādbodhasya syātparāpi yā /
daśā sā māṁ prati svāminnāsavasyeva śuktatā //11//

Have you ever tasted this liquor? Have you ever tasted liquor?

7 Swamiji uses the Hindi word "*bas*" often throughout the text, which means "enough" or "that is all." [*Editor's note*]

This is the history of liquor.

Bhavat bhaktyamṛtāsvādād bodhasya syātparāpi yā daśā. Leaving aside the taste of tasting the nectar of Your devotion, leaving that aside–leaving aside the tasting of the nectar of Thy devotion–*bodhasya syāt parāpi yā daśā*, and possessing that state, which is that supreme state of knowledge (Shaivite knowledge)–the supreme state of Shaivite knowledge you possess and leave aside that 'nectarized' state of devotion–leaving aside the 'nectarized' state of devotion and possessing the supreme state of knowledge of God consciousness, for me, this supreme state of knowledge of God consciousness is as bad, or as bad tasting, just as the *āsavasyeva śuktatā*, just like when there is some wine and there is some sourness.

DEVOTEE: Sourness.

SWAMIJI: That is sourness. That is like sourness to me, i.e., that state of supreme knowledge of God consciousness . . .

JOHN: Without devotion.

SWAMIJI: . . . without devotion. I like devotion. I want to devote always . . . I want to become [filled with] Your devotion, no matter if You appear to me or not. I want to weep for You; I want to cry for You. I want Your devotion, nothing else. I don't want knowledge.

JOHN: If knowledge means that I can't have devotion?

SWAMIJI: If knowledge is there without devotion, I don't want that knowledge.

JOHN: Yes, I don't want that kind of knowledge.

SWAMIJI:

Chapter 1 (22:14)

भवद्भक्तिमहाविद्या येषामभ्यासमागता ।
विद्याविद्योभयस्यापि त एते तत्त्ववेदिनः ॥१२॥

bhavadbhaktimahāvidyā yeṣāmabhyāsamāgatā /
vidyāvidyobhayasyāpi ta ete tattvavedinaḥ //12//

Those people who have experienced the supreme knowledge of Thy devotion–who have already experienced the supreme knowledge of Your devotion–those are only experienced in discriminating what is knowledge and what is the absence of knowledge. Knowledge and the absence of knowledge, only they can discriminate, not anybody else.

Who?

JOHN: Those who . . .

SWAMIJI: Those who have experienced the supreme knowledge of Thy devotion. Those who have experienced the supreme knowledge of Thy devotion, only they can discriminate what is real knowledge and what is not knowledge, i.e., what is ignorance.

Chapter 1 (23:19)

आमूलाद्वाग्लता सेयं क्रमविस्फारशालिनी ।
त्वद्भक्तिसुधया सिक्ता तद्रसाढ्यफलास्तु मे ॥१३॥

āmūlādvāglatā seyaṁ kramavisphāraśālinī /
tvadbhaktisudhayā siktā tadrasāḍhyaphalāstu me //13//

This expansion of the universal state of life is really a creeper, is just like a creeper, a grown creeper (*latā*). *Āmūlāt vāk latā seyaṁ kramam*, and this *vāk latā*, this vine of sound (*parā*, *paśyantī*, *madhyamā*, and *vaikharī*) . . .

> *Parā* is the supreme word. The supreme word is without differentiation. That is called *parā*, *parāvāṇī*. Next to [*parā*] is *paśyantī*, next to [*paśyantī*] is *madhyamā*, and next to [*madhyamā*] is *vaikharī*.

. . . these four-fold branches of this vine of sound, speech, are expanded in this universe.

> Sometimes you are established in the supreme word (*parā*).[8] Sometimes you are established in *paśyantī*. *Paśyantī* is when

8 "The word "*parā*" means "supreme", and *parā vāk* is the "supreme speech". It is that soundless sound which resides in your own universal consciousness. It is the supreme sound which has no sound. It is the life of the other three kinds of speech which comprise the kingdom of speech (*paśyantī, madhyamā,* and *vaikharī*) and yet it is not in this kingdom of speech." *Kashmir Shaivism–The Secret Supreme*, 6.41.

you are only looking and there is no thought in your mind. That is *paśyantī*. *Parā* is before that. *Madhyamā* is when you are looking, when you don't speak but you speak with the mind. That is *madhyamā*. *Vaikharī* is that word when you speak with words also, with the lips also. So, this is the inferior state of sound. The inferior state of sound is *vaikharī*, superior to that is *madhyamā*, superior to that is *paśyantī*, and the supreme word is *parā*.

Sometimes you are established in *parā* when you are in *samādhi*. Sometimes you are established in *paśyantī* when you are about to come out from *samādhi*. That is the state of *paśyantī*. When you are only thinking in your mind and not acting with your body, that is the state of *madhyamā*. When you are acting with the limbs also, that is the state of *vaikharī*. And this four-fold state of word (i.e., sound) is expanded in this universe.

There is one problem, one desire in me. I want my just . . . my only desire is that this creeper should be watered with the nectar of Thy devotion so that this creeper bears the fruit of Thy devotion. When it is watered with devotion, it will bear the fruit which has the taste of Thy devotion. So, I want to experience in this world, in all these four-fold states of life, only Thy devotion. This is my desire.

Chapter 1 (27:02)

शिवो भूत्वा यजेतेति भक्तो भूत्वेति कथ्यते ।
त्वमेव हि वपुः सारं भक्तैरद्वयशोधितम् ॥१४॥

śivo bhūtvā yajeteti bhakto bhūtveti kathyate /
tvameva hi vapuḥ sāraṁ bhaktairadvayaśodhitam //14//

In the *Vedās*, in the *Śiva Sūtras*, in all of those sacred books, this is said that, "you must worship Lord Śiva after becoming Lord Śiva Himself".

When you become Lord Śiva, then you are capable to worship Him. If you have become an individual, being an individual, you cannot worship that universal Being. It is out of the question.

How can a limited being get contact with unlimited Being? So, you must first become unlimited yourself and then you can worship that unlimited Being, Śiva.

But, Thy devotees have corrected it. This ruling, rules and regulations, they have corrected that. They have said, "*bhakto bhūtvā iti kathyate*", you must be devoted to Lord Śiva, then you can get contact with Him, if you are filled with devotion. If you are filled with Śiva *bhāva*, the state of Śiva, you are not capable of worshiping Śiva. When you are devotedly devoted to Śiva, then you are capable to worship Śiva. You can worship Śiva only when you are filled with devotion.

And this is correct. This is the correct way of understanding. From my point of view, this is the correct way of understanding, because *tvameva hi vapuḥ sāraṁ bhaktairadvaya śodhitam*, [Thy devotees] have clarified, they have in a real sense clarified, what is right and what is wrong. They have known, they have experienced this.

Chapter 1 (29:19)

भक्तानां भवदद्वैतसिद्ध्यै का नोपपत्तयः ।
तदसिद्ध्यै निकृष्टानां कानि नावरनाणि वा ॥१५॥

bhaktānāṁ bhavadadvaitasiddhyai kā nopapattayaḥ /
tadasiddhyai nikṛṣṭānāṁ kāni nāvaranāṇi vā //15//

Those who are Thy devotees, for those, if they want to achieve the state of God consciousness, for them, which is not the way? Even going astray also will lead them to God consciousness.

For whom?

Those who are Thy devotees.

Those who are Thy devotees, for them, in achieving You, what are not the ways, what are not the paths, to achieve that God consciousness? For them, from every corner they will travel and they will reach God consciousness. If they travel, if they go to the movies, if they will enjoy dances, by doing that also they will be diverted towards God consciousness, because they are Thy devotees. Thy devotees have never . . . they never become detached from You. They are always attached [to You]. If they are [making] love with some woman, during that period also they are diverted towards God consciousness. This is the divinity of Thy devotees.

But, on the contrary, *nikṛṣṭānāṁ*, those who are not devotedly devoted to You, *kāni na āvarṇāni*, for them, there are obstacles everywhere; everywhere for them, there are obstacles, there is hindrance. If they do *sādhanā*, by that doing *sādhanā*, they are carried away from God consciousness. If they meditate properly with one-pointedness, by meditating properly in one-pointedness, they are carried away from God consciousness. And, on the contrary, when there are Thy devotees, real devotees, they don't meditate at all and they are carried to God consciousness. This is the divinity in Thy devotees.

Now, the last one:

Chapter 1 (32:00)

कदाचित्क्वापि लभ्यो ऽसि योगेनेतीश वञ्चना ।
अन्यथा सर्वकक्ष्यासु भासि भक्तिमतां कथम् ।१६॥

kadācitkvāpi labhyo'si yogenetīśa vañcanā /
anyathā sarvakakṣyāsu bhāsi bhaktimatāṁ katham //16//

O Lord, when You are achieved by some particular *yoga* exercise or by a particular meditation, and You are achieved when a person, a devotee, is sentenced to a cave or some secluded corner [and remains] without the struggle of universal activities, then you are achieved by some particular adoption of a particular *yoga*, but this is a deceit. In a real sense, this is deceit.[9]

JOHN: To give up the world and adopt special *yogas*.

SWAMIJI: To give up the world and achieve God consciousness. You will never achieve God consciousness after shunning the

9 "When Your existence is found and realized at a particular period and at a particular place–say [within the] heart or between the two eyebrows or [some particular place] like that–and by the performance of some particular *yoga*, You are found, this kind of finding You is only a deceit to the finder. It is only a deceit or deception. Actually, they don't find You. You are not found this way." *Śivastotrāvalī* of Utpaladeva, translation and commentary by Swami Lakshmanjoo (additional audio recording, USF archives, Los Angeles, 1980).

activities of the universe. On the contrary, when you are situated in the universe and you are given to the universal activities, then there is the possibility of achieving the state of God consciousness. So, it seems that this universe is not separate from the state of God consciousness. The universe is the real manifestation of God consciousness and this universe is just the reality of His nature. If you shun this reality of His nature, how can you achieve God consciousness? So, it is deceit. It is just deceit. When you go to a cave and shun all the activities of the universe, all your activities of daily life, and [think] that you will achieve God consciousness, it is deceit, you are wrong there.

Anyathā sarvakakṣyāsu bhāsi bhaktimatāṁ. There are such devotees in this universe who are existing–and I have experienced those devotees who are existing in universal activities–they have become one with Thee in universal activities.[10]

So, you should find out the way to achieve God *in* the activity of the universe, not by shunning it. This is Shaivism.

The real way of perceiving You is to perceive You in each and every action of life.

Next:

Chapter 1 (35:01)

प्रत्याहाराद्यसंस्पृष्टो विशेषो ऽस्ति महानयम् ।
योगिभ्यो भक्तिभाजां यद्व्युत्थाने ऽपि समाहिताः ॥१७॥

pratyāhārādyasaṁspṛṣṭo viśeṣo'sti mahānayam /
yogibhyo bhaktibhājāṁ yadvyutthāne'pi samāhitāḥ //17//

There is a great difference between *yogīs* and Your devotees. *Yogīs* do find You and do realize Your nature by maintaining *pratyāhāra*[11], and meditation, and so on. Otherwise, they can't realize Your nature.

JOHN: "*Pratyāhāra*" means here?

SWAMIJI: Just to wind up all your motions from outside to inside, introverted.

10 "They perceive Your presence in each and every action of the world. In worldly actions also, they perceive Your presence." *Śivastotrāvalī* (additional audio recording, USF archives).

11 Withdrawal of the senses.

But, on the contrary, those who are Your devotees, *bhaktibhājām*, they perceive You in such a way that in *vyutthāna* also, when they are outside in the world of action, they perceive Your situation [i.e., presence] there also.

ALEXIS: *Samāhitāḥ.*

SWAMIJI: There also they find You.

Next:

Chapter 1 (36:24)

न योगो न तपो नार्चाक्रमः को ऽपि प्रणीयते ।
अमाये शिवमार्गे ऽस्मिन् भक्तिरेका प्रशस्यते ॥१८॥

na yogo na tapo nārcākramaḥ ko'pi praṇīyate /
amāye śivamārge'smin bhaktirekā praśasyate //18//

On this path of *Śiva mārga*, on this path of Lord Śiva, which is without . . . which is away from all delusion, *amāye*, which is absolutely pure and straight, on this path of Lord Śiva, no *yoga* is needed, no penance is needed, and no worship, no mode of worship, is needed. The need here is only of devotion, pure devotion. If they are really attached to You, they will find You. If they are not attached [to You], they may perform *yoga*, they may perform penance, and they may perform *pūjā*, but they cannot find You. *Bhakti*[12] is the only means to find Your nature.

ALEXIS: Passion for God consciousness.

SWAMIJI: Passion for God consciousness. *Bhakti* is "passion".

Chapter 1 (37:44)

सर्वतो विलसद्भक्तितेजोध्वस्तावृतेर्मम ।
प्रत्यक्षसर्वभावस्य चिन्तानामापि नश्यतु ॥१९॥

sarvato vilasadbhaktitejodhvastāvṛtermama /
pratyakṣasarvabhāvasya cintānāmāpi naśyatu //19//

O Lord, I am, in the real sense . . . I have, in the real sense, perceived the real nature of the universe. *Pratyakṣa sarva bhā-*

12 Faith, love, or devotion.

vasya, all the universal objective field I have perceived [clearly] because all ignorance has been shunned; all ignorance has been carried away by the light of Your devotion.

And to me, now there is only one request [that I place] before You. That is, let the phases of impression also be removed in my mind (I mean, the traces of impression of duality). The traces of duality also must be removed. This is my request before Thee.

JOHN: Duality of "I" and "this", or which duality?

SWAMIJI: "I" and "this" and "that". All these differentiated ways of perception, e.g., perceiving that, "This man is mine", "This is not mine", "This is true", "This is untrue", "This is real", "This is right", "This is wrong".

All this should vanish away from my mind, all this differentiatedness. Traces also; traces also of this should be removed. This is my request.

Chapter 1 (39:31)

शिव इत्येकशब्दस्य जिह्वाग्रे तिष्ठतः सदा ।
समस्तविषयास्वादो भक्तेष्वेवास्ति कोऽप्यहो ॥२०॥

śiva ityekaśabdasya jihvāgre tiṣṭhataḥ sadā /
samastaviṣayāsvādo bhakteṣvevāsti ko'pyaho //20//

This is a great wonder (*aho,* this is a great wonder) that when you recite only the name, this sound "Śiva", and this sound of "Śiva" resides on the tip of your tongue, *jihvāgre vasataḥ sadā*, in continuity, *samasta viṣayāsvādo bhakteṣvevāsti*, you don't realize the nectar of His name only, you realize the nectar of His touch, you realize the nectar of His embrace, you realize the nectar of His smell, you realize everything of Lord Śiva there.

ALEXIS: "*Śabda*" here with the sense of sound, *śabdanam*?

SWAMIJI: Sound, only sound.

ALEXIS: *Śiva ityeka śabdasya*; *śabda* is the sense of perhaps *parāmarśa* here?

SWAMIJI: Not from the point [of view] of Utpaladeva. You see, Utpaladeva says here that [normal sound] is only *śabda*. By *śabda*, you can hear only. By sound, you cannot have the nectar of touch, you can't have the nectar of touch by sound, you can't have the nectar of smell, nectar of that fragrance. But, the fragrance of Śiva will come by the mere reciting of the name of Lord Śiva. This is the greatness in His name that by reciting His name, you achieve the nectar of not only His name, but His touch, His fragrance, His everything. You are filled with His real existence.

ALEXIS: But, this recitation of His name is not in gross way; it is constant awareness of *ahaṁbhāva*?

SWAMIJI: Yes, *ahaṁbhāva* (I-consciousness).

ALEXIS: So, it is *utprekṣā*, it is poetical figure [of speech].

SWAMIJI: Yes, a poetical figure [of speech].

ALEXIS: It's not actually, "Śiva, Śiva, Śiva". This is continuity of awareness.

SWAMIJI: This way also. This way also, i.e., if you [utter] "Śiva" with its meaning.

ALEXIS: Awareness.

SWAMIJI: If you utter this word "Śiva" with its meaning, then it will lead you to that.

JOHN: Its meaning is awareness, *ahaṁbhāva*.

SWAMIJI: *Ahaṁbhāva*.

JOHN: That is meaning of Śiva.

SWAMIJI: Yes. Now, twenty-first [*stotra*]:

Chapter 1 (41:51)

शान्तकल्लोलशीताच्छस्वादुभक्तिसुधाम्बुधौ ।
अलौकिकरसास्वादे सुस्थैः को नाम गण्यते ॥२१॥

śāntakallolaśītācchasvādubhaktisudhāmbudhau /
alaukikarasāsvāde susthaiḥ ko nāma gaṇyate //21//

Those who are bent upon tasting that unique nectar, when they dive in the ocean of the nectar of Thy devotion, which is sweet, which is fresh, which is *śīta* . . .

Śīta means?

ALEXIS: Cool.

SWAMIJI:. . . cool, and *śāntakallola*, where there are no wavering waves, and in that ocean, those who dive their *ātman*, who dive their ego in that ocean, and are bent upon tasting the nectar of that divine bliss, *ko nāma gaṇyate*, for them, nothing remains to be counted; they don't count anything else.

"Counting" [means that] they don't feel the necessity of going towards any other corner. The journey is over there. Their journey is over. Their journey ends there.

Chapter 1 (43:22)

मादृशैः किम् न चर्व्येत भवद्भक्तिमहौषधिः ।
तादृशी भगवन्यस्या मोक्षाख्यो ऽनन्तरो रसः ॥२२॥

mādṛśaiḥ kim na carvyeta bhavadbhaktimahauṣadhiḥ /
tādṛśī bhagavanyasyā mokṣākhyo'nantaro rasaḥ //22//

Bhagavan, O Lord, those who are just like me, *mādṛśaiḥ*, why should they not taste the nectar of the herb of Your devotion? And by which taste they don't achieve the taste of that devotion only, they achieve the taste of liberation also. They are *jīvan muktas*[13] at the same time.

ALEXIS: *Anantaraḥ.*

SWAMIJI: This is attached to it. *Mokṣa rasa*, the *rasa*[14] of liberation, is attached to *bhakti rasa*. As soon as *bhakti rasa* is achieved, *mokṣa rasa* is also achieved at the same time, simultaneously.

ALEXIS: Because they are the same.

SWAMIJI: So, why should those people who are just like me not appreciate and not own this herb, this dose, of Your devotion?

Chapter 1 (44:45)

ता एव परमर्थ्यन्ते सम्पदः सद्भिरीश याः ।
त्वद्भक्तिरससम्भोगविस्रम्भपरिपोषिकाः ॥२३॥

tā eva paramarthyante sampadaḥ sadbhirīśa yāḥ /
tvadbhaktirasasambhogavisrambhaparipoṣikāḥ //23//

---

13 Liberated while embodied. [*Editor's note*]

14 Taste or nectar.

Iśa, O Lord, that wealth is only longed for and desired by those saints–that wealth is longed for and desired by those saints–[which is] the wealth that produces and strengthens the fire of desire for embracing that *bhakti rasa*, in embracing Thy nectar of *bhakti*, Thy nectar of devotion.[15]

Chapter 1 (45:43)

भवद्भक्तिसुधासारस्तैः किमप्युपलक्षितः ।
ये न रागादिपङ्के ऽस्मिंल्लिप्यन्ते पतिता अपि ॥२४॥

bhavadbhaktisudhāsārastaiḥ kimapyupalakṣitaḥ /
ye na rāgādi paṅke'smiṁllipyante patitā api //24//

Those [saints], although living and remaining in the field of *rāga*[16], greed, anger, lust, i.e., in the muddy sphere of *rāga*, etc. . . .

This is only mud. When you are attached to your family, you are attached to your son, you are attached to your husband, you are attached to your wife, this [means that] you are remaining in the mud, in the muddy sphere of the universe.

. . . although they remain in this muddy sphere of the universe, those [saints], while remaining in the muddy sphere of the universe, [they] do not get stuck by that mud, [they] do not get stuck in that mud. They are not actually stuck there. They only do these [worldly] actions but they are not stuck in that mud. Those people have actually pointed out and tasted–*upalakṣita* means "pointed out and tasted"–tasted that sharp, driving shower of Your devotion. The sharp, driving shower of Thy devotion, they have actually pointed out and tasted that shower.

Chapter 1 (47:44)

अणिमादिषु मोक्षान्तेष्वङ्गेष्वेव फलाभिधा ।
भवद्भक्तेर्विपक्काया लताया एव केषुचित् ॥२५॥

15 Swamiji explained that "*visrambha*" means *harṣa* (joy).
16 Attachment.

aṇimādiṣu mokṣānteṣvaṅgeṣveva phalābhidhā /
bhavadbhaktervipakvāyā latāyā eva keṣucit //25//

In this universe, there is only one shining creeper (a grown shining creeper), that is the creeper of Your devotion. When that creeper of Your devotion is in its full bloom, when it has bloomed perfectly, then you find in this very creeper all kinds of fruits. It bears all kinds of fruits for you, not only . . . for instance, right from the great *yogic* powers up to the great power of being liberated from repeated births and deaths (that is *mokṣa*), *aṇimādiṣu mokṣānteṣu*, all of these powers come into existence in that creeper of Your devotion. It means that the creeper of Thy devotion bears not only [the fruit of] Thy devotion, but it also bears [the fruit of] all *yogic* powers including final liberation (*mokṣa*). But, in predominance, it bears devotion; devotion is in predominance. The fruit of devotion it bears in predominance and [*yogīc* powers and *mokṣa* are] *apradhāna*.

What is *apradhāna*?

ALEXIS: Subsidiary, secondary, less important.

SWAMIJI: Yes, these are secondary fruits. Which are secondary fruits?

JOHN: Power and *mokṣa*.

SWAMIJI: These *aṇimādiṣu mokṣānteṣu*. So, he does not recognize *mokṣa* as the predominant fruit of this creeper. The predominant fruit of this creeper is only devotion for the Lord.

rudraśaktisamāveśastatra nityaṁ pratiṣṭhitaḥ /
sati tasmiṁśca cihnāni tasyaitāni vilakṣayet //
tatraitatprathamaṁ cihnāṁ rūdre bhaktiḥ suniścalā /[17]

The first sign of getting absorption in God consciousness is devotion for the Lord, attachment for the Lord. When you are attached to Lord Śiva, don't think of any other powers. All powers will come. All powers are secondary fruits for this creeper. This creeper should be owned in predominance.

Which creeper?

JOHN: The creeper of devotion.

17 *Mālinīvijaya tantra*, 8. 10-11a.

SWAMIJI: The creeper of Thy devotion.[18]

Chapter 1 (50:39)

चित्रं निसर्गतो नाथ दुःखबीजमिदं मनः ।
त्वद्भक्तिरससंसिक्तं निःश्रेयसमहाफलम् ॥२६॥

citraṁ nisargato nātha duḥkhabījamidaṁ manaḥ /
tvadbhaktirasasaṁsiktaṁ niḥśreyasamahāphalam //26//

Nātha, O desired Lord, this is also a great wonder to me that, in reality, by nature, this mind is the seed of pain, sorrow, sadness, torture. This mind is the seed of torture, sorrow, sadness–all bad things. All bad things are [produced] by this seed.

JOHN: Which is the mind.

SWAMIJI: Mind. Mind is the thinking of this and that, this, that, always, without any purpose.

But, wonder is . . . this great wonder is this to me that, by nature, this mind is the seed for . . .

Seed of what?

ALEXIS: Suffering?

SWAMIJI: . . . seed of suffering, sorrow, sadness. But this seed, when you water it with the *rasa* of Thy devotion, when it is watered by the *rasa* of Thy devotion, *niḥśreyasama*, it bears the fruit of liberation, ultimate liberation, final liberation. This is a wonder. This is a great wonder in this seed. This seed [i.e., the mind], which bears only sorrow, sadness, torture, also bears liberation in the end when it is watered by Your *bhakti rasa*, by the *rasa* of Thy devotion.

Here ends this first chapter.

18 "That master who has received this particular intensity of grace, which is known as *rūdra śakti-samāveśaḥ*, is called *rūdra śakti-samāviṣṭaḥ* because he has completely entered into the trance of *rūdra śakti*, the energy of Śiva. He exhibits five signs which can be observed by others. The first sign is his intense love for Lord Śiva." *Kashmir Shaivism–The Secret Supreme*, 10.67.

Chapter Two
Everything is Found in Everything
Sarvātmaparibhāvanākhyaṁ dvitīyam stotram

SWAMIJI: Next.
JOHN: So, next chapter is . . . what's the name?
ALEXIS: *Sarvātmaparibhāvanā.*
SWAMIJI: *Sarvātmaparibhāvanākhyaṁ. Sarvātmaparibhāvanākhyaṁ* means "you find everything in everything; everything is found in everything".
ALEXIS: *Sarvātma paribhāvana*, contemplation of absolute pervasion; *sarvātma*, everything as everything.
SWAMIJI: Yes.

Chapter 2 (00:24)

अग्नीषोमरविब्रह्मविष्णुस्थावरजङ्गम- ।
स्वरूप बहुरूपाय नमः संविन्मयाय ते ॥१॥

agnīṣomaravibrahmaviṣṇusthāvarajaṅgama- /
svarūpa bahurūpāya namaḥ saṁvinmayāya te //1//

O Lord, You are fire, You are the moon, You are the sun.

It means . . . "You are fire" [means] You have possessed subjective consciousness. "You are the moon" [means] You have possessed objective consciousness. "You are the sun" [means] You have possessed cognitive consciousness.[19] You are subjective, You are cognitive, and You are objective.

Brahmaviṣṇu, You are Brahma, You are the creator. You are Viṣṇu, You are the protector also.

---

19 "*Soma* is the moon, *agnī* is fire, *sūrya* is the sun. They indicate these three: individual (moon), *śakti* (sun), and *śiva* (fire)." *Parātriśikā Vivaraṇa* with the commentary of Abhinavagupta, translation and commentary by Swami Lakshmanjoo (original audio recordings, USF archives, Los Angeles, 1982-85).

You are [inert] and not [inert].

ALEXIS: Animate and inanimate.

SWAMIJI: Yes, *jaḍa* and *cetana*.[20]

You are universal. Actually, You are universal. I bow to Thy universal form of Thee. Actually, You are not universal. You are only consciousness. You are away from universality at the same time. Although You are universal, You are above universality, You are only consciousness (*saṁvit mayāya*).

Chapter 2 (01:54)

विश्वेन्धनमहक्षारानुलेपशुचिवर्चसे ।
महानलाय भवते विश्वैकहविषे नमः ॥२॥

viśvendhanamahakṣārānulepaśucivarcase /
mahānalāya bhavate viśvaikahaviṣe namaḥ //2//

O Lord, I bow to that supreme fire of Thee, of Thy consciousness, which is *śucivarcase*, which is absolutely glorified by pure *prakāśa* (pure light) by absorbing this universe into nothingness, by burning this universe into no substance, because this is the great fire.

He has nominated Lord Śiva as the great fire, the great abode of fire, in which this whole universe has been destroyed and burnt to ashes. And that [word] "ashes" means that they are the last traces of impressions that remain in your consciousness.

When You destroy this whole universe by Your way of *bhakti*, by Your way of devotion–it destroys the universe–but still, those traces remain that there was some universe in a previous state. That there was some universe, that impression is there, but [what] You are doing to that impression is that You absorb those ashes [of impressions] in Your Self, in Your Self of consciousness. So, those impressions also are carried away. *Anulepa śucivarcase*, by that, Your light is glorified all-around, and, in which fire of God consciousness, this universe is one offering.

It becomes one offering. It is not offered in That fire a second

20 *Jaḍa*: insentient, unconscious; *cetana*: sentient, conscious. [*Editor's note*]

time. It is only one offering, *svāhā*, one *svāhā* in That fire.[21] In one *svāhā*, it is finished. When you offer those offerings (*sāmagrī*)[22] in the fire, you recite, "*svāhā*". So, this universe becomes *svāhā* in one way, one moment, one offering.

I bow to that supreme fire of Lord Śiva.

Chapter 2 (04:58)

परमामृत सान्द्राय शीतलाय शिवाग्नये ।
कस्मैचिद्विश्वसंप्लोषविषमाय नमोऽस्तु ते ॥३॥

paramāmṛtasāndrāya śītalāya śivāgnaye /
kasmaicidviśvasaṁploṣaviṣamāya namo'stu te //3//

I bow to that supreme fire of God Consciousness, supreme fire of Lord Śiva (*śivāgnaye namaḥ*), which is *paramāmṛta sāndrāya*, which fire is cooled down by supreme nectar.

This is a cool fire. This cools down the whole system, This fire. This fire does not burn.

And, at the same time, It is very cool and It has become very hot by *kasmaicit viśva saṁploṣa viṣamāya* (*viṣamāya* means that It is hot also).

Hot in which respect?

Because, *viśva saṁploṣa viṣamāya*, It burns the differentiated perceptions of the universe. By burning the differentiated perceptions of the universe, It is hot also. And, by keeping you in the field of that 'nectarized' state of Being, It is cool. This fire is cool and, at the same time, hot. I bow to That fire.

Chapter 2 (06:27)

महादेवाय रुद्राय शङ्कराय शिवाय ते ।
महेश्वरायापि नमः कस्मैचिन्मन्त्रमूर्तये ॥४॥

21 *Svāhā*: an exclamation used while making oblations to the gods. [*Editor's note*]

22 *Sāmagrī*: sanctified offerings used in fire ceremonies. [*Editor's note*]

mahādevāya rudrāya śaṅkarāya śivāya te /
maheśvarāyāpi namaḥ kasmaicinmantramūrtaye //4//

I bow to Mahādeva, I bow to Rūdra, I bow to Śaṅkara, I bow to Śiva, I bow to Maheśvara, I bow to that unique being of God consciousness of Śiva.

This is *sarvātma paribhāvanā*,[23] this way you can see that *sarvātma paribhāvanā*, everywhere He is found.

ALEXIS: *Cinmantra mūrtaye . . .*

SWAMIJI: *Kasmaicit . . .*

ALEXIS: . . . that unique being whose form is . . .

SWAMIJI: Unique being of *mantra*, *ahaṁ parāmarśa.*

ALEXIS: . . . Self-awareness.

SWAMIJI: Yes.

Chapter 2 (07:12)

नमो निकृत्तनिःशेषत्रैलोक्यविगलद्वसा- ।
वसेकविषमायापि मङ्गलाय शिवाग्नये ॥५॥

namo nikṛttaniḥśeṣatrailokyavigaladvasā- /
vasekaviṣamāyāpi maṅgalāya śivāgnaye //5//

I bow to that Śiva *agni*, the fire of Śiva, who is *viṣama* (*viṣama* is "furious, frightening").

Śiva *agni* is frightening. Śiva *agni* means *śmaśāna agni*, where you burn those corpses, dead bodies.

JOHN: Cremation grounds.

SWAMIJI: Where dead bodies are burnt.

DENISE: Cremation grounds.

SWAMIJI: Yes. That is called *Śiva agni*, *śmaśāna agni*.

I bow to That *śmaśāna agni*, That fire where these corpses are burned.

Which corpses are burned there?

Not these individual corpses in the ordinary *śmaśāna agni*. It is not that ordinary *śmaśāna agni*. It is that *śmaśāna agni*

23 *Sarvātma paribhāvanā* means "the contemplation of absolute pervasion". This is also the title of this chapter. [*Editor's note*]

where *nikṛtta niḥśeṣa trailokya*, all of the three worlds are cut into pieces, [where] all the three worlds are being cut into pieces. The three worlds–the world of wakefulness, the world of the dreaming state, the world of sound sleep (these *bhāva*, *abhāva*, and *atibhāva*)–these three worlds are cut into pieces and thrown in that *agni*. And, when these three worlds are thrown in that *agni*, some marrow oozes out of it. The marrow of that body of the three worlds oozes out.

What is that marrow?

That marrow is those traces of impressions; impressions that there was wakefulness, there was the dreaming state, there was the dreamless state.

When you enter in that *turya* state, the fourth state, at the first time, those traces of those impressions remain in your memory–that there was something, previously there was something, i.e., there was wakefulness, there was the dreaming state, and there was the dreamless state, but now it is only *turya*; *turyānanda*, there is only the blissful state [of *turya*].[24]

Those traces are also *avaseka*, are offered in That fire in the end. Those traces of impressions are also offered in That fire. And by offering those traces in That fire, It becomes *viṣamāya* (*viṣamāya* means "frightening").

Because, you can't remain in the ground of *śmaśāna agni* at night, midnight. If I ask you to go at midnight and remain there and meditate there on the ground, you will get frightened. So, this way, in this same way, this Śiva *agni* is frightening also in that way; frightening to those who are given to the differentiated perceptions. Those who occupy and achieve and maintain differentiated perception, for those [people] it is frightening. [For those] who do not achieve differentiated perceptions, it gives them *maṅgala* (joy, happiness).

JOHN: This is an actual state?

SWAMIJI: This is the actual state of Śiva *agni*. Śiva *agni* is frightening in one way, and giving, bestowing joy, in another way. If you achieve one-pointedness and are situated in that oneness of God consciousness, it will give you *maṅgala*, it will give you joy.

JOHN: Otherwise, it is . . .

24 See appendix 3 for an explanation of *turya*.

SWAMIJI: Otherwise, it is frightening.

JOHN: And this is that state that you spoke about in those seven states of *turya* when you wrote that in rising through . . . when you feel you are dying or the house is falling?[25]

SWAMIJI: Yes, yes, that happens like that.

And, at the same time, those who are given to worldly pleasures, they don't get satisfied by diverting their attention towards God consciousness. They feel that they will die [by doing so]. And, at the same time, at the beginning, when you begin practicing this meditation on God consciousness, you feel in the beginning that you are dying, that you should leave it, that you should leave this meditation.

You have not come to that point yet that you will get frightened. That time will come, soon. It comes first and you should not get afraid of that. You should persist in meditation. And after that, you will get joy, absolute joy in the end.

JOHN: So, this is entering into full *turya* . . .

SWAMIJI: Yes.

JOHN: . . . through all these seven states?

SWAMIJI: Yes.[26]

Chapter 2 (12:51)

समस्तलक्षणायोग एव यस्योपलक्षणम् ।
तस्मै नमो ऽस्तु देवाय कस्मैचिदपि शम्भवे ॥६॥

samastalakṣaṇāyoga eva yasyopalakṣaṇam /
tasmai namo'stu devāya kasmaicidapi śambhave //6//

I bow to that unique being of Lord Śiva, whose sign of perception is perceiving Him in no way.

When you perceive Him in no way, it means you have perceived Him. If you perceive Him in some particular way, it means you have not perceived Him.

JOHN: Like in *samādhi*. If you perceive Him only in *samādhi*, then you haven't really perceived Him.

SWAMIJI: Yes, you haven't perceived Him. If you perceive Him

25 See *Kashmir Shaivism–The Secret Supreme*, 16.109.

26 See *Kashmir Shaivism–The Secret Supreme*, 16.107.

in no way, you have perceived Him. Actually, you have perceived Him then.

Yasya mataṁ, tasya mataṁ, mataṁ yasya, na veda saḥ.[27] Those who have perceived Him have not perceived Him; those who have not perceived Him have perceived Him.

Because, when He is perceived, it means you are away from It, i.e., you are not digested in That perceived thing. You are the perceiver because you have perceived Him. When you have perceived Him, you remain at the stage of perceiver and God remains at the stage of perceived. So, when there is this differentiated way of being, that you remain as the perceiver and He is perceived, it means that differentiatedness has not been removed. So, you have not perceived Him in the right way. In the right way, when you perceive Him, you will perceive Him [in such a way] that you have not perceived Him.

nāhaṁ manye suvedeti no na vedeti veda ca /
ya nastadveda tadveda no na vedeti veda ca //[28]

The disciple answers to his master, "*nāham veda suvedeti*, I don't mean that I perceive Him. O master, I don't mean by this saying, 'that I have perceived Him', I don't mean by this saying that I have perceived Him. I also don't mean that I have not perceived Him".

So, the one who actually perceives Him does not say that, "I have perceived Him", [and he] does not say that, "I have not perceived Him".

What does he say then?

Bas, he perceives Him, that is all. He perceives Him actually and does not say anything. If he says anything that, "I have not perceived Him", that way he has not perceived Him. If he says that he has perceived Him, he has not perceived Him. When he actually perceives Him, he perceives Him; actually he perceives Him and just remains in that. This is the way of perceiving the Lord.

27 *Kena Upaniṣad*, II.3.
28 *Kena Upaniṣad*, II.2.

Chapter 2 (15:57)

वेदागमविरुद्धाय वेदागमविधायिने ।
वेदागमसतत्त्वाय गुह्याय स्वामिने नमः ॥७॥

vedāgamaviruddhāya vedāgamavidhāyine /
vedāgamasatattvāya guhyāya svāmine namaḥ //7//

I bow to my Master who is absolutely against the theory of the *Vedās* and *Tantras*. I bow to that Master who is against the theory of the *Vedās* and *Tantras* and I bow to Him who is in favor of the *Vedās* and *Tantras*. I bow to Him who is actually the essence of the *Vedās* and *Tantras*. I bow to Him who is always hidden, who is always the secret to everything.

So, He is the essence of the *Vedās* and *Āgamas*, He is against the *Vedās* and *Tantras*, and He is the protector of the *Vedās* and *Tantras*.

Chapter 2 (17:04)

संसारैकनिमित्ताय संसारैकविरोधिने ।
नमः संसाररूपाय निःसंसाराय शम्भवे ॥८॥

saṁsāraikanimittāya saṁsāraikavirodhine /
namaḥ saṁsārarūpāya niḥsaṁsārāya śambhave //8//

He is the only cause of producing this wheel of repeated births and deaths (*saṁsāra*), producing the wheel of this torture of the universe. He is the only cause.

Who is the cause?

ALEXIS: *Śambhu*.

SWAMIJI: Lord Śiva. Lord Śiva is the cause of this torture of the universe, universal torture. *Saṁsāraika virodhine*, Lord Śiva is the only being who is opposite to this torture. He is the cause of this torture and He is opposite to this torture (*saṁsāraika virodhine*).

Namaḥ saṁsāra rūpāya. In fact, He is the torture. He has become the torture Himself. He has become the torture of the universe Himself. He has not manifested the torture of the universe, He has *become* the torture of the universe.

Actually, He is above this all (*niḥsaṁsārāya śambhave*). I bow to that Lord Śiva who is the only cause of the torture of the universe, who is the only opposition of the torture of the universe, and who is the reality of this torture, and who is above this torture. I bow to that Lord.

It is *sarvātma paribhāvana* (*sarvātma paribhāvana* means "He is everything"). You see, completion does not come in being complete. When you are actually complete (*pūrṇa*), it does not mean that you are only complete. You should be complete and you should be also incomplete, then you are complete. Because, in completeness, the state of incompleteness is kept aside when you are complete. So, you are not complete because incompleteness is lacking there. When you are incomplete also and complete also, then you are actually complete. This is *sarvātma paribhāvanā*.

Chapter 2 (19:39)

मूलाय मध्यायाग्राय मूलमध्याग्रमूर्तये ।
क्षीणाग्रमध्यमूलाय नमः पूर्णाय शंभवे ॥९॥

mūlāya madhyāyāgrāya mūlamadhyāgramūrtaye /
kṣīṇāgramadhyamūlāya namaḥ pūrṇāya śaṁbhave //9//

I bow to that Lord Śiva who is all-round complete (*pūrṇāya śāmbhave*). Who is found at the root, I bow to that Lord Śiva who is found at the root of everything. Who is found at *madhyāya*, who is found at the center of everything, I bow to that Lord Śiva who is found at the center of everything. I bow to that Lord Śiva who is found at the top of everything.

At the top, He will be found. At the center, He will be found. At the root, He will be found. He will be found simultaneously at the root, at the center, and at the top–simultaneously also. He will be found one by one at the root, and at the center, and at the top. He will be found simultaneously at the root, center, and top, collectively.

Kṣiṇāgra madhya mūlāya. Actually, He is not found at the root, He is not found at the center, He is not found at the top, because He is complete [laughs]. I bow to Lord Śiva that way.

Chapter 2 (21:12)

नमः सुकृतसंभारविपाकः सकृदप्यसौ ।
यस्य नामग्रहः तस्मै दुर्लभाय शिवाय ते ॥१०॥

namaḥ sukṛtasaṁbhāravipākaḥ sakṛdapyasau /
yasya nāmagrahaḥ tasmai durlabhāya śivāya te //10//

I bow to that Lord Śiva who *sukṛta saṁbhāra vipākaḥ sakṛt apyasau yasya nāmagrahaḥ*, when you recite His name only once, once in your life, if you recite His name just once in your life, *sukṛta saṁbhāra vipākaḥ*, it means all your . . .

What is opposite to sin?

ALEXIS: Virtues.

SWAMIJI: . . . all of your virtues have come in its ripening state; all of your virtues have ripened. *Sukṛta saṁbhāra vipākaḥ*, this is the sign of the ripening of all of your virtues when you just recite His name once in your life.

But, the way how to recite, it is something supreme. The recitation is not through the mouth or the tongue. The recitation of His name is through what? *Ahaṁ*, by entering in God consciousness, supreme God consciousness. That is the real way of reciting His name. If you recite His name that way only once in your life, everything is solved; nothing is to be left unsolved. And, at the same time, this is the way of His being achieved. So, this is . . . this means that He is very easy to be obtained.

But [Utpaladeva] says "*durlabhāya*". Being this way also, He is *durlabhāya*, He is very difficult to be achieved.

ALEXIS: By a miracle.

SWAMIJI: By a miracle only or by the grace of your master, He can be achieved.

Chapter 2 (23:32)

नमश्चराचराकारपरेतनिचयैः सदा ।
क्रीडते तुभ्यमेकस्मै चिन्मयाय कपालिने ॥११॥

namaścarācarākāraparetanicayaiḥ sadā /
krīḍate tubhyamekasmai cinmayāya kapāline //11//

I bow to that Lord Śiva who is the only one *cinmaya*, one conscious Being, found in all of the unconscious world, i.e., [in those] who are *pareta* [ghosts]; some are moving, some are not moving.

For instance, this body is moving; completely, this body is moving. In that also, He plays. He is found playing with that body. And some limbs of the body are not moving. There also, He is found playing.

So, actually, this body is absolutely *jaḍa*, without awareness. Awareness is only [held by] that Being. Awareness is there, awareness is playing in this body, in each and every body, not only in a *cara* (moving) body, in an *acara* (non-moving) body also, e.g., in trees, in grass, in blades of grass, in mountains. Everywhere He is found playing!

Carācarākāra pareta nicayaiḥ, just like Lord Śiva who is found playing with all *pretas*. Those *pretas* have surrounded Him all-around.

JOHN: "*Pretas*" means?

SWAMIJI: *Pretas* means those dead bodies, those ghosts who have no consciousness. Just like this [Swamiji imitates a ghost].

And, in the same way, this whole universe is only the body of *pretas*. And, in this universe, you will find Him playing in each and every movement. I bow to that Lord Śiva who is moving along with these *pretas* in this universe.

ALEXIS: *Kapāline*.

SWAMIJI: *Kapāline*, with skulls. Everywhere there is a skull. Here, in this body, He has carried a skull. He is playing with this skull, He is playing with this skull, He is playing with this skull–all skulls.

ALEXIS: So, he is like that *kāpālika*? That is the poetic meaning.

SWAMIJI: *Kāpālika*, yes. *Kāpālika* in the outside world.[29] You can see in that portrait of Lord Śiva, He has that pot (*kamaṇḍalu*) of that skull of Brahma. He has made that *kamaṇḍalu* by the skull of Brahma, with the skull of Brahma. And all of

29 *Kāpālikas* are a class of ascetics who carry a water pot made out of a human skull. [*Editor's note*]

these [*pretas*] are skulls, and they are carried by Lord Siva in each and every way of life.

Carācarākāra pareta nicayaiḥ sadā, *krīḍate tubhyam ekasmai*, and You are the only conscious Being [who is playing] in these gatherings of these *pretas*.

Chapter 2 (27:12)

मायाविने विशुद्धाय गुह्याय प्रकटात्मने ।
सूक्ष्माय विश्वरूपाय नमश्चित्राय शम्भवे ॥१२॥

māyāvine viśuddhāya guhyāya prakaṭātmane /
sūkṣmāya viśvarūpāya namaścitrāya śambhave //12//

I bow to that wonderful being of Lord Śiva who is deceitful, always deceitful, who deceives each and every being, and who is pure, straightforward; at the same time, who is straightforward.

[He is] deceitful for those who do not care to see Him, who do not care to observe Him, who do not care to perceive Him through meditation. He is deceitful for them. And for those who care to see Him, who are devoted to Him, who pray to Him, who love Him, who are attached to Him, for those He is straightforward.

[He is] deceitful for those who are worth deceiving. *Viśuddhāya*, and, at the same time, He is straightforward. *Guhyāya*, He is always hidden; hidden for those who are like that, who are worthy of that. He is hidden for those who deserve that, who deserve His being hidden to them.

Prakaṭātmane, who is always revealed, who is already revealed to everybody.

Revealed to whom?

JOHN: To those devotees who . . .

SWAMIJI: Those devotees of Lord Śiva.

Sūkṣmāya, who is very subtle; *viśvarūpāya*[30], who is very

30 "*Viśvarūpa* means "I am universal"; "I am fire, I am water, I am earth, I am a boy, I am a girl, I am a woman, I am a mountain, I am an ocean, I am sky, I am everything." *Bhagavad Gītā in a Nutshell*, (Abhinavagupta's concluding *ślokas* for each chapter), translation and com-

great. Subtle and great. I bow to that Lord Siva who is everything.

Chapter 2 (28:54)

ब्रह्मेन्द्रविष्णुनिर्व्यूढजगत्संहारकेलये ।
आश्चर्यकरणीयाय नमस्ते सर्वशक्तये ॥१३॥

brahmendraviṣṇunirvyūḍhajagatsaṁhārakelaye /
āścaryakaraṇīyāya namaste sarvaśaktaye //13//

I bow to Thee, O Lord Śiva, who is all-powerful (*sarva śaktaye*). I bow to Thee who is always possessing all powers and who does act wonderfully (*āścaryakaraṇīyāya*).

How does He act wonderfully? That wonder he [explains] in the first half of this *śloka*.

When Brahmā (the creator of the universe) creates this universe and Viṣṇu protects this universe all-round, and *nirvyūḍha*, when they have actually created [and protected] this universe with great pains, with great effort–they have created this universe and they have protected this universe–*jagata saṁhāra kelaye*, You just . . . this is Your play. In one [act of] play, You destroy this whole drama at once and You, in one movement of Your act, You destroy this whole sphere [of the universe]. This is Your play.

Brahmendra viṣṇu nirvyūḍha. *Nirvyūḍha* means "created and protected". *Brahmanā nirvyūḍham viṣṇunā pālitam*. *Brahmendra viṣṇu nirvyūḍha*, *jagat saṁhāra kelaye*, You destroy it at once. This is the act of Your wonder . . . this is Your wonderful act. And nobody is . . .

ALEXIS: Trick.

SWAMIJI: This is a trick and Your action also.

. . . and nobody has the right to oppose [Your act]. There is no opposition. Opposition party does not . . .

JOHN: Exist.

SWAMIJI: There is no opposition party; it does not arise. No opposition. Finished and finished, once and for all. "It is My will" [laughs].

---

mentary by Swami Lakshmanjoo (original audio recording, USF archives, Los Angeles, 1978).

Chapter 2 (31:12)

तटेष्वेव परिभ्रान्तैः लब्धास्तास्ता विभूतयः ।
यस्य तस्मैः नमस्तुभ्यमगाधहरसिन्धवे ॥१४॥

taṭeṣveva paribhrāntaiḥ labdhāstāstā vibhūtayaḥ /
yasya tasmaiḥ namastubhyamagādhaharasindhave //14//

I bow to Thee who is just like *agādha* (*agādha* means "unlimited ocean of God consciousness"), the unlimited ocean of Thy being. I bow to That unlimited ocean on whose shores . . .

Shores are . . . for instance, when the rise of *kuṇḍalinī* takes place, the center of the rise of *kuṇḍalinī*[31] is actually the state of This ocean, ocean of Lord Śiva. And what are the shores of This ocean?

DEVOTEE: *Iḍā* and *piṅgalā*.

SWAMIJI: No, not *iḍā* and *piṅgalā*. The shores of This ocean are the eight great *yogic* powers. Those *yogic* powers, which are achieved by . . . in the halfway [point] of maintaining this *kuṇḍalinī* rise.

ALEXIS: In *prāṇa kuṇḍalinī*?

SWAMIJI: In *prāṇa kuṇḍalinī*. In *cit kuṇḍalinī* also you can achieve this power. When *cit kuṇḍalinī* has not risen in its fullness, then you achieve powers.

ALEXIS: Not to *sarvātītā*[32] stage?

SWAMIJI: No [affirmative]. That [stage of achieving *yogic* powers] is "*taṭa*"; that is really the "shore" of This ocean. On these shores, those who travel on these shores also, they don't dive in That ocean. When they dive in That ocean, then they are gone. Their personality and their existence is over because they are digested in That, they have become one with That. But those who only tread on the shores of This ocean . . . "treading on the shores of the ocean" means enjoying your being in the enjoyment of these worldly *yogic* powers. That is actually the shore of That

31 See appendix 4 for an explanation of *kuṇḍalinī*.

32 "Established in his own nature; *sarvātītā* (beyond everything)." *Tantrāloka* of Abhinavagupta, translation and commentary by Swami Lakshmanjoo (original audio recordings, USF archives, Los Angeles, 1972-1981), 10.286.

ocean.

What?

DENISE: The eight great *yogic* powers.

SWAMIJI: Eight *yogic* powers. The shore of That ocean is the eight *yogic* powers and the utilization of those *yogic* powers. For instance, your headache does not go [away] with any medicine, so I remove it with my *yogic* power. [Therefore], I tread on that shore. I have not dived in That. If I had dived in That, then there is no question of curing you. You can't cure anybody then. How can you cure [someone]? You have dived in That, so your personality is over. You can cure only when your personality is existing. Your personality exists only on the shores. When you are inside That, finished, your [limited] being is finished.

Chapter 2 (34:26)

मायामयजगत्सान्द्रपङ्कमध्याधीवासिने ।
अलेपाय नमः शम्भुशतपत्राय शोभिने ॥१५॥

māyāmayajagatsāndrapaṅkamadhyādhīvāsine /
alepāya namaḥ śambhuśatapatrāya śobhine / / 15 / /
[first part of audio missing]

Śobhine śambhu śatapatrāya namaḥ. I bow to that beautiful lotus, lotus-like Lord Śiva.

[Utpaladeva] has given to Lord Śiva the qualification of a lotus.

He is just like a lotus as *māyāmaya jagatsāndra paṅka madhyādhivāsine*, He resides in the midst of the dense mud of the differentiated universe–dense mud–and there also He is *alepāya*, without its touch. That dense mud of differentiated perception of the universe does not affect Him at all. He is out of it just like a lotus.[33] I bow to Him.

Next:

33 "Just like that lotus leaf, although remaining in water for twenty-four hours, it is without its touch, without its impression. Those impressions do not touch that lotus leaf." *Bhagavad–In the Light of Kashmir Shaivism* (with original video), Swami Lakshmanjoo, ed. John Hughes (Universal Shaiva Fellowship, Los Angeles, 2013), 5.223.

Chapter 2 (35:52)

मङ्गलाय पवित्राय निधये भूषणात्मने ।
प्रियाय परमार्थाय सर्वोत्कृष्टाय ते नमः ॥१६॥

maṅgalāya pavitrāya nidhaye bhūṣaṇātmane /
priyāya paramārthāya sarvotkṛṣṭāya te namaḥ //16//

O Lord, I bow to Thee, who is always *maṅgala*, *maṅgala svarūpa*, and who is *pavitrāya*, who is all-round pure.

ALEXIS: *Maṅgala*?

SWAMIJI: *Maṅgala rūpatvāt, maṅgalāya.*

ALEXIS: In English?

SWAMIJI: In English [laughing]?

ALEXIS: Auspicious, joyful.

SWAMIJI: Auspicious, joyful, yes. Auspicious.

Nidhaye bhūṣaṇātmane, and He is *nidhaye*, the treasure of the universe. *Bhūṣaṇatmane*, He is the ornament of the universe. *Priyāya*, I bow to Thee, O Lord, who is *priyāya*, very dear, who is very dear to me, and *paramārthāya*, who is the real essence of the universe, and *sarvotkṛṣṭāya*, who is above all.

Chapter 2 (37:05)

नमः सततबद्धाय नित्य निर्मुक्तिभागिने ।
बन्ध मोक्षविहीनाय कस्मैचिदपि शम्भवे ॥१७॥

namaḥ satatabaddhāya nitya nirmuktibhāgine /
bandhamokṣavihīnāya kasmaicidapi śambhave //17//

I bow to that unique Lord Śiva who is always bound in the objective world, *nitya nirmukti bhāgine*, and who is always absolutely liberated from these bondages. *Bandha mokṣa vihīnāya*, and, in fact, who is without bondages and without liberation. *Kasmaicit*, it is why He is supreme, unique (*apūrva*).

Chapter 2 (37:47)

उपहासैकसारे ऽस्मिन्नेतावति जगत्त्रये ।
तुभ्यमेवाद्वितीयाय नमो नित्यसुखासिने ॥१८॥

upahāsaikasāre'sminnetāvati jagattraye /
tubhyamevādvitīyāya namo nityasukhāsine //18//

I bow to Thee only, O Lord, who is in this universe, which is the essence of *upahāsa*, which has become the root of *upahāsa*, root of nothingness, where there is only *upahāsa*.

What will you call *upahāsa*? *Upahāsa* means?

ALEXIS: It is *tuccha*, it is worthless. Therefore, it is just an object of mockery.

SWAMIJI: Mockery. "Mockery" is the real word, yes. There is only mockery in this world found in the end. In the end, there is nothing, no substance in this world, only mockery and unreality.[34]

In this universe, I bow to Thee who is the only person who is *nitya sukhāsine*, who is possessing the eternal body of beatitude, highest beatitude, highest bliss.

DEVOTEE: *Prakāśānanda ghanatvāt.*

SWAMIJI: *Prakāśānanda ghanatvāt.*[35]

---

34 "Vedānta holds that this universe is untrue, unreal, it does not really exist. It is only the creation of illusion (*māyā*). Concerning this point, Kashmir Shaivism argues that if Lord Śiva is real, then how could an unreal substance come out from something that is real? If Lord Śiva is real, then His creation is also real. Why should it be said that Lord Śiva is real and His creation is an illusion (*māyā*)? Kashmir Shaivism explains that the existence of this universe is just as real as the existence of Lord Śiva. As such, it is true, real, pure, and solid. There is nothing at all about it which is unreal." *Kashmir Shaivism–The Secret Supreme*, 15.104.

35 An appellation of Lord Śiva: concentrated (*ghana*) light of consciousness (*cit prakāśa*) and bliss (*ānanda*). See appendix 5 for an explanation of *prakāśa*.

Chapter 2 (39:15)

दक्षिणाचारसाराय वामाचाराभिलाषिणे ।
सर्वाचाराय शर्वाय निराचाराय ते नमः ॥ १९ ॥

dakṣiṇācārasārāya vāmācārābhilāṣiṇe /
sarvācārāya śarvāya nirācārāya te namaḥ //19//

O Lord, I bow to Thee who is the essence of *dakṣiṇācāra*. *Dakṣiṇācāra* is the school of Shaivism, which is the straightforward school, where no meat [nor] those unlawful things are advised to be possessed. That is *dakṣiṇācāra*.

He is the essence . . .

O Lord, You are the essence of *dakṣiṇācāra*. *Vāmācārābhilāṣiṇe*–You are not only this–*vāma ācāra abhilāṣiṇe*, You proceed to *vāmācāra* also, i.e., that way of thinking where nothing is right and nothing is wrong. In fact, *nirācāra*, there is no *ācāra* (particular conduct) in You. O Lord, I bow to You (*nirācārāya te namaḥ*).

ALEXIS: But also this *dakṣiṇa* and *vāmā* in this sense is *Bhairava tantras*[36]? They also include those *makāras*[37] and *vāma* in that sense of worship of *nityā sundarī*, that division in Shaivism.

SWAMIJI: Yes, that will also go.

JOHN: "*Ācāra*" means what here exactly?

ALEXIS: Practice.

SWAMIJI: Acting. Yes, practice, practice of *dakṣiṇācāra*, straightforward process. Where straightforward processes are explained, that is *dakṣiṇācāra*, . . .

JOHN: No *makāras*, no forbidden acts or anything like that.

SWAMIJI: . . . and where those forbidden processes are explained [i.e., prescribed], that is *vāmācāra*.

ALEXIS: Kula.[38]

---

36 Monistic *tantras*.

37 The three *makāras* (M's) are *madya* (wine), *māṁsa* (meat), and *maithuna* (sexual intercourse). [*Editor's note*]

38 "The Trika System is comprised of four sub-systems: the Pratyabhijñā system, the Kula system, the Krama system, and the Spanda system. These four systems, which form the one thought of the Trika system, all accept, and are based on, the same scriptures." *Kashmir*

SWAMIJI: And, in fact, He is *sarvācāra*, all processes reside in Him. And, in fact, there is no process at all. He is above these processes.

JOHN: *Sarvācāra*, is that Kula?

SWAMIJI: *Sarvācāra* is all *ācāras*. That is the real Trika system. Trika system does not forbid forbidden things and does not agree . . . *na kiñcit pratiṣidhyate, na kiñcit vidhīyate*,[39] there is nothing wrong, nothing right in that supreme state of thinking of the Trika system.[40]

I bow to Thee who possess all these systems.

Chapter 2 (41:40)

यथा तथापि यः पूज्यो यत्रतत्रापि योऽर्चितः ।
योऽपि वा सोऽपि वा योऽसौ देवस्तस्मै नमोऽस्तु ते ॥२०॥

yathā tathāpi yaḥ pūjyo yatratatrāpi yo'rcitaḥ /
yo'pi vā so'pi vā yo'sau devastasmai namo'stu te //20//

I bow to Thee, O Lord, who is adored in each and every way of worship, *yatra tatrāpi yo'rcitaḥ*, and who is worshiped in each and every place.

Not only in shrines, but also in the place of butchers also, He is worshiped in the real sense.

ALEXIS: In the place of?

SWAMIJI: Butchers! Where there is butchery, where there is adultery, there also He is worshiped in the real sense. He is not worshiped only in shrines, [not] only in *pūjā* rooms, not only in mosques or temples or churches. He is worshiped everywhere; everywhere His worship is being done. That is *yatra tarāpi yo'rcitaḥ yo'pi vā so'pi vā yo'sau.*

And that Personality [who is worshiped everywhere], whoever He may be–He may be Lord Śiva, He may be that person who is like that [butcher or adulterer]–I bow to that Person. He may be Lord Śiva, He may be Brahma, He may be my friend, I bow to

---

Shaivism–The Secret Supreme, 19.129. See appendix 6 for more on the Kula system and the "three M's".

39 *Tantrāloka*, 4.117.

40 See appendix 7 for explanation of "nothing wrong, nothing right".

Him. It means, I bow to that Being who is universal.

Chapter 2 (43:21)

मुमुक्षुजनसेव्याय सर्वसन्तापहारिणे
नमो विततलावण्यवाराय वरदाय ते ॥२१॥

mumukṣujanasevyāya sarvasantāpahāriṇe /
namo vitatalāvaṇyavārāya varadāya te //21//

I bow to Thee who is the bestower of boons (*varadāya*), who bestows boons to Your devotees, to Thy devotees, and who is *vitata lāvaṇya vārāya*, who is the embodiment of infinite beauty, . . .

Infinite beauty is There. Nowhere else that kind of beauty is seen–only in Lord Śiva. That is *vitatalāvaṇya* (*lāvaṇya* is "beauty, charm"; *vārāya* means "great heap").

ALEXIS: *Rāśi.*

SWAMIJI: *Rāśi.*[41]

. . . and who is *mumukṣu jana sevyāya*, who is adored by those who have the desire for being liberated (*mumukṣujana*)–those who have the desire for being liberated, He is worshiped by those–*sarvasantāpa hāriṇe*, and He who is the remover of all pains and sad[ness], sorrows.

Chapter 2 (44:49)

सदा निरन्तरानन्दरसनिर्भरिताखिल ।
त्रिलोकाय नमस्तुभ्यं स्वामिने नित्यपर्विणे ॥२२॥

sadā nirantarānandarasanirbharitākhila /
trilokāya namastubhyaṁ svāmine nityaparviṇe //22//

I bow to my Master, I bow to Thee who is my Master, and who always possesses festivals, where You have got festivals every day, every second, every moment. Festivals are [always] being functioned in Your kingdom.

There is no limited function of festivals. That is *nitya parviṇe*,

41 A heap or mass.

festivals are being functioned every second There.

JOHN: So, this means one whose whole life is, every moment is, festival.

SWAMIJI: Every moment is a festival, filled with festivals. So, there is never sadness. Always joy appears there in His kingdom.

I bow to Thee.

And [I bow to Thee] who is *sadā nirantarānanda rasanirbharitākhila trilokāya*, who has filled the whole three-fold universe by His uninterrupted and unlimited *ānanda rasa*.[42]

ALEXIS: Must we take the "three-fold universe" in all the possible senses of three here?

SWAMIJI: The three-fold universe (*triloka*) is this universe (*bhūḥ loka, bhūvaḥ loka,* and *svaḥ loka*) in the universal way of thinking.[43] If you think what is *triloka* from the individual point of view, then *triloka* is wakefulness (*jāgrat*), dreaming state (*svapna*), and dreamless state (*suṣupti*). These are *trilokas*.

And You have filled Your bliss of consciousness in all of these three worlds of mine. So, my wakefulness is overflowing with Your *ānanda*, by Your supreme bliss, and the dreaming state also, and the dreamless state also. So, I am filled with that bliss.

ALEXIS: Yes, *nirantarānanda*.

SWAMIJI: *Nirantara*, uninterrupted.

Next:

Chapter 2 (47:02)

सुखप्रधानसंवेद्यसंभोगैर्भजते च यत् ।
त्वामेव तस्मै घोराय शक्तिवृन्दाय ते नमः ॥२३॥

sukhapradhānasaṁvedyasaṁbhogairbhajate ca yat /
tvāmeva tasmai ghorāya śaktivṛndāya te namaḥ //23//

O Lord, I don't bow to Thee; I bow to Thy class of energies. I

42 *Ānanda rasa*: nectar of bliss.

43 "*Bhūḥ* means this [world], *bhūvaḥ* means this *āntarikṣa lokaḥ*, [the intermediate space between heaven and earth], and *svaḥ* is the *lokaḥ* of heavens." *Stava Cintāmaṇi* of Bhaṭṭanārāyaṇa, translation and commentary by Swami Lakshmanjoo (original audio recording, USF archives, Los Angeles, 1980-81).

bow to Thy class of energies, Thy innumerable energies who adore Thee only (*tvāmeva bhajate*, who adore Thee only) by beautiful *śabda*, *sparśa*, *rūpa*, *rasa*, and *gandha*.[44]

You strive to get beautiful things before your eyes, you strive to hear beautiful sounds in your ears, you try to smell the beautiful smell of flowers in your nose, and you want beautiful touch also with your skin. So, it means all of your senses, these are the energies of Lord Śiva. All of the five senses are the energies of Lord Śiva, and they are bent upon carrying all of these beautiful things inside and offering them to Lord Śiva who is residing in one's own heart.

So, I bow to these five senses.

ALEXIS: You translated *ghorāya śakti vṛndāya* as *saṁhāra rūpatvāt*[45]?

SWAMIJI: No. *Ghorāya* means *aghora rūpāya. Ghora śakti* means, not *ghoratarī*, not *ghora*, it is *aghora*. It is *upalakṣaṇa* (metaphor) for *aghora śaktis* here.

Ghora is frightful, but frightful for those who are ignorant. For those who are not ignorant, who are attached to Thee, who are attached to Thy devotion, it is not frightful for those [people]. It is *aghora*. [*Ghora*] is *aghora* [for Thy devotees].

Aghora energies carry you inside, *ghora* energies make you standstill, and *ghoratarī* energies kick you down. These are the three functioning actions of the three energies of Lord Śiva. One class of energies is *aghora* energies, the second class is *ghora* energies, and the third class is *ghoratarī* energies.

Here, he means [to say that] he is touching those *aghora* energies. But those *aghora* energies also are *ghora*, i.e., act [like] *ghora* for those who are ignorant, who have not given their whole [life] towards Lord Śiva. They also are kicked out.

ALEXIS: But why then does he say "*ghorāya*"? And why does Kṣemarāja, whose *parameṣṭhi guru*, Utpala[46] is, say "*sarvasaṁhartre*; *tasmai ghorāya sarvasaṁhartre*"?

SWAMIJI: *Sarvasaṁhartre*. But that won't do. *Ghora* is *aghora śakti*, because, then, all of your energies are carried towards the

44 Beautiful sound, touch, form, taste, and smell, respectively.

45 The destruction or absorption of differentiated appearances. [*Editor's note*]

46 Utpaladeva was Kṣemarāja's *parameṣṭhi guru* (great grand master). See appendix 8.

center of universal consciousness. When you collect all of these pleasures of the five senses and offer those pleasures to the Lord, then, instead of being destroyed in the differentiated perception of the universe, you are carried to that oneness of God consciousness. So, it is *ghorāya*, it is the function of *ghorāya* in the end, [i.e., to function as] *aghorāya*.

Chapter 2 (50:50)

मुनीनामप्यविज्ञेयं भक्तिसंबन्धचेष्टिताः ।
आलिङ्गन्त्यपि यं तस्मै कस्मैचिद्भवते नमः ॥२४॥

munīnāmapyavijñeyaṁ bhaktisaṁbandhaceṣṭitāḥ /
āliṅgantyapi yaṁ tasmai kasmaicidbhavate namaḥ //24//

Those who are *ṛṣis* and *munis*, who have discarded all of the pleasures of the universe, all worldly pleasures–who have kept away all worldly pleasures and directed their consciousness towards the recitation and meditation of Lord Śiva, those are called *munis*, *ṛṣis*–those *ṛṣis* also do not find Thee, O Lord. You are absolutely away from their perception. You are not perceived by them.

But, by those who are Your devotees and who are attached to Thee and who love Thee, *bhakti saṁbandha ceṣṭitāḥ* (*ceṣṭitāḥ* means "although they are given to the activities of the universe, they do everything in the daily routine of life"), in their daily routine of life, they do all worldly actions, but still they embrace You, O Lord. They, side by side, embrace You and, side by side, [they] do all of the activities of the universe. Those are real devotees.

I bow to Thee, O Lord. You are my dear. Actually, You are dear to me.

Chapter 2 (52:31)

परमामृतकोशाय परमामृतराशये ।
सर्वपारम्यपारम्यप्राप्याय भवते नमः ॥२५॥

paramāmṛtakośāya paramāmṛtarāśaye /
sarvapāramyapāramyaprāpyāya bhavate namaḥ //25//

I bow to Thee, O Lord, who is the treasure of the supreme nectar of God consciousness and who is *paramāmṛta rāśaye*, who is the *rāśi*, who is the mass of supreme nectar, who is the treasure of supreme nectar (*paramāmṛta kośāya*).

ALEXIS: So, in first, He is *viśvottīrṇa*[47] because He is the receptacle of that, and in the second, He is . . .

SWAMIJI: *Viśvamaya*.[48]

ALEXIS: . . . *viśvarūpa*.

SWAMIJI: Yes.

Sarva pāramya pāramya prāpyāya. And He is achieved only at that stage where there is the position of *sarva pāramya pāramya*, He is the topmost center of all tops.

ALEXIS: Transcendent.

SWAMIJI: Where . . . that is transcendental top, transcendental supreme limit. At the supreme limit of the transcendental state, He is achieved. He is achieved only there. When your eyes, your perceptions, and your five senses take the journey to that end and reach to that topmost transcendental point, then He is realized. Then He is realized. I bow to Thee. That is *sarva pāramya pāramya prāpyāya*.

Or, in other words, if you translate it [from the] Shaiva point of view, then *sarva pāramya* [*pāramya*] *prāpyāya* is, in each and every action, at the very source. At the very source of each and every action, He is realized–at the very source. For instance, you perceive any object, e.g., [you perceive] this is specks[49]. Before that, you perceive something like specks, and before that, you perceive some flow of perceiving where there are no specks available there in your perceiving act, and, in the very beginning, there is only the force of coming out. That is *sarva pāramya pāramya* [*prāpyāya*]. That is the source, the source of each and every perception.[50]

At the source of each and every perception, You are observed,

47 Transcendental.

48 One with the universe.

49 Eyeglasses.

50 See appendix 9 for an explanation of *nirvikalpa*.

You are achieved, my Lord. I bow to Thee.

ALEXIS: *Parā visarga.*

JOHN: This is *śāṁbhavopāya*?[51]

SWAMIJI: That is *śāmbava*, yes. *Parā visarga*, at the state of *parā visarga.*[52]

Chapter 2 (55:19)

महामन्त्रमयं नौमि रूपं ते स्वच्छशीतलम् ।
अपूर्वामोदसुभगं परामृतरसोल्वणम् ॥२६॥

mahāmantramayaṁ naumi rūpaṁ te svacchaśītalam /
apūrvāmodasubhagaṁ parāmṛtarasolvaṇam //26//

I bow to Thy form (*te rūpaṁ naumi*) who is *mahāmantra mayaṁ*, filled with the supreme *mantra*, filled with supreme I-consciousness, universal I-consciousness–who is only universal I-consciousness, I bow to Thee–and whose form is *svacchaśītalam*, whose form is always transparent, always cooling (*śītalam, ṭhaṇḍa*[53]).

ALEXIS: It is cool because of creative nectar in that metaphor?

SWAMIJI: No, It cools because there is no worry, there is no worry. Because, all worries, all worldly worries, create fire in you and you burn with that grief. For instance, I want to make love with some girl and she refuses, so I burn with the fire of the desire . . . "Oh, she hasn't accepted me. What should I do?" This is fire.

And all such fires are subsided in Your presence, when You are present. O Lord, when You are present, these fires have no opportunity to rise; no question to rise of these fires.

So, It is *śītala*; so, It is cooling down. So, divert yourself towards Lord Śiva and everything will be solved.

ALEXIS: That cool fire. And *svaccha* because It is universal reflector.

SWAMIJI: Transparent, yes. The whole universe is reflected in His being. Because, this universe, although it is separately

---

51 See appendix 2 for an explanation of the *upāyas*.

52 See appendix 10 for an explanation of *parā visarga*.

53 Hindi word for "cold".

perceived by us, but, in fact, if we could go to the depth of it, the depth of this perception, we will ultimately come to this conclusion that this whole universe is only a reflection in the mirror of God consciousness. So, you must feel that Lord Śiva is present everywhere, in each and every being in this world.

And, in addition, It is *apūrvāmoda subhagaṁ*, It is fragrant with the unique smell of God consciousness. And *parāmṛtara-solvaṇam*, and It is filled with supreme nectar.

ALEXIS: *Ulvana*, vigorous with that.

SWAMIJI: Yes. [The universe] is nourished by *parama amṛta rasa*[54] (nourished, *vardhitam*).

Chapter 2 (58:16)

स्वातन्त्र्यामृतपूर्णत्वदैक्यख्यातिमहापटे ।
चित्रं नास्त्येव यत्रेश तन्नौमि तव शासनम् ॥२७॥

svātantryāmṛtapūrṇatvadaikyakhyātimahāpaṭe /
citraṁ nāstyeva yatreśa tannaumi tava śāsanam //27//

O Lord, I bow to Thy *śāsanam*, to Thy *śāstra*, to Thy spiritual order, in which order form, nothing is written (*citraṁ nāstyeva*, nothing is written). It is only just a [blank] sheet only, a clear order form from Lord Śiva. And it is written, this order is written, on *svātantrya amṛtapūrṇa tvadaikyakhyāti*, which is the perception of Your Being, Your transcendental state, which is filled with the nectar of independence.[55] Your *svarūpa* is filled with the nectar of independence, and that nectar of independence is the sheet on which You have written orders, and on that sheet, nothing is written. I bow to that sheet, that order sheet, of Yours.

ALEXIS: *Citraṁ nāstyeva*, that great canvas on which there is no picture.

SWAMIJI: So, it means that this whole universe, although it is differentiatedly perceived–e.g., this is Sanderson, this is Denise, this is Pṛthvīnath, this is John, this is Mrs. Jah, this is Swamiji–

54 Supreme nectar of God consciousness.

55 See appendix 11 for an explanation of *svātantrya śakti*.

but actually there is nothing, no *citram*[56]. It is only universal consciousness, nothing else. Although this is a picture, this is writing, this is an order from Lord Śiva, written, but actually it is not written at all. It is only blank paper, white paper. Voidness only shines everywhere if you go to the depth of understanding this position of the universe. And [Utpaladeva] unites this picture, according to the Shaiva point of view, that although this is a picture, to us it seems it is written, it is drawn, . . .

ALEXIS: Inscribed in consciousness.

SWAMIJI: . . . inscribed in consciousness, but if you go to the basis, the root of this picture, nothing is written; there is nothing, no variety. It is only a white sheet and the white sheet, that will be perceived when you enter in that transcendental state of God consciousness. You will perceive that there is nothing; this universe is only God.

Chapter 2 (1:01:24)

सर्वाशङ्काशनिं सर्वा-
लक्ष्मीकालानलं तथा ।
सर्वामङ्गल्यकल्पान्तं
मार्गं माहेश्वरं नुमः ॥२८॥

sarvāśaṅkāśaniṁ sarvā-
lakṣmīkālānalaṁ tathā /
sarvāmaṅgalyakalpāntaṁ
mārgaṁ māheśvaraṁ numaḥ //28//

I bow to the path of Lord Śiva, the path of Lord Śiva . . .

The "path" means the avenue, from which avenue Lord Śiva could be achieved. That is the path.

. . . I bow to that path of Lord Śiva, which is *sarvāśaṅkāśaniṁ*, which is the thunderbolt to destroy all doubts; to destroy all doubts, it is a thunderbolt. It acts like a thunderbolt, where all doubts are destroyed, shattered. *Sarva alakṣmī kālānalaṁ*, and all *alakṣmī* (*alakṣmī* means *daridhratā*), for all misfortunes, this

56 Differentiation.

path of Lord Siva acts like *kālāgnirudra*, great fire so that all these misfortunes are fired to ashes.

So, all doubts are gone and all misfortunes are over just when you step on the path of Lord Śiva.

And *sarvā amaṅgalya kalpāntaṁ*, where *amaṅgala* (absence of joy), where absence of . . . for absence of joy, it is *kalpānta*, it is just destruction, the way of destroying all absence of joy.

So, joy comes.

I bow to that path of Lord Śiva.

Chapter 2 (1:03:26)

जय देव नमो नमोऽस्तु ते
सकलं विश्वमिदं तवाश्रितम् ।
जगतां परमेश्वरो भवान्
परमेकः शरणागतो स्मि ते ॥२९॥

jaya deva namo namo'stu te
sakalaṁ viśvamidaṁ tavāśritam /
jagatāṁ parameśvaro bhavān
paramekaḥ śaraṇāgato'smi te //29//

O Lord, be victorious! *Jayadeva*! O Lord, be victorious! *Namo namo'stu te*, I bow to Thee again and again. *Sakalaṁ viśvamidaṁ tavāśritam*, all this world is dependent on You. *Jagatāṁ parameśvaraḥ bhavān*, You are the Master of all the three worlds. I am the only person who has come and taken Your refuge.

Bas?

Paramekaḥ śaraṇamāgato'smi, here ends the chapter of Your explanation.[57]

Bas!

57 "Your explanation" in the sense of explaining how *sarvātmaparibhāvanākhyaṁ*, Lord Śiva is found everywhere. [*Editor's note*]

Chapter Three
Pleasing the Lord in Humble Ways
Praṇaya prasādākhyaṁ tṛtīyaṁ stotram

SWAMIJI: This is the third chapter. [It is nominated as] "*praṇaya prasādākhyaṁ tṛtīyaṁ stotram*". The meaning of "*praṇaya prasāda*" is just to attempt to make God pleased by various ways; not furious ways, but various bowing ways, by various humble ways. You try to please the Lord by humble ways. It is *praṇayah prasāda*, e.g., "please, please, please".

ALEXIS: Supplication.

SWAMIJI: Yes, that is *praṇaya prasāda*.

Chapter 3 (00:53)

सदसत्त्वेन भावानां युक्ता या द्वितयी गतिः ।
तामुल्लङ्घ्य त्रितीयस्मै नमश्चित्राय शम्भवे ॥ १ ॥

sadasattvena bhāvānāṁ yuktā yā dvitayī gatiḥ /
tāmullaṅghya tritīyasmai namaścitrāya śambhave //1//

I bow to that wonderful Lord Śiva.

Citrāya means "wonderful, marvelous" Lord Śiva.

Actually, *sadasattvena bhāvānāṁ yuktā yā dvitayī gatiḥ*, there are two aspects of the processes of the universe; the universe moves in two ways. One universe is that of existence and the other universe is that of non-existence.

For instance, the existing universe is *nīla pītādi*[58], all this objective world is the existing universe, and the non-existent universe is imaginary, when you imagine so many things, e.g., that, "I will have this much", "I will have that thing", etc. This is the imaginary world. That is the non-existent world.

ALEXIS: But, from point of view of consciousness, it is

58 Lit., blue, yellow, etc. That is, the existing universe is comprised of differentiated objects of perception. [*Editor's note*]

existent.

SWAMIJI: Non-existent is also existent because as long as you perceive [something] in your own mind, [then it is existing]. I can create things in the dreaming state also, which are non-existent. In the dreaming state, the world is non-existent, but I ride in a motorcar there also in the non-existent world; and where the motorcar is my own imagination, and the road on which the motorcar is driven is my own imagination, and to the point where the motorcar is being driven, that is also my own imagination. So, with my own imagination, I create this universe and that is the [so-called] "non-existent universe". That is found in the dreaming state.[59] That is found in drunkards. Drunkards also create–drunkards, those people–also create those worlds of their own.

ALEXIS: And lovers.

SWAMIJI: Lovers also. They are always blind. They also create their own worlds.

And this [existing] universe is the creation of God and that [non-existent universe] is the creation of the individual being, in their own minds. And that [creation of God] is the *sat* world and this [creation of the individual] is *asat* world, the existing world and the non-existent world.

Tvāṁ ullaṅghya, just having crossed these two worlds, when you cross these two worlds (the existing world and non-existent world), then you get entry in the world which is the third world, the third way of the world. That is *sat asat bhāva rahitam*, *sat asat bhāva atītam*, He is beyond existing things and non-existent things. And that is Lord Śiva.

ALEXIS: Swamiji, this "existent" and "non-existent" can also be taken in logical way. When I say–in the nature of *vikalapa*–when I say, "this is a pot", although that is just positive from the point of view of consciousness, in order to make that conception, I have to have negation in my mind, "this is not not a pot". *Apohana śakti.*

SWAMIJI: That is also [correct], yes. *Apohana śakti* is also the

59 "The main explanation of dreaming state is, when you are dreaming, and that dreaming state, when you are in that world, when you are put in that world of dreaming state, that world is not experienced by any other person. It is your own world, your own personal world. It is not experienced by someone else." *Tantrāloka*, 10.251 (USF archives).

non-existent world.[60]

ALEXIS: So, from that non-discursive point of view, it is neither *sat* (existent) nor *asat* (non-existent).

SWAMIJI: Yes.

But You, You are above it.

ALEXIS: As a perceiver.

SWAMIJI: You are neither *sat*, nor above, nor *asat*. And that is the state which can't be described. It is wonderful (*citraya śambhave*). I bow to that Śiva state.

Chapter 3 (05:02)

आसुरर्षिजनादस्मिन्नस्वतन्त्रे जगत्रये ।
स्वतन्त्रास्ते स्वतन्त्रस्य ये तवैवानुजीविनः ॥२॥

āsurarṣijanādasminnasvatantre jagatraye /
svatantrāste svatantrasya ye tavaivānujīvinaḥ //2//

In fact, in this triple universe, three-fold universe, everyone is dependent, everyone is *asvātantrya*, without *svātantrya*, without independence. It is dependent! The whole body of the three worlds is dependent to this thing or that thing.

ALEXIS: Dependently originated.[61]

SWAMIJI: Yes, dependent.

And, in this dependent world, in this dependent three-[fold] world, those people only are independent who serve You who are the absolute embodiment of independence. Only Your *sevaks*, your devotees, are independent in this dependent universe, *te svatantrya ye tava svatantrasya anujīvinaḥ*, who follow, who are the followers of Thyself who are the absolute embodiment of independence.

Right from the *devarṣijana*[62] to this earth, all are dependent, all are seen dependent to one thing or another thing. In this dependent, fully dependent world, only those people are indepen-

60 *Apohana* means reasoning/discerning, removal/forgeting. [*Editor's note*]

61 See the Buddhist doctrine of *pratītyasamutpāda*, dependent origination. [*Editor's note*]

62 Race (*jana*) of celestial saints/sages (*devarṣi*). [*Editor's note*]

dent who serve Thee [who art] independent.

ALEXIS: This other world is the world of causality.

SWAMIJI: Because, Lord Śiva is the only embodiment of independence, and those persons who worship Lord Śiva become independent. They also are independent.

Chapter 3 (06:58)

अशेषविश्वखचितभवद्वपुरनुस्मृतिः ।
येषां भवरुजामेकं भेषजं ते सुखासिनः ॥ ३ ॥

aśeṣaviśvakhacitabhavadvapuranusmṛtiḥ /
yeṣāṁ bhavarujāmekaṁ bheṣajaṁ te sukhāsinaḥ //3//

Those who possess only one dose [of medicine] for getting rid of the universe of difference, *bhava roga* . . .

Bhava roga means "that disease, which can't be cured by any medicine". This is the disease of the universe, the disease of differentiated perception. When you perceive differentiatedly, that is the disease, which you can't get rid of in any way, except there is only one dose, one dose for relieving this trouble.

Which trouble?

ALEXIS: *Bhinnavedyatā.*

SWAMIJI: *Bhinnavedyatā*, differentiated perception, the disease of perceiving differentiatedly in this universe is the greatest disease we have.

. . . and those persons who have, who possess, this dose . . .

[What] is that dose?

Aśeṣa viśva khacita bhavadvapur anusmṛtiḥ. Just to memorize their minds towards Thy *svarūpa*, Thy being of God consciousness, which is filled with universality, where the whole universe is existing. This whole universe is, in fact, existing in God consciousness, and to create memory, and to put memory, on that God consciousness is the dose for removal of this trouble, this disease.

ALEXIS: So, "memory" here means . . . *anusmṛti* means "constant flow of awareness in That".

SWAMIJI: Yes, uninterrupted flow of meditation.

JOHN: This is *śāktopāya*.

SWAMIJI: This is *śāktopāya*, yes.[63]

Chapter 3 (09:08)

सितातपत्रं यस्येन्दुः स्वप्रभापरिपूरितः ।
चामरं स्वर्धुनीस्रोतः स एकः परमेश्वरः ॥४॥

sitātapatraṁ yasyenduḥ svaprabhāparipūritaḥ /
cāmaraṁ svardhunīsrotaḥ sa ekaḥ parameśvaraḥ //4//

He only is Lord Śiva, He only is the real master of the universe (*sa ekaḥ parameśvaraḥ*, He only is the master of the universe) who has used the moon as an umbrella, who has used the moon as an umbrella for Him[self]. *Sitātapatraṁ yasyendu*, the moon is, for Him, [used] as an umbrella. [He] who has got the moon in the place of an umbrella and *cāmaraṁ svardhunīsrotaḥ*, and this Milky Way is an electric fan (*cāmaraṁ*[64]). The Milky Way is an electric fan for that Being. For whom the Milky Way serves as an electric fan (*cāmara*) and this moon serves in place of an umbrella, *sa ekaḥ parameśvaraḥ*, He is the only master existing in this universe.

Sitātapatraṁ yasyendu svaprabhā paripūritaḥ.

Now will come the next, second meaning.

When this universal objective state is infused by your God consciousness, . . .

The universal objective state is *indu* (moon). The universal objective state is called *soma* (moon) from the Shaiva point of view–universal objectivity is *soma*–and you have to inject in that *soma*, in that objective world, *svaprakāśa*, your own God consciousness. You have to inject that with God consciousness.

. . . and then *soma* will get, will possess, another formation. *Soma* will not become *soma*; *soma* will become the abode of nectar for him. And *cāmaraṁ svardhunīsrotaḥ* (*svardhunīsrotaḥ* means "the rise of *kuṇḍalinī*"), the rise of *kuṇḍalinī* [functions like] a *cāmara*.

[For He] who has got the rise of *kuṇḍalinī* as a *cāmara*, as an electric fan, and [for whom] this universal objective [world, which

63 See appendix 2 for an explanation of the *upāyas*.

64 Lit., fly-whisk.

is] injected already with God consciousness, is an umbrella, *sa ekaḥ para*[*meśvaraḥ*], He is the real Lord, He is the real master, He is the real Lord Śiva. There is no other Lord Śiva.

ALEXIS: So, here, *parabīja* is *udāra*; this is *para bījodāra*[65]. This *indu* is *sa-kāra*, this *svardhunī srota* is *au-kāra,* and *sa ekaḥ parameśvara* is *visargaḥ* [*aḥ*].[66]

SWAMIJI: [laughs] Yes, that way also you can take it. Yes, you can take it that way also.

Chapter 3 (12:22)

प्रकाशां शीतलामेकां शुद्धां शशिकलामिव ।
दृशं वितर मे नाथ कामप्यमृतवाहिनीम् ॥५॥

prakāśāṁ śītalāmekāṁ śuddhāṁ śaśikalāmiva /
dṛśaṁ vitara me nātha kāmapyamṛtavāhinīm //5//

O desired Lord (*Nātha*, O desired Lord), throw Your kind glance on me (*dṛśaṁ vitara me*, throw Your kind glance on me), and that glance which is *prakāśām*, filled with light, *śītalām*, which is filled with coolness–and with only one glance; I want only one glance of Thee–and which is always all-round purified (*śuddhām*) just like *śaśikalām*, just like the ray of the moon, the *kalā* of the [moon]. Throw that glance on me, O Lord, which is *kāmapi*, which is a unique glance, and *amṛtavāhinī*, which flows, which will flow out, floods of nectar on me.

ALEXIS: *Unmīlanā krama.*

SWAMIJI: It is *unmīlanā*, yes.[67]

---

65 The rise of "*sauḥ*" (*sa+au+aḥ*).

66 See appendix 12 for an explanation the *mantra* "*sauḥ*".

67 "*Unmīlanā samādhi* is experienced in *turyātita* and *nimīlanā samādhi* is experienced in *turya*. This is the difference between *turya* and *turyātita*. *Nimīlanā samādhi* means absorption of universal consciousness; when universal consciousness is absorbed in your nature, that is *turya*. When universal consciousness is expanded every-where, that is *turyātita* [viz., *unmīlanā samādhi*]." *Tantrāloka* (USF archives) 10.288. See appendix 3 for an explanation of *turya* and *turyātīta* and appendix 17 for more on *unmīlanā* and *nimīlanā samādhi*.

Chapter 3 (13:38)

त्वच्चिदानन्दजलधेश्च्युताः संवित्तिविप्रुषः ।
इमाः कथं मे भगवन्नामृतास्वादसुन्दराः ॥ ६ ॥

tvaccidānandajaladheścyutāḥ saṁvittivipruṣaḥ /
imāḥ kathaṁ me bhagavannāmṛtāsvādasundarāḥ //6//

Here, the commentary of Kṣemarāja is not being digested by me, i.e., the commentary of Kṣemarāja for this *śloka*.[68]

[Utpaladeva] says, "*Tvad cidānanda jaladheścyutāḥ saṁvittivipruṣaḥ imāḥ*, this whole universe, this whole universe is actually *tvad cidānanda jaladheh saṁvittivipruṣaḥ*, these are drops, which have come out from the ocean of Thy being who is the embodiment of *cit* (consciousness) and *ānanda* (bliss). From the body of the embodiment of *cidānanda*, *cidānanda rasa*[69], these drops have come out in this universe and this universe is created. This whole universe [is created by] a few drops, which have come out from that ocean of God consciousness. *Kathaṁ me bhagavan na amṛtāsvāda sundarāḥ*, why don't I taste from these [drops] that nectar of God consciousness? Why that nectar of God consciousness is absent here for me? Why don't I get God consciousness? Why don't I find God consciousness here also?"

But Kṣemarāja has commentated upon it in another way. He has commentated that actually this whole universe has come out . . . these are drops, which have come out from that center, from that universal ocean of God consciousness. This universal objective world are the drops, which have come out from that ocean, [and Utpaladeva is saying], "*Kathaṁ me bhagavan na amṛta*, how cannot this universe become 'nectarized' for me? This is already 'nectarized' for me!" But this is not the meaning. [Utpaladeva] wants this universe to be 'nectarized' with God consciousness [because] he does not perceive that 'nectarized' state of this universe.

ALEXIS: His devotion is the desire for that to be 'nectarized'.

SWAMIJI: Desire for that. But this desire is neglected by the

68 That is to say, Swamiji does not agree with Kṣemarāja's commentary on this *śloka*. [*Editor's note*]

69 The nectar (*rasa*) of consciousness (*cit*) and bliss (*ānanda*).

commentator here.

ALEXIS: So, he takes it as a *kāku*, some intonation?

SWAMIJI: Yes. *Kathaṁ me bhagavan na* [*amṛtā*] *svād . . . bhavantyeva*! But that is not the real commentary for this.

Chapter 3 (16:31)

त्वयि रागरसे नाथ न मग्नं हृदयं प्रभो ।
येषामहृदया एव तेऽवज्ञास्पदमीदृशाः ॥७॥

tvayi rāgarase nātha na magnaṁ hṛdayaṁ prabho /
yeṣāmahṛdayā eva te'vajñāspadamīdṛśāḥ //7//

O my Master, those whose mind has not dived into the nectar of Thy devotion, *ahṛdaya eva te*, they have no mind. From my point of view, they have no mind. Those persons are mindless, absolutely mindless. *Avajñāspadamīdṛśāḥ*, such people are absolutely *avajñāspadam*, to be thrown away, just like ordinary stones.

Chapter 3 (17:11)

प्रभुणा भवता यस्य जातं हृदयमेलनम् ।
प्राभवीणां विभूतीनां परमेकः स भाजनम् ॥८॥

prabhuṇā bhavatā yasya jātaṁ hṛdayamelanam /
prābhavīṇāṁ vibhūtīnāṁ paramekaḥ sa bhājanam //8//

[One] who has achieved the oneness of heart with Thee, O Master, O my Master, he who has achieved the oneness of heart with Thee, he is the only person who is worthy of enjoying the nectar of Thy state, Thy state of God consciousness. The nectar of Thy glorious state is tasted by him only.

ALEXIS: So, *hṛdayamelanam* is fusion of awareness in the Lord.

SWAMIJI: No. *Hṛdayamelanam* [means] "whatever you think, I think the same".

ALEXIS: So, that *hṛdayam*, that awareness, is identical.

SWAMIJI: That is identical; identity with heart. The state of being the slave of a master is not a joke. The state of being [a slave of] a master must be in such a way that, when you are a slave to your master, your master must not [have to] ask you to do such and such a thing. You must know what he thinks in his mind and you must do that. This is the actual position of being a slave. That is the oneness of *hṛdaya* (heart). Whatever [your master] thinks, that thought must come in your mind. [For example], that master thinks at this time for [drinking] tea, at this time for [eating] cake, at this time for [having] *kaṭahal*[70], and so on. You should not give him the trouble to [ask for these things]. Before that, you should act according to his choice. His choice must be known to you, then you are his slave. Otherwise, you are engaged, an engaged *coolie*[71].

Chapter 3 (19:11)

हर्षाणामथ शोकानां सर्वेषां प्लावकः समम् ।
भवद्ध्यानामृतापूरोनिम्नानिम्न भुवामिव ॥९॥

harṣāṇāmatha śokānāṁ sarveṣāṁ plāvakaḥ samam /
bhavaddhyānāmṛtāpūro nimnānimnabhuvāmiva //9//

O Lord, *bhavat dhyāna amṛtāpūraḥ*, the great flood of the nectar of Thy meditation–meditating upon You is the flood of nectar that flows out (*bhavat dhyāna amṛtāpūra*)–the large flood of the nectar of Thy meditation is *harṣāṇāmatha śokānāṁ sarveṣaṁ plāvakaḥ samam*, it floods, in the same level, all joys and all sorrows, just like *nimnānimna bhuvāmiva*, just like low and high grounds are flooded in the same river by a great flood. The flood levels [cover] the ups and downs of the grounds so it is in one level.

JOHN: Flood evens the ground.

SWAMIJI: Evens the ground.

In the same way, the flood of the nectar of Thy meditation keeps in the same level, all joys and all sorrows, all torture (*bhavat dhyāna*; *dhyāna* is meditation, contemplation).

---

70 Jackfruit.

71 An unskilled laborer.

ALEXIS: *Dhyānam* is used here in the highest sense of *samāveśa*[72] or just in the lowest sense of gross contemplation?
SWAMIJI: No, higher sense.[73]

Chapter 3 (21:07)

केव न स्याद्दशा तेषां सुखसम्भारनिर्भरा ।
येषामात्माधिकेनेश न क्वापि विरहस्त्वया ॥१०॥

keva na syāddaśā teṣāṁ sukhasambhāranirbharā /
yeṣāmātmādhikeneśa na kvāpi virahastvayā //10//

Īśa, O Lord, for those persons, those who are exceptions [amongst] these human beings, those who are an exception, to whom *ātmādhikena tayā na kvāpi virahaḥ*, You are, for them, You are more than their [own] lives, more than their own existence, more than their own existence in this universe–You are more than that for them–for those persons, all states of their lives are filled with the excess of joy, every now and then[74]. *Teṣāṁ sukha sambhāradaśā kā eva na syāt*, constantly, by the excess of joy, filled with the excess of joy, all states, for them, all states of their livelihood are filled with the excess of joy, always. They are filled with joy. They never become sad. For whom You are more than their lives, and they are not separated, they don't remain away from You for even one second–*na kvāpī virahastvayā*, they don't remain away from You, away from Your consciousness–for

72 Trance or absorption.
73 "The one who experiences this state of the absorption (*samāveśa*) of *krama mudrā* experiences this whole universe melting into nothingness in the great sky of God Consciousness (*cid-gagana*). Although he opens his eyes and perceives that everything is melting into that state, yet when he strives to come out of that state, it becomes very difficult for him. As it is very difficult for us to enter into that state, in the same way, it is very difficult for that *yogi* to come out of it." *Self Realization in Kashmir Shaivism–The Oral Teachings of Swami Lakshmanjoo*, ed. John Hughes (State University of New York Press, Albany, 1995), 5.114. See appendix 13 for an explanation of *krama mudrā*.
74 Swamiji often uses "every now and then" to mean "repeatedly" or "continuously". [*Editor's note*]

those [people], all states of their lives are filled with the excess of joy, always.

Chapter 3 (23:20)

गर्जामि बत नृत्यामि पूर्णा मम मनोरथाः ।
स्वामी ममैष घटितो यत्त्वमत्यन्तरोचनः ॥ ११ ॥

garjāmi bata nṛtyāmi pūrṇā mama manorathāḥ /
svāmī mamaiṣa ghaṭito yattvamatyantarocanaḥ / / 11 / /

As You are my *atyanta rocanaḥ*, You are always dearest to me (*atyanta rocanaḥ*)–I love You, I long for Your presence (*atyanta rocanaḥ*)–as You who are so loved by me, [You are thereby] devised or solved for me. You are devised or solved for me. So, You have come and You are present with me. You are always with me now because You are *ghaṭita*, attained, solved. The problem is solved. This was my problem, i.e., to attain You, and that I have achieved. This was the only problem in my life to attain You, to attain Your presence, and That presence is solved for me. Hence, *garjāmi*, I will emit a deep thundering sound now with joy (*garjāmi*) and *bata nṛtyāmi* (*nṛtyāmi* means "I will dance").

It does not mean an ordinary dance. Dance means *nṛti*. The verbal root for *nṛti* is *nṛti gātra vikṣepe*, I will shatter all of the limited limbs of my body. I will shatter away–*nṛti gātra vikṣepe*–I will shatter all the limitations of/from my body now because You are solved now, because You were the only One for whom I was craving for.

Chapter 3 (25:24)

नान्यद्वेद्यं क्रिया यत्र नान्यो योगो विदा च यत् ।
ज्ञानं स्यात् किन्तु विश्वैकपूर्णा चित्त्वं विजृम्भते ॥ १२ ॥

nānyadvedyaṁ kriyā yatra nānyo yogo vidā ca yat /
jñānaṁ syāt kintu viśvaikapūrṇā cittvaṁ vijṛmbhate / / 12

Where there is no other object of perception, where there is no other action, where there is no other *yoga*, practice of *yoga*, and where there is no other way of thinking, and where there is no other knowledge than Thee, than the knowledge of Thy own nature, there only the kingdom of consciousness is glorified, shines from all sides, in which consciousness this whole differentiated world becomes one offering in That fire of consciousness.

ALEXIS: *Svāhā.*

SWAMIJI: *Svāhā.*[75] In one *svāhā*, it is finished, i.e., this whole differentiated perception of the world.

ALEXIS: *Pūrṇā* is *pūrṇā āhuti.*

SWAMIJI: *Pūrṇāhuti*, yes.[76]

Chapter 3 (26:43)

दुर्जयानामनन्तानां दुःखानां सहसैव ते ।
हस्तात्पलायिता येषां वाचि शश्वच्छिवध्वनिः ॥१३॥

durjayānāmanantānāṁ duḥkhānāṁ sahasaiva te /
hastātpalāyitā yeṣāṁ vāci śaśvacchivadhvaniḥ //13//

Those persons in whose mouth this sound of "Śiva" is residing eternally, without any break–those who recite this *mantra* of "Śiva" without any break, in continuity–those persons have escaped from the grip of unlimited and uncontrollable *duḥkha's* (the tortures of the universe). The tortures of the universe, which are numberless and which are uncontrollable, which you can't conquer, they can't be conquered, and they have escaped from the grip of those tortures in an instant, all of a sudden, i.e., in whose mouth this *Śiva dhvani*[77] is continuously flowing.

ALEXIS: But not only *vaikharyāṁ vāci.*

75 Each offering into the sacrificial fire (*havan*) is traditionally concluded by the recitation of the word "*svāhā*", which means "hail", "hail to", or "may a blessing rest on". [*Editor's note*]

76 The *pūrṇāhuti* (lit., "complete oblation") is the culmination of the *havan* ceremony. It is said to contain the complete essence and purpose of the *havan* within it. [*Editor's note*]

77 The sound of "Śiva".

SWAMIJI: Even *vaikharyāṁ vāci* also.[78]

ALEXIS: But the main sense is a higher sense of awareness.

SWAMIJI: No. When you utter the sound of "Śiva" with its meaning in *vaikharī* also, it doesn't matter, it will carry you to that God consciousness in the end.

ALEXIS: But Utpala means here primarily *parāmarśa*.

SWAMIJI: Yes, *parāmarśa* is the chief, [it is] predominant there. *Śivā dhvani* means entry in Śiva in the real sense.[79]

Chapter 3 (28:52)

उत्तमः पुरुषोऽन्योऽस्ति युष्मच्छेषविशेषितः ।
त्वं महापुरुषस्त्वेको निःशेषपुरुषाश्रयः ॥१४॥

uttamaḥ puruṣo'nyo'sti yuṣmaccheṣaviśeṣitaḥ /
tvaṁ mahāpuruṣastveko niḥśeṣapuruṣāśrayaḥ //14//

Actually, in this world of action, there are three persons existing, grammatically. One is first person, the other is second person, and the other is third person. First person, second person, and . . . first person indicates "I", second person indicates "you", third person indicates "he". *Uttamaḥ puruṣo*, but it is already admitted in this world of actions that whenever you three–for instance, you, this woman, and this woman–do some work jointly and you have to . . . when you [want to say] to me that "we are working jointly", you don't say "I am working jointly, she is working jointly, and she is working jointly". What do you say there? "*We* are working!" So, the first person is predominant in all these three persons from the grammatical point of view. First person is the chief. So, we attribute first person for all of these three persons, i.e., for him, for you, and for myself. We say, "we are reading". *Uttamaḥ puruṣa.* In the same way, *uttamaḥ*

78 *Vaikharī* is the gross level of speech. Swamiji explains the levels of speech in his commentary in Chapter 1, verse 13.

79 *Parāmarśa* is a synonym for *vimarśa*, reflective Self-awareness. "It is the *parāmarśa* of fullness, the fullness of Being. Where there is *parāmarśa* of the fullness of Being, there is no question of rise of *idaṁ* (this-ness) or *ahaṁ* (I-ness) . . . and it is thus nominated as "*ahaṁ*" that way." *Tantrāloka*, 3.203 (USF archives).

puruṣa, this first person is *anya*, [more] supreme than *yuṣmat śeṣaviśeṣitaḥ*, than the second person and the third person.

But, O Lord, You are neither first person, nor second person, nor third person. You are *mahā puruṣa*! You are *mahā puruṣa* because You are the life of all these three persons, *tvaṁ mahāpurusaḥ tu eka niḥśeṣa puruṣāśrayaḥ*, because You are the basis of all of these three persons. All of these three persons flow out in this manifestation because of You.

Chapter 3 (31:17)

जयन्ति ते जगद्वन्द्या दासास्ते जगतां विभो ।
संसारार्णव एवैष येषां क्रीडामहासरः ॥१५॥

jayanti te jagadvandyā dāsāste jagatāṁ vibho /
saṁsārārṇava evaiṣa yeṣāṁ krīḍāmahāsaraḥ //15//

Jagatāṁ vibho, O Lord of the three worlds (he calls Him "the Lord of the three worlds"), they are victorious, those persons are victorious, who are Thy slaves, who art Thy slaves, who are Your slaves. And they are actually Your slaves, but, on the contrary, they are respected by the whole universe. Although they are Your slaves, they are honored and respected by all of the three worlds. Everybody respects them because they are Your slaves. The slaves of the Lord are respected by everybody.

In Kashmiri, it is said, "*yus khoci tasa tamisa khoci ālama*, the one who prostrates before Lord Śiva is prostrated [before by] the whole universe". Everybody takes refuge in him because he has taken refuge in that supreme Being, the creator of the universe.

So, although they are Your slaves, they are *jagat vandyā*, they are respected by the whole universe. And for whom, *yeṣāṁ eṣa saṁsāra arṇava eva*, for whom this great ocean of the universe, the great ocean of torture, sadness, ups and downs of this universe–this is an ocean; he has nominated this universe as an ocean of torture, ocean of sadness, ocean of everything bad–for whom this ocean of torture of the universe is *krīḍāmahāsaraḥ*, it just appears . . . for them, it appears just like enjoyment in . . . as you get enjoyment in a bathing pool, e.g., when you go to swim in

Naginbagh[80].

Chapter 3 (33:59)

आसतां तावदन्यानि दैन्यानीह भवज्जुषाम् ।
त्वमेव प्रकटीभूया इत्यनेनैव लज्ज्यते ॥ १६ ॥

āsatāṁ tāvadanyāni dainyānīha bhavajjuṣām /
tvameva prakaṭībhūyā ityanenaiva lajjyate //16//

Those who are Thy devotees, who are Your devotees, who have taken refuge in Your Being, let other miserable states or griefs remain unsolved for them (*tāvad anyāni dainyānīha*, other miserable states or griefs in this world).

There are so many griefs and miserable states and conditions. For instance, I want a wife, but I don't get a wife; I want money, but I don't get money; I want a car, but I don't get a car; I want peace of mind, but I don't get peace of mind. There are so many miserable states in this universe to be solved.

Let them be unsolved for the time being. O Lord, I am not going to solve those miserable states of this universe. Only one thing is to be solved for me and that is everything for me. That is, *tvameva prakaṭībhūyā*, let You reveal Your nature to me. I only want Thy presence before me. If You reveal Your nature to me, *ityanenanaiva*, all of those miserable states will vanish off by itself, by themselves, automatically. So, the only problem is, for me, to be solved . . .

What is that problem?

DEVOTEE: To be one with that Lord.

SWAMIJI: Not to be one with that Lord. Don't talk of Shaivism always [laughter]. This is a devotional book.[81]

---

80 A lake in the vicinity of Srinagar, Kashmir. [*Editor's note*]

81 Devotion, or *bhakti*, implies duality, and Kashmir Shaivism teaches an uncompromising monism. Swamiji does say, however, that "*bhakti* is when you see that each and every object is the glamour of one's own consciousness". *Bhagavad Gita–In the Light of Kashmir Shaivism*, 4.203.

Chapter 3 (35:56)

मत्परं नास्ति तत्रापि जापकोऽस्मि तदैक्यतः ।
तत्त्वेन जप इत्यक्षमालया दिशसि क्वचित् ॥१७॥

matparaṁ nāsti tatrāpi jāpako'smi tadaikyataḥ /
tattvena japa ityakṣamālayā diśasi kvacit //17//

O Lord, there is one painting of Your form available in the market.

You have seen that [image] where the Lord is seated with crossed legs, eyes closed, with beads, moving beads [i.e., performing *japa*], and eyes closed, and thinking of something else. There is one [image of] Lord Śiva in *samādhi*, in the posture of *samādhi*, with eyes closed and thinking of something other, higher than His being. [Lord Śiva appears to be] worshiping some other deity.

But, [Utpaladeva] says here, "*matparaṁ nāsti*". By that *akṣamālā*, by those beads, moving those beads in that *kvacit*, in some photograph of Yours, in some paintings of Yours, You reveal to us, You make us understand, that "*matparaṁ nāsti*, there is no other higher being than Me (*matparaṁ nāsti*), but still I recite the *mantra* of something else".

So, the recitation of *mantra* is not reciting a *mantra* for other lords. You must recite the *mantra* for your own Self. [Lord Śiva is saying], "I am reciting the *mantra* for my own nature. I am not diverted towards [some other] higher being. There is no higher being because *matparaṁ nāsti*, there is no other higher being than Me. *Tatrāpi jāpako'smi*, even then, I recite a *mantra*".

So, in fact, the recitation of *mantra* means reciting *mantra* to reveal your own Self.

Tattvena [*japa*] *iti akṣamālayā diśasi*. This You teach in that photograph, in that photograph of Yours, that you must recite *mantra* for your own Self; you must recognize your own nature. You must not go astray to all other *devatās* (gods).

Chapter 3 (38:28)

सतोऽवश्यं परमसत्सच्च तस्मात्परं प्रभो ।
त्वं चासतस्सतश्चान्यस्तेनासि सदसन्मयः ॥१८॥

sato'vaśyaṁ paramasatsacca tasmātparaṁ prabho /
tvaṁ cāsatassataścānyastenāsi sadasanmayaḥ //18//

Prabho, O Master, *sato'vaśyaṁ paramasat*, it is a fact that an existing thing is absolutely other than a non-existent object; that existent object is other than a non-existent object. *Sat* (existence) is other than *asat* (non-existence), *sato avaśyaṁ paraṁ asat*, *sat ca tasmāt paraṁ prabho*, and that existent object is other than a non-existent object. *Tvaṁ cāsatassataścānya*, but You are something else. You are neither existent nor non-existent. You are neither existing nor non-existing. *Tvaṁ cāsatassataścānya*, You are above existence and non-existence.

But Lord Śiva, our Lord Śiva of Shaivism, is both existing and non-existing also, because the complete embodiment of Lord Śiva is because He is complete and not complete. The one who is complete only and not incomplete, he is not complete; he is incomplete because incomplete is not there. When there is incomplete also and complete also (both are existing there), this is the completion, this is the fullness.

ALEXIS: Existence comes there, too–*mahā sattā*.

SWAMIJI: That is *mahā sattā*[82].

Sato aveśyam paraṁ asat. *Asat*, a non-existent thing is other than an existent thing. *Sat ca tasmātparaṁ prabho*, and this existent thing is other than a non-existent thing.

Tvaṁ ca asata sataśca anya, You are above these non-existent and existent things. *Tenāsi sadasanmayaḥ*, this is why You are both; You are existing also and not existing also. You are both.

Chapter 3 (40:59)

सहस्रसूर्यकिरणाधिकशुद्धप्रकाशवान् ।
अपि त्वं सर्वभुवनव्यापकोऽपि न दृश्यसे ॥१९॥

sahasrasūryakiraṇādhikaśuddhaprakāśavān /
api tvaṁ sarvabhuvanavyāpako'pi na dṛśyase //19//

82 Absolute Being.

Although, O Lord, You are more brilliant and shining (*adhika śuddha prakāśavān*) than *sahasra sūryakiraṇā*, than the simultaneous rise of the rays of one thousand suns, . . .

Just imagine one thousand suns have risen and how many rays, brilliant rays, it will produce.

. . . You are more brilliant than those rays, although You are more brilliant and vividly revealed in each and every corner of this universe, and *api tvaṁ sarva bhuvanavyāpako'si*, although You have pervaded this whole universe (the existent universe and the non-existent universe), . . .

Do you know what is the existent universe? The existent universe is this.[83] What is the non-existent universe? The imaginary world.

. . . although You have pervaded both of the worlds, the existing world and the non-existing world, *tathāpi na dṛśyase*, it is a wonder for me how it is that You are not seen anywhere.

ALEXIS: *Śuddhaprakāśavān.*

SWAMIJI: You are not seen anywhere. Nobody can perceive You in this universe. You are absolutely . . . You have kept [Yourself] absolutely secret.

ALEXIS: Utpala suggests the reason in the first line: *śuddha prakāśavān*, because That *prakāśa* is absolutely pure, absolutely universal.[84]

SWAMIJI: Yes, because It can't be an object. The one who is absolutely pure, purely subjective, It will never become the object of anybody. It will never be revealed because It is the revealer. He sees everything.

Vijñātāramare kena vijānīyāt[85], the knower can't be known. The knower knows everybody, but nobody knows the knower. The knower is the Thing. This is the embodiment of knower-ship.

Chapter 3 (43:21)

जडे जगति चिद्रूपः किल वेद्येऽपि वेदकः ।
विभुर्मितेे च येनासि तेन सर्वोत्तमो भवान् ॥२०॥

83 The objective world, which is common to all subjects. [*Editor's note*]

84 See appendix 5 for an explanation of *prakāśa*, the light of consciousness.

85 *Bṛhadāraṇyaka Upaniṣad.*

jaḍe jagati cidrūpaḥ kila vedye'pi vedakaḥ /
vibhurmite ca yenāsi tena sarvottamo bhavān //20//

O Lord, as You are *jaḍe jagati*, in the unconscious world, in the world of unconsciousness, You are filled with consciousness. *Jaḍe jagati cidrūpaḥ*, in the unconscious world, You are filled with consciousness and filled with awareness. In the unaware world, You are aware.

Kila vedye'pi vedakaḥ, in the world of objectivity, You are the knower. You are the knower in the world of the known. *Kila vedye'pi vedakaḥ*, in the objective world, You are the subject.

Vibhurmite ca yenāsi, as You are all-pervading in limitation–in the world of limitation, You are unlimited–as You are such, *tena sarvottamo bhavān*, so You are the greatest and the highest being existing in this universe.

Chapter 3 (44:41)

अलमाक्रन्दितैरन्यैरियदेव पुरः प्रभोः ।
तीव्रं विरौमि यन्नाथ मुह्याम्येवं विदन्नपि ॥२१॥

alamākranditairanyairiyadeva puraḥ prabhoḥ /
tīvraṁ viraumi yannātha muhyāmyevaṁ vidannapi //21//

Let other lamentations, or weeping, or crying bitterly, *ākranditaiḥ*, let those remain untouched [i.e., ignored]. Let other lamentations and weeping for Thee, for Thyself, for achieving Thy nature, . . .

Because, I am always weeping for achieving Thy nature. I am always filled with lamentations to achieve Thee. I am always weeping, I am always distressed, because of Thy separation.

. . . let those distresses remain untouched. I don't want to touch those. *Alamākranditairanyairiyadeva puraḥ prabhoḥ*, I want to weep bitterly before You only for this point . . .

I am not touching those points of my weeping and lamentations. I am not touching them. Let them remain untouched.

. . . I want to weep and cry loudly before You only for this purpose: *tīvraṁ viraumi yat nātha*, O Lord, *muhyāmyevaṁ vidannapi*, although I know how to attain You, although I know how to hold You, I leave You aside and go for worldly pleasures for the time being. For *this* point I want to weep bitterly before You, i.e., why I am doing so. I should not have done this. I should have only sought Your presence all-around, everywhere.

Alam ākranditair anyaiḥ, let other lamentations and crying before Thee remain untouched. Only for this very purpose I am crying wholeheartedly that although I know how to hold You, although I know how to own You, I disown You; at the same time, I disown You and go after worldly pleasures. For this, I am going to weep bitterly before You! I will cry! I am crushed! I will end my life before You!

DEVOTEE: As to why I am going astray.

SWAMIJI: Yes. This *stotra* is over.

Chapter Four
Attachment for Lord Comes by Itself
Surasodbalākhyāṁ caturthaṁ stotram

SWAMIJI: *Surasodbalākhyāṁ caturthaṁ stotram*. This is the fourth chapter. It is nominated as "*surasa-udbala*". *Surasa udbala* means that *rasa*, that attachment for the Lord, comes by itself. It does not come by adoption [of any practice].

JOHN: "By adoption" means doing some particular thing, then you will get that fruit of that. Some . . . it never comes by any . . .

STEPHANIE: Means.

JOHN: Or for any reason.

SWAMIJI: Just, it comes. It just comes. If it comes, that is all, finished.

JOHN: If it doesn't come?

DENISE: You can't make it come.

SWAMIJI: You can't make it come.

DENISE: By pure action, by pure thoughts, by meditation.

SWAMIJI: [Not] by meditation of . . . it is divine grace that makes it flow in you, and grace also does not depend upon your action, good or bad. If you do good actions, it is not possible that . . . it is not [certain] that you will get grace. If you do bad actions, it is not [certain] that you won't get grace. You can get grace anywhere, whenever He so wishes.

DEVOTEE: In other words, is one chosen to receive grace? Is there like a predestination?

SWAMIJI: Destiny is due to *karmas*; destiny takes place due to your past actions. [Grace] has nothing to do with your actions. It just comes! This is called *haṭha śaktipāta*. *Haṭha śaktipāta*, you know? *Haṭha śaktipāta* is that grace which makes you go even if you don't agree; if you are not willing, if you are not prepared, [still] it will carry you. This is *haṭha śaktipāta*. This forcibly carries you there without your . . . even if you don't like.

DENISE: Doesn't matter.

SWAMIJI: Doesn't matter [laughter]. You have to reach there, you have to go [there when this grace comes].

JOACHIM: Is *haṭha śaktipāta* the same like *tīvra tīvra śaktipāta*?[86]

SWAMIJI: Yes, it is *tīvra tīvra śaktipāta.*

JOHN: With this *haṭha śaktipāta,* a person can have this grace and not leave his body.

SWAMIJI: Huh?

JOHN: A person can have this . . .

SWAMIJI: No, *haṭha śaktipāta* is attributed to all *śaktipātas*, all the twenty-seven *śaktipātas.*[87]

JOHN: All those are *haṭha śaktipāta.*

SWAMIJI: *Haṭha śaktipāta.*

JOHN: That means that when that grace comes, you are forced to love Lord Śiva. You can't help it . . .

SWAMIJI: Yes, you can't help it.

JOHN: . . . but get on the path in order to be close to Him.

SWAMIJI: You can't do anything afterwards. You don't like anything [else]. It is why those *yogīs* have turned about to that consciousness.

Chapter 4 (02:56)

चपलमसि यदपि मानस
तत्रापि श्लाघ्यसे यतो भजसे ।
शरणानामपि शरणं
त्रिभुवनगुरुमम्बिकाकान्तम् ॥ १ ॥

capalamasi yadapi mānasa
tatrāpi ślāghyase yato bhajase /
śaraṇānāmapi śaraṇaṁ
tribhuvanagurumambikākāntam //1//

He calls his mind: "O mind, O my mind (*mānasa*), O my mind,

86 "The first and highest level of grace is called "*tīvra tīvra śaktipāta*". *Tīvra tīvra śaktipāta* means "super-supreme-grace". When Lord Śiva bestows super-supreme grace on anyone, then that person becomes perfectly self-recognized. He knows his real nature completely and in perfection." *Kashmir Shaivism–The Secret Supreme*, 10.66.

87 Ibid., chapter 10.

capalamasi yadapi, although you are flickering, always you are restless, *tatrāpi ślāghyase*, even then you are glorified because, at times, whenever you direct your nature towards the remembrance of Lord Śiva, you direct it wholeheartedly. So, you are glorified. So, you are victorious. You are victorious because *tribhuvanagurum*, because you achieve the nearness of the Master of the three worlds."

I mean, Lord Śiva.

ALEXIS: *Tribhuvana*?

SWAMIJI: *Tribhuvanagurum*, the Master of the three worlds.

ALEXIS: *Jāgrat*, *svapna*, and *suṣupti*.

SWAMIJI: *Jāgrat*, *svapna*, and *suṣupti* . . . yes, spirituality. The world of wakefulness, the world of the dreaming state, and the world of the dreamless state, who has mastery over these three worlds. Do you know what is mastery, what is the sign of being a master of these three worlds?

For instance, you have to gain mastery over the other two worlds first, in the beginning. In the beginning, you have to gain mastery [over] the dreaming state first. Whatever you dream, this dream must occur according to your choice, not according to the choice of the *niyati śakti*[88] of Lord Śiva. Whatever you like to dream, you must dream that. This is *svapna svātantrya.*[89] *Svapna svātantrya* must take place. If *svapna svātantrya* takes place, whatever you wish to dream, you dream that dream. That is *svapna svātantrya*. And that *svapna svātantrya*[90] means you have

88 *Niyati* is one of the five *kañcukas* (coverings) that confines the individual soul to a particular place, time, or situation. "The function of *niyati tattva* is to put the impression in *puruṣa* that he is residing in a particular place and not in all places. You are residing in Kashmir. You are not residing simultaneously in Australia or Canada. This is the limitation which *niyati tattva* causes for *puruṣa*, that one is residing in a particular place and not everywhere." *Kashmir Shaivism–The Secret Supreme*, 1.7.

89 "The independent world of the dreaming state." *Shiva Sutras–The Supreme Awakening*, Swami Lakshmanjoo, ed. John Hughes (Universal Shaiva Fellowship, Los Angeles, 2002), 1.19.61.

90 "Perfect *svapna svātantrya* is when you see Lord Śiva existing before you." *Spanda Kārikā* of Vasugupta with the *nirṇaya* (commentary) of Kṣemarāja, translation and commentary by Swami Lakshmanjoo (original audio recording, USF archives, Los Angeles, 1975), 3.2.

mastery [over] the dreaming state.

And, at the same time, you must achieve afterwards mastery over dreamless sound sleep (*suṣupti*). And when mastery over sound sleep also [is achieved], the state of sound sleep comes in your hold, then you can become a master of wakefulness (*jāgrat*).

JOHN: What is the master of sound sleep?

SWAMIJI: As long as you remain in *suṣupti*, you remain aware that, "I am in *suṣupti*, peacefully". That is *vijñānākalā*.[91] When you have gained mastery over these two states, [i.e., dreaming and deep sleep], then you can gain mastery over this wakefulness. When you have once gained mastery over this [state of] wakefulness, then you are no other than Lord Śiva. You are Lord Śiva Himself.

JOHN: Which comes first, mastery in *suṣupti* or mastery in *svapna*?

SWAMIJI: First mastery in *svapna* (dreaming state), then mastery in *suṣupti* (dreamless sleep), then mastery in wakefulness (*jāgrat*).

And because you [i.e., my mind] remember that Master who is the master of all these three worlds, three states . . . sometimes, when you have mind [i.e., awareness], you focus yourself towards that supreme master, so you are victorious. Although, you are . . . in the real sense, you are restless, always going astray, here and there, but still you are victorious because at times you remember the Lord of lords who is the Master of all the three worlds, three states.

ALEXIS: *Śaraṇānāmapiśaraṇam*

SWAMIJI: *Śaraṇānāmapiśaraṇam*, who is the refuge of all refuges. *Tribhuvanaguram*, who is the Master of the three worlds. *Ambikā kāntam*, who is dear to Pārvatī,

ALEXIS: *Ambikā śakti kāntam*, embraced by *śakti*.

SWAMIJI: Yes . . . embraced by *parāśakti*, the supreme *śakti*. That is Pārvatī.[92]

ALEXIS: Consciousness.

---

91 See appendix 14 for an explanation of the seven perceivers. See also *Kashmir Shaivism–The Secret Supreme*, "The Seven Processes of the Seven Perceivers".

92 The supreme energy of Lord Śiva is also known as *svātantrya śakti*, His energy of absolute freedom. See appendix 11 for an explanation of *svātantrya*.

Chapter 4 (07:26)

उल्लङ्घ्य विविधदैवत-
सोपानक्रममुपेयशिवचरणान् ।
आश्रित्याप्यधरतरां भूमिं
नाद्यापि चित्रमुज्झामि ॥२॥

ullaṅghya vividhadaivata-
sopānakramamupeyaśivacaraṇān /
āśrityāpyadharatarāṁ bhūmiṁ
nādyāpi citramujjhāmi //2//

O Lord, this is the great torture for me. This is the great story of torture for me.

What is that story?

That story is *ullaṅghya vividhasopānakramam*, I have crossed all of the steps of *yogic* exercise, *yogic* practices, all *sādhanās*. I have crossed all of those steps and I have come to this supreme, uppermost limit of that step-less state (*ullaṅghya vividhasopānakramam*). And, not only that. I have achieved *upeyaśivacaraṇānāśrityāpi*, I have touched the lotus feet of Lord Śiva also. But, the great torture, the great story of torture, is still existing for me and that is *adharatarāṁ bhūmiṁ nādyāpi citramujjhāmi*, I again go after these worldly pleasures and worldly senses. After achieving this highest state also, I hanker after these worldly enjoyments. This is the great story of my torture in this universe. So, there is one request:

Chapter 4 (9:13)

प्रकटय निजमध्वानं
स्थगयतरामखिललोकचरितानि ।
यावद्भवामि भगवं-
स्तव सपदि सदोदितो दासः ॥३॥

prakaṭaya nijamadhvānaṁ
sthagayatarāmakhilalokacaritāni /
yāvadbhavāmi bhagavaṁ-
stava sapadi sadodito dāsaḥ //3//

Bhagavan, O Lord, O my Master, *prakaṭaya nijamadhvānaṁ*, keep Your ways open for me; keep Your ways, keep Your avenues, open for me. I don't ask You to keep the avenues always open; just for the time being, as long as I would pass through them and reach at Your feet (*prakaṭaya nijamadhvānaṁ*). And, at the same time, simultaneously, *sthagayatarām akhila lokacaritāni*, and close all of the doors of this tortured . . . the world of torture, the world of differentiated perception, the world of hankering after sensual pleasures. Keep them closed for the time being, *yāvad bhavāmi bhagavan*, as long as I would become Your slave. Till then, You have to do these two things for me.

What are these two things?

Just to keep Your avenues open, widely open, so that they don't hinder me while passing. And, on the right side, on the left side, there are so many hindrances that appear, and those hindrances are *loka caritāni*, hindrances of hankering, going after [worldly pleasures].

Because, side-by-side, you are confused, you are confused every now and then in this universe. Although you have developed desire and devotion for Lord Śiva, at the same time, the other side also is appearing to show you some attractive figure, some attractive smell, some attractive taste, so that your attention is diverted towards [worldly pleasures].

Keep those doors closed for the time being, O Lord, as long as I would reach before Your lotus feet (*yāvadbhavāmi*, as long as I would reach before Your lotus feet). But I don't [mean to] say, "as long as". Please, make it possible for me to reach at Your lotus feet now.

I want to serve You wholeheartedly. This is my only desire in my . . . this is the only pleasure for me. Not desire. Pleasure.

Chapter 4 (12:01)

प्रकटय निजमध्वानं
स्थगयतरामखिललोकचरितानि ।

यावद्भवामि भगवं-
स्तव सपदि सदोदितो दासः ॥३॥

prakaṭaya nijamadhvānaṁ
sthagayatarāmakhilalokacaritāni /
yāvadbhavāmi bhagavaṁ-
stava sapadi sadodito dāsaḥ //3//

O Lord, please clear Your path for me. I want . . . because Your path has become blunt to me, i.e., it is not clarified. I can't see, I can't see Your path. So, my journey is stuck. *Prakaṭaya nijamadhvānaṁ*, please clear Your path and *sthagayatarām-akhila lokacaritāni*, and conceal all other activities of the universe for me for the time being, till I achieve the state when I will become Your devoted slave. This is my desire in the end.

Chapter 4 (13:07)

शिव शिव शम्भो शङ्कर
शरणागतवत्सलाशु कुरु करुणाम् ।
तव चरणकमलयुगल-
स्मरणपरस्य हि सम्पदोऽदूरे ॥४॥

śiva śiva śambho śaṅkara
śaraṇāgatavatsalāśu kuru karuṇām /
tava caraṇakamalayugala-
smaraṇaparasya hi sampado'dūre //4//

O Lord Śiva, O Śambho, O Śaṅkara, O *Śaraṇāgatavatsala*, O [You who are] dear to those who have sought Your refuge (that is *śaraṇāgatavatsala*), *āśu kuru karuṇām*, keep Your *karuṇā* (*dayā*), keep Your grace on me in a speedy way. Don't hesitate, don't hesitate to bless me. Bless me soon, and now, *āśukuru karuṇām*, because, if You don't bless me soon, I will be blessed automatically. I'll be blessed automatically because I have got so much craving to get blessings from You that I can't remain without it. I can't live without Your grace! So, if You want to maintain Your honor and prestige, then You must bless me as soon as You can. Otherwise, I will be blessed naturally. I will be blessed because I am craving for that!

There is no way out because, *tava caraṇa kamala yugala smaraṇaparasya*, I am bent upon remembering Your nature. I am bent upon remembering and reciting Your *mantra*. I am bent upon . . . I have diverted my whole attention towards Thy form, Thy divine form. *Sampado udūre*, because those glories of being with You are very near to me, [they] have come very near to me, so it is for You to decide if You [will] do it Yourself or have it done automatically.

Chapter 4 (15:21)

तावकाङ्घ्रिकमलासनलीना
ये यथारूचि जगद्रचयन्ति ।
ते विरिञ्चिमधिकारमलेना-
लिप्तमस्ववशमीश हसन्ति ॥५॥

tāvakāṅghrikamalāsanalīnā
ye yathārūci jagadracayanti /
te viriñcimadhikāramalenā-
liptamasvavaśamīśa hasanti //5//

Īśa, O Lord (these are devotional songs), O Lord, those people . . .

You know what is the functioning of Brahma? Brahma creates. He cannot protect, he cannot destroy, he cannot conceal, and he cannot reveal. He creates only. His job is to create the universe. And Brahma is residing in the lotus, in the lotus of Viṣṇu['s navel].

You have heard that theory? Viṣṇu is asleep, resting on those thousand heads of Śeṣanāga[93], he is resting there, and a lotus comes from [Viṣṇu's] naval and, at the time of creation, in that

93 Lord Viṣṇu is traditionally depicted as lying on the bed of a thousand-headed serpent called Śeṣanāga. [*Editor's note*]

lotus appears Brahma, and he creates the whole universe. This is our tradition of this theory. So, it is why Brahma is called *kamala āsana* (*kamala āsana* means "whose seat is a lotus"). His seat is a lotus; the seat of Brahma is a lotus. But there are some other Brahmas also. This devotee [i.e., Utpaladeva] says here, "there are other Brahmas also who are residing in the lotus of Your feet". He addresses Śiva, the feet of Śiva, the lotus-like feet of Śiva: "those who reside there, those are also Brahmas."

. . . *tāvaka āṅghri kamalāsanalīnā ye*, those Brahmas who are residing in the lotus of Your feet, O Lord Śiva, *yathārūci jagat racayanti*, they do not only create the universe. They create the universe, they protect the universe, they destroy the universe, they conceal their nature, and they reveal their nature to people. They do all the five actions just like Śiva, i.e., those Brahmas, those Brahmas who reside in Your lotus feet, in Thy lotus feet. *Te viriñcim adhikāra malānāliptam asvavaśam*, and that Brahma who is bent upon creating only, he cannot protect, he cannot destroy, he cannot reveal, and he cannot conceal. He has only to create.

Who?

DENISE: Brahma.

SWAMIJI: Ordinary Brahma.

Those Brahmas who are residing in the lotus feet of Thine, they *hasanti*, they just abuse those [other] Brahmas. They think that these Brahmas are worthless.

JOHN: Who can only create.

SWAMIJI: Who can only create. And they can create only according to *karmas*. And these Brahmas who are residing in the lotus feet of Yours, they create with their free will, not *karmas*. This is the difference between those Brahmas and this Brahma.

Chapter 4 (19:35)

त्वत्प्रकाशवपुषो न विभिन्नं
किंचन प्रभवति प्रतिभातुम् ।
तत्सदैव भगवन् परिलब्धो-
ऽसीश्वर प्रकृतितोऽपि विदूरः ॥६॥

tvatprakāśavapuṣo na vibhinnaṁ
kiṁcana prabhavati pratibhātum /
tatsadaiva bhagavan parilabdho
'sīśvara prakṛtito'pi vidūraḥ //6//

O Lord, nothing can exist if it is separated from Your glamorous form of *cit* (all consciousness, all knowledge, and all bliss). If anything is separated from that being of Yours, *kiṁcana prabhavati pratibhātum*, it cannot exist. So, everything, whatever exists, is one with that being of Your consciousness.

Tat sadaiva bhagavan parilabdho. So, what is . . . I have no worry to think that I have not attained You. I have already attained You, wherever You are. You are everywhere, so I have attained You already. Although You are away from me, although internally You are away from me, I don't see You, but still I am with You.

It is just [for the sake of] satisfying his self. Otherwise, he [feels that he] is away from Him. He says, "from [the viewpoint of] this philosophy, it is obvious that I am with You because nothing exists, which is separated from You. Everything is with You, everything is united with You, so I am also united with You. I have also achieved You. So, there is no worry for That achievement for me. But still, You are away from me".

It is madness!

Chapter 4 (21:48)

पादपङ्कजरसं तव केचिद्
भेदपर्युषितवृत्तिमुपेताः ।
केचनापि रसयन्ति तु सद्यो
भातमक्षतवपुर्द्वयशून्यम् ॥७॥

pādapaṅkajarasaṁ tava kecid
bhedaparyuṣitavṛttimupetāḥ /
kecanāpi rasayanti tu sadyo
bhātamakṣatavapurdvayaśūnyam //7//

Thine devotees are classified in two ways. *Pādapankañja-rasam*, those who drink the nectar of Your lotus feet by sips, e.g., just [taking] one sip, then talk, then another sip, then do some other thing, then another sip . . . like that, successively. They drink in the nectar of Thine lotus feet . . .

How?

JOHN: Successively.

SWAMIJI: Successively. So, it does not remain so fresh. That nectar that comes from Your lotus feet is not fresh that they take [successively]. The freshness is ruined there. The freshness of that nectar is ruined there for those people who drink that nectar in that way.

But there are some devotees of Thine who drink that nectar *kecanāpi rasayanti sadyo bhātam akṣatavapur dvaya śūnyam*, they just begin to drink it and they drink it forever. They never are separated from that drinking of that nectar. So, those are really godly persons.

JOHN: So, these people who drink sometimes are people who remember Him now and then, and when they go to temples, or when they . . .

SWAMIJI: . . . go to the factory [laughter] and then come in the evening and then drink That nectar, and then sleep, do sex, get up and drink nectar, take tea and drink nectar, take lunch and drink nectar. This kind of drinking is not so fresh drinking. Freshness will come only when you drink It altogether, *bas*! Don't do any other job, just go on drinking. So, That nectar always remains fresh for them.

Another *śloka*:

Chapter 4 (24:34)

नाथ विद्युदिव भाति विभाते
या कदाचन ममामृतदिग्धा ।
सा यदि स्थिरतरैव भवेत्तत्
पूजितोऽसि विधिवत्किमुतान्यत् ॥८॥

nātha vidyudiva bhāti vibhāte
yā kadācana mamāmṛtadigdhā /
sā yadi sthirataraiva bhavettat
pūjito'si vidhivatkimutānyat //8//

Nātha, O Master, Your shining formation appears to me–That shining formation, which is soaked with nectar, soaked with the supreme nectar of joy, ecstasy; that is Your formation–and That [formation], already soaked with nectar, that formation of Thine appears to me sometimes, very seldom, not always.

Now, O Master, I would like to perceive That formation, which is soaked with that supreme nectar. *Sā yadi sthirataraiva bhavet*, if That formation would remain established for some time more, would remain stationery for some time more, not just like lightening, the lightening of clouds . . .

It appears to me just like the lightening of clouds, just [in one flash], *bas*, then It is finished. Not that way. I would like to perceive It just in the stationary formation, just for one minute more, *sā yadi sthiratarairva bhavet* (*taraiva* means that; *taraiva* means just "for some more time"). Not only for one second. Just say, ten seconds.

. . . then, what would I do? *Tat pūjito'si vidhivat kimutānyat*, then I would worship Thee, O Lord. I would be able to worship You. [Presently, just as] I am going to worship You and [my perception of] It is finished [laughter]. When I see [Your formation], It is just like lightening; I want to worship It and It is gone. How can I worship? If It would remain for sometime more, then I would be able to worship Thee, O Lord.

So, do it! *Kimutānyat*, what is there [laughter]? *Kimutānyat*, what is there [in doing that for me]? There is nothing to do for You. It is not so much [of a] job for You. You could do it very easily.

Chapter 4 (27:32)

सर्वमस्यपरमस्ति न किंचिद्
वस्त्ववस्तु यदि वेति महत्या ।
प्रज्ञया व्यवसितोऽत्र यथैव
त्वं तथैव भव सुप्रकटो मे ॥९॥

sarvamasyaparamasti na kiṁcid
vastvavastu yadi veti mahatyā /
prajñayā vyavasito'tra yathaiva
tvaṁ tathaiva bhava suprakaṭo me //9//

In fact, from the Shaivite point of view, You are everywhere. This is one hundred percent truth that You are everywhere (*sarvamasi*). And You are residing in every object, each and every object. You are there always. *Na kiṁcit*, there is nothing existing except You. This is a fact. This is a fact discussed and proved in Shaivism. *Prajñayā vyavasthito'tra yathaiva*, and this I have noticed, this I have concluded, that this is the real fact, that You are everywhere, You are everything, You are residing in each and every object, but why don't You appear like that to me? I would like You to appear like that. It is only theory. Theoretically, I understand it but it must appear to me practically. That is what I long for.

Now, You would say, "Get out from this place. I don't want you". Now, You will sometimes be worried because I am always after You, I am always troubling You.

Chapter 4 (29:25)

स्वेच्छयैव भगवन्निजमार्गे
कारितः पदमहं प्रभुणैव ।
तत्कथं जनवदेव चरामि
त्वत्पदोचितमवैमि न किंचित् ॥१०॥

svecchayaiva bhagavannijamārge
kāritaḥ padamahaṁ prabhuṇaiva /
tatkathaṁ janavadeva carāmi
tvatpadocitamavaimi na kiṁcit //10//
[not recited in full]

Svecchayaiva bhagavannijamārge, I have never told You to put me on the roadside, on the path of Your abode, Your spiritual abode. I never told You . . . I never asked You to carry me on the path of Yours. You have done it Yourself! *Kāritaḥ padamahaṁ prabhuṇaiva*, You have put me on the path and now You are refusing to appear.

Tat kathaṁ janavadeva carāmi, if I have been kept and carried on the path of Thine, why do I act like ordinary, worldly people? Why don't I sink in that glamour of Thine glory, filled with consciousness and all bliss? How is it?

Bas?

STEPHANIE: One more, we want to know the answer.

SWAMIJI: One more [laughter]?

Chapter 4 (30:33)

कोऽपि देव हृदि तेषु तावको
जृम्भते सुभगभावः उत्तमः ।
त्वत्कथाम्बुदनिनादचातका
येन तेऽपि सुभगीकृताश्चिरम् ॥ ११ ॥

ko'pi deva hṛdi teṣu tāvako
jṛmbhate subhagabhāvaḥ uttamaḥ /
tvatkathāmbudaninādacātakā
yena te'pi subhagīkṛtāściram //11//

But this is the greatness of Thine, O Lord, O Master, that in those hearts of those blessed devotees of Thine, that fineness of Thy devotion is perceived, appears. That fineness of Thy devotion appears in the hearts of those people–that kind of fineness. Although they are away from that consciousness of Thine, but when some other person explains the fineness of Yours before them–some other person explains, puts forth, the fineness of Your joy and Your bliss and they hear–. . .

Who [is hearing]?

DENISE: Those devotees.

SWAMIJI: Those devotees who have got those fine hearts.

. . . they hear only [and just] by hearing, they get entry in their God consciousness at once, by hearing only. This is the fineness of their heart.

Yena tepi subhagākṛtāściram. If you only explain the ways of

God consciousness [to those blessed devotees], by hearing the ways of God consciousness, they get entry in that God consciousness. This is the fineness of their heart that they have attained.

Chapter 4 (32:27)

त्वज्जुषां त्वयि कयापि लीलया
राग एष परिपोषमागतः ।
यद्वियोगभुवि सङ्कथा तथा
संस्मृतिः फलति संगमोत्सवम् ॥ १२ ॥

tvajjuṣāṁ tvayi kayāpi līlayā
rāga eṣa paripoṣamāgataḥ /
yadviyogabhuvi saṅkathā tathā
saṁsmṛtiḥ phalati saṁgamotsavam //12//

Tvajjuṣām, those devotees of Thine, in those devotees of Thine, *kayāpi līlayā*, by the divine grace of Thine, the *rāga*, the attachment for Thee, is so much intense in those devotees of Thine. [This occurs] not by their actions, not by their continuous practice of *yoga*, but how?

ERNIE: Devotion.

SWAMIJI: No, by Your grace.

It is grace only that can carry you to God consciousness. It is not your actions. Actions won't do. Action is always limited. Action done by the limited soul will always remain limited. How can that limited action carry you to that unlimited abode of truth? So, for achieving that unlimited abode of truth, you need unlimited grace, and that will come, that will be divine, that will be from your master. Who is your master? Lord Śiva.

Tvajjuṣāṁ tvayi kayāpi līlayā. So, by that supreme *līlā*, supreme play of Thine . . .

It is Your play that You can [bestow grace]. It is not . . . You have not to do [anything]. You have not to put money, put workers, for that, i.e., when You induce grace on somebody. It is just a play. If You [would], You could do it now.

. . . so, when You put that grace in some person, *rāga eṣa paripoṣamāgataḥ,* they are so much attached afterwards to Thee.

They are so much intensely attached to Thee that, although they are away from You, [although] they are not in *samādhi*, they don't remain in *samādhi* for always–they are talking, walking, smiling, laughing–at the time they are laughing, [or while] they are talking, or [while] they are doing some other household works, when somebody only reminds them of Lord Śiva, they get entry in that God consciousness at once! There and then, on that very pathway, they get entry. This is the greatness of that attachment that is created in their heart through Your divine grace.

Chapter 4 (35:37)

यो विचित्ररससेकवर्धितः
शङ्करेति शतशोऽप्युदीरितः ।
शब्द आविशति तिर्यगाशये-
ष्वप्ययं नवनवप्रयोजनः ॥ १३ ॥

yo vicitrarasasekavardhitaḥ
śaṅkareti śataśo'pyudīritaḥ /
śabda āviśati tiryagāśaye-
ṣvapyayaṁ navanavaprayojanaḥ / / 13 / /

When this sound, this sound "Śiva" is recited one hundred times–"Śaṅkarā, Śaṅkarā, Śaṅkarā, Śaṅkarā . . . ", like that, one hundred times–and this sound *āviśati tiryagāśayeṣu*, this sound enters in the heart of the animal world, the animal kingdom . . .

You know the animal kingdom? Animals or animal-like persons. Animal-like persons means duffers, those who have beastly understanding. That is also the animal kingdom; they also reside in the animal kingdom.

. . . and this sound, this sound of "Śiva", this "Śaṅkara", when it is recited one hundred times and this [sound] gets entry in those animal-like hearts, in those hearts also it creates always fresh and new profits and glamour. So, they find that a new application is applied in their hearts; a new and joyful application. They will also understand . . . those animal duffers will also feel that joy.

JOHN: Something has happened to them.

SWAMIJI: Something has happened to them. This is the greatness of this sound "Śiva".

Now . . .

Chapter 4 (37:53)

ते जयन्ति मुखमण्डले भ्रमन्
अस्ति येषु नियतं शिवध्वनिः ।
यः शशीवप्रसृतोऽमृताशयात्
स्वादु संस्रवति चामृतं परम् ॥ १४॥

te jayanti mukhamaṇḍale bhraman
asti yeṣu niyataṁ śivadhvaniḥ /
yaḥ śaśīvaprasṛto'mṛtāśayāt
svādu saṁsravati cāmṛtaṁ param //14//
[not recited in full]

Now, those persons on whose lips this sound "Śiva" is residing twenty-four hours–this "Śiva" is residing [on their lips] for twenty-four hours [a day], while walking, doing everything, talking, bathing, eating, drinking, meditating, not meditating–and they feel that this sound is appearing to them on their lips always . . .

What is the greatness of that sound? *Yaḥ śaśīva prasṛta-amṛtā'śayāt*, that sound of "Śiva", when once uttered, when you utter this only once, you feel that it has come out, flown out, from the abode of nectar, just like]*śaśīva*, just like the moon, just [like] the moonlight, which has come from the abode of nectar, and it soothes your heart, soothes your appearance. You are soothed. You are made comfortable, peaceful, when you look at the moon. In the same way, that sound, when it is uttered once only, you feel that it has come out, it has flown out, from that abode of nectar and it sprinkles and bathes you with that nectar in fullness.

. . . and that sound, when it is recited by those persons for twenty four hours [per day], they are actually glorified. What can I say to them? *Te jayanti*, they are glorified, they are victorious, always.

Next. These [*ślokas*] are two in one.

Chapter 4 (40:23)

परिसमाप्तमिवोग्रमिदं जगद्
विगलितोऽविरलो मनसो मलः ।
तदपि नास्ति भवत्पुरगोपुरार्-
गलकवाटविघट्टनमण्वपि ॥ १५ ॥

parisamāptamivogramidaṁ jagad
vigalito'viralo manaso malaḥ /
tadapi nāsti bhavatpuragopurār-
galakavāṭavighaṭṭanamaṇvapi //15//

O Lord, this whole universe of differentiated perception–e.g., he is Bruce Hughes, he is John Hughes, she is another Hughes, and he is Pollack, he is everything–this differentiated perception, this world of differentiated perception, has totally come to its end. It is a fact, to me. To me, I feel that this differentiated perception is over, for good. So there is nothing applicable for that. *Vigalito'viralo manaso malaḥ*, and the internal impurity of *āṇavamala* (that subtle impurity, that is *āṇavamala*), that, too, is also finished, to me. The differentiated perception, the mode of differentiated perception is also finished.[94]

So, it is due that You must appear to me! It is now due because this differentiated perception exists no more and *āṇavamala* exists no more. I have no impurity now. *Kārmamala* and *māyīya-mala* are gone. *Āṇavamala* also there was . . . some impressions of *āṇavamala*, there were some impressions, but those, too, those impressions are also shattered to pieces. Now, Your appearance to me is due. *Tadapi*, even though, even then, *nāsti bhavatpurar-galakavāṭavighaṭṭanamaṇvapi*, the external door of Your abode of [Your] kingdom does not open a bit, even then! It does not even get a slight opening also. It is not yet . . .

94 "There are three impurities existing in the ignorant being. What is that? *Āṇavamala*, *māyīyamala*, and *kārmamala*. *Kārmamala* is concerned with our activities, *māyīyamala* is concerned with our impressions, *āṇavamala* is concerned with our self, the ignorance of Self." *Parātriśikā Vivaraṇa* (USF archives). See appendix 15 for a further explanation of the *malas* (impurities).

JOHN: Even a crack.

SWAMIJI: . . . even a crack.

What is there? I am confused. What has happened to me? I have done all of these things. I have come across all of these things. All of this differentiated perception is gone and this impurity is also over, but still there is no hope of entering into that kingdom of Thine because there is not even a slight crack in that external door, gate, gate-door.

Next. These are *ślokas* like that. There is no philosophy in this, you see.

Satataphullabhavan . . . it is just a cry, a crisis.

Chapter 4 (43:51)

सततफुल्लभवन्मुखपङ्कजो-
 दरविलोकनलालसचेतसः ।
किमपि तत्कुरु नाथ मनागिव
 स्फुरसि येन ममाभिमुखस्थितिः ॥ १६ ॥

satataphullabhavanmukhapaṅkajo-
 daravilokanalālasacetasaḥ /
kimapi tatkuru nātha manāgiva
 sphurasi yena mamābhimukhasthitiḥ //16//
[not recited in full]

O Lord, I have got only one craving and longing. My mind longs and craves for–for what?–*bhavad mukha paṅkaja udara vilokana*, just to see the depth of Your mouth, the depth of Your face; just to see and get entry in the depth of Your face, That face which is *satataphulla*, which is blooming always, not like lotuses [that bloom] only in the daytime and at night they are closed–Thine lotus-shaped *mukha* (face) is always blooming. It is a lotus, day and night–blooming lotus. And I have got only this much craving in my mind, just to see in the center of That lotus, just to go on observing the depth of that lotus of Your face. So, this craving and this longing is there always. So, do something for me! *Kimapi tat kuru*, do something, somehow, at any cost. Do that thing.

What thing?

O my Master, *manāgiva*, for You it is not too much. It is just a play. You can do it in [an act of] play, *sphurasi yena mamābhimukhasthitiḥ*, by which You could appear to me always, face to face. This is my ambition.

Next:

Chapter 4 (45:59)

त्वद् विभेदमतेरपरं नु किं
सुखमिहास्ति विभूतिरथापरा ।
तदिह तावकदासजनस्य किं
कुपथमेति मनः परिहृत्य ताम् ॥ १७॥

tvad'vibhedamateraparaṁ nu kiṁ
sukhamihāsti vibhūtirathāparā /
tadiha tāvakadāsajanasya kiṁ
kupathameti manaḥ parihṛtya tām //17//

This is a fact, O Lord, this is a fact, this is an admitted fact, that when *tvad abhedamateḥ*, when that conclusive perception comes, appears in one's mind, . . .

What conclusive perception? Conclusive perception of perceiving oneness everywhere (*abheda*).

. . . for him, what [other] pleasure could he have? What other pleasure than that or what [other] glory than that? That is the best glory and that is the best pleasure for him.

What is the best pleasure and glory?

DENISE: Oneness.

SWAMIJI: Oneness. Oneness of Thine. Oneness of Your nature. Perceiving the oneness of Your nature is the real pleasure, it is the real glory.

If already I know that–from my master, I know that–but why then sometimes do I go to sex, sometimes I go to other worldly pleasures, sometimes I am attached to some other things, e.g., *tzamin*[95] (*panir*), everything. What is that? It should not have happened. *Kupatham eti manaḥ*, [my mind] goes in diversion, it

95 Kashmiri cheese (*panir*) dish.

goes in diversion another way, *pariḥrityatām*, and leaves that aside; leaves that glamour of that oneness of Your nature aside and goes towards other pleasures of the world. Why does it happen? It should not have happened but it happens to me.

Chapter 4 (48:22)

क्षणमपीह न तावकदासतां
प्रति भवेयमहं किल भाजनम् ।
भवदभेदरसासवमादराद्-
अविरतं रसयेयमहं न चेत् ॥ १८॥

kṣaṇamapīha na tāvakadāsatāṁ
prati bhaveyamahaṁ kila bhājanam /
bhavadabhedarasāsavamādarād-
aviratam rasayeyamahaṁ na cet //18//

If I would not have tasted the nectar of Thy glorious feet, lotus-like feet–*abheda rasam*, that is *abheda rasam*, the oneness of that *rasa*–if that oneness of *rasa* I would not have tasted with great honor, with great love, with affection, and in continuity, . . .

I have done that; previously, I have done that. What have I done? I have tasted the nectar of that oneness of Thine glory, in continuity, with honor, with respect, with love, with affection.

. . . if I would have not done that, what would have happened to me? *Kṣaṇamapīha na tāvaka dāsatām*, then I was not destined to become Your slave for even one second as if I have . . . as I have become. Now I have become Your slave for one second or two seconds in twenty-four hours. That is enough for me, that is great for me. That is enough for me. I am happy that way. If I would have not done this beforehand, . . .

What?

JOHN: Have the continuity of that experience of His oneness.

SWAMIJI: With honor, with respect, and with love.

. . . if I had not done that, I would not have been honored in becoming Your slave for one second also. [But now it is] as if I have become Your slave.

It is some other point to say if I see You at all. I don't see You at all, but I have become Your slave. That is a great thing for me, that is a great consolation for me that I have become Your slave. And this is due to my previous behavior that I have tasted the nectar of Your oneness with respect, with honor, and love, and in continuity.

If I would have not done this exertion to drink the nectar of Your oneness with devotion, with honor, and in continuity, then I would have not been able to become Your slave for one second also.

I would have not been Your slave even for one second (*kṣaṇamapi*). But, for one second, I am Your slave. Sometimes, for instance, sometimes, for one minute, I see You [once] in twelve months. That is enough. That is a great thing for me. That overjoys me and intoxicates me for my whole life.

You see, if you once experience the state of that state of Śiva, only in a flash, say for one second, it will soak you for your whole life, that joy. You will be soaked. You are always intoxicated. It is so joyous!

ERNIE: So, that's why he is crying all of the time?

SWAMIJI: He is crying . . . there is no other way; [it would be impossible for him] not to cry. Because, as soon as he remembers the position of being [God's] slave–the position of being a slave [to God] is to get soaked in that pleasure–and he must cry, he must become mad for that. Sometimes he says, "I am mad but I am fortunate also!" I have become . . . "

JOHN: At least I've had one . . . at least I've had something . . .

SWAMIJI: Yes, something.

JOHN: . . . it's not nothing.

SWAMIJI: *Bas*?

DENISE: But even when you are soaked, you want more. You want to be soaked more?

SWAMIJI: Yes [laughter].

DENISE: So, it becomes worse and worse as you go along.

SWAMIJI: Worse and worse [laughter].

DENISE: It doesn't get better [laughter].

SWAMIJI: That worse-ness also . . .

DENISE: Is sweet.

SWAMIJI: . . . is sweet.

Chapter 4 (53:28)

न किल पश्यति सत्यमयं जन-
स्तव वपुर्द्वयदृष्टिमलीमसः ।
तदपि सर्वविदाश्रितवत्सलः
किमिदमारटितं न शृणोषि मे ॥ १९ ॥

na kila paśyati satyamayaṁ jana-
stava vapurdvayadṛṣṭimalīmasaḥ /
tadapi sarvavidāśritavatsalaḥ
kimidamāraṭitaṁ na śṛṇoṣi me //19//

It is true. I confess it, my Lord. It is true and I confess it, that these worldly people (*ayaṁ janaḥ*, these people) are given to worldly pleasures, *dvaya dṛṣṭi malīmasaḥ*, and they are made impure; they are made impure by the impurity of differentiated perception of worldly . . . differentiated worldly perception of worldly joys. It is true.

JOHN: Who?

SWAMIJI: These worldly people. These worldly people are given to these worldly joys and they are always residing in differentiated perception, in the field of differentiated perception. It is true!

So, they are not . . . it is not possible for them to see You. They can't see You because they are so . . . they are kept away from God consciousness by being attached to worldly pleasures and differentiated perceptions. It is true. I believe in this thing.

But, *tadapi*, even then, You know everything. You know the position of each and every soul in this world. You know me also, in which position I am living. *Tadapi sarvavid*, You are all-knowing. *Āśritavatsalaḥ*, and You are holding . . . You are the protector of those who have surrendered in You (*āśritavatsalaḥ*, those who have surrendered in You), unconditional surrender in You. You protect them. It is true.

Kimidamāraṭitam, why [does] my cry of this [desire for] being with You . . . this cry [of mine], where does it go? In which pit [does] it go? It does not get entry in Your ear. You don't hear my cries. Where [does] this cry and this *chaṭapaṭī* . . .

Chaṭapatī means . . .

ERNIE: Anguish.

SWAMIJI: . . . anguish-ness goes? It goes in some pit and it vanishes. It does not reach You. I am crying for this.

You must know that I am not like those worldly people who are given to these worldly enjoyments. So, it is due that their being separated from You is due. But for me, it is not due. I am always longing for You. I have nothing [other] than You. You are everything for me and still this cry does not reach You. What shall I do?

Bas, these are only mad things!

DENISE: Is he going to say what? He isn't going to say what to do?

SWAMIJI: No. *Bas*, there ends this story. One story begins in one *śloka* and ends in that *śloka*, because this is madness of . . .

JOHN: Loving God.

SWAMIJI: . . . madness of loving God.

Chapter 4 (57:09)

स्मरसि नाथ कदाचिदपीहितं
विषयसौख्यमथापि मयार्थितम् ।
सततमेव भवद्वपुरीक्षणा-
मृतमभीष्टमलं मम देहि तत् ॥२०॥

smarasi nātha kadācidapīhitaṁ
viṣayasaukhyamathāpi mayārthitam /
satatameva bhavadvapurīkṣaṇā-
mṛtamabhīṣṭamalaṁ mama dehi tat //20//
[not recited]

Smarasi nātha kadācidapīhitaṁ. Just remember, my Lord, just remember, just think and go deep in previous [thoughts and actions] of mine, think and see if there was any moment when I have longed and craved for worldly enjoyments; if there is a day, there is a moment, there is one moment, that kind of one moment at which moment I have acted or longed for worldly pleasures. You won't find any moment like that! I have always been asking for Your love, for Your nearness, for Your . . . I want to get entry in You. I have nothing else. In this world, I have no taste. I don't feel anything, just only You.

Samarasi nātha kadācidapīhitam. If I have . . . it is a promise, I promise You that if there was one moment, at which moment I have played or acted or longed for worldly pleasures, then well and good, don't see me at all, discard me! If there is not one moment in my whole life like that . . . I have always been longing for Your nearness. There is nothing else I have longed for. So, *mama dehi tat*, give me that; give me that nearness of Thine, nothing else. I don't want anything else.

Chapter 4 (58:54)

किल यदैव शिवाध्वनि तावके
कृतपदोऽस्मि महेश तवेच्छया ।
शुभशतान्युदितानि तदैव मे
किमपरं मृगये भवतः प्रभो ॥२१॥

kila yadaiva śivādhvani tāvake
kṛtapado'smi maheśa tavecchayā /
śubhaśatānyuditāni tadaiva me
kimaparaṁ mṛgaye bhavataḥ prabho //21//
[not recited completely]

Prabho, O Master, *yadaiva tāvake śivādhvani*, O Master, O my Lord (*maheśvara* means "O my Lord"; *prabho* means "O my Master"), O my Master, O my Lord, at that moment, when I have been made to step on the path of Your supreme nectar, when I have stepped on the path of Your abode (*śivādhvani*, the path of *śiva bhāva*), I have not stepped on That path myself. *Tavecchayā*, it was Your desire that I should step on That path.

From that very moment, O Lord, You must understand that *śubhaśatānyuditāni tadaiva me*, from that very moment, thousands and *lakhs*[96] of glories have risen in my nature–from that very moment. *Kimaparaṁ mṛgaye bhavataḥ*, why should I ask

96 One *lakh* is equal to one hundred thousand.

for some other thing from Thee, O my Lord! I only ask for You. I want You and nothing else. As soon as I have stepped in on the path of Your supreme *śiva bhāva*–by Your own will, by Your own free will–from that very moment, thousands and hundreds of glories have risen in my nature. Why should I crave for other things [other than] You? I crave only You. I want You and nothing else. *Bas*!

Chapter 4 (1:01:21)

यत्र सोऽस्तमयमेति विवस्वांश्-
    चन्द्रमः प्रभृतिभिः सह सर्वैः ।
कापि सा विजयते शिवरात्रिः
    स्वप्रभाप्रसरभास्वररूपा ॥२२॥

yatra so'stamayameti vivasvāṁś-
    candramaḥ prabhṛtibhiḥ saha sarvaiḥ /
kāpi sā vijayate śivarātriḥ
    svaprabhāprasarabhāsvararūpā //22//

Where that stage, that place, that abode of Your 'nectarized' residence, where *astamayameti vivasvān*, this functioning of the sun stops altogether, the sun does not function . . .

JOHN: "Sun" means here?

SWAMIJI: There is no sunlight there. Sunlight has nothing to do there. Sunlight is not . . . it is subsided sunlight.

JOHN: Sunlight does not mean in terms of *pramātṛ*, *prameya*, *pramāṇa*?[97]

SWAMIJI: Yes, yes. The external meaning of sunlight is sunlight. The internal meaning is when the outgoing breath has stopped.

. . . *candrama prabhṛtibhḥ saha sarvaiḥ*, and where the moonlight has also taken its end . . .

JOHN: Ingoing breath it would be.

97 Fire (*pramātṛ*, subject), moon (*prameya*, object), and sun (*pramāṇa*, cognition). [*Editor's note*]

SWAMIJI: Ingoing breath.[98]

. . . *prabhṛtibhiḥ saha sarvaiḥ*, and all notions of thought also have stopped totally, notions of thought . . .

JOHN: "Notions of thought" means actual thoughts themselves or even thinking of . . . ?

ERNIE: Even the seeds.

SWAMIJI: No, all thoughts.

JOACHIM: Any thinking activity.

SWAMIJI: Things other than spirituality, other than Lord Śiva. Those thoughts also have ended and the ingoing breath and the out-coming breath, these also have stopped.

. . . where these have stopped and all those notions of mind have stopped, that is *Śiva rātri*, that supreme *Śiva rātri*. That unique *Śiva rātri* is glorified. There, that *Śiva rātri* is glorified, [which generally occurs on] the dark half of the *phālguna* month.[99] *Śiva rātri* you know?

JOHN: *Śiva rātri* is the night of Śiva that comes in . . .

SWAMIJI: The night of Śiva that is the dark half of *phālguna*, the fourteenth day of the dark half of *phālguna* month.

JOHN: What does that mean? It means that on the fourteenth day it's the darkest night of the . . .

SWAMIJI: The darkest night.

JOHN: . . . of the moon?

SWAMIJI: Yes.

JOHN: Where the moon is just a . . .

SWAMIJI: Just a . . .

JOHN: . . . a sliver?

SWAMIJI: Yes. That is *Śiva rātri*, [external] *Śiva rātri*.

[Internal] *Śiva rātri* is the rise of *cidānanada*, the rise of God consciousness. Because, the rise of God consciousness will never take place unless there is [cessation of] breathing in and out. And that will never take place . . .

JOHN: If there is breathing.

SWAMIJI: . . . when there is breathing in and out and when there are also so many notions and thoughts residing in your mind, that *Śiva rātri* won't take place. That *Śiva rātri* takes place only when these three sections end altogether. Which

98 That is, when the ingoing breath has also stopped. [*Editor's note*]

99 February-March.

sections? Ingoing breath, out-coming breath, and all thoughts.[100]

DENISE: So, that is the real marriage of Śiva and Pārvati?

SWAMIJI: Yes.

Svaprabhāprasara bhāsvara rūpa, and that *Śiva rātri* is shining with Her own glory, with Its own glory. It is not perceived by some other foreign light or some other foreign torch. It is glorified by Its own light.

This is one way of his understanding. He does not say this to Lord Śiva. He says it to his own self, that this is the glorious *Śiva rātri*.

Now, he addresses Lord Śiva now. Next:

Chapter 4 (1:05:53)

अप्युपार्जितमहं त्रिषु लोके-
ष्वाधिपत्यममरेश्वर मन्ये ।
नीरसं तदखिलं भवदङ्घ्रि-
स्पर्शनामृतरसेन विहीनम् ॥ २३ ॥

apyupārjitamahaṁ triṣu loke-
ṣvādhipatyamamareśvara manye /
nīrasaṁ tadakhilaṁ bhavadaṅghri-
sparśanāmṛtarasena vihīnam //23//

Amareśvara, O God of gods, O God of all gods (*amareśvara* means "who is the God of all gods, who is the master of all gods"), if I have attained and achieved and possessed a kingdom in all of the three worlds, if I possess the state of a kingdom of all the three worlds, even then, that whole kingdom appears to me as rubbish. That kingdom appears to me as rubbish and without any taste.

JOHN: Three worlds are?

100 "Because breath is the cause of thought; breath produces thoughts. . . . This breath movement will create thoughts only when it knows there is nobody watching it." *Bhagavadgītārthasaṁgraha* of Abhinavagupta, translation and commentary by Swami Lakshmanjoo (original audio recording, USF archives, Los Angeles, 1978), 16.1.

SWAMIJI: There are three worlds: *bhūḥ*, *bhuvaḥ*, and *svaḥ* (*bhūrloka*, *bhuvarloka*, and *svarloka*). This is one world (*bhūrloka,* earth); where there are stars, moons, that is another world (*bhuvarloka*); and above that, there is heaven, that is the third world (*svarloka*).

If I achieve the kingdom, if I become ruler of all the three worlds, but I am detached–*bhavat aṅghri sparśanā amṛtarasena*–detached, deprived of being near [You] or with[out] the touch of Your *aṅghri sparśa* (*aṅghri sparśa* means "the touch of Your lotus feet")–when Your lotus feet I don't touch, when I am away from touching Your lotus feet, and I have achieved the kingdom of all the three worlds–that whole kingdom appears to me tasteless and it worries me. I don't like to have that kingdom. When there is nearness of sitting near Your lotus feet, that is everything for me. I want to be near Your feet and nothing else.

Now, there is another problem for me:

Chapter 4 (1:08:34)

बत नाथ दृढोऽयमात्मबन्धो
भवदख्यातिमयस्त्वयैव क्लृप्तः ।
यदयं प्रथमानमेव मे त्वाम्-
अवधीर्य श्लथते न लेशतोऽपि ॥२४॥

bata nātha dṛḍho'yamātmabandho
bhavadakhyātimayastvayaiva klṛptaḥ /
yadayaṁ prathamānameva me tvām-
avadhīrya ślathate na leśato'pi //24//

Nātha, O my Master, this is the greatest worry in me.

What?

Dṛḍho'yamātmabandha, this bondage of *mala* (impurity) is so strong![101] And this bondage of impurity is created by You; *bhavad akhyātimaya stvayaiva klṛptaḥ*, it is created by You, my Lord. You have created this impurity and this impurity is so strong that *ayam prathamānameva me tvām*, [although] You are ap-

101 See appendix 15 for an explanation of the *malas*.

pearing to me, You appear to me, You are in front of me, You are shining before me, and still this tight . . . this bondage does not get loosened. It does not care for Your appearing; [this impurity does not] care for You! So, this bondage is so strong it disrespects You also. You appear to me and still it is tight; still this bondage is tight with me. You could have shattered it into pieces, but it is not shattered; before You also, it is not shattered. So, this bondage of impurity in me is so strong. You appear to me and still it is tight.

Chapter 4 (1:10:22)

महतामरमरेश पूज्यमानोऽ-
  प्यनिशं तिष्ठसि पूजकैकरूपः
बहिरन्तरपीह दृश्यमानः
  स्फुरसि द्रष्टृशरीर एव शश्वत् ॥२५॥

mahatāmamareśa pūjyamāno-
  'pyaniśaṁ tiṣṭhasi pūjakaikarūpaḥ /
bahirantarapīha dṛśyamānaḥ
  sphurasi draṣṭṛśarīra eva śaśvat //25//
[not recited completely]

O God of gods, there is one thing, which is unique regarding Your nature when You are worshiped by great souls. When great souls worship You and You are worshiped by those great souls, You take the seat of being the worshiper, not the worshiped. There, You are the worshiper, not the worshiped. If You are worshiped by those great souls, when they worship You, You are worshiped, actually You are worshiped, but, in fact, You are the worshiper Yourself. You are the worshiper.

Understand?

DENISE: Yes.

SWAMIJI: *Bahirantarapīha dṛśyamānaḥ*, if great *yogīs* perceive You internally and externally quite vividly, there also You remain as the perceiver, not the perceived.

This is Shaivism. He has touched Shaivism in this.

There, You are the perceiver, not the perceived. Although they perceive You in their heart, they perceive You in their heart at the time of *samādhi*, but actually You are not perceived, You are the perceiver. When they worship You and You are worshiped, but actually You are not worshiped, You are the worshiper.

Chapter Five
Longing for the Strength of Ones's Own Nature
Svabalanideśanākhyaṁ pañcamaṁ stotram

Next *stotra*, fifth [chapter]:

Chapter 5 (00:04)

त्वत्पादपद्मसम्पर्कमात्रसंभोगसङ्गिनम् ।
गलेपादिकया नाथ मां स्ववेश्म प्रवेशय ॥ १ ॥

tvatpādapadmasamparkamātrasaṁbhogasaṅginam /
galepādikayā nātha māṁ svaveśma praveśaya //1//

O Master, *tvatpādapadma samparkamātra saṁbhogasaṅginam*, I am always attached to Your lotus feet. As You know that I am attached to Your lotus feet and this is my weakness–I have no other weakness in this world [except] only this weakness that I want to be near Your lotus feet, to be attached with Your lotus feet–but I can't reach there. The problem is, I can't reach there. How can I reach? How can individuality get entry in universality? Individual consciousness can never reach universal consciousness. So, there is no hope for me to reach there and to be near Your lotus feet. So, there is one request. You should fulfill that, my Lord. That is, *galepadikayā nātha māṁ svaveśma praveśaya*, drag me to that abode of Thine [regardless of] my desires also, i.e., if I don't want it, if I have no strength to go there, [still] You [must] carry me, drag me there, at once.

JOHN: Because I can't go there myself.

SWAMIJI: I can't go. But I have only the craving to reach there. How can the individual go there?

JOHN: Can you tell us what the name of this chapter is? What is it?

SWAMIJI: "*Svabalanideśanākhyaṁ pañcamaṁ stotram*": just longing for his own nature, longing for his own nature of strength, strength of nature. Or pointing out, pointing out his own power.

JOHN: So, he is longing for the strength to point out his own power?

SWAMIJI: Power, yes, because he is powerless. He cannot attain that power but he longs for that power. How can he reach there? But he has attachment for that, to be near [Lord Śiva's] lotus feet, but he can't reach there [on his own]. So, he requests Him, "Lord, drag me there!"

Chapter 5 (02:40)

भवत्पादाम्बुजरजोराजिरञ्जितमूर्धजः ।
अपाररभसारब्धनर्तनः स्यामहं कदा ॥२॥

bhavatpādāmbujarajorājirañjitamūrdhajaḥ /
apārarabhasārabdhanartanaḥ syāmahaṁ kadā //2//

When will that glorious day come to me, my Lord, when *bhavatpādāmbujarajo rājirañjitamūrdhajaḥ*, I will be with You, I will remain with You and Your lotus feet, and I will take Your lotus feet, hold Your lotus feet, and take off the dust from Your lotus feet, and that dust I would apply on my head and hair wholeheartedly and *apārarabhasaḥ*, and I will get intoxicated in fullness and I would dance? I would dance always when that glorious day will come to me.

Chapter 5 (03:47)

त्वदेकनाथो भगवन्नियदेवार्थये सदा ।
त्वदन्तर्वसतिर्मूको भवेयं मान्यथा बुद्धः ॥३॥

tvadekanātho bhagavanniyadevārthaye sadā /
tvadantarvasatirmūko bhaveyaṁ mānyathā buddhaḥ //3

I have only one master and that is Thyself (*tvadekanātha*). I have nothing. I know nobody else. I know You. You are my master. You are everything to me! You are my wife, You are my husband, You are my father, You are my mother, You are my everything! You are my attaché. You are everything to me!

So, *iyadevārthaye sadā*, O Lord, I crave only for this, this much . . . what is that craving? *Tvadantarvasatirmūko*, let me remain dumb.

You know "dumb"?

[One] who cannot speak, who is just like, "just let me remain an idiot, but residing in You". I would reside in Thee and become an idiot to others. Let people call me an idiot and I would be residing in Yourself. I would like to be an idiot in that way. *Mānyathā buddhaḥ*, I don't like wisdom. I don't welcome that wisdom when that wisdom comes when I am far away from Thy nearness. I don't want that wisdom. I want this idiot-ship also, i.e., idiot-ship only when I am with You.

Chapter 5 (05:33)

अहो सुधानिधे स्वामिन् अहो मृष्ट त्रिलोचन ।
अहो स्वादो विरूपाक्षेत्येव नृत्येयमारटन् ॥४॥

aho sudhānidhe svāminn aho mṛṣṭa trilocana /
aho svādo virūpākṣetyeva nṛtyeyamāraṭan //4//

I wish to dance! I wish to dance wholeheartedly. I crave to dance wholeheartedly and I would like to sing with sounds, clear sounds.

Aho sudhānidheḥ, O my Lord, You are *sudhānidheḥ*, You are the ocean of nectar for me. *Svāmin*, You are my master. *Aho mṛṣṭaḥ*, You are tasty (*mṛṣṭa* means "tasteful"). *Trilocana*, You have got three eyes. *Aho svādo*, O my Master, You are sweet, sweet in words, sweet in action, compassionate, everything. You are always sweet. You are sweet to me. You are tasty also. I get taste also with You. *Virūpākṣa*, You have got a third eye. And, in this way, I would cry and sing Your glory and dance altogether, always.

Chapter 5 (07:08)

त्वत्पादपद्मसंस्पर्शपरिमीलितलोचनः ।
विजृम्भेय भवद्भक्तिमदिरामदघूर्णितः ॥५॥

tvatpādapadmasaṁsparśaparimīlitalocanaḥ /
vijṛmbheya bhavadbhaktimadirāmadaghūrṇitaḥ //5//

I would like to drink, taste the liquor of Your devotion[102]. The liquor of Your devotion, I would like to taste. When I would taste the liquor of Your devotion, and by that devotion, *ghūrṇitaḥ*, I would get intoxicated–I would like to get intoxicated–and then, *tvatpādapadmasaṁsparśaḥ*, and I would be near Your lotus feet. And by the touch of Your lotus feet, *parimīlitalocanaḥ*, my eyes would be closed altogether and I would be intoxicated for twenty-four hours [a day]. Like that, I wish that.

And when I would taste the liquor of that devotion, and by that liquor, I will get intoxicated, and by intoxication, in that intoxication, I would be near Your lotus feet. So, there would be no other thought in me except Your lotus feet and [all of] my organs would get closed.

Because, when you taste like that, you just close your eyes, i.e., when something you taste is tasty. That is what he wants.

Chapter 5 (09:03)

चित्तभूभृद्भुवि विभो वसेयं क्वापि यत्र सा ।
निरन्तरत्वत्प्रलापमयी वृत्तिर्महारस ॥६॥

cittabhūbhṛdbhuvi vibho vaseyaṁ kvāpi yatra sā /
nirantaratvatpralāpamayī vṛttirmahārasā //6//

O Lord, I would like one thing: I would like to reside in the secluded, isolated place, of that mountain of the mind; some isolated place of the mind, I would like to reside in that. Isolated place of the mountain of the mind, on the peak of the mountain, there would be that isolated place of that mind where there are

102 That is, Utpaladeva's devotion for Lord Śiva.

no other thoughts coming. There I would like to reside.

And then, what I would like to do there?

Just to cry for Your nearness–*nirantara tvat pralāpamayī–tvatpralāpamayī*, just crying for Thee. If I have already achieved the nearness of You, still I would cry, still I would like to cry for You. I would like to cry and cry and cry and cry for always. That is my ambition and that would be very tasteful for me.

Chapter 5 (10:28)

यत्र देवीसमेतस्त्वमासौधादा च गोपुरात् ।
बहुरूपः स्थितस्तस्मिन्वास्तव्यः स्यामहं पुर ॥७॥

yatra devīsametastvamāsaudhādā ca gopurāt /
bahurūpaḥ sthitastasminvāstavyaḥ syāmahaṁ pure //7//

O Lord, where You reside along with Your better half, where You are residing along with Your better half, Pārvatī, not only in the secluded place of *samādhi*, not only in the secluded place of Your residential abode of God consciousness, no, from That point to *ā ca gopurāt*, up to the point of *vaikharī*[103], up to the point of worldly activities, I wish You [would] appear to me along with Your Pārvatī, right from *samādhi* to worldly activities.

Bahurūpa sthitaḥ, and whatever I would come across, I think . . . for instance, when I would see Ernie on the roadside, I would like to see God in Ernie. I would like to see God in Denise. I would like to see God on the pathway. I would like to see God in a motorcar. I would like to see You [everywhere], You along with Your Pārvati.

JOHN: So, this is moving from that internal state to that . . .

SWAMIJI: Internal state to external state.

JOHN: *Jagadānanda*.

SWAMIJI: *Jagadānanda.*[104]

---

103 *Vaikharī* is the grossest level of speech. Swamiji explains the levels of speech in his commentary in Chapter 1, verse 13.

104 Lit., "rejoicing the world". See appendix 16 for an explanation of *jagadānanda*.

Chapter 5 (12:19)

समुल्लसन्तु भगवन् भवद्भानुमरीचयः ।
विकसत्वेष यावन्मे हृत्पद्मः पूजनाय त ॥८॥

samullasantu bhagavan bhavadbhānumarīcayaḥ /
vikasatveṣa yāvanme hṛtpadmaḥ pūjanāya te //8//

I want to give You one trouble only, only for . . . not always, not for always. I am troubling You only for some considerable period. That is . . .

What trouble?

. . . I want to give You this much trouble, *samullasantu bhagavan*, O Lord, *bhavad bhānu marīcayaḥ*, You are the sun, You are just like the sun, You are shining just like the sun, and those rays of Your sun, go on producing those rays, go on producing those rays of Thine on me. Not on me, on my heart; not on my heart, on my lotus in the heart. There is a lotus in my heart and the lotus is just shrunk; it is not in its blooming nature. My lotus-like heart wants this penetration of those rays of You, Your sun . . .

[Utpaladeva] thinks of Him as the sun and he wants His rays to penetrate his lotus in the heart.

. . . so that, *yāvat me hṛtpadmaḥ vikasatu*, as long as it has bloomed nicely. *Bas*, after that, You can withdraw Your rays. Let it bloom first, because I have nothing to do for my [self]; this is not my own thing. This is for You, because if it is bloomed, then I would offer it to Your lotus feet, i.e., this heart [of mine].

JOHN: In other words, he is saying, "I can't do this. Bloom this".

SWAMIJI: How can it . . . it is shrunk. It wants sun rays. And That sun is something [like a] supernatural sun and That sun is Lord Śiva.

Chapter 5 (14:52)

प्रसीद भगवन् येन त्वत्पदे पतितं सदा
मनो मे तत्तदास्वाद्य क्षीवेदिव गलेदि ॥९॥

prasīda bhagavan yena tvatpade patitaṁ sadā /
mano me tattadāsvādya kṣīvediva galediva //9//

O Lord, be pleased with me. And, by that, what will happen? *Tvatpade patitaṁ sadā*, my mind [will] always be at Your lotus feet. Let You be pleased with my mind, and when it is . . . when Your pleasure, Your joy, will penetrate my mind, what will happen in my mind? *Tattadāsvādya*, my mind will experience many of those many supernatural states of being, and my mind will get intoxicated, and my mind will get dissolved in some supreme Being. So, let You be pleased with my mind in that way.

Chapter 5 (16:06)

प्रहर्षाद्वाथ शोकाद्वा यदि कुड्याद्घटादपि ।
बाह्यादथान्तराद्भावात्प्रकटीभव मे प्रभो ॥१०॥

praharṣādvātha śokādvā yadi kuḍyādghaṭādapi /
bāhyādathāntarādbhāvātprakaṭībhava me prabho //10//

O my Master, appear to me! I don't mind if You appear to me in happiness, by giving happiness. If I am happy and You appear to me, well and good. If I am in crisis and You appear to me, well and good. Let me remain in crisis, but appear to me! *Śokādvā*, if I am grieved, totally grieved, if I have lost all of my relatives, all of my kith and kin, and I am discarded from all of my company, and You appear to me, well and good. *Praharṣādvātha śokādvā yadi kuḍyād*, if You appear to me from a wall, well and good; *ghaṭādapi*, if You appear to me from some pot, well and good; *bāhyāt*, if You appear to me from outside, well and good; *antarādbhāvāt*, if You appear to me from inside, well and good.

Appear to me! Just appear to me. I don't want anything else. Appear to me. I don't keep any binding [as to how You appear to me].

JOHN: No conditions.

SWAMIJI: Appear to me in pleasure, in pain, whatever it is. If I am put in crisis and You appear to me, that is nectar for me; that crisis is nectar for me.

Chapter 5 (17:40)

बहिरप्यन्तरपि तत्स्यन्दमानं सदास्तु मे ।
भवत्पादाम्बुजस्पर्शामृतमत्यन्तशीतलम् ॥ ११ ॥

bahirapyantarapi tatsyandamānaṁ sadāstu me /
bhavatpādāmbujasparśāmṛtamatyantaśītalam //11//

Bhavatpāda ambuja sparśa amṛtam. The nectar, which appears by the touch of Your divine lotus feet–that nectar that rises from the touch of Your lotus feet–and that nectar which is *atyanta śītalam*, soothing and very cooling–the touch of Your lotus feet, the nectar of that touch of Your lotus feet, is very soothing and cooling–O Lord, *bahirapyantarapi tat syandamānaṁ sadāstu me*, let that divine nectar remain flowing outside and inside to me always–that nectar.

So, it means I would like to be attached with the touch of that, i.e., Your divine lotus feet, because that produces that nectar, which is cooling and soothing.

And let that nectar flow for twenty-four hours [a day] to me, outside and inside. "Outside" means in worldly activities; "inside" means in *samādhi* also, at the time of meditation.

JOHN: *Unmīlanā* and *nimīlanā samādhi.*

SWAMIJI: *Unmīlanā* and *nimīlanā*, both.[105]

Chapter 5 (19:34)

त्वत्पादसंस्पर्शसुधासरसोऽन्तर्निमज्जनम् ।
कोऽप्येष सर्वसम्भोगलङ्घी भोगोऽस्तु मे सद ॥ १२ ॥

tvatpādasaṁsparśasudhāsaraso'ntarnimajjanam /
ko'pyeṣa sarvasambhogalaṅghī bhogo'stu me sadā //12//

I would like to have that enjoyment, that unique enjoyment, that unique pleasure. I would like to have that unique pleasure, always.

105 See appendix 17 for an explanation of *unmīlanā* and *nimīlanā samādhi.*

What is that unique pleasure?

Just, I would like to drown . . .

You know "drown"?

JOACHIM: Yes, *nimajjanam*.

SWAMIJI: *Nimajjanam*. *Nimajjanam* means "drowning".

. . . I would like to drown in the pool (*saras*), in the *sara* (*sara* means "lake"), in the lake of that nectar, which comes . . . which is filled with the touch of Your lotus feet. The touch of Your lotus feet is nectar and filled with that nectar is that lake. In that lake, I would like to be drowned. If I am drowned in that lake, that is not actually drowning. I won't die in that way.

Ko'pyeṣa sarvasambhoga laṅghī bhoga. This enjoyment is unique enjoyment, and this [is the] unique enjoyment that defeats all other enjoyments of the world.

You know "defeating"?

BRUCE P: Overcomes.

SWAMIJI: Overcomes.

JOACHIM: Overcomes (*laṅghī*); jumps over (*laṅghī*).

SWAMIJI: Yes, *laṅghī*.

JOHN: "Overcomes" is good.

SWAMIJI: Overcomes.

Sarvasambhogalaṅghī, that enjoyment I would like to have for twenty-four hours [a day], always.

Chapter 5 (21:38)

निवेदितमुपादत्स्व रागादि भगवन्मया ।
आदाय चामृतीकृत्य भुङ्क्ष्व भक्तजनैःसमम् ॥१३॥

niveditamupādatsva rāgādi bhagavanmayā /
ādāya cāmṛtīkṛtya bhuṅkṣva bhaktajanaiḥ samam //13//

O Lord, I have come to You. I am before You at Your feet. I have got some present for You. I have carried some present for You. Would you accept it?

And that present is what I have acquired in my past life ("past life" means up to this point). I have attained those things, which I have gathered now at this moment, just to offer at Your feet. This is a great present for You, if You would accept that present, and that present is worldly enjoyments, craving for worldly enjoyments. I have been craving for worldly enjoyments up to this point. When I was born, from my very birth, to this point when I am [present] before You, I have only collected those cravings in my whole life. And I have collected them and I want to offer them to You, at Your feet.

Ādāya cāmṛtīkṛtya, I don't want that You should keep [them] for Yourself because You don't need it [laughs]. I would like You to possess [them] for some time, *amṛtīkṛya*, and nectarize [them] with Your consciousness, with Your God consciousness. Nectarize those cravings for worldly enjoyment and *bhuṅkṣva bhaktajanaḥ samam*, and You take one spoonful from those enjoyments and distribute it amongst Your devotees. We will also then take it.

It means that [these] worldly enjoyments, I don't want to have, I don't want to use, these worldly enjoyments in dryness. These worldly enjoyments I would like to have when they are 'nectarized' with Your God consciousness. When they are 'nectarized', I have no harm to . . . I have no hesitation to have them. I would enjoy them afterwards. And You also take one or two spoonfuls and distribute it amongst us.

JOHN: So, he means, by 'nectarized' here, he means to enter into *jagadānanda*, to have that consciousness in all these actions.

SWAMIJI: Yes, *jagadānanda*. This is *jagadānanda*, yes. [That is] what he wishes.

Chapter 5 (24:29)

अशेषभवनाहारनित्यतृप्तः सुखासनम् ।
स्वामिन् गृहाण दासेषु प्रसादालोकनक्षणम् ॥१४॥

aśeṣabhavanāhāranityatṛptaḥ sukhāsanam /
svāmin gṛhāṇa dāseṣu prasādālokanakṣaṇam //14//

Now, You will say, O Lord, that You have so much to do, "I can't attend to you so soon". O Lord, if You will say that, that You have so much to do, that You have got worldly matters, so many things to be done, so many things to be adjusted, but, in fact, You have done all those things, *aśeṣabhuvanāhāranityatṛptaḥ*, because You are always full. Your stomach is always full because this whole universe is Your own food. You have already possessed that. *Sukhāsanam*, You are seated peacefully now. So, what is the harm if You don't [neglect to] hear my demand?

Because, those great kings who are seated on a throne, they attend those demands of people one-by-one, successively, because they have no time to do all things. [The king] will tell you, "come tomorrow". To [someone else], he will say, "come after eight days, or come after one month. I will do your things".

But, [for You], there is nothing. You have finished Your own household things. For instance, You have already taken food. That is *jagadānanda*. You are always filled with *jagadānanda*. So, food You have already taken and all of Your activities You have done. So, *aśeṣabhuvana āhāranityatṛptaḥ*, You are always full, *sukhāsanam*, and You are seated in peace.

Dāseṣu prāsāda alokanakṣaṇam gṛhāṇa. Now, You [must] divert Your attention towards us also because You are full, You have done everything which was to be done. You have done that and [so] You hear our things now, our demands now.

Chapter 5 (27:10)

अन्तर्भक्तिचमत्कारचर्वणामीलितेक्षणाः ।
नमो मह्यं शिवायेति पूजयन् स्यां तृणान्यपि ॥१५॥

antarbhakticamatkāracarvaṇāmīlitekṣaṇāḥ /
namo mahyaṁ śivāyeti pūjayan syāṁ tṛṇānyapi //15//

O Lord, I would like to have that state, that supreme state, when *antar bhakti camatkāra carvaṇa āmīlitekṣaṇā*, I would be experiencing the internal joy of God consciousness, internal joy of Your nearness. And, by experiencing that internal joy, all of my organs would [become] closed (*mīlitekṣanā*). And then, *namo mahyaṁ śivāyeti*–then I would be doing what?–*namo mahyaṁ śivāyeti*, let prostrations be to my own Self, prostrations be to my own Self. In this way, I would like to prostrate before my own nature and I would be worshiping even blades of grass in this universe. Everything I would like to worship afterwards.

JOHN: So, that means he is asking that first let him know his own nature . . .

SWAMIJI: Yes.

JOHN: . . . and worship that, and unfold that, then he would like to come out and worship everything in that, in that light.

SWAMIJI: Worship everything. For instance, when he sees, looks at John, he won't look at John, he will look at his own nature. When he tastes some cheese, he won't taste cheese, he would taste that God consciousness, the divine nectar of God consciousness. In each and every act of daily life, [he would perceive God consciousness].

Chapter 5 (29:12)

अपि लब्धभवद्भावः स्वात्मोल्लासमयं जगत् ।
पश्यन् भक्तिरसाभोगैर्भवेयमवियोजितः ॥१६॥

api labdhabhavadbhāvaḥ svātmollāsamayaṁ jagat /
paśyan bhaktirasābhogairbhaveyamaviyojitaḥ //16//

When that day will come (*api* means "when that day, when that glorious day will come to me"), when that glorious day will come to me when *svātma ullāsam ayaṁ jagat paśyan*, I would perceive this whole universe as the outcome of my own nature's glory, *bhakti rasā bhogair bhaveyam aviyojitaḥ*, and I will become one with that ecstasy, ecstasy of *bhaktirasa*, ecstasy of tasting the nectar of devotion. I would be one with . . . in tasting the ecstasy of Your devotion when that day will come to me.

Chapter 5 (30:18)

आकाङ्क्षणीयमपरं येन नाथ न विद्यते
तव तेनाद्वितीयस्य युक्तं यत्परिपूर्णता ॥१७॥

ākāṅkṣaṇīyamaparaṁ yena nātha na vidyate /
tava tenādvitīyasya yuktaṁ yatparipūrṇatā //17//

O Lord, *śāstras* (scriptures) hold that You are full, You are always full. I think it is a fact. I think it is a fact that You are always full because *ākāṅkṣaṇīyam aparaṁ*, full is that person who has nothing to do, who has nothing to seek, who has nothing to get, who has nothing to achieve–he is full.

And, because You have nothing to achieve, You don't desire anything because You have everything. You possess everything, so You don't desire anything. If there is craving for money, that is [already] there. If there is craving for a motorcar, that is [already] there. Everything You have possessed, so there is nothing to be longed for.

If this is the way, if this is the theory, in connection with Thee, O Lord, then You are the only unique person who is filled with fullness–exact, real fullness.

Chapter 5 (32:52)

हस्यते नृत्यते यत्र रागद्वेषादि भुज्यते ।
पीयते भक्तिपीयूषरसस्तत्प्राप्नुयां पदम् ॥१८॥

hasyate nṛtyate yatra rāgadveṣādi bhujyate /
pīyate bhaktipīyūṣarasastatprāpnuyāṁ padam //18//

O Lord, I would like to achieve that state of being where *hasyate*, You are filled with laughter, where You are filled with laughter, You always laugh, *nṛtyati*, You always dance, *rāgadveṣādi bhujyate*, You always eat the craving of worldly enjoyments"at" means subsiding; "eating worldly enjoyments" means subsiding worldly enjoyments).

So, in the outward world also, the real enjoyment lies in eating, dancing, and laughing.

JOHN: "Dancing" means here?

JOACHIM: *Nṛtyati*.

JOHN: Yes, but I mean what does it mean in the . . . ?

SWAMIJI: I will tell you. *Hasyate* means to laugh, laughing. *Nṛtyate* means when there is dance. When you are laughing always, when you are dancing, and when you are eating many varieties [of food], and when you are drinking, these four things make you complete. The completion of your life is done by these four things: when you are laughing, when you are dancing . . . dancing is there, laughing is there, eating all varieties [of food] is there, and drinking Scotch whisky worth five hundred rupees a bottle [laughter].

JOHN: This has other meaning, these . . . ?

SWAMIJI: The other meaning is *hasyate*. *Hasyate* means when you laugh at the worldly people, when you laugh at/on these worldly peoples [and think], "what are they doing? They are only wasting their time in going here and there. This activity is all false activity". So, you laugh at them.

Nṛtyate. *Nṛtyate* means *nṛti gātra vikṣepe* (this is the verbal root from *nṛti*). *Gātra vikṣepe* means "you shatter, you shatter away all of your limbs". "All of your limbs" means all attachments. When all attachments, bodily attachments (e.g., bodily attachment is with Viresh, with John, with your master, with all your surroundings, with house, with motorcar, with swimming– these are your limbs), when these limbs are all shattered to pieces, that is *nṛtyate*, that is dancing, that is real dancing.

Rāgadveṣādi bhujyate, and what is "eating"? [Eating] varieties is eating, just absorbing attachment and hatred. Love, hatred, all of these things, when they are absorbed, when they are consumed inside, in God consciousness, that is "eating".

Pīyate bhaktipīyūṣa rasaḥ. *Pīyate* means "drinking", but not that Scotch whisky. *Bhaktipīyūṣa rasa*, just being attached to your divine nature, when you are attached to your divine nature, that is the real drink.

Where this is being done, I would like to achieve that state of being. When shall I achieve that state?

Chapter 5 (36:11)

तत्तदपूर्वामोद त्वच्चिन्ताकुसुमवासना दृढताम् ।
एतु मम मनसि यावन्नश्यतु दुर्वासनागन्ध ॥१९॥

tattadapūrvāmodatvaccintākusumavāsanā dṛḍhatām /
etu mama manasi yāvannaśyatu durvāsanāgandhaḥ / / 19

O Master, in my mind there is a foul smell, always. In my mind, in the space of my mind, there is always a foul smell. And that "foul smell" means that *durvāsanā*, various thoughts, various desires of life, e.g., I would like to go there, I would like to do this, that, swimming, attending movies, music, everything. And all of these desires have created a hell in my mind. They have created a hell of a bad smell. This is a bad smell.

DEVOTEES: [laughter]

SWAMIJI: Yes, because he says it is *durvāsanā gandha. Durvāsanā gandha* means "this is a hell of a bad smell in my mind".

So, I would like to remove [this smell], have it removed, but it is not in my power, Sir. O Lord, *tattad apurvāmoda tvaccintā kusuma vāsanā*, and there is only one way to get rid of this foul smell in my mind. That is by always remembering Your lotus feet. I do try [to do] that. I do remember Your lotus feet always because those lotus feet create *apūrva āmoda*, fragrance, divine fragrance. [From Thy] lotus feet flows out fragrance; divine fragrance flows out from Thy lotus feet. And when you remember those lotus feet, divine fragrance is there.

But this divine fragrance in my mind comes and goes, so it is not established, it is not established in my mind. As soon as it goes, again this foul smell arises in my mind and it has created a hell of that bad smell. I am actually drowned in that bad smell. What can I do? How can I get rid of that?

So, I would like one . . . I would ask one favor from Thee, O my Lord. That favor is, just establish this remembrance of Thy lotus feet, fragrance of [Thy] lotus feet. If it remains established and stationary for, say, two or three hours only, then this bad smell would get washed [away]. This is my desire.

Chapter 5 (39:14)

क्व नु रागादिषु रागः
क्व च हरचरणाम्बुजेषु रागित्वम् ।
इत्थं विरोधरसिकं
बोधय हितममर मे हृदयम् ॥२०॥

kva nu rāgādiṣu rāgaḥ
kva ca haracaraṇāmbujeṣu rāgitvam /
itthaṁ virodharasikaṁ
bodhaya hitamamara me hṛdayam //20//

Amara, O divine Lord, my mind, I know my mind, it is *virodharasikaṁ*; *virodharasikaṁ*, sometimes [my mind] likes to be [involved] in the enjoyment of worldly pleasures, sometimes [my mind] wants to meditate. Sometimes it happens in my mind, just this desire comes just to meditate wholeheartedly on that one-pointedness. Sometimes it appears in my mind just to go after worldly pleasures, worldly enjoyments. But this is North Pole and South Pole. There is no meeting of these things; they don't meet. How can they meet? This is North Pole and this is South Pole.

What is North Pole?

North Pole is just to be attached to Your lotus feet; attachment with Your lotus feet is the North Pole. Attachment with worldly pleasures is the South Pole. Sometimes the attachment with Your lotus feet rises in my mind. Sometimes, in the next moment, the attachment for worldly pleasures rises in my mind. So, my mind is *virodharasikam*, my mind is attached to two opposite things.

O my Lord, just initiate my mind not to do these mischievous doings. I can't teach my mind; it is out of my reach. My mind is always like this. So, *amara*, O immortal Being, You teach my mind to be attached to only one point, not to go in two opposite directions.

Because, there is no fun in that, i.e., just to be attached with God consciousness [in one moment and then to be] degraded [with attachment to worldly pleasures in the next moment].

Who is to get married?

STEPHANIE: Dilshad[106].

SWAMIJI: Dilshad. To be attached to Dilshad. To be attached to God and to be attached to Dilshad–two opposite things–it should not happen in my mind. If I am attached to God, he must think, my mind must think, that you are attached to God! Remember God! God is the only highest being in the universe and above the universe. You should not get [attached in] two directions.

Please teach my mind so that it comes to its senses, my mind comes to its senses.

106 A girl from Swamiji's the local village.

Chapter 5 (42:34)

विचरन्योगदशास्वपि विषयव्यावृत्तिवर्तमनोऽपि ।
त्वच्चिन्तामदिरामदतरलीकृतहृदय एव स्याम ॥२१॥

vicaranyogadaśāsvapi viṣayavyāvṛttivartamano'pi /
tvaccintāmadirāmadataralīkṛtahṛdaya eva syām //21//

Vicaran yoga daśāsvapi. Although I am roaming in the various states of *yoga*, although I am bent upon depriving my mind from attachment towards worldly pleasures–I am doing that; I am extracting my mind from worldly enjoyments and I am roaming in the states of *yoga*–I am doing this, it is true, but I don't like this kind of struggle.

Tvat cintāmadirāmadataralī kṛta hṛdaya eva syām. I would like to be intoxicated in Your desire only, the desire of being attached to Your lotus feet. Only this desire must remain. I don't like these states of *yoga*. I don't like to withdraw worldly thoughts from my mind.

You see, you can't meditate when you don't withdraw these worldly thoughts in your mind. You have to withdraw those [thoughts].

But this botheration I would not like; not this botheration nor that botheration.

What botheration?

GANJOO: Going into those *yoga daśas* (*yogic* states).

SWAMIJI: Going into the states of experiences of *yoga*. Sometimes *mūlādhāra cakra*[107] is rising, the *cakra* in the navel is rising, the *cakra* in the heart is rising, the *cakra* in *kaṇṭha* (throat) is rising, [or] the *cakra* in *bhrūmadhya*[108] is rising [while] experiencing these various states of *yoga*. This is also one thing. And another thing is to withdraw your energy from worldly pleasures and focus your mind towards one point of God consciousness.

Although I do these things, it is true, but there is no happiness in these two things. I would like to remember being attached to Your lotus feet twenty-four hours [a day]. That is my only

107 The *mūlādhāra cakra* is located just near the rectum.

108 *Bhrūmadhya*: between the two eyebrows.

[desire]! I don't want to achieve anything [else]. Just remembrance. This remembrance, remembering Your lotus feet, nearness of Your lotus feet, always, I would like to have that.

JOHN: This "remembering the nearness of His lotus feet" is?

SWAMIJI: Just to be one with that, just to be one with that, mad after [His] lotus feet.

JOHN: He wants to just have that.

SWAMIJI: Yes, not the states of *yoga*.

JOHN: Or *siddhis*, or . . .

SWAMIJI: Just to subside and propagate in the world that I am a powerful *yogi*, I don't like that. I [just] want to die in that nearness of Your lotus feet.

Chapter 5 (45:56)

वाचि मनोमतिषु तथा शरीरचेष्टासु करणरचितासु ।
सर्वत्र सर्वदा मे पुरःसरो भवतु भक्तिरस ॥२२॥

vāci manomatiṣu tathā śarīraceṣṭāsu karaṇaracitāsu /
sarvatra sarvadā me puraḥsaro bhavatu bhaktirasaḥ //22

O Lord, I would like to have this [one] thing.

What is that?

Vāci mano matiṣu śarīra ceṣṭāṣu karaṇa racitāsu. When I talk (*vāci* means "when I begin to talk with others"), *mano*, when my mind is functioning ("functioning" means when my mind is thinking of various things of the world), *matiṣu*, when my intellect is confirming what to do and what not to do, e.g., "O, this should be done" [or] "No, don't do this" (these differentiated things are done by the intellect, the doings of the intellect), *tathā śarīraceṣṭāsu*, and the activities of my body, in the activities of my body (in speech, in mind, in intellect, and in the activities of my body), and *karaṇaracitāsu*, and in the activities of my organs (*śabda*, *sparśa*, *rūpa*, *rasa*, and *gandha*; in seeing, in touching, in hearing, in all of these), in all of these activities, I would like the . . .

Puraḥ saraḥ means "easily approached, easily achieved, not with struggle", e.g., when there is in your mind to have this fountain pen and, at that very moment, I offer this fountain pen [to you]. It is easily achieved, without craving, without struggling. That is *puraḥ saraḥ*.

. . . in all things, always let me have the *rasa* (*rasa* means "the nectar of Your devotion") in all of these activities. I would like to have and possess the nectar of Thy devotion in all of these activities of mine: in speech, in mind, in intellect, in bodily activities, and in organic activities.

JOHN: Effortlessly.

SWAMIJI: Effortlessly. *Puraḥ saraḥ* means that, "effortlessly achieved".

Chapter 5 (49:00)

शिवशिवशिवेति नामनि
तव निरवधि नाथ जप्यमानेऽस्मिन् ।
आस्वादयन् भवेयं
कमपि महारससमपुनरुक्तम् ॥२३॥

śivaśivaśiveti nāmani
tava niravadhi nātha japyamāne'smin /
āsvādayan bhaveyaṁ
kamapi mahārasasamapunaruktam //23//

Nātha, O my Master, I would like to have this [one] thing.

What is that?

I would like to recite Your name, "Śiva, Śiva", and I would like to recite this "Śiva, Śiva", the name of Thine, *niravadhi* (*niravadhi* means "endlessly").

Endlessly means . . .

GANJOO: Without a break.

SWAMIJI: Without a break, in continuity.

And I would like to recite only this *mantra* of "Śiva" always. And internally I would like to experience the nectar of that supreme nectar of that unique thing, which I can't repeat, repeat, and repeat. I can't repeat [it because] it is beyond my explanation. I can't repeat what would happen to me afterwards when I would recite Your name, "Śiva, Śiva", in continuity, always.

Chapter 5 (50:42)

स्फुरदनन्तचिदात्मकविष्टपे
परिनिपीतसमस्तजडाध्वनि ।
अगणितापरचिन्मयगण्डिके
प्रविचरेयमहं भवतोऽर्चिता ॥२४॥

sphuradanantacidātmakaviṣṭape
parinipītasamastajaḍādhvani /
agaṇitāparacinmayagaṇḍike
pravicareyamahaṁ bhavato'rcitā //24//

O Lord, I would like to reside, I would like to live, in that country, I would like to live in that country–in which country?–*sphurad ananta cidātmaka viṣṭape*, which country is filled with numberless hutments of God consciousness.

You know "hutments"?

DENISE: No.

SWAMIJI: Small huts.

DENISE: Oh.

SWAMIJI: Small huts.

JOHN: Cottages.

SWAMIJI: Cottages, small cottages. If you enter in one cottage, [you will find] God consciousness. In another cottage, [you will find] God consciousness. In another cottage, it is filled with God consciousness. Everywhere [there is] God consciousness and nothing else.

And, in that country, I would like to live. In that country, I would like to live and roam and walk and have a daily walk, go around here and there. Wherever I go, I'll find that small hut [filled] with God consciousness; everywhere [I would find] God consciousness (that is *ananta cidātmaka viṣṭape*). *Ananta*, and those hutments, those huts, I would like to have numberless.

"Numberless" means, when[ever] I perceive . . . e.g., when I talk to Ernie, I wouldn't talk to Ernie at that time. What would I do? I would get entry in that hut of God consciousness. If I talk to some other gentleman, that would make me enter in another hut.

DENISE: Of God consciousness.

SWAMIJI: So, everywhere, whatever I do, [be it] *śabda*, *sparśa* (smell, touch), everything, whatever I do in my worldly life, I would like to feel only the hutments of God consciousness. Hutments means small huts.

JOHN: Cottages.

SWAMIJI: Cottages, cottages of [God consciousness]; *sphurad ananta cidātmaka viṣṭape.*

And *parinipīta samasta jaḍādhvani*, and those hutments would be producers of the strength of awareness.

He desires, he longs, to taste the nectar of that God consciousness with awareness. And awareness would also come out from those huts.

Parinipīta samasta jaḍa adhvani. And dullness would be totally absent. Where, in which country, dullness of everything, in all ways, in all ways and walks of life, the dullness would disappear to me.

Agaṇita pracinmaye gaṇḍike. And I would like to go into another country just to visit another country other than this country of God consciousness, and I would not find any other country. I would find only this country [of God consciousness] and no other country existing. I would like to have such a kind of thing. And, in That country, I would like to roam and live and shine.

JOHN: This is *śāktopāya* practice?

SWAMIJI: This is *śāktopāya*[109].

Chapter 5 (54:52)

स्ववपुषि स्फुटभासिनी शाश्वते
स्थितिकृते न कमप्युपयुज्यते ।
इति मतिः सुदृढा भवतात् परं
मम भवच्चरणाब्जरजः शुचेः ॥२५॥

svavapuṣi sphuṭabhāsinī śāśvate
sthitikṛte na kamapyupayujyate /

109 See appendix 2 for an explanation of the *upāyas*.

iti matiḥ sudṛḍhā bhavatāt paraṁ
mama bhavaccaraṇābjarajaḥ śuceḥ //25//

It is a fact–there is no doubt in this understanding–that Your nature, when It is *sphuṭa bhāsini*, when It appears clearly, when It appears clearly to anybody, . . .

What?

JOHN: Your nature.

SWAMIJI: Your nature.

. . . and It appears *śāśvate* (*śāśvate* means "it is established, this appearance is established"), when This appearance is established firmly, confirmed, and when you are also established in that God consciousness, *na kim api upayujyate*, then nothing remains to be done afterwards. When you are once established in that God consciousness, what remains to be done afterwards? Nothing. This is right.

Iti matiḥ, this understanding in me is existing. But, [although] this understanding I have, but sometimes I make love, sometimes I go in a *shikara*[110] for pleasure, sometimes I go for dinner, for lunch, but that is not establishment, that is not real establishment in that [understanding]. If it would have been [real establishment], I would have been established in that, in that understanding.

Which understanding?

JOHN: Of Your nature.

SWAMIJI: That when once you are established in Your nature, then there is nothing to be done, there is nothing to be sought after. So, this understanding in me is already existing but it is not *dṛḍha*, it is not confirmed, it is not established. Let it be established, my Lord! Not because of my qualities. I have no qualities. I have . . . this is not due to me. *Bhavat caraṇa ambuja rasaḥ śuceḥ*, because I think of Your feet, and thinking of Your feet makes me fit, not because of my qualities. I have no qualities–that is true–and I don't deserve this kind of achievement, but I deserve it because I am purified with the nearness of Your lotus feet.

110 A type of small boat used in Kashmir. [*Editor's note*]

Chapter 5 (57:44)

किमपि नाथ कदाचन चेतसि
स्फुरति तद्भवदङ्घ्रितलस्पृशाम् ।
गलति यत्र समस्तमिदं सुधा-
सरसि विश्वमिदं दिश मे सदा ॥२६॥

kimapi nātha kadācana cetasi
sphurati tadbhavadaṅghritalaspṛśam /
galati yatra samastamidaṁ sudhā-
sarasi viśvamidaṁ diśa me sadā //26//

Nātha, O my Master, *bhavat aṅghritala spṛśam*, those fortunate souls who are always residing near Thy lotus feet, those fortunate ones who are always residing near Your lotus feet, in those minds, in the minds of those fortunate people who reside near Your lotus feet, something happens to them, which I cannot explain. Something unique happens to them in their minds; in their minds, something flows out. And, by which thing, by which flow, *galati yatra samastamidaṁ sudhā sarasi*, where all other worries of the world are shattered to pieces and dissolved in that supreme ocean of nectar. Give me that, please. I would like to achieve that.

Bas, there ends this chapter

Chapter Six
Clearance of the Path
Adhvavisphuraṇākhyaṁ ṣaṣṭham stotram

SWAMIJI: Now, this chapter is [called] "*adhva visphuraṇākhyaṁ ṣaṣṭhaṁ stotram*", the sixth. *Adhva visphuraṇākhyaṁ.*

BRUCE P: What does that mean?

SWAMIJI: *Adhva visphuram* means, if I am on the path, I am treading on the path, on the path of Thee, Thy path, just to achieve You, just to get entry in Your kingdom, the happenings on the path, other happenings on the path, that are a disturbance, those disturbances he wants to get removed.

It is only madness in this *stotra*.

Adhva visphuraṇākhyaṁ ṣaṣṭhaṁ stotram. He wants clearance of his path (*adhva visphuraṇ*). *Adhva visphuraṇa* means, he wants his path on which he is treading, just [to obtain] clearance, so that [he] could tread nicely.

Chapter 6 (01:18)

क्षणमात्रमपीशान वियुक्तस्य त्वया मम ।
निबिडं तप्यमानस्य सदा भूया दृशः पदम् ॥ १ ॥

kṣaṇamātramapīśāna viyuktasya tvayā mama /
nibiḍaṁ tapyamānasya sadā bhūyā dṛśaḥ padam //1//

Īśāna, O Lord, *mama tvayā viyuktasya*, when I become separated from Your Self, *kṣaṇamātram api*, even for one second–when I become separated, when I am placed away from You even for one second, one moment–*nibiḍaṁ tapyamānasya*, You must understand that I catch fire of sadness, at once. I am burnt in the fire of sadness at that moment.

Sadā bhūyāḥ dṛśaḥ padam. So, it is worthwhile for You, my Lord, to remain in front of me always. Because, when I am kept away from Your Self, even for one moment, I get burnt with sadness, the fire of sadness. So, *sadā bhūyā dṛśaḥ padam*, be in front of me, remain in front of me, always.

Chapter 6 (02:51)

वियोगसारे संसारे प्रियेण प्रभुणा त्वया ।
अवियुक्तः सदैव स्यां जगतापि वियोजित ॥२॥

viyogasāre saṁsāre priyeṇa prabhuṇā tvayā /
aviyuktaḥ sadaiva syāṁ jagatāpi viyojitaḥ //2//

It is a fact that this world (*saṁsāre*), this world is *viyogasāre*, it is to be . . . there is separation in the end. In this universe, there is separation. You are being separated from your kith and kin. You have to . . . *viyogasāre saṁsāre*, this *saṁsāre*, the essence of this world, is to [experience] separation. Separation will take place in the end. Everybody will be separated.

JOHN: "Separated" means death.

SWAMIJI: Yes. There is no contact afterwards.

So, this is the essence of the world–that I believe–but I have not attachment for my kith and kin. If I am separated from them, I don't mind. But I have got attachment for Thee, my Lord. *Priyeṇa prabhuṇā tvayā*, You are my only thing. You are my wished and longed personality. I am craving for You.

Aviyuktaḥ sadaiva syāṁ jagatāpi viyojitaḥ. If I am separated from my relatives and kith and kin in the end, [I don't mind]. I wish I was inseparable from Thee. I wish I was one with Thee, always. This is my earnest desire in my mind.

Chapter 6 (04:39)

कायवाङ्मनसैर्यत्र यामि सर्वं त्वमेव तत् ।
इत्येष परमार्थोऽपि परिपूर्णोऽस्तु मे सदा ॥३॥

kāyavāṅmanasairyatra yāmi sarvaṁ tvameva tat /
ityeṣa paramārtho'pi paripūrṇo'stu me sadā //3//

Ityeṣa paramārtho'pi. This is the real science of our philosophy, *ityeṣa paramārtho'pi*, this is our true philosophy, that wherever I go, *yatra yāmi*, wherever I go through body, through speech, or through mind, wherever I go, wherever I move (*kāya* means "through body", *vāṅ* means "through speech", *manasaiḥ* means "through mind"), wherever I move, in fact, *sarvaṁ tvameva tat*, in fact, that place is always one with Thee. *Sarvaṁ tvameva tat*, wherever I move, e.g., if I move to a picture house, that picture house is one with [Thee]. I am not away from Thy presence there. Wherever I go, wherever my body goes, wherever my speech goes, whatever my speech says, whatever my mind thinks, that is Your nature, that is Your divine Self. This is the reality of our philosophy. *Ityeṣa paramārtho'pi*, this is the reality. It is a fact that this is the reality. *Paripūrṇo'stu me sadā*, but I don't get satisfaction. I would like to get satisfaction in this understanding. I understand this is true, but this does not appear to me practically. I want this to appear in practical shape.

Chapter 6 (06:51)

निर्विकल्पो महानन्दपूर्णो यद्वद्भवांस्तथा ।
भवत्स्तुतिकरी भूयाद्अनुरूपैव वाङ्मम ॥४॥

nirvikalpo mahānandapūrṇo yadvadbhavāṁstathā /
bhavatstutikarī bhūyādanurūpaiva vāṅmama //4//

O Lord, You are *nirvikalpa*, You have no *vikalpas.*[111] *Mahānanda pūrṇa*, You are filled with supreme ecstasy. This is the reality of Your nature. You are *nirvikalpa* and You are filled with supreme ecstasy, always.

But, I am Your singer, I sing Your glory. But, I would like that whatever I sing, whatever glory I sing of Thee, it must become like that. It must not become shrunk. I must not sing Your glory in a shrunken way. I must sing Your glory just as You are. You are *nirvikalpa*, and my singing also must be *nirvikalpa*. And You are *mahānanda pūrṇa*, You are filled with ecstasy, and my singing must also be filled with ecstasy. That is what I wish, long for.

---

111 See appendix 9 for an explanation of *nirvikalpa*.

Chapter 6 (08:17)

भवदावेशतः पश्यन् भावं भावं भवन्मयम् ।
विचरेयं निराकाङ्क्षः प्रहर्षपरिपूरितः ॥५॥

bhavadāveśataḥ paśyan bhāvaṁ bhāvaṁ bhavanmayam /
vicareyaṁ nirākāṅkṣaḥ praharṣaparipūritaḥ //5//

Paripūritaḥ, I would wish one thing, *bas*. Just as a ghost enters into somebody and that person becomes one with the ghost, he talks like the ghost afterwards, . . .

Do you believe in these things?

JOHN: I do.

SWAMIJI: . . . and, in the same way, I want You to get entry in my body. My Lord, *bhavadāveśataḥ*, when You enter in my body, in my self, then what will happen to me in my perception? My perception will be something else. It will be absolutely different [than] it was before.

Bhāvaṁ bhāvaṁ bhavan mayaṁ paśyan. I wish I would see, I would perceive, each and every object, every object I would see one with Thee. And *vicareyaṁ nirākāṅkṣaḥ*, I would roam in this world, *nirākāṅkṣaḥ*, without any desire and filled with supreme joy. This is my desire, i.e., how I will live in this world afterwards when You will enter into me just like a ghost and I will become one with You.

Chapter 6 (10:06)

भगवन्भवतः पूर्णं पश्येयमखिलं जगत् ।
तावतैवास्मि सन्तुष्टस्ततो न परिखिद्यसे ॥६॥

bhagavanbhavataḥ pūrṇaṁ paśyeyamakhilaṁ jagat /
tāvataivāsmi santuṣṭastato na parikhidyase //6//

Bhagavan, O Lord, there is one desire in me, which always knocks in the background of my consciousness, and that is, I would like to perceive this whole universe filled with Your consciousness, filled with Your supreme consciousness. This whole universe, I would like to perceive already filled with supreme consciousness. *Tāvataivāsmi santuṣṭaḥ*, that is my ambition. That, my ambition, will be completed that way. I take an oath, my Lord, then I won't trouble You further. Afterwards, I won't trouble You. I won't give You any trouble in asking for more and more things. This is the only one thing that I ask, once and for all. Let me see this whole universe as one with Thee and I will be satisfied. I won't trouble You any more afterwards.

Chapter 6 (11:26)

विलीयमानास्त्वय्येव व्योम्नि मेघलवा इव ।
भावा वीभन्तु मे शश्वत्क्रमनैर्मल्यगामिन ॥७॥

vilīyamānāstvayyeva vyomni meghalavā iva /
bhāvā vībhantu me śaśvatkramanairmalyagāminaḥ //7//

Let me feel this objective world, this universe of objectivity, as it is lying in the ether of Your God consciousness; in the ether of Your consciousness, just like clouds. As clouds . . . as there are heaps of clouds in the sky, in the same way, let me feel this universal world as masses of clouds in the sky of God consciousness, in the sky of God consciousness.

In which action?

Vilīyamānā, just as clouds fade by and by–by and by they fade and there is only blue sky afterwards–afterwards there remains only blue sky and clouds are felt no more existing, in the same way, this universe would appear to me. *Bhāvā vibhāntu me śaśvat krama nairmalya gāminaḥ*, and [this objective world] will become purified and become one with Thee in the end. Let me feel that way.

Chapter 6 (12:55)

स्वप्रभाप्रसरध्वस्तापर्यन्तध्वान्तसन्ततिः ।
सन्ततं भातु मे कोऽपि भवमध्याद्भवन्मणि ॥८॥

svaprabhāprasaradhvastāparyantadhvāntasantatiḥ /
santataṁ bhātu me ko'pi bhavamadhyādbhavanmaṇiḥ //8

Svaprabhā prasara, O Lord, I have this desire that when, by the effulgent light of Your consciousness, the effulgent light of Your flow of consciousness, *dhvasta aparyanta dhvānta santatiḥ*, all of my ignorance, all of the masses of ignorance, . . .

No, not [masses]. *Santati* means . . .

JOHN: Layers, like layers?

SWAMIJI: Layers.

. . . the layers (*santatiḥ*) of those darknesses [of my ignorance] will vanish by the effulgent flow of the light of Your consciousness, always. And, *bhātu me ko'pi bhavamadhyād bhavanmaṇiḥ*, and I will find–in the very action of this universe–I will find a great universal jewel of Thy formation. That universal jewel will appear to me *in* the universe.

JOHN: In the action of the universe, not separate from it.

SWAMIJI: Yes, not separate from it.

Chapter 6 (14:21)

कां भूमिकां नाधिशेषे किं तत्स्याद्यन्न ते वपुः ।
श्रान्तस्तेनाप्रयासेन सर्वतस्त्वामवाप्नुयाम् ॥९॥

kāṁ bhūmikāṁ nādhiśeṣe kiṁ tatsyādyanna te vapuḥ /
śrāntastenāprayāsena sarvatastvāmavāpnuyām //9//

O Lord, what is that stage, which You don't possess? All stages are possessed by Thee. *Kiṁ tat syāt yanna*, and what is that formation, which is not Your formation? All formations are possessed by You. All forms of You are Yours.

I am really exhausted now [because] I can't find You (*śrāntas*, exhausted). So, *tena aprayāsena sarvatas tvām avāpnuyām*, let me perceive the presence of Your consciousness, let me perceive the presence of Your Being, in my own home, in my own room. I don't want to roam and roam and [try to] find out . . . in search of Thee. Because, You are everywhere; Your appearance is possible anywhere. So, why not appear in my own bedroom?

He is actually tired now, exhausted. He does not want to search for Him.

Chapter 6 (15:53)

भवदङ्गपरिष्वङ्गसम्भोगः स्वेच्छयैव मे ।
घटतामियति प्राप्ते किं नाथ न जितं मया ॥१०॥

bhavadaṅgaparisvaṅga sambhogaḥ svecchayaiva me /
ghaṭatāmiyati prāpte kiṁ nātha na jitaṁ mayā //10//

Nātha, O Master, just by my will[112]–not by action–just when I desire, *bhavadaṅga parisvaṅga saṁbhogaḥ*, let the joy of becoming embraced with Thee appear automatically. I don't want to embrace You. You must embrace me! This is what I desire. *Bhavat aṅga pariṣvaṅga saṁbhogaḥ svecchayaiva me ghaṭatām*, not by embracing, but by being embraced. I must get embraced by You.[113]

Iyati prāpte, when this is done, when this appears to me, *kiṁ nātha na jitaṁ mayā*, I have conquered everything in this world (*kiṁ nātha na jitam*, I have conquered everything). Each and everything that is to be conquered, that was to be conquered, I have conquered [by Thy embrace].

Chapter 6 (17:09)

प्रकटीभव नान्याभिः प्रार्थनाभिः कदर्थनाः ।
कुर्मस्ते नाथ ताम्यन्तस्त्वामेव मृगयामहे ॥११॥

prakaṭībhava nānyābhiḥ prārthanābhiḥ kadarthanāḥ /
kurmaste nātha tāmyantastvāmeva mṛgayāmahe //11//

---

112 *Śāmbhavopāya* or *icchopāya*, the path (*upāya*) of will. See appendix 2 for an explanation of the *upāyas*.

113 "Fruitless practice and meditation is under your control. Fruitful meditation and concentration is under His control. You see, when you meditate for sometime and your mind is not one-pointed, it means you [have] put your own effort–grace is not there. When you meditate and automatically you get one-pointed, you must know that it is His grace that you are pushed in." *Tantrāloka*, 13.109 (USF archives).

"Once you are embraced by Him, there is no problem for your meditation." Ibid, 15.77.

O Master, appear to me! Now, appear to me! *Nānyābhiḥ prārthanābhiḥ kadarthanāḥ te kurmaḥ*, I will never ask any other thing as long as I am living. As long as I am in this world, I will ask nothing. I ask only that You should appear to me.

Tāmyantaḥ. I am *tāmyantaḥ* (*tāmyantaḥ* means "one who is craving and longing in excess"), I am craving and longing in excess.

[For example], when you are both in love, extreme love, and you are away from each other–say twenty-thousand miles away–and you want to meet with each other, what happens in your mind? That is called [*tāmyantaḥ*], craving and longing, desire. Desiring to meet.

And this desiring and longing is possessed by us. So, we desire only You and nothing else. So, let You become . . . let You appear . . . You must appear before us. I won't ask other things from You. It is a promise. I will never ask for anything. I ask only one thing: just appear to me, that is all.

Chapter Seven
Conquering Helplessness
Vidhuravijaya nāmadheyaṁ saptamaṁ stotram

Now, this *stotra* is [nominated as] "*vidhura vijaya nāmadheyam*". "*Vidhura*" means that he wants to conquer helplessness. Helplessness is due to separation from the Lord. *Vidhura* means *vyākulatā*.[114]

When you are not successful in un-minding your mind, recite these [following] two or three *ślokas* and your mind will get focused on that point peacefully. You want to break that unpeaceful atmosphere in your mind. That is the aim of this *stotra*.

Chapter 7 (00:48)

त्वय्यानन्दसरस्वति
समरसतामेत्य नाथ मम चेतः ।
परिहरतु सकृदियन्तं
भेदाधीनं महानर्थम् ॥ १ ॥

tvayyānandasarasvati
samarasatāmetya nātha mama cetaḥ /
pariharatu sakṛdiyantaṁ
bhedādhīnaṁ mahānartham //1//

O my Master (*nātha* means "O my Master"), *mama cetaḥ*, I would like that my mind (*mama cetaḥ*), my mind would act like this.

And what is that way?

Tvayi ānanda sarasvati samarasatāmeti. First, my mind should get entry, take a dive, in the lake of Your consciousness. In the lake of Your consciousness, my mind should dive.

---

114 One who is bewildered, confounded, perplexed, or troubled. [*Editor's note*]

You know "dive"?

DENISE: Dive.

SWAMIJI: In that lake of God consciousness, [my mind] should dive first. Then, *pariharatu sakṛdiyantaṁ bhedādhīnaṁ mahānartham*, and then, just for good, for good that mind of mine should leave aside all of the ups and downs of duality; the ups and downs of dual perceptions of the world [would be discarded] when it will dive in That. And that duality, perceiving in dualization (*bheda*), differentiated perception, [my mind] would throw away altogether. I would like that.

Chapter 7 (02:48)

एतन्मम न त्विदमिति
  रागद्वेषादिनिगडदृढमूले ।
नाथ भवन्मयतैक्य-
  प्रत्ययपरशुः पतत्वन्तः ॥२॥

etanmama na tvidamiti
  rāgadveṣādinigaḍadṛḍhamūle /
nātha bhavanmayataikya-
  pratyayaparaśuḥ patatvantaḥ //2//

And there is another problem in me, and that is, O my Master, "this is mine" (*etan mama*, this is mine), "I possess . . . this is my property" and "*na tu idam*, this is not mine", "this is mine and this is not mine" . . .

[For example, you say], "Viresh is mine and Jyoti's son is not mine" (*etan mama na tu idaṁ iti*). It is *rāga dveṣa* (*rāga* means "attachment"; *dveṣa* means "detachment"). You are detached from Jyoti's son; you are attached to Viresh. It is *rāga dveṣa*, and this is bondage. Actually, this is bondage, i.e., to be detached in one way and to be attached in one way, another way.

. . . and this is attachment . . . this attachment [and detachment] is a great bondage, and, in this great bondage of that chain, which has tied [me], which is tied around my mind, O my Master, I would like that, *bhavan mayataikya pratyayaparaśuḥ patatvantaḥ*, the *pratyaya paraśuḥ*, the perception of perceiving one God consciousness in both, perceiving one God consciousness in both of the sides (e.g., the Viresh side and this side), and, which has bound . . .

ERNIE: By chain?

SWAMIJI: . . . which is absolutely tight in a chain, and on that chain, chain-strip, let that axe of the oneness of God consciousness fall and cut it into pieces, into two, so that this *pratyaya* will get it's unification.[115]

JOHN: So, in reality, you see that everything is yours and nothing is yours, and also nothing is yours and everything is . . . . which? Both? Everything?

SWAMIJI: No. Either perceive that everyone is mine or perceive nobody is mine [laughter]. One thing. Not "This is mine and this is not mine". This way you should not perceive. You should perceive in one way. For instance, everybody is mine or nobody is mine.

JOHN: This doesn't mean . . . this isn't the *saṇyāsi* point of view that, "I give up everything". This is real perception here.

SWAMIJI: Yes, perception.

JOHN: But the *yogi* still would own things of his own, would he not? Would he own anything? He wouldn't have his own razor? He'd say, "This is my razor"? He wouldn't have . . . ?

SWAMIJI: No, as long as he perceives that, "This is my razor", this is his.

BRUCE P: With attachment

SWAMIJI: This is attachment. This is being away from God consciousness.

ERNIE: So, the best point of view is "Everything is mine".

SWAMIJI: "Everything is mine or nothing is mine. I just use it, it is not mine. I just use it, I don't mind."

JOHN: So, you can still own that thing without that being attached to it.

SWAMIJI: Yes, yes.

JOHN: You can own something . . .

SWAMIJI: Yes, yes. A Shaivite can own.

JOHN: . . . without being attached to it.

SWAMIJI: Yes, just as I do [laughs].

---

115 The firm conviction or certainty (*pratyaya*) that God consciousness is equally present in all things. [*Editor's note*]

DEVOTEES: [laughter]
ERNIE: Or, what is his attitude when [he feels], "Everything is mine"?
SWAMIJI: Or "Nothing is mine".
ERNIE: But, "When nothing is mine", he just uses it.
SWAMIJI: Yes, yes.
ERNIE: But, when everything is his . . .
DENISE: Then he uses everybody else's things, too?
SWAMIJI: No. He feels that if you shave, it is also my shaving, in that universal way.

galatu vikalpakalaṅkāvalī
samullasatu hṛdi nirargalatā /3a

This is the cutting down into pieces of these differentiated entanglements, chains, chains by which you are bound.

Chapter 7 (06:52)

गलतु विकल्पकलङ्कावली
समुल्लसतु हृदि निरर्गलता ।
भगवन्नानन्दरस-
प्लुतास्तु मे चिन्मयी मूर्तिः ॥३॥

galatu vikalpakalaṅkāvalī
samullasatu hṛdi nirargalatā /
bhagavannānandarasa-
plutāstu me cinmayī mūrtiḥ //3//

Bhagavan, O Lord, let *vikalpa kalaṅkāvalī galatu*, let the *kalaṅkāvalī* (*kalaṅkāvalī*, the chain of this darkness, the darkness of differentiated perceptions, the chain of the darkness of differentiated perceptions), let the chain of the darkness of differentiated perceptions get destroyed altogether.

Samallastu hṛdaye nirargalatā. Let the *nirargalatā* (unboundedness, freedom, universal freedom), let universal freedom rise in my heart, always–bloom.

O my Lord, let *ānandarasaplutāstu me cinmayī mūrtiḥ*, let

this individuality of mine become soaked with the *rasa* of the bliss of God consciousness.

These three things he wants here.

First thing is, let *vikalpa kalaṅkavalī*, the black darkness of differentiated perception should be washed off. Next, in my heart, the *nirargalatā*, freedom from all sides should bloom out. And then, my individuality, the individuality of the self, must be soaked in universal God consciousness.

JOHN: Is this "freedom in the heart", does that mean . . . is that the experience that my will is God's will? That I am doing, that everything I do, is God's will?

SWAMIJI: Yes, God's will. Whatever happens is divine.

BRUCE H: Are these successive things that happen?

JOHN: Is that successive (*krama*)?

SWAMIJI: No, simultaneously. Simultaneously, these three things must happen. It is not successive (*krama*).

Rāgādimaya . . . there is one more problem:

Chapter 7 (09:12)

रागादिमयभवाण्डक-
 लुठितं त्वद्भक्तिभावनाम्बिका तैस्तैः ।
आप्याययतु रसैर्मां
 प्रवृद्धपक्षो यथा भवामि खगः ॥४॥

rāgādimayabhavāṇḍaka-
 luṭhitaṁ tvadbhaktibhāvanāmbikā taistaiḥ /
āpyāyayatu rasairmāṁ
 pravṛddhapakṣo yathā bhavāmi khagaḥ //4//

I am just like an egg, a bird egg.

JOHN: *Tul*[116]. Egg, yes.

SWAMIJI: *Tul*. I am just like an egg, and that egg, which is [externally] made by the universal egg. I am an egg in the universe, and that egg, the outer substance of that egg, is . . .

STEPHANIE: Shell.

116 Kashmiri word for "egg". [*Editor's note*]

SWAMIJI: Is it called shell?

STEPHANIE: Yes, that outside?

SWAMIJI: Outside.

STEPHANIE: Yes, shell.

SWAMIJI: . . . and that shell is made with the substance of attachment and detachment (*rāga* and *dveṣa*), *kāma* and *krodha* (desire and wrath), *lobha* and *moha* (greed and illusion). [With] all of these differentiated things of the universe, that shell is made of that egg.

ERNIE: For the individual

SWAMIJI: Individual.

JOHN: Him? He is talking about himself?

SWAMIJI: Yes, for himself [i.e., Utpaladeva].

And, in that egg, I am *luṭhitam* (*luṭhitam* means "I am going here and there"), I am moving here and there, inside. Inside that egg, I am moving here and there, because, when it rolls like this, the substance inside also moves. That means, sometimes I am born, sometimes I am old, sometimes I am young, sometimes I am a youth, a child, death; and then again birth, then again childhood, then youth, then old age, then death. And, like this, I move in this egg.

JOHN: But always in this egg.

SWAMIJI: Always in this egg.

There is one problem for me now, here in this egg. I am entangled inside that egg, which is . . . the substance of that shell of the egg is made of *rāga* and *dveṣa*, *kāma* and *krodha*, *lobha* and *moha*–all of these differentiated things. *Tvad bhakti bhāvanāmbikā*, I want a mother, I want a mother bird for this egg. And that mother bird is Your attachment, Your devotion. Being devoted to Thee, O Lord, being devoted to Thee is the mother. That will make me shine in this . . . that will solve my problem.

What she will do?

Tvat bhakti bhāvanāmbikā, that mother of Thy devotion must come and heat that egg and give that shooting of those warm delicate sparks, sparks of those [sentiments of] devotion. Because the embodiment of that mother is only devotion, Your devotion–that is the mother, the mother bird–and that mother bird will put those sparks of devotion on the shell of that egg and it must continue that sparking on the shell, warming that egg by those sparks, by which way, *pravṛdha pakṣo yathā*, I will become a bird, I will come out of this shell and become a bird and fly in the sky, the sky of God consciousness.

Chapter 7 (12:43)

त्वच्चरणभावनामृत-
　　रससारास्वादनैपुणं लभताम् ।
चित्तमिदं निःशेषित-
　　विषयविषासङ्गवासनावधि मे ॥५॥

tvaccaraṇabhāvanāmṛta-
　　rasasārāsvādanaipuṇaṁ labhatām /
cittamidaṁ niḥśeṣita-
　　viṣayaviṣāsaṅgavāsanāvadhi me //5//

And there is another problem in me. That problem is, *tvat caraṇa bhāvana amṛta rasasārāsvāda naipuṇaṁ*. There is one thing to be done. That thing is–what is to be done in this world?–*tvat caraṇa bhāvana amṛta*, to taste the nectar of remembering Your lotus feet. This is to be done in this world. Just to taste the nectar of the remembrance of Your lotus feet; always taste the nectar of remembering Your lotus feet. But, the technique of tasting the nectar of Your lotus feet, the technique I don't know, i.e., how to taste it. Let You teach me that technique! You teach me how to taste that nectar of [Your] lotus feet (*naipuṇam* means "the trick of that technique, the trick of understanding that technique").

Not me. My mind! My mind is absolutely ignorant of that technique. My mind does not know that technique of how to taste the nectar of Your oneness of [Thy] lotus feet. Let that technique be taught to my mind, not only today but *cittam idaṁ niḥśeṣāta viṣayaviṣa vāsanā saṅga avadhiḥ me*, up to that point until, in my mind, all of the differentiated attachments towards worldly pleasures will get destroyed for good. Up to that point, You have to teach me. You have to go on teaching my mind the technique of how to do it.

Do you understand?

Tvadbhaktitapanadhīdhiti . . . there is another problem.

Tvadbhakti tapana . . . it is only the world of problems in me!

Chapter 7 (15:21)

त्वद्भक्तितपनधीधिति-
संस्पर्शवशान्ममैष दूरतरम् ।
चेतोमणिर्विमुञ्चतु
रागादिकतप्तवह्निकणान् ॥ ६ ॥

tvadbhaktitapanadhīdhiti-
saṁsparśavaśānmamaiṣa dūrataram /
cetomaṇirvimuñcatu
rāgādikataptavahnikaṇān //6//

Actually, my mind is just like *sūryakānta*.

Sūryakānta you know? That glass.

GANJOO: Magnifying glass.

JOHN: Yes, rays of sun go through it and yes, it burns.

SWAMIJI: The rays of the sun go through it, penetrate, and it burns; the substance underneath burns. That is magnifying glass?

JOHN: Yes, sir.

SWAMIJI: My mind is just like that. *Cetomaṇiḥ*, my mind is a magnifying glass. But, there is always . . . this sky [of my mind] is always clouded; no sun rays, no sun is visible anywhere. What will it burn? It will burn nothing. *Cetomaṇiḥ*, let this magnifying glass of my mind be penetrated by *tvad bhakti tapanadhīdhiti saṁsparśavaśāt*, be penetrated by the rays of the sun of Your devotion.

Not this [celestial] sun. The sun of God's attachment. Being attached to God is the "sun". That being attached to God is the sun and the sun of devotion, the sun of Thine devotion is the sun.

Let that sun of Thy devotion produce rays, go on producing rays, in continuity, without the disturbance of clouds in between, so that my mind, which is a magnifying glass, will remove, already burnt[117], all attachments and detachments, and pleasures,

117 That is, "already burnt" by the rays of the sun of my devotion for Thee.

pain, everything of the world.

These sorrows, sadnesses, pleasures, happiness, attachments, all of these things will get burnt altogether and thrown into those *tambaris*, sparks. It will only produce sparks and it will get removed. All of those [impressions] of being attached and detached and everything that happens in this world [will get removed].

But, as long as my magnifying glass of the mind does this function, till then, Your sun of devotion–Thy devotion is the sun–that sun must produce, go on producing, rays on that glass so that it burns everything aside.

[Now], another problem [laughter]. I am crazy in producing this problem before You, but still, it is a problem for me.

Chapter 7 (18:23)

तस्मिन्पदे भवन्तं
सततमुपश्लोकयेयमत्युच्चैः ।
हरिहर्यश्वविरिञ्चा
अपि यत्र बहिः प्रतीक्षन्ते ॥७॥

tasminpade bhavantaṁ
satatamupaślokayeyamatyuccaiḥ /
hariharyaśvaviriñcā
api yatra bahiḥ pratīkṣante //7//

I would like to reside at that point of divinity (*tasmin pade bhavantam*) and I would reside at that point of divinity and *satatam upaśloka yeyaṁ atyuccaiḥ*, and I would sing Your glory outside, outside That abode, the abode of God consciousness. Outside that abode of God consciousness, I will sing Your . . .

Not outside. Inside. When God is seated here, I am in front of God and singing His glory, and singing His glory loudly, so that everybody else hears from outside that I am singing [His] glory secretly. Nobody is with me.

. . . I want to sing that glory of Thee in Your presence at that stage where *hariharyaśvaviriñcā*, where Indra, Nārāyaṇa, and all of those gods and goddesses are waiting outside, and they will hear my cry from inside, and they will get impressed [and wonder], "who is that important person inside singing the glory of God?" That is my problem [i.e., desire].

JOHN: What does he mean here?

SWAMIJI: Just to impress them. Just to . . .

JOHN: Because he is so devoted.

SWAMIJI: So devoted. [He is saying], "I want to become Your only devotee".

JOHN: Even more than they [i.e., the gods].

SWAMIJI: Even more than they.

Where they are not allowed inside, where those gods are not allowed inside, there I would like to sing Your glory.

JOHN: "Inside" means that he is sitting with God . . .

SWAMIJI: God, one with God.

JOHN: . . . and they are kept outside.

SWAMIJI: Yes.

Tasmin pade bhavantaṁ satatam upaśloke. In songs, I would sing Your glory in songs. *Hariharyaśva viriñcā* (*hari* means Nārāyaṇa, *haryaśva* means Indra, *viriñcā* means Brahma), [they] are *yatra bahiḥ pratīkṣante*, are waiting outside. No entry, no possibility of their entry inside. This is my problem. This must be solved.

Chapter 7 (20:50)

भक्तिमदजनितविभ्रम-
वशेन पश्येयमविकलं करणैः ।
शिवमयमखिलं लोकं
क्रियाश्च पूजामयी सकलाः ॥८॥

bhaktimadajanitavibhrama-
vaśena paśyeyamavikalaṁ karaṇaiḥ /
śivamayamakhilaṁ lokaṁ
kriyāśca pūjāmayī sakalāḥ //8//

There is another problem and that problem is, I want madness. I want to get mad. I want to turn mad, absolutely mad! Mad for Thy devotion, *bhaktimada* (*bhaktimada* is madness for

Your love). *Bhaktimada janita vibhramavaśena*, and, by that madness, I must feel absolutely different, from others (*vibhrama-vaśena*).

Because, mad people don't see actual things. Mad people will see, e.g., "O, this is a big mountain!" When he is intoxicated, he will feel that this [small object] is a big mountain, [that it] is just one thousand miles high. He will feel that. [Or] he will feel the mountain just, oh, just like a pot, small pot, i.e., the mountain. This is the point of view of those mad people.

And I want to become mad like that; mad by tasting the nectar of Thy devotion. *Bhaktimada janita vibhrama*, and then there will be . . . my point of perceiving will change altogether.

What I will perceive then?

Śivamayaṁ akhilaṁ lokaṁ, when I will see two persons actually quarreling with each other, fighting with each other [over] worldly matters, I would not feel that. I would feel that they are quarreling for attaining God consciousness. If somebody is making sexual intercourse with somebody else, I'll find they are going into [the state of] divinity. I'll feel like that because I would get myself maddened by Your devotion. I'll feel everything, whatever is happening in the outside world, I would feel that it is all divine.

JOHN: Full of Śiva, full of God.

SWAMIJI: Yes, *śivamayaṁ akhilaṁ lokaṁ.*

And *kriyāśca*, all actions also, I would feel that all actions, whatever good or bad, all actions are just Your worship, Thy worship, nothing else.

Another problem (the last one):

Chapter 7 (23:45)

ममकमनोगृहीत-
त्वद्भक्तिकुलाङ्गनाणिमादिसुतान् ।
सूत्वा सुबद्धमूला
ममेति बुद्धिं दृढीकुरुताम् ॥९॥

mamakamanogṛhīta-
tvadbhaktikulāṅganāṇimādisutān /
sūtvā subaddhamūlā
mameti buddhiṁ dṛḍhīkurutām //9//

My mind is a boy, a young boy. My mind is just like a young boy in his perfect youth and he has–my mind, that boy–has *gṛhīta*, possessed *tvad bhakti kulāṅganā*, a wife, and that is Your devotion. Your devotion is a beautiful girl. [My mind] has possessed that beautiful girl.

Which girl?

Your devotion. Your devotion is my wife, which is possessed by my mind, who is . . .

STEPHANIE: Young boy.

SWAMIJI: . . . a young boy. But, there is a problem in that. Although he is married–my mind is married to that wife–but the problem is this girl always goes astray; [she] does not remain with me. The problem is she does not remain with me. She is always outside. She goes here and there. Sometimes [she goes] outside. "Where is my wife?" I ask my boy or boy-servant, "where is my wife?" [He replies], "master, she went out and didn't say where she was going". And I am waiting, wasting my time for my wife. This is my problem. She does not get focused.

But, I come to the understanding that the problem is because she has no issue [i.e., offspring]. If she had an issue, a son, she would stay always at home. So, let her have an issue, and that is *aṇimādi sutān* (*aṇimā*, *mahimā*, etc., the great *yogic* powers). *Aṇimā*, *mahimā*, *laghimā*, . . . all of those eight great powers must be produced by that wife.

ERNIE: By that devotion . . . which is the devotion.

SWAMIJI: Devotion, yes.

And, by that wife who is devotion, Your devotion, these sons would be produced. Eight sons would be produced by that wife.

Where would she go afterwards?

She would always remain with me. *Subaddhamūlāṁ mameti buddhiṁ dṛḍhīkurutām*, and she will get entangled in my own home and say, "Oh, my son, [he] is here and another son is outside", and she would get him, drag him inside, and always remain with me and this, my problem, would be solved like that.

STEPHANIE: So, the sons are those eight *yogic* . . . ?

SWAMIJI: Eight *yogic* powers. Because, you have been practicing all of these techniques of mine. If you don't achieve *yogic* powers, some *yogic* powers, you are always sluggish in meditation, you become always sluggish in meditation. For instance, you meditate and get something, achieve something inside, then you get vigor to practice for more and more time; you give more time [to your practice] afterwards.

DENISE: It is encouraging.

SWAMIJI: It is encouraging.

When she will produce those eight powers, it will be encouraging to her and she will encourage me also, and remain with me always.

There ends our lesson.

DENISE: So, those eight *yogic* powers are to be sought after?

SWAMIJI: No, they must come, they must come.

BRUCE H: They strengthen one-pointedness.

SWAMIJI: Yes.

BRUCE H: But also, it's easy to get caught in those, isn't it?

SWAMIJI: No, the eight *yogic* powers are classified in two sections. One [section of] eight *yogic* powers are godly and the other eight *yogic* powers are worldly. [Utpaladeva] does not point out those worldly eight powers.[118]

Atra abhedasārā eva aṇimādayaḥ abhipretāḥ, these are the divine eight great powers, not those other powers which entangle a *yogi*.[119]

---

118 The eight worldly powers are: *aṇimā* (the power to make one's body extremely small), *mahima* (the power to make one's body infinitely large), *garima* (the power to become infinitely heavy), *laghima* (the power to become weightless), *prāpti* (the power to be anywhere), *prākāmya* (the power to achieve any desire), *īśtva* (the power to possess absolute sovereignty), and *vaśitva* (the power to subjugate). [*Editor's note*]

119 See appendix 18 for an explanation of the entanglements of the *yogic* powers.

Chapter Eight
Supernatural Power
Alaukikodbalanākhyamaṣṭamaṁ stotram

यः प्रसादलव ईश्वरस्थितो
  या च भक्तिरिव मामुपेयुषी ।
तौ परस्परसमन्वितौ कदा
  तादृशे वपुषि रूढिमेष्यतः ॥१॥

yaḥ prasādalava īśvarasthito
  yā ca bhaktiriva māmupeyuṣī /
tau parasparasamanvitau kadā
  tādṛśe vapuṣi rūḍhimeṣyataḥ //1//

O Lord, *yaḥ prasādalava īśvaraḥ sthitaḥ*, one thing is just these *lava*.

Lava means "drops of nectar of being blessed by Lord Śiva". Those are drops, very tiny particles, of those blessings of Lord Śiva.

Yā ca bhaktiriva māmupeyuṣī. And there is another thing, which is residing in me. That is, in some way, attachment for Thee, *bhakti*, devotion for Thee, my devotion. My devotion for Thee is one thing–I devote all of my time in remembering You–and that is existing in me, that is residing in me (*mām upeyuṣī bhaktiriva*). It is not real devotion. Actually, it is not actual devotion in me. It is just so-called devotion because if it were exactly devotion, then it would have [produced] the fruit of that devotion. And that, the fruit of devotion, is Your nearness, and as long as Your nearness has not happened to me and devotion is [supposedly] there, so this is nominal devotion in me.

So, this nominal devotion, which is residing in me, and grace, which is residing in You, when the time will come, when that time, that golden time, golden opportunity, will come, when these two things will be united with each other? I will [offer] my devotion and You will go on showering grace on me, both simultaneously. They will work simultaneously, *tādṛśe vapuṣi rūḍhimeṣyataḥ*, and it will be established in me. So, as soon as I will continue [offering] my devotion, the grace will continue showering on me. This I would like! I would not like this kind of [nominal] devotion [by which] I devote all my time for You and nothing happens.

This is what [Utpaladeva] wishes.

Chapter 8 (03:14)

त्वत्प्रभुत्वपरिचर्वणजन्मा
कोऽप्युदेतु परितोषरसोऽन्तः ।
सर्वकालमिह मे परमस्तु
ज्ञानयोगमहिमादि विदूरे ॥२॥

tvatprabhutvaparicarvaṇajanmā
ko'pyudetu paritoṣaraso'ntaḥ /
sarvakālamiha me paramastu
jñānayogamahimādi vidūre //2//

Tvat prabhutva paricarvaṇa janmā ko'pi udetu paritoṣa raso antaḥ sarvakāla. Always let that kind of *paritoṣa rasaḥ*, that kind of the *rasa* (the taste of satisfaction, real satisfaction), let the taste of that real satisfaction rise always in me; that real satisfaction when I will be really satisfied, when I will be really full, I will get myself filled with that satisfaction.

What is that satisfaction? What kind of that satisfaction?

Tvat prabhutva paricarvaṇa janmā. Just this kind of satisfaction: I have a master and that is Lord Śiva. I have a master [who is] Lord Śiva. This satisfaction. Let this satisfaction always reside in me.

ALEXIS: Complete tasting of that Lordship.

SWAMIJI: Yes, I would like to taste that, taste that perception, perceiving state.

What perceiving state?

"My master is Lord Siva!" *Bas*, this kind of taste. I would like this kind of taste always residing in me.

Jñāna yoga mahimādi vidūre. Being informed in Shaivism, being informed in Vedānta, Trika, all of these philosophies, or doing meditation, doing practice of *prāṇāyāma*, breath control, etc., let them remain aside, let them remain away from me. I only wish this kind of *rasa* in me that I have a master, I have got a master, and that is Lord Śiva.

Chapter 8 (05:25)

लोकवद्भवतु मे विषयेषु
स्फीत एव भगवन्परितर्षः ।
केवलं तव शरीरतयैतान्
लोकयेयमहमस्तविकल्पः ॥३॥

lokavadbhavatu me viṣayeṣu
sphīta eva bhagavanparitarṣaḥ /
kevalaṁ tava śarīratayaitān
lokayeyamahamastavikalpaḥ //3//

Bhagavan, O Lord, I don't want that these hankerings after worldly pleasures should be discarded in me. Let this state of hankering after worldly objects remain in me. I don't want that they should vanish altogether.

What?

JOHN: Hankering after worldly objects.

SWAMIJI: Hankering after worldly objects.

Let these *viṣayeṣu paritarṣaḥ–viṣayeṣu* (in these worldly objects), *paritarsaḥ* (taste, enjoyment, desire)–let that desire remain in me. I don't want to discard that desire. Let that desire remain always in me. But, let only one thing happen in this case: *kevalaṁ tava śarīratayaitān lokayeyam*, only one thing should remain there, that I should perceive these worldly desires for worldly objects just as one with You, just one with You.

JOHN: Just as one with You or one with the desire for wanting You? Which?

SWAMIJI: No, this desire for these worldly objects, I must perceive as *tavaśarīra*, as Your body, Your body of universal consciousness.

ALEXIS: *Etān viṣayān?*

SWAMIJI: *Etān viṣayān.*

ALEXIS: These objects of my desire, these things.

SWAMIJI: Yes.

JOHN: So, these things become one, and these things become one in Lord Śiva then.

SWAMIJI: Yes.

ALEXIS: So, this is really *pañcadaśavidyā.*[120]

SWAMIJI: Yes.

Chapter 8 (07:25)

देहभूमिषु तथा मनसि त्वं
प्राणवर्त्मनि च भेदमुपेते ।
संविदः पथिषु तेषु च तेन
स्वात्मना मम भव स्फुटरूपः ॥४॥

dehabhūmiṣu tathā manasi tvaṁ
prāṇavartmani ca bhedamupete /
saṁvidaḥ pathiṣu teṣu ca tena
svātmanā mama bhava sphuṭarūpaḥ //4//

O Lord, there are four sections of states. One section is the section of *deha pramātṛ bhāva*, when you are residing in wakefulness (*jāgrat*). Another section is when you are residing in the world of thought, that is *svapna* (the dreaming state). Another is the world of *prāṇa*, when you are residing in dreamless sleep.

Prāṇavartmani ca bhedamupete, and these differentiated three states of life, three states of being–that is *deha-bhūmi* (*deha-bhūmi* is called the state of wakefulness), *manasi* is the state of dreaming state, and *prāṇa vartmani* is the state of dreamless [sleep] . . .

JOACHIM: *Suṣupti.*

---

120 The fifteen-fold science of rising. See *Kashmir Shaivism–The Secret Supreme*, 9.58.

SWAMIJI: *Suṣupti.*

. . . and *saṁvidaḥ pathiṣu* means *turya*[121], *saṁvidaḥ pathiṣu* means the path of perception, real perception–in these four sections, let my self remain one with You. Let my self remain one with You. I don't want oneness shining only in *turya*, only in the path of consciousness. Let oneness with You remain in my wakefulness, let oneness remain in my dreaming state, oneness remain in my dreamless state, and oneness remains in *turya*.

Chapter 8 (09:20)

निजनिजेषु पदेषु पतन्त्विमाः
करणवृत्तय उल्लसिता मम ।
क्षणमपीश मनागपि मैव भूत्-
त्वदविभेदरसक्षतिसाहसम् ॥५॥

nijanijeṣu padeṣu patantvimāḥ
karaṇavṛttaya ullasitā mama /
kṣaṇamapīśa manāgapi maiva bhūt-
tvadavibhedarasakṣatisāhasam //5//

O Lord, let my organs work in their own senses. I don't want to withdraw them from sensual pleasures. Let them work on their sensual objects.

ALEXIS: Let them flow out. Let them flow, *patantu.*

SWAMIJI: Flow out, *patantu.* Yes, flow out, flow out on their sensual objects, because their nature is to flow out; because the nature of my organs, the nature of all organs, is to flow out.

ALEXIS: *Ullasitā.*

SWAMIJI: *Ullasitā*[122]. The nature of the organs is *ullasitā.* They are always . . . the mood of organs is to flow out on their objects.

Let them do that. I have no harm in that [occurring]. Only one thing, one thing is a problem. That problem is, *kṣaṇamapīsa manāgapi maiva bhūta tvadavibhedarasakṣatisāhasam*, for one

121 See appendix 3 for an explanation of *turya.*

122 Coming forth, rising, appearing.

moment also, Your oneness should shine along with this function. When this organic function takes place, Your oneness of God consciousness must shine. And if It does not shine for even one moment, if for one moment it breaks, let me lose my courage. I must lose my courage altogether. This is what I want. I want to lose my courage altogether. If I am away from [Your oneness] only for one second, I must lose my courage [for attaining oneness with Thee].

Let these sensual pleasures happen to me. Let these sensual pleasures take place, but sensual pleasures must take place in Your oneness. The oneness with You must shine altogether in these sensual pleasures.

For instance, if for some moment there will be the breakage of oneness with You in this act, let me lose courage at that moment, i.e., let me not make myself [believe] that, "Next time, I will get oneness with God, after a while. Don't worry". No, I must not have that much courage.

What courage?

BRUCE H: To know that It'll come back.

JOHN: To not care about this moment, because . . .

SWAMIJI: No, this moment, this one-hundredth part of a moment also must not be without [Your oneness]. If it is without that, I must lose my courage, I must be courage-less.

DENISE: I *must* lose my courage, or I *will* lose my courage?

SWAMIJI: No, I *must* lose my courage. I must not be courageous at that time. I must not be courageous. I must not hold my senses, hold my temper. I must lose everything.

ALEXIS: So, he says, let them flow out, provided that not even for a moment should there be that *sāhasam*, in the sense of outrage; outrage of losing for a moment that bliss of union with You.

SWAMIJI: Yes.

ALEXIS: *Sāhasam* in that sense.

SWAMIJI: Yes, courage.

ALEXIS: But that would mean, "Let there not be even for a moment of that courage of abandoning the bliss of union with You".

SWAMIJI: [Let there not be the] courage of being away from You for even one second also.

JOHN: You mean that when that one second is there . . .

SWAMIJI: One second is a gap.

JOHN: . . . you should be outraged that that happens. You should be completely distraught.

ALEXIS: Shocked, *sāhasa*.

SWAMIJI: Shocked, shocked, yes.

ALEXIS: Let there not be, even for a moment, the shock of breaking that bliss, *rasakṣati*.

SWAMIJI: Yes.

JOHN: Not thinking that, "Well, this doesn't matter because I will get that oneness back in five minutes". That shouldn't happen.

SWAMIJI: That shouldn't happen.

I must get a great shock and I must die at that very moment; I must lose my body, I must lose everything, if it breaks only for one second or one-hundredth part of a second. So, it must continue; oneness with You must continue during the enjoyment of worldly pleasures.

Chapter 8 (14:02)

लघुमसृणसिताच्छशीतलं
भवदावेशवशेन भावयन् ।
वपुरखिलपदार्थपद्धतेर्-
व्यवहारानतिवर्तयेय तान् ॥६॥

laghumasṛṇasitāchaśītalaṁ
bhavadāveśavaśena bhāvayan /
vapurakhilapadārthapaddhater-
vyavahārānativartayeya tān //6//

Akhila padārtha paddhateḥ vapur bhāvayan. I must perceive all of the formations of all of the objective world in this way: *laghu* (very light), *masṛṇa* (very soft), *sita* (absolutely white, without any dots), *acha* (very pure), *śītalaṁ* (cooling).

How?

Bhavad āveśa vaśena, when I get entry in Your Self. When I get entry in Your Self during worldly sensations, during enjoyment of worldly sensations, I must get entry in Your nature. And that entry in Your nature is what? Like what?

ERNIE: Soft.

SWAMIJI: It is soft, it is light, it is white, it is pure, and it is cooling. It cools down all of your body, all of your mind. And *akhila padārtha paddhateḥ vapur*, and all of the formations of all worldly objects must remain like this (i.e., cooling, soft, everything), because they will enter in Your God consciousness. They must enter in Your God consciousness. *Tān vyavahārānativartayeya*, and I will get rid of all of those differentiated perceptions of the world. I would get rid of the differentiated perceptions of the world.

JOHN: So, he's saying that he wants to enter all of these, or soak all of these objects, in God consciousness, so that they have this nature of being cooling and peaceful . . .

SWAMIJI: Nature of being . . . yes.

Chapter 8 (16:21)

विकसतु स्ववपुर्भवदात्मकं
    समुपयान्तु जगन्ति ममाङ्गताम् ।
व्रजतु सर्वमिदं द्वयवल्गितं
    स्मृतिपथोपगमेऽप्यनुपाख्यताम् ॥७॥

vikasatu svavapurbhavadātmakaṁ
    samupayāntu jaganti mamāṅgatām /
vrajatu sarvamidaṁ dvayavalgitaṁ
    smṛtipathopagame'pyanupākhyatām //7//

Let my individuality shine in the *svarūpa* of Your universality. Let my individual consciousness shine in the *svarūpa*[123] of Your universal consciousness.

JOHN: Nature of universal consciousness.

SWAMIJI: Nature of consciousness.

Samullasantu [*samupayāntu*] *jaganti mamāṅgatām*. Let this

123 *Svarūpa* literally means "self-form or shape", but Swamiji generally translates *svarūpa* as "one's nature", i.e., the nature of consciousness. [*Editor's note*]

whole universe, let all of the three worlds[124], become the parts and particles of my body, universal body. Let all of this universe become the parts and particles of my body. *Vrajatu sarvaṁ idaṁ dvayavalgitaṁ*, and the *dvayavalgitaṁ*, the expansion of differentiated perception, which took place before this experience, which had taken place before this experience, . . .

What?

ALEXIS: *Valgitaṁ* literally is . . .

SWAMIJI: *Vikasa*[125].

ALEXIS: . . . "dancing and jumping about". *Valgita.*

SWAMIJI: Yes, dancing, expansion.

. . . expansion of differentiated perception, which took place before this perception . . .

Which perception?

JOHN: Perception that, "I am this universe, my universal body, and that I am a . . . "

SWAMIJI: Yes. So, it is in the past [where] that [experience] was residing. That was existing.

GANJOO: Duality.

SWAMIJI: Dualistic perception.

. . . let that dualistic perception not remain in my past remembrance also.

ALEXIS: In past memory.

SWAMIJI: *Smṛtipatha upagame api anupākhyatām.* I am terrified by this dualistic perception, so much that I don't want to remember it now at all, i.e., that there was dualistic perception. No, this remembrance also must vanish. I must not think of it.

GANJOO: Memory also must go.

SWAMIJI: This memory also must be vanished.

JOHN: Is that *anupāya*[126] perception that once you perceive

124 "This is one world (*bhūrloka,* earth); where there are stars, moons, there is another world (*bhuvarloka*); and above that, there is heaven. That is the third world (*svarloka*)." See chapter 4, verse 23.

125 Expansion.

126 "The word "*anupāya*" means "no *upāya*". In *anupāya*, the aspirant has only to observe that nothing is to be done, be as you are. If you are talking, go on talking. If you are sitting, go on sitting. Do not do anything, only reside in your being. This is the nature of *anupāya*." *Kashmir Shaivism–The Secret Supreme*, 5.40.

anupāya perception, that once you experience that, "I was this, I am this, I always was . . . ", then all that memory leaves and you always remember that you always were That?

SWAMIJI: Yes.

JOHN: Is that the same thing as that?

SWAMIJI: Yes.[127]

Chapter 8 (19:08)

समुदियादपि तादृशतावका-
ननविलोकपरामृतसम्प्लवः ।
मम घटेत यथा भवदद्वया-
प्रथनघोरदरीपरिपूरणम् ॥८॥

samudiyādapi tādṛśatāvakā-
nanavilokaparāmṛtasamplavaḥ /
mama ghaṭeta yathā bhavadadvayā-
prathanaghoradarīparipūraṇam //8//

Tādṛśa tāvaka ānana viloka parāmṛta samplavaḥ. Let that great flood occur on me. Let me be flooded with that great flood.

Flood of what?

That kind of flood, the flood of the water of supreme nectar. Let that flood of the water of supreme nectar take place on me. And that flood is *ānana viloka*; *tāvaka ānana viloka*, just to observe Your face, just to see Your face. Whenever I see Your face, I am flooded with that nectar.

ALEXIS: Face here *mukham*, energy? Face here is energy?

SWAMIJI: *Cit śakti*, *ānanda śakti*, *icchā śakti*, *jñāna śakti*, and *kriyā śakti* is "face". *Pañca mukha.*[128]

---

127 "When he perceives the realization of God consciousness, he perceives, "Oh, I was perceiving It beforehand also!" This memory comes in him. This memory comes in his brain at that very moment of realization that, "It was already existing with me". At the time of realization, he understands that, at the time of ignorance also, he was perceiving That." *Tantrāloka*, 13.17 (USF archives).

128 The five faces/energies of Lord Shiva are: consciousness, bliss, will, knowledge, and action, respectively. [*Editor's note*]

And this face, when I perceive Your divine face, that will flood me, I will get that flood. Let me be flooded by that *rasa* of nectar. Will that flood ever come to me? *Samudiyāt api*, will that flood ever come in my lifetime?

He is asking if it would be flooded sometime.

I don't mean now. Sometime, if this kind of flood would take place in me, then *bhavad advaya aprathana ghoradarī paripūrṇam ghaṭeta*, then separation, *advaya aprathana ghoradarī*, this separation of being away from You, separation of being away from You, that has created a great abyss . . .

For instance, there is a wound, a terrible wound. When this wound prolongs, it becomes an abyss, just like an abyss. This wound goes deeper and deeper, deeper and deeper, deeper and deeper, and it becomes an abyss, and it is cureless then. You can't cure it.

. . . these kind of wounds I have created by Your separation. These wounds I want to get filled with that nectar.

ALEXIS: So, it's that terrible abyss of perceiving the absence of unity within you.

SWAMIJI: Yes, absence of . . .

ALEXIS: *Advaya aprathana.*

SWAMIJI: Yes, *advaya aprathana*. That oneness . . .

ALEXIS: Non-manifestation.

SWAMIJI: The non-manifestation of oneness has created those wounds in me. Let those wounds be filled with that nectar so they are healed up.

Chapter 8 (22:31)

अपि कदाचन तावकसङ्गमा-
मृतकणाच्छुरणेन तनीयसा ।
सकललोकसुखेषु पराङ्मुखो
न भवितास्म्युभयच्युत एव किम् ॥९॥

api kadācana tāvakasaṅgamā-
mṛtakaṇācchuraṇena tanīyasā /
sakalalokasukheṣu parāṅmukho
na bhavitāsmyubhayacyuta eva kim //9//

[some audio missing in 1st line]

O Lord, the nearness of Thy consciousness, of that nectar, divine nectar, takes place in my mind very seldom, not always, not each day. *Tāvakasaṅgama amṛta kaṇa ācchuraṇena*, the soaking or being sprinkled by the divine nectar of Your nearness of Your consciousness, it is *tanīyasā*, and that sprinkling is also a very minute sprinkling.

ALEXIS: By the slightest sprinkling of that.

SWAMIJI: Slightest, not more. Just tiny drizzling. And that too is *kadācana*, very seldom, not each day.

And, at the very first [moment] when I experience this sprinkling of that nectar, I have lost the charm for all of the worldly excitements. *Sakala loka sukheṣu parāṅmukhaḥ*, I have become totally, absolutely, away from hankering after worldly pleasures. Those worldly pleasures have taken their real end [at] that very point. So, I have no interest in worldly pleasures.

Then–this is a fact–I have no interest in worldly pleasures, well and good, but there must be some[thing else] in its place. In its place, that sprinkling, again that sprinkling must come. That does not come. But now, there is apprehension in my mind. *Sakala loka sukheṣu parāṅmukhaḥ*, I have turned about from all of the worldly pleasures from that very point when this first sprinkling took place, i.e., sprinkling of that nectar.

Actually, this nearness of God consciousness is so much dense nectar that you lose all taste of worldly pleasures, at that very moment.

Sakalaloka sukheṣu parāṅmukhaḥ, na bhavitāsmyubhayacyuta eva kim. Now, there is apprehension in my mind that I may become deprived of both things, i.e., deprived of God consciousness (the divine nectar of God consciousness won't be existing [for me] at all) and I have already become deprived of [enjoying] worldly pleasures. But that should not happen. I must not become deprived from both things. This is my apprehension.

ALEXIS: So, you are translating "may I" as *api na bhavitā.*

SWAMIJI: *Na bhavitā api* [means] "won't that be that I will be deprived of both?"

Now, there is the possibility of my being deprived from both sides. I will be gone, I will be ruined for good. "Won't I be ruined?" This is what he asks. "Won't I get ruined from both sides?"

Chapter 8 (26:07)

सततमेव भवच्चरणाम्बुजा-
करचरस्य हि हंसवरस्य मे ।
उपरि मूलतलादपि चान्तरा-
दुपनमत्वज भक्तिमृणालिका ॥१०॥

satatameva bhavaccaraṇāmbujā-
karacarasya hi haṁsavarasya me /
upari mūlatalādapi cāntarā-
dupanamatvaja bhaktimṛṇālikā //10//

In fact, I am just like that swan. I am *haṁsavara* (*haṁsavara* means "just like a swan").

And a swan is always residing, swimming in lakes. And his ambition is to find out–in lotus lakes–to find out the *nadroo* at the root of the lotus.[129] *Nadroo* is the desired object, it is his food. He wants this food. He is fond of this food, fond of *nadroo*.

I am just like that swan and I swim, I roam, I reside, not in that lake where there are *nadroos*, these gross *nadroos*, but *bhavaccaraṇa ambuja ākara carasya hi haṁsavarasya*, I reside in the *ākara*, in the lake of Your lotus feet. Where Your lotus feet are existing, in that lake I reside. I am that kind of *haṁsa*, that kind of swan. And I must get that *nadroo* there. I don't want Your lotus feet because they are only . . . those are lotuses. I want to find the *nadroo* wherefrom these lotuses grow.

Wherefrom these grow, these lotuses?

GANJOO: From the root.

SWAMIJI: From the root.

And the "root of Your lotus feet" is what?

Thy devotion. Thy devotion, Thy love. Intense love for You is the root of those lotus feet. Those lotus feet will grow when there is intense love for Thy lotus feet. When there is intense love, that is the *nadroo*.

So, *upari*, I don't want to dive there and go to the bottom and find *nadroo* and eat it.

129 *Nadroo* is the edible rhizome of the lotus plant. [*Editor's note*]

Nadroo. What *nadroo*?
ALEXIS: *Bhakti nadroo*.
DEVOTEES: Devotion.
SWAMIJI: Devotion.

Your intense devotion must appear to me, not at the place of the root, but at the place of the lotus (*upari* means "in the upper surface of that plant"; *upari,* in the space of the root), *mūlatalādapi ca*, and in the center also. I must get *nandroo* everywhere. I must get *nadroo* . . .

Nadroo. What is *nadroo*? Thy devotion.

. . . Thy devotion must appear to me at Your lotus feet, in the center of Your lotus feet, and in the root of Your lotus feet. I must observe only devotion.

GANJOO: Everywhere.

SWAMIJI: I want that devotion. I don't want to see the lotus without devotion. Your lotus feet must appear to me with devotion, everywhere.

Chapter 8 (30:04)

उपयान्तु विभो समस्तवस्तून्यपि
चिन्ताविषयं दृशः पदं च ।
मम दर्शनचिन्तनप्रकाशा -
मृतसाराणि परं परिस्फुरन्तु ॥११॥

upayāntu vibho samastavastūnyapi
cintāviṣayaṁ dṛśaḥ padaṁ ca /
mama darśanacintanaprakāśā -
mṛtasārāṇi paraṁ parisphurantu //11//

Vibho, O my Master, I don't want to discard this objective world or the impressions and thoughts and desires for this objective world, or not to perceive this objective world. Let it be perceived. Let thoughts come regarding the same. Let this objective world remain present for twenty-four hours [a day] before me. I don't want to discard it.

But, *darśana cintana prakāśa amṛta sārāṇi* [*paraṁ*] *parisphurantu*, this objective world, the appearance of this objective world, and the state of utilizing this objective world, must become to me, must appear to me, as *prakāśanāmṛta*, as the shining of Your *svarūpa* and that divinity, that taste. That taste and the shining of Your *svarūpa* must appear [to me] in each and every act of this universe. This is what I want.

Chapter 8 (31:31)

परमेश्वर तेषु तेषु कृच्छ्रे-
ष्वपि नामोपनमत्स्वहं भवेयम् ।
न परं गतभीस्त्वदङ्गसङ्गाद्-
उपजाताधिकसम्मदोऽपि यावत् ॥१२॥

parameśvara teṣu teṣu kṛcchre-
ṣvapi nāmopanamatsvahaṁ bhaveyam /
na paraṁ gatabhīstvadaṅgasaṅgād-
upajātādhikasammado'pi yāvat //12//

O Lord Śiva, *teṣu teṣu kṛcchreṣu api nāma upanamatsu*, let all those crises fall only on me. Crises of the world, depressions of the world, ruins of the world, disastrous things of the world, let those fall on me. I welcome them. But, *tvad aṅga saṅga*, I must be embraced with You. My body must be embraced with You.

Let all of those crush me. *Teṣu teṣu kṛcchreṣu api nāma upanamatsu*, those *kṛcchra* (*kṛcchra* means those [happenings], which are unbearable, disastrous things), let them . . . I welcome them. Let them fall on me. Let my self be soaked in that.

JOHN: Unbearable woes of the world.

SWAMIJI: Yes.

Let me not remain only *gatabhī* (*gatabhī* means "without any fear, fearless"). I don't want to become only fearless at that state, in those states.

In which states?

DENISE: When catastrophes come and it's bad . . .

SWAMIJI: How?

Tvat aṅga saṅgāt, when I will be in Your arms, in Thy arms, when I will be in Your arms, I won't become only fearless, *upajātādhika sammada api yāvat*, I will become intoxicated also by those disastrous flows on me.

JOHN: He will love them, in other words.

SWAMIJI: I will love them. I will welcome them. Let those disastrous things fall on me, attack me. I welcome them.

Chapter 8 (33:43)

भवदात्मनि विश्वमुम्भितं
यद् भवतैवापि बहिः प्रकाश्यते तत् ।
इति यद्दृढनिश्चयोपजुष्टं
तदिदानीं स्फुटमेव भासताम् ॥ १३ ॥

bhavadātmani viśvamumbhitaṁ
yad bhavataivāpi bahiḥ prakāśyate tat /
iti yaddṛḍhaniścayopajuṣṭaṁ
tadidānīṁ sphuṭameva bhāsatām //13//

From the philosophical point of view, I have understood that this whole universe is one with Thee. *Bhavad ātmani viśvam umbhitam*, this whole universe is woven in Your consciousness. That is a fact to me. And I read this in all of these spiritual books that this universe is woven in Your consciousness. And, at the same time, *bahiḥ prakāśyate*, one feels like that. One feels the universe . . . that person who is fully aware, he feels that, he feels that way of the universe. But this I have concluded [intellectually]; this is my conclusion in [intellectual] understanding. But this is only [intellectual] understanding that I have understood this way of the existence of the universe. I want to experience it! Let me experience it. Give me the capacity to experience this in a practical way. That is all. *Tadidānīm sphuṭameva bhāsatām*, let me experience this way of the actual position of the universe.

ALEXIS: I have enjoyed this in the form of a conviction, let me now experience it manifestly.

SWAMIJI: Conviction, yes. Let me experience it in manifestation.

Chapter Nine
The Victory of Absolute Freedom
Svātantrya vijayākhyaṁ navamaṁ stotram

SWAMIJI: This is "*svātantrya vijayākhyaṁ*": nothing is in his hands. Nothing is in the hands of the devotee but he wants to possess everything, all power–the devotee.

Chapter 9 (00:15)

कदा नवरसार्द्रार्द्रसम्भोगास्वादनोत्सुकम् ।
प्रवर्तेत विहायान्यन् मम त्वत्स्पर्शने मनः ॥ १ ॥

kadā navarasārdrārdra sambhogāsvādanotsukam
pravarteta vihāyānyan mama tvatsparśane manaḥ //1//

O Lord, when that time will come before me when *navasārdrārdra sambhoga āsvādana utsukam*, when *mama manaḥ* (my mind), which is *navasārdrārdra sambhoga āsvādana utsukam* . . . it is already like that. My mind is already like that. [My mind] is fond of *navarasa ārdrārdra sambhoga*, just to enjoy the taste of the always new taste of the nectar of the Lord's devotion. [My mind] has got fondness of tasting the nectar of the nearness of God consciousness.

JOHN: Already.

SWAMIJI: He is already . . . it is [the mind's] qualification.

My mind's qualification is this. [My mind] is fond of taking that *rasa*, *navarasa*, which is always new (*navarasa*), and *ārdra ārdra bhāva*, and which is always wet, which is not dry; where there is no dryness in that *rasa*. He wants to . . . [my mind] is fond to taste that *rasa* where there is no dryness in that *rasa* and where that *rasa* is always fresh, it remains always fresh.

That is the *rasa* of the love of God consciousness, love of God, attachment for God. Attachment for God creates that *rasa*, that fresh *rasa*.

ALEXIS: So, *utsukam* means "yearning", more truly.

SWAMIJI: Yes, he is fond of.

ALEXIS: Fond, not in the sense that he is familiar with it, but like a lover who is separated, he yearns, has *autsukyam*, yearning for that taste.

SWAMIJI: Yes, yearning.

And this is the position of my mind. But he does not get that joy, never. *Svātantryam vijayākhyam*, he wants that *svātantrya*. He wants to own that *svātantrya*[130].

Pravarteta vihāyānyan mama tvat sparśane. And that *rasa* will only come when I touch Your body; *tvat sparśane*, when I touch Your body, when I touch Your spiritual body. When my mind will touch Your body? Because, my mind is fond of yearning for that attaining and tasting the *rasa* of Your devotion. And that devotion will come only by Your touch. I want to embrace You and that embrace will give me that joy of that *rasa*, tasting that *rasa*.

When that time will come? I want to ask You, when that day will come for me, when that day will appear, when I will leave all other things, all of the other activities of the world, and be focused only to that point, i.e., just to embrace You and taste the nectar of that nearness of that devotion, love? When that day will come for me? Tell me.

Chapter 9 (04:05)

त्वदेकरक्तस्त्वत्पादपूजामात्रमहाधनः ।
कदा साक्षात्करिष्यामि भवन्तमयमुत्सुकः ॥२॥

tvadekaraktastvatpādapūjāmātramahādhanaḥ /
kadā sākṣātkariṣyāmi bhavantamayamutsukaḥ //2//

Tvadekaraktaḥ. I am *utsukaḥ*, I am *utsukaḥ*. This, myself, I am *utsukaḥ*. "I am" means I am (*aham*) *utsukaḥ*, who is *utsukaḥ*, who is fond of, or who is yearning.

What is the position of myself?

Tvad eka raktaḥ, I am always attached to You. I am always attached to You (*tvad eka raktaḥ*). *Tvad pāda pūjā mātra ma-*

130 See appendix 11 for an explanation of *svātantrya*.

hādhanaḥ, and I only possess the wealth of adoring You. I have no other wealth, no other bank balance. I have only the wealth just to adore You. This is my wealth! This is the qualification of me. I have only one wealth and that is Your adoration. I want to adore You. That is my wealth. That is what I want to possess. And *tvad eka raktaḥ*, and attachment I have not for other things except Thee (*tvad eka raktaḥ*). I am attached to You, to Thee, and I have only this wealth.

What?

JOHN: Of Your devotion.

SWAMIJI: Of Your devotion, of adoring You.

Kadā sākṣāt kariṣyāmi bhavantam. So, when shall I see You? When that day will come to me when I shall see You, I shall perceive You, I shall own You? Tell me that day.

Chapter 9 (06:06)

गाढानुरागवशतो निरपेक्षीभूतमानसोऽस्मि कदा ।
पटपटिति विघटिताखिलमहार्गलस्त्वामुपैष्याम ॥३॥

gāḍhānurāgavaśato nirapekṣībhūtamānaso'smi kadā /
paṭapaṭiti vighaṭitākhilamahārgalastvāmupaiṣyāmi //3//

When that day will come to me?

This *stotra* is always "when", questioning when, when that day will come.

Gāḍha anurāgavaśataḥ nirapekṣībhūta mānasaḥ kadā asmi. When that day will come when, by the intensity of Your love, *gāḍha anurāga-vaśataḥ*, by the intensity of, denseness of, Your love . . .*

ALEXIS: "Your love" means love for You.

SWAMIJI: Yes. Because I love You. You don't love me. You don't love me. I love You.

ṣṛṇu deva prārthaneyaṁ nātha tavāhaṁ namāma kena / [131]
sāmudro hi taraṅgāḥ kvacana samudro na tāraṅgaḥ // [132]

O Lord, just hear one word from me: *śṛṇu deva prārthaneyaṁ nātha tavāham*, I am Yours, *na māmakena aham*, You are not mine. I am Yours. You are not mine.
How?
Sāmudro hi taraṅgāḥ, the tide is of the ocean. The tide belongs to the ocean. The ocean does not belong to the tide.
This is what he says.

*. . . *gāḍha anurāgavaśataḥ nirapekṣībhūta mānasaḥ*, when that day will come when *gāḍha anurāgavaśataḥ*, by the intensity of Your love, attachment, *nirapekṣībhūtamānasaḥ*, my mind will vacate all other thoughts away? My mind will exclude all other thoughts by the intensity of Your love.

And *paṭa paṭiti vighaṭita mahārgalaḥ*, and I will become *paṭapaṭiti vighaṭita mahārgalaḥ,* I will become such a being that, when in my presence, that big door, which is locked already between You and me, between Your residence and my self (I am outside and You are inside and there is a door) . . .

ALEXIS: There is a bar across the door. *Argalā*. Is this a bar across?

SWAMIJI: Yes.

ALEXIS: Horizontal bar.

SWAMIJI: Bolt, big bolt!

ALEXIS: Yes, yes.

SWAMIJI: . . . and by the main presence of mine there, because I would be with that qualification . . .

With what qualification?

With the intensity of Thy devotion and by the exclusion of all other anxieties, all other attachments, all other thoughts. I will remain like that.

. . . and by that qualification, what would happen? This *argala*, this bolted, barred door, will break into pieces, *tvāmupaiṣyāmi*, and I will embrace You inside. When that day will come?

ALEXIS: He will break it? He will do the breaking?

131 Unknown source.
132 From Śaṅkara's *Ṣaṭpadī Stotra*. This *stotra* begins with the following line: *satyapi bhedāpaga me nātha tavāham na māmakī na stvaṁ.*

SWAMIJI: No, it will break by itself because of [Utpaladeva's] presence.

ALEXIS: *Vighaṭitākhilamahārgala* is *bahuvrīhi.*[133]

SWAMIJI: Yes.

Because, *mahārgalaḥ ahaṁ*, by my presence, this [locked door] will break into pieces and *tvāmupaiṣyāmi*, You will be seated in my lap.

ALEXIS: So, "*paṭa paṭiti*" is the sound of it breaking.

SWAMIJI: Sound, sound of breakage.

Chapter 9 (10:13)

स्वसंवित्सारहृदयाधिष्ठानाः सर्वदेवताः ।
कदा नाथ वशीकुर्यां भवद्भक्तिप्रभावतः ॥४॥

svasaṁvitsārahṛdayādhiṣṭhānāḥ sarvadevatāḥ /
kadā nātha vaśīkuryāṁ bhavadbhaktiprabhāvataḥ //4//
[not recorded completely]

All of my *devatās*, *sva saṁvit sāra hṛdaya adhiṣṭānāḥ sarvadevatāḥ*, all of these deities, all these deities [which are] organic[134] deities–my eyes, my ears, my nose, my throat, my tongue, my body, my skin–actually, *sva saṁvit sara hṛdaya adhiṣṭhānāḥ*, they are residing in one's own consciousness. *Sva saṁvit sāra hṛdaya adhiṣṭhānāḥ sarvadevatā*, all of this organic section, organic class of organs, all of these organs, are actually *sva saṁvit sāra hṛdaya adhiṣṭhānā*, they are residing on the basis of God consciousness. They are residing on the basis of God consciousness.[135]

---

133 Literally meaning "much rice", a *bahuvrīhi* compound signifies a referent by the specification of a particular quality. [*Editor's note*]

134 Of, or pertaining to, the organs. [*Editor's note*]

135 "Your own organs are gods. *Karaṇeśvaryo devatā*, these organs, your bodily organs, are all *devās*. *Rahasyaśāstraprasiddhaḥ*, they are nominated [as such] in the *Rahasya śāstra*, Shaivite books. *Tā anena karmaṇā tarpayat*, your organs, you should feed by these *karmas*, by giving them good food, good taste, good enjoyment, *ghee*, *paratha*, *palau* (fried rice), everything, whatever fine [thing] you can get for them, for your own organs. Feed them with many delicious things. Give them delicious

When that day will come to me when all of these organs I will get under control by the glory of Your devotion? When that time will come to me? This will be the cause of controlling all of my organs. [The cause] will be Thy intense devotion. When that day will come to me? Tell me.

Chapter 9 (11:49)

कदा मे स्यात्विभो भूरि भक्त्यानन्दरसोत्सवः ।
यदालोकसुखानन्दी पृथङ्नामापि लप्स्यते ॥५॥

kadā me syātvibho bhūri bhaktyānandarasotsavaḥ /
yadālokasukhānandī pṛthaṅnāmāpi lapsyate //5//

Vibho, O Lord, when that day will come to me when I will possess *bhūri bhaktyānanda rasotsavaḥ*, I will possess the intensity, the *utsavaḥ*, the intense festival of Your devotion?

ALEXIS: Of the bliss of Your devotion.

SWAMIJI: Bliss of Your devotion.

And that festival will take place in me, that great festival. This is the only festival for me, i.e., to get Your devotion, to achieve Your devotion. This is the only festival for me. I have no other festival, no charm in other festivals. When that festival will appear to me?

I want to ask You, *yadāloka sukhānandī pṛthak nāmāpi lapsyate*, when will I get entry in *prathamābhāsa*, when will I get entry in universal God Consciousness, *loka sukha ānandī*?

ALEXIS: *Ālo.*

SWAMIJI: *Āloka sukha, āloka sukha.*

ALEXIS: *Prathamāloka.*

SWAMIJI: Yes, *prathamābhāsa. Prathamābhāsa* means "the appearance of God consciousness in universal objectivity".[136]

---

food." *Bhagavad Gītā–In The Light of Kashmir Shaivism*, 3.11.

"Your own organs are your masters. They will direct you towards God consciousness. Those are your masters." Ibid 4.34.

136 "This starting point (*prathamābhāsa*) is found just at the beginning of any perception or thought, before it has become determinate." *Vijñāna Bhairava–The Manual for Self Realization*, Swami Lakshmanjoo,

ALEXIS: In this *ālocana*[137] moment.

SWAMIJI: Yes.

Pṛthak nāmāpi lapsyate, and when differentiated names and forms and speeches also will vanish for good.

ALEXIS: So, that God consciousness there is flowing up from that first moment of perception like a fountain?

SWAMIJI: Yes, the first moment–fountain. That is *nirvikalpa*.[138]

Another request:

Chapter 9 (14:04)

ईश्वरमभयमुदारं पूर्णमकारणमपह्नुतात्मानम् ।
सहसाभिज्ञाय कदा स्वामिजनं लज्जयिष्याम ॥ ६ ॥

īśvaramabhayamudāraṁ
pūrṇamakāraṇamapahnutātmānam /
sahasābhijñāya kadā svāmijanaṁ lajjayiṣyāmi //6//

Actually, Lord Śiva, You who are Lord Śiva, You are *abhaya*, You have no fear, You are fearless. *Udāram*, You are extravagant, You spend in Your own way. You don't ask anybody's decision, e.g., "should I spend this much or that much?" *Īśvaram abhayam udāram*, fearlessness is with You and *udāram*, this extravagance, the qualification of being extravagant . . . extravagance is in You. *Pūrṇam*, and still You are *pūrṇa*, You are filled always, i.e., there is nothing lacking [in You]. *Akāraṇam*, and You have no father and mother. You are absolutely . . . absolutely, You have come from incorrect sex.[139] It is why You have possessed so many disqualifications. You are "disqualified" because You have [no] fear, You don't fear anybody, and *udāram*, You are extravagant.

---

ed. John Hughes, (Universal Shaiva Fellowship, Los Angeles, 2007), Introduction, xxvi.

137 In this instance, "'*ālocana*' refers to the very first sensation of any perception before it reaches the state of knowledge." Ibid., 92, fn138.

138 See appendix 9 for an explanation of *nirvikalpa*.

139 *Akāraṇa* literally means "without cause".

This is also a disqualification.[140] *Pūrṇam*, and this is a misfortune for me that You are always full.

GANJOO: I can't offer anything.

SWAMIJI: You don't accept [anything] because You are full always (*pūrṇam*). *Akāraṇam*, and You have no father and mother. *Apahnuta*, O, this is . . . I know this is why You have kept Yourself hidden because You are not worth being known to anybody [because of] these disqualifications.

Now, there is one longing and craving in me. When that day will come to me when *sahasā abhijñāya*, I will perceive You in an instant? Instantaneously I will perceive You. *Śvāmijanam*, I will perceive You who are my Master, *lajjayiṣyāmi*, and I will make everybody . . . I will take You in a cart and everywhere everybody will see You. You will be ashamed. I will shame You, everywhere.

ALEXIS: *Svāmijanam* means *tvam*?

SWAMIJI: Yes, *svāmijanam* means "my Master."

I will shame You, my Master. [Everyone will say], "O, this is that debauched, extravagant [One]! This [One] is without father and mother!"

ALEXIS: I will break Your cover.

SWAMIJI:

Chapter 9 (17:00)

ईश्वरमभयमुदारं पूर्णमकारणमपह्नुतात्मानम् ।
सहसाभिज्ञाय कदा स्वामिजनं लज्जयिष्याम ॥ ६ ॥

īśvaramabhayamudāraṁ
pūrṇamakāraṇamapahnutātmānam /
sahasābhijñāya kadā svāmijanaṁ lajjayiṣyāmi //6//
[verse repeated]

So, I will shame You and You will be ashamed everywhere.

It means, in the background of his consciousness, Utpaladeva has this thought that everybody should perceive God.

ALEXIS: I will make a scandal of You.

SWAMIJI: Scandal of You. I will show You to everybody.

---

140 That is, Lord Śiva is "disqualified" from the realm of mere mortals. [*Editor's note*]

ERNIE: But he . . . isn't that an outrageous thing to say to God? Isn't that an outrageous thing to say?

SWAMIJI: Everything is fine because it is [said] through love.

ERNIE: No, I know, I am just saying.

SWAMIJI: Through love. *Bhaktiviṣe na kaścit doṣaḥ*, wherever there is devotion and love, you can say anything. It is fine. You can also kill your master! So many [devotees] have smashed shoes on the head of *iṣṭadevās*[141] because of love.

> [Once, a] master had told [his disciple] to shoot [Lord Śiva] eleven times each day on the head–this *liṅga*, *śivaliṅga*–and he used to go there and shoot Him with his shoes.
>
> **ERNIE:** Hit Him.
>
> **SWAMIJI:** Hit Him, yes. And a flood came once, one flood came. It was all flooded and that *liṅga* had gone under water. How could he reach there? He had to hit Him with shoes because he had made this possible to go everyday, each day (morning), and hit Him eleven times and come back. This was his *pūjā*, worship, *sādhanā*. And there, that day also, he [dove into the water and] he somehow reached that place [where the *liṅga* was] and hit Him with [his] shoes. And, at that very moment, He appeared, Lord Śiva appeared to him, and showed him His real form, divine form.

There are so many ways of devotion.

Chapter 9 (19:29)

कदा कामपि तां नाथ तव वल्लभतामियाम् ।
यया मां प्रति न क्वापि युक्तं ते स्यात्पलायितुम् ॥७॥

kadā kāmapi tāṁ nātha tava vallabhatāmiyām /
yayā māṁ prati na kvāpi yuktaṁ te syātpalāyitum //7//

Alright, leave everything aside! Don't come to me! But only there is one request. I want to ask You, I want to own that intensity of love for You, intense love, extremity of love for Thee. When

141 A chosen tutelary deity, a favorite god, one particularly worshiped. [*Editor's note*]

that state of extremity of love for Thee will rise in me? When that day will come when there will be [such] extreme love for Thee, by which extremity of love (*yayā*, by which), *māṁ prati na kvāpi yuktaṁ*, there will be no way for You to hide from me? There will remain no excuse for You to hide from me because of my intensity of love. My intensity of love will make You always remain in front of me. When that day will come?

Chapter 9 (20:48)

तत्त्वतोऽशेषजन्तूनां भवत्पूजामयात्मनाम् ।
दृष्ट्यानुमोदितरसाप्लावितः स्यां कदा विभो ॥८॥

tattvato'śeṣajantūnāṁ bhavatpūjāmayātmanām /
dṛṣṭyānumoditarasāplāvitaḥ syāṁ kadā vibho //8//

Vibho, O Lord, in fact (*tattvato* means "in fact"), *aśeṣajantunāṁ bhavat pūjā mayātmanām*, everybody, each and everybody, not knowingly or knowingly, worships You. Everybody worships You!

If anybody is giving bad names to another person, he is not [actually] giving bad names to anybody. He is just worshiping You. If anybody is doing sex, he is just worshiping You. If anybody is quarreling with [another], he is worshiping You. In fact, in the real sense, this is Your worship. Whatever is done is Your worship. *Aśeṣa jantūnāṁ*, everybody, *tattvataḥ*, in fact, *bhavat pūjā mayātmanām*, just worship, they just worship [You].

Dṛṣṭyā anumodita rasa. Now, there is one problem in me. That problem in me is that, when that time will come when I will actually *feel* that Your worship is being done everywhere? I will feel myself that whatever is done by anybody is Your worship; it is just Your worship and I would feel it myself clearly and *anumoditarasā*, and would confirm it in my mind that really the Lord is being worshiped everywhere. *Plāvitaḥ syāṁ kadā*, when that day will come when I will be flooded by this joy that the Lord is only worshiped everywhere? Whatever is being done, it is just Your worship.

This is what he wants to [know]: when that day will come when I will be flooded with the joy of this confirming that Your *pūjā* is being adopted, nothing else?[142]

I will become *rasena āplāvitaḥ syām*, flooded by that *rasa*. That flood will come and *bas*, throw me into that joy!

ALEXIS: The bliss of confirmation.

SWAMIJI: Confirmation that Your worship is being done. Whatever is . . . if bad names are given to You, that is Your worship, nothing else.

Jñānasya paramā bhūmir . . .

Why do you laugh?

JOHN: It's so great. Its our Shaivism.

SWAMIJI:

Chapter 9 (23:43)

ज्ञानस्य परमा भूमिर्योगस्य परमा दशा ।
त्वद्भक्तिर्या विभो कर्हि पूर्णा मे स्यात्तदर्थिता ॥९॥

jñānasya paramā bhūmiryogasya paramā daśā /
tvadbhaktiryā vibho karhi pūrṇā me syāttadarthitā //9//

Vibho, O Lord, O pervading, all-pervading Lord, really Your devotion, this is Your devotion that is the supreme state of knowledge and that is the supreme state of *yoga*. The supreme state of *yoga* and the supreme state of knowledge is just Your devotion, that is all. Just Your love.[143]

And that love, *karhi*, when that day will come when *pūrṇā me syāt tadarthitā*, that love will shine and take place and *tadarthitā* (*tadarthitā* means "longing for that love") will be fulfilled? When that day will come? *Tadarthitā pūrṇā syāt*, that longing of love, longing of that love . . .

Which love?

DENISE: Your love. Love for God.

SWAMIJI: Which love?

. . . which is the supreme state of knowledge, the supreme state of *yoga*. When that day will come when this longing for that love will be fulfilled in me?

---

142 *Anumodanam* means "confirmed".

143 That is, love for God.

Chapter 9 (25:23)

सहसैवासाद्य कदा गाढमवष्टभ्य हर्षविवशोऽहम् ।
त्वच्चरणवरनिधानं सर्वस्य प्रकटयिष्यामि ॥१०॥

sahasaivāsādya kadā gāḍhamavaṣṭabhyaharṣavivaso'ham /
tvaccaraṇavaranidhānaṁ sarvasya prakaṭayiṣyāmi //10//

Now, there is another problem. That is, *tvat caraṇa vara nidhānam*, the treasure of Your divine feet (that is that supreme state treasure) . . .

ALEXIS: *Svātantrya.*

SWAMIJI: *Svātantrya.*[144]

. . . the supreme treasure of Your divine feet, It is really known *not* in succession. It is never known in succession.

It is never known successively [like knowing] that your bank [account] will be 2000 rupees, then 3000 rupees, then 4000 rupees, then five, six, seven, eight, nine, then one *lakh*, two *lakhs*, three *lakhs*, like that, [where] successive treatment is there, successive attainment.

ALEXIS: Accumulation?

SWAMIJI: Accumulation.

But, in this spiritual field of Your science, knowing Your feet, the treasure of Your feet, is not successive. When It is known, It is known just once, just once.

Sahasaiva, so, when that day will come when I will come to understand Your treasure, Your treasure of Your divine feet (*sahasaiva* means "suddenly"). When that day will come that suddenly I will know, I will come to know, the treasure of Your divine feet, and *gāḍhamavaṣṭambhya*, and I will embrace It with me? That treasure I will hold with my own nature, *gāḍhamavaṣṭambhya*, and then that supreme joy will flow in me! I won't know what to do with It or how to handle It! *Sarvasya prakaṭayiṣyāmi*, I will distribute amongst the whole world, this treasure. When that day will come?

This is the ambition that he wants to . . . he wanted that everybody should know This treasure.

144 See appendix 11 for an explanation of *svātantrya*.

Chapter 9 (27:56)

परितः प्रसरच्छुद्धत्वदालोकमयः कदा ।
स्यां यथेश न किञ्चिन्मे मायाच्छायाबिलं भवेत् ॥११॥

paritaḥ prasaracchuddhatvadālokamayaḥ kadā /
syāṁ yatheśa na kiñcinme māyācchāyābilaṁ bhavet //11//

Īśa, O Lord, when that day will come when *paritaḥ prasarat śuddha tvad ālokamayaḥ syāṁ*, Your light will be so flooded in me that I would become one with That light, one with that light of Thy consciousness, by which light, *na kiñcit me māyāt chāyā bilaṁ bhavet*, there will be no traces of any darkness of illusion? No traces of the darkness of illusion will remain there. When that day will come to me?

Chapter 9 (29:00)

आत्मसात्कृतनिःशेषमण्डलो निर्व्यपेक्षकः ।
कदा भवेयं भगवंस्त्वद्भक्तगणनायकः ॥१२॥

ātmasātkṛtaniḥśeṣamaṇḍalo nirvyapekṣakaḥ /
kadā bhaveyaṁ bhagavaṁstvadbhaktagaṇanāyakaḥ //12

O Lord, O Bhagavan, O Lord, *ātmasāt kṛta niḥśeṣa maṇḍalaḥ*, I would like to achieve that state when I will be united with this whole universal consciousness, universe, all of the universe. This universal consciousness will be united with me; I will be united with universal consciousness.

And then, what I will do?

Kadā bhaveyaṁ bhagavan, O Lord, when that day will come, I will be the leader of all of Your devotees, leading them towards Your abode. "Come on! Come on this way! I will show you. I will lead you." I want to become the leader of all of Your devotees! When that day will come to me?

Chapter 9 (30:13)

नाथ लोकाभिमानानाम्-अपूर्वं त्वं निबन्धनम् ।
महाभिमानः कर्हि स्यां त्वद्भक्तिरसपूरितः ॥ १३ ॥

nātha lokābhimānānāmapūrvaṁ tvaṁ nibandhanam /
mahābhimānaḥ karhi syāṁ tvadbhaktirasapūritaḥ //13//

This I-ness, this ego, [which] is found in this universe, the sensation of ego comes from You. In fact, this sensation of ego, which is found in each and every individual, it has flown out from You. It is You who has produced this ego in each and every being. But I don't want *that* ego. That kind of ego, I don't want. *Mahābhimānaḥ karhi syāṁ*, I would like that universal I-consciousness, the ego of universal I-consciousness. When that day will come when I will achieve that ego of universal I-consciousness and when I will be *bhakti rasa pūritaḥ*, I will be soaked in the *rasa* of Your devotion?

Chapter 9 (31:27)

अशेषविषयाशून्यश्रीसमाश्लेषसुस्थितः ।
शयीयमिव शीताङ्घ्रिकुशेशययुगे कदा ॥ १४ ॥

aśeṣaviṣayāśūnyaśrīsamāśleṣasusthitaḥ /
śayīyamiva śītāṅghrikuśeśayayuge kadā //14//

There is one problem in me, in my life. *Aśeṣa viṣaya aśūnya śrī samāśleṣasusthitaḥ*, *śītāṅghri kuśeśayayuge*, Your two feet, which are very cooling, *aṅghri*, and these feet are just like lotuses, two lotuses, I would like to sleep on them. When that day will come when I will sleep on those two lotuses, already having embraced the woman of liberation, the woman who is the embodiment of liberation? Because, when I will embrace [her], when I will lie down on those lotus feet of Yours, I will be liberated. So, that liberation–liberation he has [described] as a beautiful girl–and that liberation, that Lakṣmī (the goddess of spiritual wealth), I would embrace on that bed.

Which bed?

ALEXIS: Lotus feet.

SWAMIJI: Your lotus feet.

And that bed, which is not deprived from worldly enjoyments, where all worldly enjoyments are existing (*aśeṣa viṣaya aśūnya*).

ALEXIS: That *śrī*, that spiritual . . .

SWAMIJI: Goddess of spiritual wealth.

Chapter 9 (33:25)

भक्त्यासवसमृद्धायास्त्वत्पूजाभोगसम्पदः ।
कदा पारं गमिष्यामि भविष्यामि कदा कृती ॥१५॥

bhaktyāsavasamṛddhāyāstvatpūjābhogasampadaḥ /
kadā pāraṁ gamiṣyāmi bhaviṣyāmi kadā kṛtī //15//

Bhaktyāsava smṛddhāyāḥ tvat pūjā bhoga sampadaḥ. Thy devotion, Thy worship, this is the great wealth, this is the great treasure, this is really the great treasure. Enjoyment of that treasure is enjoying that treasure.

Which treasure?

Thy devotion. Thy worship.

And that worship is *smṛddhāyā*, it rises, *bhaktyāsava*, by taking the liquor of being attached to You, Your attachment. Thy attachment is liquor. To be attached to You is liquor. I take the liquor, that is, I remain attached with You, and by that attachment, that liquor, it rises; this enjoyment rises, the enjoyment of worshiping You. When that day will come when I will reach the last end of that last resting point of that worship? And when that day will come when all of my desires will be fulfilled like that?

Chapter 9 (35:05)

आनन्दबाष्पपूरस्खलितपरिभ्रान्तगद्गदाक्रन्दः ।
हासोल्लासितवदनस्त्वत्स्पर्शरसं कदाप्स्यामि ॥१६॥

ānandabāṣpapūraskhalitaparibhrāntagadgadākrandaḥ /
hāsollāsitavadanastvatsparśarasaṁ kadāpsyāmi //16//

When that *rasa* of Thy *sparśa*, Thy embrace, will shine in me? When shall I enjoy this fragrance, Thy sweetness of Your embrace (*tvat sparśa rasaṁ*)? *Kadāpsyāmi*, when shall I achieve that?

Now, he thinks what would happen at that time.

I would be *ānanda bāṣpa pūrṇa*, by great joy, tears would be rolling down from my cheeks by that great joy, *skhalita*, and I would not be able to perceive anyone in front of me because those [tears] will . . .

JOHN: Tears will flood his eyes, obscure his vision.

SWAMIJI: . . . those [tears] will [be an] obstacle, they will block my vision (*skhalita*), *paribhrānta*, and I would be *paribhrānta* (*paribhrānta* means "intoxicated"), and *gadgadākrandaḥ* [Swamiji makes the sound of sobbing].

DENISE: Sobbing.

SWAMIJI: I would be sobbing. *Hāsollāsa*, and I would be laughing loudly at the same time. This would take place simultaneously. I would be laughing and, at the same time, I would be sobbing. I would be . . .

DENISE: Tears would be rolling.

SWAMIJI: Tears would be rolling down from my cheeks and I would be *skhalita* and intoxicated. When that day will come to me?

Chapter 9 (37:04)

पशुजनसमानावृत्ताम्-अवधूय दशामिमां कदा शम्भो ।
आस्वादयेय तावकभक्तोचितमात्मनो रूपं ॥१७॥

paśujanasamānāvṛttāmavadhūya
daśāmimāṁ kadā śambho /
āsvādayeya tāvakabhaktocitamātmano rūpaṁ //17//

Śambho, O Lord Śiva, really it is disgraceful! Not only for me, it is also for You disgraceful. It is disgraceful [because] You know I am Your devotee and still, *paśujana samāna vṛttām daśām*, I am just like others, just like ignorant persons, roaming from door to door like an ordinary worldly person.

Paśujana samāna vṛttām imām daśām. This state, this degraded state, which I have possessed, which I ought not to have possessed, and I have possessed by Your negligence. Because I am your devotee, it does not look nice that I possess this degraded state.

So, when that day will come that this degraded state, I will shake it aside (*avadhūya* means "I will shake down this aside") and *āsvādayeya tāvaka bhaktocitam*, and I would enjoy the reality of the nectar of Your nearness, which is due to Your devotees? That is due to your devotees. [Your] devotees must have that.

Chapter 9 (38:57)

लब्धाणिमादिसिद्धिर्विगलितसकलोपतापसन्त्रासः ।
त्वद्भक्तिरसायनपानक्रीडानिष्ठः कदासीय ॥१८॥

labdhāṇimādisiddhirvigalitasakalopatāpasantrāsaḥ /
tvadbhaktirasāyanapānakrīḍāniṣṭhaḥ kadāsīya //18//

When that day will come, my Lord, when I would have possessed, achieved, all of those eight *yogic* powers, *vigalita sakala upatāpa santrāsaḥ*, and I will be . . . all *upatāpa* (all torture) and *trāsaḥ* (fear), all dread and torture would be vanished, would get vanished, *tvad bhakti rasāyana pāna krīḍāniṣṭhaḥ*, and I would play, I would be playful, joyful, in drinking the nectar of Your devotion? *Kadāsīya*, when this state will come to me?

ALEXIS: *Rasāyana* is that thing, which gives eternal life.

SWAMIJI: Yes.

Chapter 9 (40:03)

नाथ कदा स तथाविध आक्रन्दो मे समुच्चरेद् वाचि ।
यत्समनन्तरमेव स्फुरति पुरस्तावकी मूर्तिः ॥१९॥

nātha kadā sa tathāvidha ākrando me samuccared vāci /
yat samanantarameva sphurati purastāvakī mūrtiḥ //19//

O my dear *nātha*, O my dear [Lord], when that day will come when I will cry, only in one word, "O my Lord! O my Lord", in such a way . . . when that day will come that I will produce this one cry, one cry only, one cry, in such a way that You will have no excuse to ignore me at all, and You will just appear before me at that very moment when I cry? At the next moment, You will appear, Your *mūrti*, Your beautiful shape and beautiful body, will appear to me, in front of me, by that one cry. When that such cry I will utter? When that day will come when I will utter such a cry, only one cry, by which cry, *samantarameva sphurati puraḥ*, You will have no excuse to hide?

Chapter 9 (41:20)

गाढगाढभवदङ्घ्रिसरोजा-
लिङ्गनव्यसनतत्परचेताः ।
वस्त्ववस्त्विदमयत्नत एव
त्वां कदा समवलोकयितास्मि ॥२०॥

gāḍhagāḍhabhavadaṅghrisarojā-
liṅganavyasanatatparacetāḥ /
vastvavastvidamayatnata eva
tvāṁ kadā samavalokayitāsmi //20//

There is one desire in me, my Lord. *Gāḍha gāḍha bhavat aṅghri saroja āliṅgana vyasana tatparacetāḥ*, I would like to be, to take this state of my position, that *gāḍha gāḍha bhavat aṅghri saroja*, Thy lotus feet, I would *gāḍha gāḍha āliṅgana*, . . .

DEVOTEE: Embrace.

SWAMIJI: . . . embrace tightly. I would embrace tightly Your lotus feet; not only embrace [once], *vyasana tat paracetāḥ*, embrace and just [continue to] embrace, embrace [Swamiji demonstrates] . . .

DENISE: Again and again.

SWAMIJI: Again and again (*vyasana tat*). Just this embracing again and again, that is *vyasana tat paracetāh.*

When that day will come?

Then, what would happen to me?

Vastu avastu idam ayatnata eva. Though You are not existing, though You are existing–You may exist [or] You may not exist–

[still] I would achieve Thee by this action. When that day will come when I will embrace Your feet like this? [I will] embrace, then disconnect those [embraces] in front, and then [again] embrace, then embrace, then embrace, then embrace . . . and die after it.

Chapter Ten
The Continuity of God Consciousness is Broken
Avicchedabhaṅgākhyaṁ daśamaṁ stotram

SWAMIJI: "*Avicchedabhaṅgākhyaṁ daśamaṁ stotram*".[145] This is the tenth *stotra*. It is nominated as "*avicchedabhaṅga*". *Avicchedabhaṅga* means he feels that the continuity of God consciousness does not remain.

ALEXIS: The break of that continuum (*avicchedabhaṅga*).

SWAMIJI: It breaks. His continuity of God consciousness breaks every now and then. So, he is crying for that [continuity] in this *stotra*.

Chapter 10 (00:27)

न सोढव्यमवश्यं ते जगदेकप्रभोरिदम् ।
माहेश्वराश्च लोकानामितरेषां समाश्च यत् ॥ १ ॥

na soḍhavyamavaśyaṁ te jagadekaprabhoridam /
māheśvarāśca lokānāmitareṣāṁ samāśca yat //1//

Jagadeka prabhor. O, the only Lord of the universe, the only Lord of the universe–You are the only Lord of this universe–how do You tolerate this, that Your slaves (Your devotees) and other worldly people reside on the same level? It should not happen that Your devotees tread on the same path and they remain on the same level where ordinary worldly people are. How do You tolerate this? You should not tolerate this.

Chapter 10 (01:27)

ये सदैवानुरागेण भवत्पादानुगामिनः ।
यत्र तत्र गता भोगांस्ते कांश्चिदुपभुञ्जते ॥ २ ॥

145 "*Avicchedabhaṅgā*" is missing from the audio.

ye sadaivānurāgeṇa bhavatpādānugāminaḥ /
yatra tatra gatā bhogāṁste kāṁścid upabhuñjate //2//

Lord, those people who are always following the pathway on which Your lotus feet travel–they are following that pathway–and those people who are following that pathway with great love and affection, *yatra tatra gatāḥ*, never mind if they are situated in any [particular] position, in any worldly state, *te kāṁcit bhogān upa-bhuñjate*, they enjoy some supreme *camatkāra*, supreme taste, supreme spiritual taste. So, they don't worry about that.[146]

Chapter 10 (02:41)

भर्ता कालान्तको यत्र भवांस्तत्र कुतो रुजः ।
तत्र चेतरभोगाशा का लक्ष्मीर्यत्र तावकी ॥३॥

bhartā kālāntako yatra bhavāṁstatra kuto rujaḥ /
tatra cetarabhogāśā kā lakṣmīryatra tāvakī //3//

Where *kālāntakaḥ*, the destroyer of the lord of death . . .

Lord Śiva is the destroyer of the lord of death. He has killed the lord of death. *Kāla* means the lord of death.

. . . and where the destroyer of the lord of death is in the background, is [the] helping hand, remains as a helping hand, where that *kālāntaka* (the destroyer of the lord of death) is helping, *tatra kuto rujaḥ*, where is there the possibility of any disease? No disease will appear to him when He is protecting him.

Who?

DENISE: Lord Śiva

SWAMIJI: Lord Śiva who . . .

ALEXIS: Destroys death.

SWAMIJI: . . . who is the destroyer of death.

Tatra ca itara bhogāśā kā lakṣmīḥ yatra tāvakī. Yatra tāvakī lakṣmīḥ, where there is Your Lakṣmī (Lakṣmī means the goddess of wealth, Your goddess of wealth), where Your goddess of wealth

146 That is, they don't worry about being situated in worldly states because they actually attain spiritual enjoyment from them. [*Editor's note*]

is existing, there is no possibility of any desire for any other enjoyments. All enjoyments end there!

JOHN: Why is that, sir? Why do all enjoyments end where the goddess of wealth . . .

SWAMIJI: All [worldly] enjoyments seem nothing before that.

DENISE: Goddess of spiritual wealth.

SWAMIJI: Yes, spiritual wealth.

Chapter 10 (04:53)

क्षणमात्रसुखेनापि विभुर्येनासि लभ्यसे ।
तदैव सर्वः कालोऽस्य त्वदानन्देन पूर्यते ॥४॥

kṣaṇamātrasukhenāpi vibhuryenāsi labhyase /
tadaiva sarvaḥ kālo'sya tvadānandena pūryate //4//

Kṣaṇamātra sukhenāpi vibhur yenāsi labhyase. When Thou, Lord, is achieved by some person, though in just a flash of super-sexual joy, only a flash of super-sexual joy (it means only for half a second), that flash of joy, super-sexual joy,[147] rises only for *kṣaṇa* . . .

Kṣaṇa means . . .

GANJOO: Momentary.

ALEXIS: Instant.

SWAMIJI: . . . five breaths, the span of time of five breaths.

. . . only for that time, if Your super-sexual joy of Your *svarūpa*, Your existence, is experienced by anybody, *tadaiva sarvaḥ kālo 'sya tva*, no matter if he does not achieve that joy up to his death time afterwards, but still, the whole span of time of his life is filled with the intoxication of that joy, for his lifetime. This is the greatness of that joy. That joy remains forever, up to his death.

147 In the ordinary sexual course, one experiences a single drop of the bliss of God consciousness. Here, experiencing the Lord's nature (*svarūpa*) in just one flash, the devotee feels the intoxication of that super-sexual joy of God consciousness for the rest of his or her lifetime. [*Editor's note*]

Chapter 10 (06:40)

आनन्दरसबिन्दुस्ते चन्द्रमा गलितो भुवि ।
सूर्यस्तथा ते प्रसृतः संहारी तेजसः कण ॥५॥
बलिं यामस्त्रितीयाय नेत्रयास्मै तव प्रभो ।
अलौकिकस्य कस्यापि माहात्म्यस्यैकलक्ष्मण ॥६॥

ānandarasabinduste candramā galito bhuvi /
sūryastathā te prasṛtaḥ saṁhārī tejasaḥ kaṇaḥ //5//
baliṁ yāmastritīyāya netrayāsmai tava prabho /
alaukikasya kasyāpi māhātmyasyaikalakṣmaṇe //6//

You see this moon that shines in the sky, that is only one drop of the nectar of Your spiritual bliss. It is only one drop, which shines . . . the shining of the moon. You find this moon so pleasing and so soothing to everybody, and this is only one drop of that super-sexual joy, [which] has entered in that substance [of the] moon.

And *sūryastathā te prasṛtaḥ saṁhārī tejasaḥ kaṇaḥ*, and the sun that shines in the sky is only one spark of Your *prakāśa*, one spark of Your light, destructive light. One spark of Your destructive light is existing in that *sūrya*, and you see how much light it produces, burning light.

JOHN: Why "destructive light" here?

SWAMIJI: That *tejas* (light) is destructive. If you look on that *teja,* you will go blind.

ALEXIS: But also in the sense that *sūrya* is the course of withdrawal, is it not?

SWAMIJI: Yes.

JOHN: It destroys individuality and gives universality.

SWAMIJI: Yes, universality.

ALEXIS: The course of *saṁhāra bhairava.*

SWAMIJI: But I, [Utpaladeva], leave these two substances of this *prakāśa* aside. I have nothing to do with [i.e., I am not concerned with] these two *prakāśās*. One is filled with joy [i.e., the moon] and one is filled with destructive light [i.e., the sun].

And that represents, this *candramā* (moon) represents, Your left eye and *sūrya* (the sun) represents Your right eye. I have nothing to do with these two eyes of Yours. These are Your two eyes shining in this world.

There is a third eye, which is situated in between Your two eyebrows. That is the eye of *agni* (fire)*, pramātṛ bhāva*[148]. I want to offer my whole everything to that.

There is one appropriate word in Kashmiri for that "*baliṁ yāmaḥ*". *Baliṁ yāmaḥ* means *balāya lāgun* [in Kashmiri]. *Balāya lāgun* is just to dispose of your everything for that.

GANJOO: Sacrifice everything in its name.

JOHN: Without reservation.

SWAMIJI: Yes, that is *baliṁ yāmaḥ*.

I want to do that to Your third eye. And which is *alaukika*, which is beyond the universe, above the universe, and it has great glory in that, and it is glorified in that . . . the sign of that glory is there (*lakṣmaṇe* means "sign").

Chapter 10 (10:41)

तेनैव दृष्टोऽसि भवद्दर्शनाद्योऽतिहृष्यति ।
कथञ्चिद्यस्य वा हर्षः कोऽपि तेन त्वमीक्षित ॥७॥

tenaiva dṛṣṭo'si bhavaddarśanādyo'tihṛṣyati /
kathañcidyasya vā harṣaḥ ko'pi tena tvamīkṣitaḥ //7//

In the real sense, he has actually perceived and seen You who, by seeing You, will become *atihṛṣyati* (*atihṛṣyati* means "his joy will find no bounds"). He will be out of bounds in joy.

It is not that when you perceive God consciousness and you relate/explain your perception before your master: "O master, I have seen God consciousness today by your grace and it was so nice. It was very beautiful." This is not the way of experiencing That.

DENISE: It's like you experienced It and It was over?

SWAMIJI: No, when you experience It and relate It to your master, you can't relate anything. You will just weep before him. You can't say even one word. You will be so filled with joy that you can't speak, you can't utter any word for That. You will just

148 *Pramātṛ bhāva* (subjective state, fire), *pramāṇa bhāva* (cognitive state, sun), and *prameya bhāva* (objective state, moon). [*Editor's note*]

weep before him. And that is the sign that you have actually perceived that God consciousness. If you say that, "it was very beautiful, I have perceived it", it is all a fraud.

DENISE: Because it is some limited experience then.

SWAMIJI: Yes.

So, *bhavaddarśanāt yo atihṛṣyati*, that person who becomes *atihṛṣyati* (*atihṛṣyati* means "his joy is so much dense that he cannot explain anything"), *tenaiva dṛṣto'si*, in fact, he has perceived You. *Kathañcidyasya vā harṣaḥ*, and that joy does not come just by meditating on That. *Kathañcit*[149], *bas*, that joy comes only by the grace of God, by *śaktipāta*. So, he has seen You, he has actually seen You, not anyone else.

Chapter 10 (13:08)

येषां प्रसन्नोऽसि विभो प्रभो यैर्लब्धं हृदयं तव ।
आकृष्य त्वत्पुरत्तैस्तु बाह्यमाभ्यन्तरीकृतम् ॥८॥

yeṣāṁ prasanno'si prabho yairlabdhaṁ hṛdayaṁ tava /
ākṛṣya tvatpurattaistu bāhyamābhyantarīkṛtam //8//

Vibho[150], O Lord, to whom You are actually pleased, with whom You are pleased, *yairlabdhaṁ hṛdayaṁ tava*, and those who have achieved and perceived Your heart, Your internal heart, those persons only have done this thing.

What they have done?

They have extracted this whole universe from Your nature of God consciousness and then soaked it again in that God consciousness. They have done this. They have extracted this universe from the state of God consciousness and then again united it with God consciousness.

JOHN: What is that "extracting the universe from God consciousness" mean?

SWAMIJI: This duality does not come from duality. This duality comes from unity. From unity they have extracted this duality

149 Somehow.

150 In his recitation of this verse, Swamiji sings "*prabho*" instead of "*vibho*". The two words have the same meaning. In Swamiji's Sanskrit/Hindi publication, "*vibho*" appears in the text. [*Editor's note*]

and then again, this duality they have united with unity again. They have done this job.

DENISE: Who?

ERNIE: The seekers.

SWAMIJI: To whom You are pleased, with whom You are pleased, and those who have actually perceived Your essence, [they] have done this thing.

Chapter 10 (14:59)

त्वदृते निखिलं विश्वं समदृग्यातमीक्ष्यताम्
ईश्वरः पुनरेतस्य त्वमेको विषमेक्षणः ॥९॥

tvadṛte nikhilaṁ viśvaṁ samadṛgyātamīkṣyatām /
īśvaraḥ punaretasya tvameko viṣamekṣaṇaḥ //9//

[Except for] Thee, this whole universe, everybody sees, observes this universe, with two eyes in a dualistic way, [except for] You. [Except for] You, everybody perceives this universe in a dualistic way, with two eyes. But only You are that person who perceives this [universe] with one eye, only the third eye, in a monistic way. This is the difference (*viṣamekṣaṇaḥ*).[151]

Chapter 10 (15:51)

आस्तां भवत्प्रभावेण विना सत्तैव नास्ति यत् ।
त्वद्दूषणकथा येषां त्वदृते नोपपद्यते ॥१०॥

āstāṁ bhavatprabhāveṇa vinā sattaiva nāsti yat /
tvaddūṣaṇakathā yeṣāṁ tvadṛte nopapadyate //10//

Bhavat prabhāveṇa vinā sattaiva nāsti yat. This is a fact that without Thy glory, without the existence, appearance, of Your glory, nothing can exist in this universe. This is a real fact that without Your glory, nothing can exist. There must be Your glory for existence. If this [microphone] exists, it exists only because of Your glory. Your glory is there, so it exists.

151 The difference in perception. [*Editor's note*]

Let it remain. Let this fact remain on one side.

But only one thing is, *tvaddūṣaṇa kathā yeṣāṁ tvadṛte nopapdyate*, those persons who deny Your existence–Cārvāka, atheists, they deny Your existence, those persons–the denying of Your existence cannot be explained without Your existence. If they deny Your existence, that denying way of explaining cannot exist without Your existence. There also they need Your existence to deny You to say, "there is no God". To say, "there is no God", this saying only will exist when there is God.[152]

Chapter 10 (17:34)

बाह्यान्तरान्तरायालीकेवले चेतसि स्थितिः ।
त्वयि चेत्स्यान्मम विभो किमन्यदुपयुज्यते ॥११॥

bāhyāntarāntarāyālīkevale cetasi sthitiḥ /
tvayi cetsyānmama vibho kimanyadupayujyate //11//

O Lord, *vibho*, O Lord, if my mind is established in Thy Self, if my mind is established, becomes established, in Thy Self, and my mind will take the position of being detached from outward universality (the outward universe), the introverted universe, and the void universe, then the outward universe, the introverted universe, and the void universe will not exist in my mind.[153] My mind will be absolutely away from these three sections of universes. *Arthāt*[154], the outward universe won't exist in my mind, the introverted universe won't exist in my mind, and the

152 "If you say that God does not exist, I ask you, who is saying that God does not exist? It is God that says that God does not exist. So it is God Himself who is trying to prove that He does not exist. Why? Because that person who disproves the existence of Lord Śiva, by his very attempt to disprove His existence, proves His existence. This is because that person who is asking the question is Lord Śiva, who exists even before the question of His existence arises." *Self Realization in Kashmir Shaivism*, 3.58.

153 *Jāgrat* (wakefulness), *svapna* (dreaming), and *suṣupti* (dreamless sleep), respectively. [*Editor's note*]

154 *Arthāt*: according to the state of the case, according to the circumstance, as a matter of fact. [*Editor's note*]

void universe won't exist in my mind. And, in that mind, if You prevail, Your existence shines, establishes [Itself], *kimanyadupayujyate*, what do I need then? I need nothing then! My needs are complete, altogether.

Chapter 10 (19:26)

अन्ये भ्रमन्ति भगवन्नात्मन्येवातिदुःस्थिताः ।
अन्ये भ्रमन्ति भगवन्नात्मन्येवातिसुस्थिता ॥१२॥

anye bhramanti bhagavannātmanyevātiduḥsthitāḥ /
anye bhramanti bhagavannātmanyevātisusthitāḥ //12//

O Lord, some people . . .

There are two meanings of this word "*bhramanti*". First *bhramanti* means [those who] just waste their time in going here and there. Second *bhramanti* means [those who] enjoy. [The second] *bhramanti* means *vikasanti*. The first *bhramanti* means *bhramanti*, actually *bhramanti*. The second *bhramanti* means *vikasanti*. The first *bhramanti* means *bhramanti*, actually.

ALEXIS: To wander about pointlessly.

SWAMIJI: Yes.

Because, O Lord, *na ātmani eva ati duḥsthitāḥ*, they are situated in that being which is not God. They are situated in that being which is not actually God. So, *ati duḥsthitā*, they remain there *ati duḥsthitā*, always scattering, with scattered mind.

Anye, and there are some people who shine, who are glorified, *ātmanyeva*, there, *ātmanyeva*, *na ātmanyeva*, *bhagavan*, O Lord, *ātmanyeva ātisusthitāḥ*, because they take . . . they are established in their own nature.[155]

Chapter 10 (21:19)

अपीत्वापि भवद्भक्तिसुधामनवलोक्य च ।
त्वामपीश त्वत्समाचारमात्रात्सिद्ध्यन्ति जन्तवः ॥१३॥

155 The two lines of this verse contain a subtle play on words between the two possible readings of "*bhagavan na ātmani*" and "*bhagavan ātmani*". [*Editor's note*]

apītvāpi bhavadbhaktisudhāmanavalokya ca /
tvāmapīśa tvatsamācāramātrātsiddhyanti jantavaḥ //13//
[the audio of the first part of this verse is missing]

O Lord, *bhavad bhakti sudhām apītvāpi*, those who have not tasted the nectar of Your devotion, who have not tasted the nectar of Your devotion and *anavalokya ca tvām*, who have not experienced the state of Your God consciousness–those people who have not experienced the state of God consciousness and those people who have not tasted the nectar of Your devotion–but still, *tvat samācāramātrā*, by hearing Your name from the outside world also, they get entry in God consciousness! There are such people who, without getting entry in God consciousness and without adoption of devotion for Thee–they have not tasted the nectar of Your devotion and they have not entered in the state of God consciousness–but still, they are so fine and they are so close to You that by hearing Your one name from outside, from some[one's] lips, they get entry. They are so great!

JOHN: So, there is no prerequisites for who . . .

SWAMIJI: Huh?

JOHN: There is no prerequisites of devotion or anything . . .

SWAMIJI: No [affirmative].

JOHN: . . . or anything for who gets this? It's all grace!

SWAMIJI:

Chapter 10 (23:00)

भृत्या वयं तव विभो तेन त्रिजगतां यथा ।
बिभर्ष्यात्मानमेवं ते भर्त्तव्या वयमप्यलम ॥१४॥

bhṛtyā vayaṁ tava vibho tena trijagatāṁ yathā /
bibharṣyātmānamevaṁ te bharttavyā vayamapyalam //14

O Lord, we are Your slaves. There is no doubt that we are slaves. *Tena*, so, *trijagatāṁ yathā bibharṣi* . . .

Bhṛtya means "slaves". *Bhṛtya* does not mean "servant, paid servant". [*Bhṛtya* means] without . . . "an unpaid servant".

ALEXIS: Completely supported by a master.

SWAMIJI: Completely supported by a master, that is *bhṛtya*.

ALEXIS: *Tasmai dīyate sarvaṁ.*

SWAMIJI: *Hāṁ*[156]. *Dhāryate poṣyate ca. Dhāryate poṣyate*, [one] who is looked after in each and every respect by a master, he is a *bhṛtya*; and who has no other support than his master, he is a *bhṛtya*. So he is a slave.

JOHN: He depends completely on his master.

SWAMIJI: Yes. He doesn't want . . . he doesn't need money. He needs just the support of his master.

And we are Your *bhṛtya*, we are Your slaves. And, as it is obvious that You take care of all of these three worlds, considering them as Your *bhṛtya*, considering these three worlds as Your *bhṛtyas*, in the same way, it is Your duty to take our care. You have to take care [of us] and see that we don't need anything. You have to fill and complete our needs. You have to do that because You are our master.

Chapter 10 (25:00)

परानन्दामृतमये दृष्टेऽपि जगदात्मनि ।
त्वयि स्पर्शरसेत्यन्ततरमुत्कण्ठितोस्मि ते ॥१५॥

parānandāmṛtamaye dṛṣṭe'pi jagadātmani /
tvayi sparśarase'tyantataramutkaṇṭhito'smi te //15//

Although, O Lord, I have seen You and I have experienced the state of Your being, which is filled with the supreme nectar of bliss, but still there is some need in my mind just to embrace You. I want to just embrace You. And this is always tickling in the background of my desire (*icchā śakti*) that I want to embrace You.

Bas, only there is this much: I have seen You, I have experienced You, but I want to embrace You.

ALEXIS: "*Jagadātmani*", where does this come in?

SWAMIJI: *Tvayi.*

ALEXIS: *Tvayi jagadātmani sparśa rase.*

SWAMIJI: No, it will go both ways: *tvayi jagadātmani parā-*

156 Hindi word for "yes".

nandāmṛtamaye dṛṣṭe'pi.

ALEXIS: It is not that I have seen You in *uttīrṇā* form, i.e., *viśvottīrṇa* (transcendent) form, now I wish to embrace You in the world. Is it not like that?

SWAMIJI: Yes, yes. It is. Yes.

ALEXIS: It is like that. There is that opposition there in this verse?

SWAMIJI: Yes.

Chapter 10 (26:23)

देव दुःखान्यशेषाणि यानि संसारिणामपि ।
धृत्याख्यभवदीयात्मयुतान्यायान्ति सह्यताम ॥१६॥

deva duḥkhānyaśeṣāṇi yāni saṁsāriṇāmapi /
dhṛtyākhyabhavadīyātmayutānyāyānti sahyatām //16//

O Lord, *saṁsāriṇām api yāni aśeṣāni duḥkhāni*, those tortures and those pains, sorrows, sadnesses, in this universe, what[ever tortures] come here, and they are tolerated by everybody. [They] are tolerated only . . . the cause of this tolerance is just Your nearness. You are near to them, so they tolerate it. Otherwise, nobody would tolerate any sadness, any torture, in this universe. It is tolerated only because of Thy presence. You are present and so it is tolerated.

JOHN: How does that make it tolerable?

SWAMIJI: Huh?

DENISE: Because it makes it sweet also?

SWAMIJI: Because it is sweet. Because He is always sweet, He is all-round sweet [laughter]! Yes, you are right.

GANJOO: It is very correct.

JOHN: But he is speaking about every person, isn't he? Devotees, everybody.

SWAMIJI: Every person.

ALEXIS: So, even the person with no love of God, when they are in extreme pain, they feel some attachment to I-consciousness.

SWAMIJI: Yes, I-consciousness.

ALEXIS: So they don't despair entirely.

SWAMIJI: They tolerate. They tolerate because of that . . .
ALEXIS: There is some God consciousness there.
SWAMIJI: That is I-consciousness existing [in them], that God consciousness.
ALEXIS: Universal devotion.
SWAMIJI: Yes.

Chapter 10 (27:51)

सर्वज्ञे सर्वशक्तौ च त्वय्येव सति चिन्मये ।
सर्वथाप्यसतो नाथ युक्तास्य जगतः प्रथा ॥ १७ ॥

sarvajñe sarvaśaktau ca tvayyeva sati cinmaye /
sarvathāpyasato nātha yuktāsya jagataḥ prathā //17//

The existence of the universe, in fact, is *sarvathā api asataḥ*, it is not existing. This existence of the universe is false, it is unreal, it should not exist!

Why does it exist? These [spectacles] should not exist. Why does it exist?

It exists only *sarvajñe sarvaśaktau ca tvayyeva sati*, when You are there. When Your existence is there shining, then it exists. This existence of the universe–the [would-be] non-existent universe–this existence of the [would-be] non-existent universe is only possible when You are shining. So, [because] You are shining, everything is fine [laughter].

JOHN: Why does he say this universe should not exist?
SWAMIJI: Because duality is not existing. Duality is existing only when non-duality is shining there. Non-duality is shining in duality.
ALEXIS: He says it doesn't make sense to imagine the world being dependent simply on time, space, and form.[157] It makes no sense.
SWAMIJI: No, it makes no sense.
ALEXIS: It has no authority to exist on those grounds.
SWAMIJI: That is Shaivism.

157 "All these three (time, space, and form) are only the glory of God. They don't exist in their own way [i.e., independently]." *Tantrāloka*, 11.105 (USF archives).

त्वत्प्राणिताः स्फुरन्तीमे गुणा लोष्टोपमा अपि ।
नृत्यन्ति पवनोद्धूताः कार्पासपिचवो यथा ॥१८॥
यदि नाथ गुणेष्वात्माभिमनो न भवेत्ततः ।
केन हीयेत जगतस्त्वदेकात्मतया प्रथा ॥१९॥

tvatprāṇitāḥ sphurantīme guṇā loṣṭopamā api /
nṛtyanti pavanoddhūtāḥ kārpāsapicavo yathā //18//
yadi nātha guṇeṣvātmābhimano na bhavettataḥ /
kena hīyeta jagatastvadekātmatayā prathā //19//

O Lord, *ime guṇā*, these senses (senses of action and senses of cognition), these five senses of action and five senses of cognition, they are actually *loṣṭopamā api*, just like a rock. They have no life. All of these ten senses have no life. They are just like *loṣṭa* (*loṣṭa* means this "ball of earth"), just a dead ball of earth. But, *tvatprāṇita*, when You inject Your consciousness in them, *sphuranti*, they do their acting.

ALEXIS: *Sphuranti*? They shine. They vibrate.

SWAMIJI: *Sphuranti, svaṁ svaṁ kāryaṁ kurvanti. Sphuranti* [means] "they shine, they vibrate, they do everything".

The eyes are just like that earthen ball, i.e., dead. When You inject Your God consciousness in the eyes, they perceive this form, each and every form. In the same way, all of the organs act when they are injected by Your God consciousness. So, *nṛtyanti*, they dance just like *pavanoddhūtāḥ kārpāsa picavaḥ*, i.e., when *kārpāsa picavaḥ*, the smallest particles of cotton, cotton fibers [i.e., lint], move here and there in the ether by the force of the wind. So, You are that wind.

ALEXIS: *Picavaḥ*?

SWAMIJI: *Picavaḥ* means *leśāḥ*, particles, small particles of those cotton fibers.

In the same way, *yadi nātha guṇeṣu ātmābhimāno na bhavet*, if, in these organs, in these ten organs, there was not the adjustment of God consciousness, if there would have not been the adjustment of God consciousness, who would come down from the state of God consciousness? Nobody! Everybody would take hold of God consciousness, always. Nobody would come in this universal existence.

Have you understood?

JOHN: No.

SWAMIJI: It means we are enjoying, we have got ten organs (five organs of action, five organs of cognition), and we enjoy the worldly life. Nobody would accept enjoying the worldly life if God consciousness would not have been adjusted in this state also. Nobody would care for this universe.

DENISE: The joy comes from God consciousness.

SWAMIJI: The joy comes from that I-consciousness.

ALEXIS: *Virodhābhāsa*, here.

SWAMIJI: Huh?

ALEXIS: *Virodhābhāsa*, apparent contradiction.

SWAMIJI: *Virodhābhāsa*, yes.

ALEXIS: Because God establishes that self-identity in those organs.

SWAMIJI: Yes.

ALEXIS: So they think, "this is me!"

SWAMIJI: Yes.

And so, God consciousness is there. If God consciousness they would not have found in this state of life, nobody would have come down in this state of life. Everybody would have remained in God consciousness, always. What is there in that? But they find Your presence there also, so they enjoy.

JOHN: So, That presence is in the form of, "I am enjoying?"

ALEXIS: *Ātmābhimānaḥ.*

SWAMIJI: Yes, *ātmābhimānaḥ, na bhavet.*

Kena hīyeta jagatas tvadekātmatayā prathā. Who would abandon that state of spirituality of God consciousness? No one would have abandoned That place. But everybody has abandoned It because they have found that God consciousness is here also.[158]

JOHN: This is Shaivism.

SWAMIJI: Yes [laughs].

ALEXIS: This is not Vedānta.

SWAMIJI:

---

158 In the state of worldly life, *saṁsāra*. [*Editor's note*]

Chapter 10 (34:01)

वन्द्यास्तेऽपि महीयांसः प्रलयोपगता अपि ।
त्वत्कोपपावकस्पर्शापूता ये परमेश्वर ॥२०॥

vandyāste'pi mahīyāṁsaḥ pralayopagatā api /
tvatkopapāvakasparśāpūtā ye parameśvaraḥ //20//

O *parameśvaraḥ*, O Lord, *pralayopayatā api tvat kopa pāvaka sparśapūtā*, those who have been killed by You with wrath . . .

For instance, Rāvaṇa was killed by God; the lord of death (Yama) was killed by God; the lord of love (Kāma) was killed by God.

. . . *pralaye*, although they were killed by Your wrath, but still, because Your nearness was there, so they are worthy of salutations from us. We salute them because they had Your nearness. You had fought with them with Your hands. Your divine hands touched them. So, they are divine.

ALEXIS: So, love is divine.

SWAMIJI: Yes.

ALEXIS: *Kāma*.

SWAMIJI: Absolutely.

Chapter 10 (35:16)

महाप्रकाशवपुषि विस्पष्टे भवति स्थिते ।
सर्वतोऽपीश तत्कस्मात्तमसि प्रसराम्यहम ॥२१॥

mahāprakāśavapuṣi vispaṣṭe bhavati sthite /
sarvato'pīśa tatkasmāttamasi prasarāmyaham //21//

It is a fact that Your existence is everywhere found, *mahāprakāśa vapuṣi*, because it is all-light, all-consciousness, everywhere. Your existence is found everywhere. But, although it is found by me also everywhere, why do I roam in darkness every now and then? What is the cause of that, that I am existing in only darkness, dense darkness?

Chapter 10 (36:02)

अविभागो भवानेव स्वरूपममृतं मम ।
तथापि मर्त्यधर्माणामहमेवैकमास्पदम ॥२२॥

avibhāgo bhavāneva svarūpamamṛtaṁ mama /
tathāpi martyadharmāṇāmahamevaikamāspadam //22//

Actually, You are universal, You are everywhere, and my body is one with Your body. My body is one with Your 'nectared' body. But still, it is a wonder for me why I am given to all aspects, which are mortal aspects, e.g., I have got headache, I have got nasal trouble, I have got boils, I have got everything, I have got all sadnesses. All sadnesses, all sorrows come to me. This is a wonder.

Chapter 10 (37:05)

महेश्वरेति यस्यास्ति नामकं वाग्विभूषणम् ।
प्रणामाङ्कश्च शिरसि स एवैकः प्रभावित ॥२३॥

maheśvareti yasyāsti nāmakaṁ vāgvibhūṣaṇam /
praṇāmāṅkaśca śirasi sa evaikaḥ prabhāvitaḥ //23//

That person whose tongue is glorified with Thy name, whose tongue always recites Your name, *maheśvara iti yasa asti nāmakam*, "O Lord", "O Maheśvara", "O Bhagavān", "O God", "O Śiva", "O my dear", "dearest", these names are glorified in that tongue, and *praṇāmāṅkaśca śirasi*, and the sign of bowing down on the earth before You, and the sign on the forehead of bowing . . .

[For example], when they bow before me and they do *praṇāma*[159] and that sign comes on their knee cap, that dust. But no, that dust should come on the forehead when you bow down before your master.

. . . and those people whose tongue is glorified by Your name,

159 Obeisance.

by constant recitation of Your name, and whose forehead is glorified by the sign of bowing before You, he is actually fortunate. He is actually fortunate and no one else.

Chapter 10 (38:59)

सदासच्च भवानेव येन तेनाप्रयासतः ।
स्वरसेनैव भगवंस्तथा सिद्धिः कथं न म ॥२४॥

sadāsacca bhavāneva yena tenāprayāsataḥ /
svarasenaiva bhagavaṁstathā siddhiḥ kathaṁ na me //24

O Lord, this is a fact that You are, in existing objects, You are existing, and in non-existent objects, You are existing. In those objects, which are not existing, You exist; in those objects, which are existing, You exist. In those objects, which are fully lighted, You exist; in those objects, which are in the dark, You exist. You are in darkness, You are in light. You are in existing objects and You are in non-existent objects.

Why don't I perceive You without doing any effort then? If it is a fact that You are everywhere–You are existing everywhere in non-existent things and existing things–why don't I perceive Your state without any effort? Why should I make effort to perceive You? You are everywhere so You must shine [everywhere to] me. This is a problem in me.

Chapter 10 (40:30)

शिवदासः शिवैकात्मा किं यन्नासादत्येसुखम् ।
तर्प्योऽस्मि देवमुख्यानाम् अपि येनामृतासवैः ॥२५॥

śivadāsaḥ śivaikātmā kiṁ yannāsādayetsukham /
tarpyo'smi devamukhyānām api yenāmṛtāsavaiḥ //25//

I am a slave of Lord Śiva. It is a fact. I am just His slave. I am not only a slave, I am myself Śiva, *śivaikātmā* [laughter]! *Kiṁ yat nā sādayet sukham*, and that person who has become like that, he will enjoy all sorts of enjoyments, all sorts of bliss. So, it is a fact that *deva mukhyānāma*, all these five great lords have to come and devote [themselves] to me.

JOHN: Which five Lords?

SWAMIJI: The five lords of the five great actions: creation, protection, destruction, [concealing, and revealing]. The creating lord is Brahma, the protecting lord is Nārāyaṇa, and the destructing lord is Rūdra, and the concealing lord is Īśvara, and the revealing lord is Sadāśiva.

ALEXIS: *Pañca kāraṇa.*

SWAMIJI: And these five *kāraṇas*, five great lords, *have* to come before me and prostrate before me. They don't know me, who I am.

DENISE: He's becoming bolder, isn't he?

SWAMIJI: [laughing] Yes, in some places.

DENISE: All the time he is becoming stronger and stronger.

ALEXIS: *Amṛtāsavaiḥ.*

SWAMIJI: *Amṛtāsavaiḥ*, by those liquors, which are filled with divine *amṛta*, divine nectar.

JOHN: How does that fit into the verse here?

SWAMIJI: They have to worship me [with divine nectar]! They *have* to worship me! They are bound to worship me!

Chapter 10 (42:21)

हृन्नाभ्योरन्तरालस्थः
प्राणिनां पित्तविग्रहः ।
ग्रससे त्वं महावह्निः
सर्वं स्थावरजङ्गमम् ॥२६॥

hṛnnābhyorantarālasthaḥ
prāṇināṁ pittavigrahaḥ /
grasase tvaṁ mahāvahniḥ
sarvaṁ sthāvarajaṅgamam //26//

O Lord, You have become that fire, which is existing in the center of the belly of each and every being; that fire, which is situated in the center of each and every being, in the belly, in the center of the belly of each and every being, and there You eat whatever is moving and whatever is not moving. You eat everything! Everything goes [in that fire] and is digested by You.

For instance, You have to eat filth. How do you eat filth, You, Lord Śiva? By taking the formation of a dog. You eat nectar, You eat milk, You drink milk, by taking the formation of a baby. You eat meat by taking the formation of tigers, lions, beasts, and those who . . . actually, those who take meat, they are beasts.

Chapter Eleven
Longing for the Nearness of God
Autsukyaviśvasitanāmaikādaśaṁ stotram

Autsukyaviśvasitanāmaikādaśaṁ stotram.

ERNIE: Swamiji, why is it that he said that, "I am in darkness", and then, in the very next verse, he says, "I am Lord Śiva"?

SWAMIJI: [laughter] Because he feels like that. This is the maddened state of spirituality that he had.

ERNIE: One time, he is in complete darkness . . .

SWAMIJI: One time, he is dust; another time, he is the Lord Himself [laughter].

ALEXIS: These verses are produced one by one at different moments of his spiritual experience and then somebody else collected them together.

SWAMIJI: Yes. *Saṁgraha stotra* and *Bhakti stotra* and *Jaya stotra* he has collected himself.

ALEXIS: *Saṁgraha stotra, jaya stotra, bhakti stotrāṇi.*

SWAMIJI: *Bas*, these three. *Saṁgraha stotra* and *Bhakti stotra* . . .

ALEXIS: And *Jaya stotra.*

SWAMIJI: *Jaya stotra,* yes. *Jaya stotra* is fine!

BRUCE P: Swamiji, he asked that since everything that exists and things that don't exist are all Lord Śiva, why does he have to make effort to perceive Him?

SWAMIJI: He asked that. Why should he do any effort at all if it is a real thing?

ERNIE: Bruce is asking the same question.

BRUCE P: What's the answer? He asks but there was no answer.

SWAMIJI: No answer comes. He is just dumb. He does not say anything.

JOHN: Can you tell us the answer, sir?

BRUCE P: What is the answer to that? Why is that?

SWAMIJI: [Because] it is not actually felt like that. As long it is not felt like that, [that perception] does not come. If you actually feel that [Lord Śiva] is always there in non-existent things also, it will shine [as such].

[This *stotra* is nominated as] "*Autsukyaviśvasitanāmaikādaśaṁ stotram*". *Autsukyaviśvasita*. [*Autsukya*] means "desire, longing for nearness of God"; *viśvasita*, and "consolation", e.g., "no, don't worry". *Autsukya*, first longing, then [*viśvasita*], "don't worry". That comes from above. "Don't mind, it will come."

Chapter 11 (02:07)

जगदिदमथ वा सुहृदो
बन्धुजनो वा न भवति मम किमपि ।
त्वं पुनरेतत्सर्वं यदा
तदा कोऽपरो मेऽस्तु ॥१॥

jagadidamatha vā suhṛdo
bandhujano vā na bhavati mama kimapi /
tvaṁ punaretatsarvaṁ yadā
tadā ko'paro me'stu //1//

This whole universe, my kith and kin, my friends, my relatives, I have no one in this world. I have no universe, I have no baby, no Viresh, no John, nothing [belongs] to me. I have no concern with anything, [no] concern with anybody here in this universe.

You are my John, You are my Viresh, You are my everything, You are my master, You are my everything, You are my husband, You are my everything. *Tvaṁ punaretatsarvaṁ*, You are in their place for me. You are in their place.

Yadā tadā ko'paro me astu. Not only at this moment of intense desire for Your nearness; always, for always, You are my everything. You are husband for me, You are my friend, You are my son, You are my everything. I have nothing [other] than You.

Chapter 11 (03:30)

स्वामिन्महेश्वरस्त्वं साक्षात्सर्वं जगत्त्वमेवेति ।
वस्त्वेव सिद्धिमेत्विति याञ्चा तत्रापि याञ्चैव ॥२॥

svāminmaheśvarastvaṁ sākṣātsarvaṁ jagattvameveti /
vastveva siddhimetviti yācñā tatrāpi yācñaiva //2//

O my Master, You are the Lord of lords. It is a fact, You are the Lord of lords. *Sākṣāt sarvaṁ jagattvameveti*, this whole universe is just one with You. Why should I ask for anything from You? Why should I ask for anything? Give me everything! I don't want one thing [laughter]. Give me everything! You are Maheśvara, You are the Lord of lords. Everything will come out [from You]. Why should I ask for some particular thing from You? I will never ask [You for] a particular thing.

JOHN: So, "everything" means being one with that universal consciousness?

SWAMIJI: Yes, yes.

ALEXIS: And a particular thing is, e.g., "please, my son needs a better job".

SWAMIJI: I won't ask for these things.

JOHN: So, when you ask your master to give you your own nature, you are asking him for everything, isn't it?

SWAMIJI: Yes.

Chapter 11 (04:35)

त्रिभुवनाधिपतित्वमपीह यत्-
तृणमिव प्रतिभाति भवज्जुषः ।
किमिव तस्य फलं शुभकर्मणो
भवति नाथ भवत्स्मरणादृते ॥३॥

tribhuvanādhipatitvamapīha yat-
tṛṇamiva pratibhāti bhavajjuṣaḥ /
kimiva tasya phalaṁ śubhakarmaṇo
bhavati nātha bhavatsmaraṇādṛte //3//

Nātha, O Master, this *tribhuvanādhi pati tvam api*, in this world, the kingdom of all the three worlds appears to Thy devotees, to Thy *bhavat juṣaḥ*, adorers.

ALEXIS: Those who adore You.

SWAMIJI: Adorers, worshipers, yes.

ALEXIS: Those who taste You.

SWAMIJI: Those who taste You, yes.

. . . and this kingdom of all the three worlds appears to them just like a neglected, dried grass; a dried blade of grass, one blade of grass. So, *tasya śubhakarmaṇaḥ*, that person who is always conducting that divine action–which divine action?–just to adore You, Thy worship, what [other] enjoyment he will have, he will own, except Thy remembrance (*bhavat smaranādṛte*)?

ALEXIS: There is no other *phalam*, no other reward for him than just to remember You.

SWAMIJI: Just to remember Him, *bas*, he enjoys that only.

Tasya, that devotee who is *śubhakarmi* (*śubhakarmi* means "[one] who does this divine action, the divine action of worshiping You"), what fruit he will own? Only he will own [the fruit of] just remembering You.

Chapter 11 (06:48)

येन नैव भवतोऽस्ति विभिन्नं
किञ्चनापि जगतां प्रभवश्च ।
त्वद्विजृम्भितमतोऽद्भुतकर्मस्व-
प्युदेति न तव स्तुतिबन्धः ॥४॥

yena naiva bhavato'sti vibhinnaṁ
kiñcanāpi jagatāṁ prabhavaśca /
tvadvijṛmbhitamato'dbhutakarmasva-
pyudeti na tava stutibandhaḥ //4//

It is a fact that *bhavataḥ vibhinnaṁ kiñcana na asti*, there is nothing outside Your *svarūpa*, there is nothing existing without Thee. Only You are existing and nothing else in this world. And *jagatāṁ prabhavaśca tvad vijṛmbhitam*, the handlers of this whole universe, those five handlers of this universe–creators, protectors, destroyers, concealers, and revealers (Brahma, Viṣṇu, Rudra, Īśvara, and Sadāśiva)–those great gods, those five handlers of this universe, are also *tvatvijṛmbhitam*, just offshoots of Your divine divinity. [They] are only offshoots, just sparks of Thy divinity.

So, *adbhuta karmasu api tava. Tava adbhuta karmasu*, whatever You do, whatever great thing You are doing–You are conducting any great thing in this universe–for that great thing, there is no space [i.e., reason] for singing Thy glory, i.e., singing the glory of You, that You have done a wonderful thing. Nothing is a wonder to You.

Have you understood?

Nothing is wonderful for You! Everything is very easy for You! Because, this expansion of Yours . . . those sparks of [Your] divinity are found in these five great gods who are handling this whole universe. So, *adbhuta karmasu api*, in Your surprising acts also, we are not supposed to sing glory to You, that You have done such and such [thing], You are doing such and such . . .

ERNIE: Miracles.

SWAMIJI: . . . miracles. It is Your nature to do this. It is not a new thing for You.

I think you have understood.

Chapter 11 (9:20)

त्वन्मयोऽस्मि भवदर्चननिष्ठः
सर्वदाहमिति चाप्यविरामम् ।
भावयन्नपि विभो स्वरसेन
स्वप्नगोऽपि न तथा किमिव स्याम् ॥५॥

tvanmayo'smi bhavadarcananiṣṭhaḥ
sarvadāhamiti cāpyavirāmam /
bhāvayannapi vibho svarasena
svapnogo'pi na tathā kiṁiva syām //5//

O Lord, there is one problem in me. That is, there is [never] such a moment when I don't adore You, when I don't adore You wholeheartedly! *Tvanmayo'smi*, I am always with You! I am always thinking of You. I am always possessing You. Every now and then[160], I am with You and I am worshiping You always. *Iti cāpi avirāmambhavayannapi*, and this I am perceiving in this universe, that I am worshiping You as my Lord, dearest Lord, and that, I perceive that.

O Lord, there is one problem in me still. If I do all of these things, still, why [is it that] when I go to sleep, I see other dreams also? I get merged in that dreaming world and I dream some peculiar things. That should not happen. If I am always [worshiping You] from four o'clock in the morning up to the late hour of twelve o'clock, I am with You, and after twelve [o'clock], I rest a little and dream those dreams, which are not concerned with Your worship . . . this should not happen to me! I must worship You in the dreaming state also. This is my problem.

Chapter 11 (11:20)

ये मनागपि भवच्चरणाब्जोद्-
भूतसौरभलवेन विमृष्टाः ।
तेषु विस्रमिव भाति समस्तं
भोगजातममरैरपि मृग्यम् ॥ ६ ॥

ye[161] *manāgapi bhavaccaraṇābjod-*
bhūtasaurabhalavena vimṛṣṭāḥ /
teṣu visramiva bhāti samastaṁ
bhogajātamamarairapi mṛgyam //6//

Those people who are touched by *bhavat caraṇābja udbhūta saurabhalavena*, who have got contact with the fragrance, with just a small particle of the fragrance, which has come out from the lotus feet of Thee, from Your lotus feet–that fragrance, that pollen, which has come out from Thy lotus feet–and with that

160 Here, Swamiji uses "every now and then" in a completely literal sense to mean "all of the time". [*Editor's note*]

161 Swamiji corrected "*yena*" as it mistakenly appears in his Hindi/Sanskrit publication to read "*ye*". [*Editor's note*]

pollen, by that pollen, those who are *manāgapi*, just slightly *vimṛṣṭaḥ*, touched (*vimṛṣṭaḥ* means "just touched"), and in those people, *teṣu visramiva bhāti samastaṁ bhogajātam*, all that enjoyment found in *amaraiḥ,* found by the gods in heaven, that enjoyment, all that enjoyment, the world of enjoyment appears to them as *visram* (*visram* means "[having] a foul smell"). They just think of that enjoyment and put this [Swamiji covers his nose]. They can't look at it.

Who?

Those who have got the *slightest* touch of that particle of that pollen of Your lotus feet. But, they think the other enjoyments are tasteless.

Chapter 11 (13:24)

हृदि ते न तु विद्यतेऽन्यदन्यद्-
वचने कर्मणि चान्यदेव शंभो ।
परमार्थसतोऽप्यनुग्रहो वा
यदि वा निग्रह एक एव कार्यः ॥७॥

hṛdi[162] *te na tu vidyate'nyadanyad-*
vacane karmaṇi cānyadeva śaṁbho /
paramārthasato'pyanugraho vā
yadi vā nigraha eka eva kāryaḥ //7//

You see, I am a simple man, I have no fraud in me. You know that. You must also possess that state. But, You seem to be a fraud sometimes! Because, *hṛdi te na tu vidyate*, it is not a fraud[ulent] action when whatever [you] do is also existing in your mind; *hṛdi te*, the same thing must exist in your speech, in your word. Whatever is existing in your mind, the same thing must exist in your word and the same thing must exist in your action. But, I feel that in Your mind, You have some [idea] of doing something [else] in connection with Your devotees. You say, outwardly You say, "I will do it" but internally You think, "I won't do it".

162 Swamiji corrected "*hṛti*" to read "*hṛdi*". [*Editor's note*]

Just as I did with Mother Alice [when I told her], "I will come to America". But, this is not the real way of being straightforward. This is a fraud.

Vacane, and in action You'll do something else. It should not happen that You will fix up . . . that Your resolution in Your mind will be something else, in speech something else, in action something else. It should not happen. *Paramārtha sato*, I am a simple man. Lord, I am a simple man. You must also act like that. *Anugraho vā*, if You have not to uplift me, if You have not to elevate me, then kick me down, but once and for all! *Anugraho vā nigrahaḥ*, if You elevate me, well and good, but say that in Your mind, say that in Your speech, and do that in [Your] action. Don't do these contradict[ions].

JOHN: Don't tease me.

SWAMIJI: Don't tease me. Tell me frankly that, "I won't do it. I will kick you out". That is all. That is all. I will sit in some corner and repent for my whole life [afterwards]. But You are telling me that, "I will do it, I will do it tomorrow, I will do it the day after tomorrow", but internally You [don't want] to do it at all. Internally You are going . . .

ALEXIS: Another course.

SWAMIJI: Yes.

Yadi vā nigraḥ eka eva, do one thing, do one thing: *anugraḥ* or *nigraḥ*, elevate me or destroy me!

Chapter 11 (16:49)

मूढोऽस्मि दुःखकलितोऽस्मि जरादिदोष-
भीतोऽस्मि शक्तिरहितोऽस्मि तवाश्रितोऽस्मि ।
शंभो तथा कलय शीघ्रमुपैमि येन
सर्वोत्तमां धुरमपोज्झितदुःखमार्गः ॥८॥

mūḍho'smi duḥkhakalito'smi jarādidoṣa-
bhīto'smi śaktirahito'smi tavāśrito'smi /
śaṁbho tathā kalaya śīghramupaimi yena
sarvottamāṁ dhuramapojjhitaduḥkhamargaḥ //8

O Lord, I am dull-headed. Actually, I am dull-headed. I don't know how to talk with You (*mūḍho'smi*). You see, I am *duḥkha kalito'smi*, I am overwhelmed with sadness. I am always sad. I am dull-headed. It is a fact that I am dull-headed and I am sad.

Jarādidoṣa bhīto'smi, I am afraid of the pains of this universe and this old age and death. I am afraid of these three things (troubles): diseases, old age, and death. I am afraid of these three things.

Śakti rahita, I am . . . nothing is in my power. Nothing is in . . . I can't do anything. I can't do any remedy for all of these things. I am dull and this dullness won't go even if I do some effort. I am overwhelmed with sadnesses, sorrows, torture, but I can't get out of that torture. *Jārādi doṣaḥ*, I am afraid of these three things.

What three things?

Old age, diseases, and death.

Śakti rahito'smi, I have no power; it is not . . . nothing is in my power. *Tavāśrita*, I have taken Your support; I have taken Your support. I have to! *Śambho tathā kalaya*, so, do that way, so act that way, *tathā kalaya* (*tathā kalaya* [means] "do that way, act that way"), *śīghramupaimi yena*, by which way I would achieve rapidly (*śīghram*, instantaneously), I would achieve *sarvottamāṁ paraṁ*, the highest and the greatest state of being, *apojjhita duḥkha mārgaḥ*, which is deprived [i.e., free] from all tortures, where there is no torture at all. Do that!

Chapter 11 (19:41)

त्वत्कर्णदेशमधिशय्य महार्घभावम्-
आक्रन्दितानि मम तुच्छतराणि यान्ति ।
वंशान्तरालपतितानि जलैकदेश-
खण्डानि मौक्तिकमणित्वमिवोद्वहन्ति ॥९॥

tvatkarṇadeśamadhiśayya mahārghabhāvam-
ākranditāni mama tucchatarāṇi yānti /
vaṁśāntarālapatitāni jalaikadeśa-
khaṇḍāni mauktikamaṇitvamivodvahanti //9//

O Lord, just as *vaṁśāntarāla patitajalaikadesa khaṇḍāni*,

when there is a soft rain and those drops of rain fall into the hollow of that bamboo, the bamboo hollows (i.e., the bamboos [which] are burnt by *dāvānala*), . . .

ALEXIS: By forest fire.

SWAMIJI: Forest fire. And there are some *ḍaṇṭhalas* left of bamboos.

ALEXIS: Stumps.

SWAMIJI: Stumps.

. . . and in those hollows, those drops of rain fall, and after some particular period [of time], they are converted [into] jewels, they become pearls.

Vaṁśāntaralapatitāni jalaikadeśa khaṇḍāni, but this water [in and of itself] has no fun in it, there is no cost of it. They are . . . there is no [innate] value to it. But [those drops of water] become valuable when they fall into the hollow space of [the burnt] bamboo trees and they become . . . they take the formation of pearls.

In the same way, my crying, my torture–and I am always crying, weeping for Your nearness–and this weeping, it is useless weeping. My crying is useless [because] *tucchatarāṇi*, it has no value. My weeping for You, for Your nearness, to get [Your] nearness, has no value. But this cry, when this cry, this sound, reaches in the hollow of Your ears, in the hollow part of Your ears, *mahārghabhāvaṁ yānti*, *mahārgabhāvam*, they become valuable, they become precious. *Mauktika maṇitvamiva*, just as those drops of water in those bamboos become pearls and jewels, in the same way, my useless crying becomes valuable and it bears the fruit of *mukta*, *muktātmā* (*muktātmā* means "I get liberated").

Chapter 11 (22:50)

किमिव च लभ्यते बत न तैरपि नाथ जनैः
क्षणमपि कैतवादपि च ये तव नाम्नि रताः ।
शिशिरमयूखशेखर तथा कुरु येन मम
क्षतमरणोऽणिमादिकमुपैमि यथा विभवम् ॥१०॥

kimiva ca labhyate bata na tairapi nātha janaiḥ
kṣaṇamapi kaitavādapi ca ye tava nāmni ratāḥ /
śiśiramayūkhaśekhara tathā kuru yena mama
kṣatamaraṇo'ṇimādikamupaimi yathā vibhavam //10//

Nātha, O Lord, *kimiva ca labhyate vata na tairapi nātha janaiḥ*, those people, can't they achieve [anything]? They can achieve everything! Those people can achieve everything! Whatever is possible and whatever is impossible, they will achieve that. Who? *Kṣaṇamapi kaitavādi api ca ye tava*, those who have diverted their minds in Your remembrance, not with devotion, but with deceit, just to please You.

ALEXIS: Fraud.

SWAMIJI: Fraud. Fraudulently they are reciting Your name. Those people who are fraudulently reciting Your name, those people also achieve a great thing, the greatest thing, i.e., those who play fraud with You also.

DENISE: Why would they do that? They would recite God's name for what reason?

SWAMIJI: Yes, for the sake of making money. That is not from the core of his heart. He does not recite the name of God from the core of his heart. If he would have recited the name of [God from] the core of his heart, he would have entered in God consciousness.

But Your name is so great that, for him also, he also achieves everything. *Kimiva na labhayate vata na tairapi nātha janaiḥ.* Those people also achieve those tremendous and valuable things.

Who?

Kṣaṇamapi, only for one moment, *kaitavāt api*, even out of fraud, *ye tava nāmni ratāḥ*, those people who are given to Your name, who are remembering You [by reciting], "*oṁ gluṁ gaṁ gaṇapataye namaḥ, gaṁ gaṇapataye namaḥ, . . .*"

What is there in it? Actually, what is there in it?

This was called Ṛṣibher. Kashmir was, from ancient times, called Ṛṣibher, the place of *ṛṣis* (seers) and saints.

GANJOO: Garden of *ṛṣis.*

SWAMIJI: Orchard of *ṛṣis*. And [among] those *ṛṣis*, one saint was sitting at one place and another saint came to see him. He said, "*oṁ namaḥ śivāya*". He sighed and said, "*oṁ namaḥ śivāya*". What was there in it? There was nothing in that. He just recited "*oṁ namaḥ śivāya*" just purely, not out of deceit.

ALEXIS: Because he was sitting down and sighing.

SWAMIJI: Yes, sighing, "*oṁ namaḥ śivāya*". [The other saint] said, "couldn't you digest this "*oṁ namah śivāya*" within [yourself]? You have not the capacity to digest it. Why do you recite it outwardly? Digest it within [yourself]. Don't throw it outside".

DENISE: But don't they also gain fruit by reciting that?

SWAMIJI: They also, they also gain [fruit because] this is so great, i.e., His name.[163]

ALEXIS: But people say "*oṁ namaḥ śivāya*" every time they sit down and groan or anything.

SWAMIJI: But that is not the right way! You must say "*oṁ namaḥ śivāya*" only when you are sitting in one corner, a secluded corner, in your own room. You must not say "*oṁ namaḥ śivāya*" in public. But if you say in public also, "*oṁ namaḥ śivāya*," this will also bear fruit.

DENISE: Then it doesn't matter?

SWAMIJI: No, this [outward recitation] won't get that [highest] reward.

DENISE: *Acha* (okay), but some.

SWAMIJI: Some.

ERNIE: It still gets reward, but not the same.

SWAMIJI: Yes.

Chapter 11 (27:13)

शिशिरमयूखशेखर तथा कुरु येन मम ।
क्षतमरणोऽणिमादिकमुपैमि यथा विभवम् ॥ १० ॥

śiśiramayūkhaśekhara tathā kuru yena mama /
kṣatamaraṇo'ṇimādikamupaimi yathā vibhavam //10//
[repeated, not recited in full]

Śiśiramayūkhaśekhara. You have got . . . Your forehead is beautified with that crescent moon. *Tāthā kuru*, so do something for me. Do that thing for me [whereby] *yena kṣatamaraṇa*, I will get relieved from old age, diseases, and death. I would get re-

163 See appendix 19 for a discussion on the efficacy of *mantra*.

lieved from old age, diseases, and death, and *aṇimādikamupaimi yathā vibhavam*, and those internal eight *yogic* powers I would achieve.[164]

Chapter 11 (28:00)

शम्भो शर्व शशाङ्कशेखर शिव त्र्यक्षाक्षमालाधर
श्रीमन्नुग्र कपाल लाञ्छन लसद्भीमत्रिशूलायुध ।
कारुण्याम्बुनिधे त्रिलोकरचनाशीलोग्रशक्त्यात्मक
श्रीकण्ठाशु विनाशयाशुभभरानाधत्स्व सिद्धिं पराम् ॥११॥

śambho śarva śaśāṅkaśekhara śiva tryakṣākṣamālādhara
śrīmannugrakapālalāñchana lasadbhīmatriśūlāyudha /
kāruṇyāmbunidhe trilokaracanāśīlograśaktyātmaka
śrīkaṇṭhāśu vināśayāśubhabharānādhatsva siddhiṁ parām //11

O Lord Śiva! O destroyer of the whole universe! *Śaśāṅkaśekhara*, O holder of the crescent moon on Your forehead! O Śiva! O Śiva! *Tryakṣa*, O holder of three eyes! *Akṣamālā dharaḥ*, O holder of these beads (*japa malā*)! *Śrīman*, O holder of the wealth of liberation! *Ugra kapāla lāñchana*, O holder of the terrifying *kapāla* (skull)!

Skull, you know whose skull?

ALEXIS: Brahma.

SWAMIJI: Brahma.

ALEXIS: Filled with Viṣṇu's blood.

SWAMIJI: Yes.

Lasadbhīmatriśūlāyudha, and the terrifying *triśūla*, [He] who has this weapon in His hand! *Kāruṇyāmbunidhe*, who is the ocean of compassion, the ocean of *dayā*! Compassion. *Triloka racanā śīla*, and who has got terrifying energies. You also hold [terrifying energies].

JOHN: He has the capacity of holding all of the three worlds?

SWAMIJI: Yes . . . no, arranging the three worlds.

164 See appendix 18 for an explanation of the *yogic* powers.

ALEXIS: *Prameya*, *pramāṇa*, and *pramātṛ*.[165]

SWAMIJI: *Pramātṛ* also.

Śrīkaṇṭha, *O Śrikaṇṭhanātha* (this is all calling[166]), *āśu vināśaya aśubha bharān*, please destroy all of my tortures (*aśubha bharān*, the burden of tortures, the burden of crisis) existing in me. Please destroy the burden of crisis existing in me, *ādhatsva siddhiṁ parām*, and please bestow Your divine divinity of God consciousness to me.

ALEXIS: The ultimate *siddhi, siddhiṁ parām.*

SWAMIJI: Yes, *parām* (supreme).

JOHN: The divinity of God consciousness. What's he doing with Brahma's head?

SWAMIJI: Just terrifying others. He has got such and such power. *Hariṁ śūlaḥ protaḥ*, and [with the] *triśula*, He has *protam* (impaled) Nārāyaṇa, and got it.[167] He is just like a mad, mad boy, i.e., Lord Śiva.

DENISE: Is He really?

SWAMIJI: Yes, He doesn't care for anything.

ALEXIS: *Unnata Bhairava*!

SWAMIJI: *Unnata Bhairava* [laughter][168]. But He is so compassionate, so loving, so beautiful–shining!

Chapter 11 (31:20)

तत्किं नाथ भवेन्न यत्र भगवन्निर्मातृतामश्नुते
भावः स्यात्किमु तस्य चेतनवतो नाशास्ति यं शंकरः ।
इत्थं ते परमेश्वराक्षतमाहाशक्तेः सदा संश्रितः
संसारेऽत्र निरन्तराधिविधुरः क्लिश्याम्यहं केवलम् ॥ १२ ॥

tatkiṁ nātha bhavenna yatra bhagavannirmātṛtāmaśnute
bhāvaḥ syātkimu tasya cetanavato nāśāsti yaṁ śaṅkaraḥ /

---

165 *Pramātṛ bhāva* (subjective state), *pramāṇa bhāva* (cognitive state), and *prameya bhāva* (objective state). [*Editor's note*]

166 Śrikaṇṭhanātha is a form of Lord Shiva. [*Editors's note*]

167 The skull of Brahmā is described as being filled with Nārāyaṇa's (Viṣṇu's) blood. [*Editors' note*]

168 *Unnata* figuratively means "high, elevated, eminent, sublime, great, noble". [*Editor's note*].

itthaṁ te parameśvarākṣatamāhāśakteḥ sadā saṁśritaḥ
saṁsāre'tra nirantarādhividhuraḥ kliśyāmyahaṁ kevalam //12
[incomplete recording]

Nātha, O Lord, *tat kiṁ bhavet*, *yatra bhagavān nirmātṛtām na aśnute*, what is that object where Lord Śiva (or You, Thou) art not the creator? You create everything. Whatever is existing in this universe, You are its creator. And *bhāvaḥ syāt kimu tasya cetanavato nāśāsti yaṁ śaṅkaraḥ*, and what is that object, which is not governed and ruled out by You, Śaṅkara?

Itthaṁ te parameśvara akṣata mahā śakteḥ sadā saṁśritaḥ. In this way, I have taken refuge in Thee who possesses all power, and unending all-power, eternal all-power, and I have taken refuge in Thee.

Still, it is shameful for You, not for me, that in this world, I am overwhelmed with . . . overwhelmed and scattered and tortured with *ādhi* (*ādhi* means those mental diseases). I am tortured by mental diseases in continuity. This is my state. This is the fruit of my taking refuge in Thee and *kliśyāmi aham*, and I become only the object of pain and sorrow. I don't experience any joy in this world. This is the fruit of my surrendering everything to You and taking refuge in You.

And You are the greatest! You have got the highest power. Your power is never ending and whatever object exists in this world, You are its creator, and whatever object is existing in this world, You are ruling [over] it, i.e., You are governing that object. So, You are governing this whole universe and You have got that supreme unending power, and I have taken refuge in Thee, and the fruit of that I have got, and that is, I am tortured with unending pain and sorrow. This is Your greatness.

Chapter 11 (34:39)

यद्यप्यत्र वरप्रदोद्धततमाः पीडाजरामृत्यवः
एते वा क्षणमासतां बहुमतः शब्दादिरेवास्थिरः ।
तत्रापि स्पृहयामि सन्ततसुखाकाङ्क्षी चिरं स्थास्नवे
भोगास्वादयुतत्वदङ्घ्रिकमलध्यानाग्र्यजीवातवे ॥१३॥

yadyapyatra varapradoddhatatamāḥ pīḍājarāmṛtyavaḥ
ete vā kṣaṇamāsatāṁ bahumataḥ śabdādirevāsthiraḥ /
tatrāpi spṛhayāmi santatasukhākāṅkṣī ciraṁ sthāsnave
bhogāsvādayutatvadaṅghrikamaladhyānāgryajīvātave / / 13

Varaprada, O bestower of boons ("*varaprada*" is *āmantraṇam*[169]), O bestower of boons, O Lord Śiva, although in this universe, *pīḍā* (crisis, pain, unending pain), *jarā* (old age), and *mṛtyava* (death) are supposed to be *uddhatatamāḥ*, frightening (*uddhata tamāḥ*, very, extremely, frightening, unbearable)–sadness, old age, and death–*ete vā kṣaṇamāsatām*, let [us not] touch upon this topic. Let these three things remain aside, on one side.

Bahumataḥ śabdādireva asthiraḥ. Now, there was some side of pleasure also in this universe. That is, hearing (*śabda*), *sparśa* (touching), *rūpa* (perceiving form, beautiful forms), *rasa* (tasting, e.g., cheese or *pulau*), all of these [sensations]. *Śabdādireva*, and this by which we get pleasure, and that, too, is *asthiraḥ* (not stable). That, too, is going and vanishing.

Tatrāpi, so, in this position, *spṛhayāmi santata sukhākāṅkṣī*; *santata sukhākāṅkṣī*, in fact, I am that person who needs that pleasure, which will remain, which will be established, for always, for eternity. I want *that* joy! So, I ask for that joy (*ciraṁ sthāsnave*).

And what is that joy?

Ciraṁ sthāsnave, that [joy that] will remain for eternity. *Bhogāsvādayuta tvad aṅghri kamala dhyānāgryajīvātave*, and that joy will come only by maintaining, by possessing, *āgrya jīvātave*, a delightful life consisting of enjoying the nectar of Your worship. I would like that kind of life, in which life I would only worship You always and enjoy that worshiping action throughout my whole life. This is what I need in this universe because this *pīḍā* (*pīḍā* means "pain, old age, and death") is fearful. So, there is no question of [desiring] that. And worldly enjoyments, they also do not remain; they are *asthiraḥ* (unstable). So, I want this.[170]

---

169 The vocative case. [*Editor's note*]

170 That is, a delightful life consisting of enjoying the nectar of Your worship. [*Editor's note*]

Chapter 11 (38:44)

हे नाथ प्रणतार्तिनाशनपटो
श्रेयोनिधे धूर्जटे
दुःखैकायतनस्य जन्ममरणत्रस्-
तस्य मे साम्प्रतम् ।
तच्चेष्टस्व यथा मनोज्ञविषया-
स्वादप्रदा उत्तमाः
जीवन्नेव समश्नुवेऽहमचलाः
सिद्धीस्त्वदर्चापरः ॥ १४ ॥

he nātha praṇatārtināśanapaṭo
śreyonidhe dhūrjaṭe
duḥkhaikāyatanasya janmamaraṇatras-
tasya me sāmpratam /
taccesṭasva yathā manojñaviṣayā-
svādapradā uttamāḥ
jīvanneva samaśnuve'hamacalāḥ
siddhīstvadarcāparaḥ //14//

He nātha, O my Master, *praṇatārtināśanapaṭah*, O my Lord who is bent upon removing and destroying the torture of those who have taken Your refuge–[for those] who have taken Your refuge, You are bent upon destroying their pain, torture–*śrey-onidhe*, O ocean of peace (*kalyāṇa,*[171] beatitude; *śreyaḥ* means "beatitude"; beatitude is final liberation), *dhūrjaṭe*, O *jaṭā juta*, *dhūrjaṭe*, who has got (*dhūrjaṭe* means those [matted locks that] you find in *sādhus*[172]) . . .

DENISE: Matted.

ALEXIS: They comb it and put some . . .

JOHN: What do they put in it?

ALEXIS: . . . soil.

---

171 Literally *kalyāṇa* means 'good fortune, happiness, prosperity'. [*Editor's note*]

172 A holy man, saint, sage, or seer.

SWAMIJI: Yes, without combing . . .

ALEXIS: Actually, it takes them many years to get it, with soil and things.

DENISE: They never wash it?

SWAMIJI: They never wash it, no. They wash it, *bas*!

DENISE: They never comb it.

SWAMIJI: No. Because, this is the way of Lord Śiva's make-up and He puts those ashes on it and rubs it in as powder.

DENISE: And it's nice.

SWAMIJI: Yes.

. . . *duḥkhaikāyatanasya,* O such Lord, *duḥkhaikāyatanasya*, I have become only the victim of pain, sorrow, sadness, and torture. *Janma maraṇa trastasya me*, I am afraid of birth and death; I am afraid of repeated births and deaths. So, for me, *sāmpratam*, at present, *tat ceṣṭāsva*, You should do this thing: *yathā*, You should act in such a way, *yathā*, by which way, *manojñāviṣayāsvādapradā uttamāḥ siddhi tvadarcāparaḥ siddhīḥ jīvanneva aham samaśnuve*, so that, in this very life, I would get those powers, those great powers.

What are those powers?

Manojña viṣayāsvāda pradā, they give you the taste of what you have been longing for. They give you that taste of what you have been longing for, those tasteful powers. And those tasteful powers are *acalāḥ* (permanent), permanent tasteful powers, and those tasteful powers are just to worship, just to worship You, and those powers, I should achieve *jīvanneva,* in this very life, in my lifetime, not after my death!

Chapter 11 (42:29)

नमो मोहमहाध्वान्तध्वंसनानन्य कर्मणे ।
सर्वप्रकाशातिशयप्रकाशायेन्दुलक्ष्मणे ॥१५॥

namo mohamahādhvāntadhvaṁsanānanya karmaṇe /
sarvaprakāśātiśayaprakāśāyendulakṣmaṇe / / 15 / /

I bow to Thee who has only this much to do.

What You are going to do?

You have only one work. That is, *moha mahādhvānta dhvaṁ-*

sanānanya karmaṇe–moha means "illusion, forgetfulness" of your being, your existence; that is *mahādhvāntaḥ*, great darkness, dense darkness–and You are bent upon removing that dense darkness. You have only this much to do. This thing, it is Your only work. I bow to Thee.

Sarvaprakāśa atiśaya prakāśāya, and who is more delightful and possessing more radiant light than all of the other lights–the light of fire, the light of the moon, the light of the sun; more than that light, which is effulgent light–more than these three lights, and *indu lakṣmaṇe*, and who has this mark of the crescent moon on His forehead, I bow to Thee.

ALEXIS: Sir, you have written this Hindi note on this crescent moon. What does it say?

SWAMIJI:

> *'indu lakṣmane' – yaha mahādeva kā nāma atyanta sārthaka hai / isase sūcita hotā hai ki bhagavān śaṁkara prakāśa phailā kara andhakāra ko dūra karane kī pūrī kṣamatā rakhate hai /*[173]

He is the only bestower of light to everybody because He has got the crescent moon that's shining on His forehead.

173 "The name of "Mahādeva" is highly advantageous, meaningful. It reveals that Lord Śaṅkara is completely capable of destroying the darkness/ignorance of this universe by revealing his supreme energy or *prakāśa*." *Śivastotrāvalī* of Utpaladevācaryā, with the Sanskrit commentary of Kṣemarāja, edited with Hindi commentary by Rājānaka Lakṣmaṇa (Swami Lakshmanjoo) (Chowkhamba Sanskrit Series 15, Varanasi, 1964), ref. 11.15.164.

Chapter Twelve
Revealing the Secret
Rahasyanirdeśanāma dvādaśaṁ stotram

Rahasyanirdeśanāma dvādaśaṁ stotram, the twelfth *stotra*. *Rahasyanirdeśa* [means] the revealing of a secret.

Chapter 12 (00:15)

सहकारि न किञ्चिदिष्यते
भवतो न प्रतिबन्धकं दृशि ।
भवतैव हि सर्वमाप्लुतं
कथमद्यापि तथापि नेक्षसे ॥ १ ॥

sahakāri na kiñcidiṣyate
bhavato na pratibandhakaṁ dṛśi /
bhavataiva hi sarvamāplutaṁ
kathamadyāpi tathāpi nekṣase //1//

Bhavato dṛśi, for finding You, my Lord, for finding You out, for experiencing Your nature, *sahakāri na kiñcit iṣyate*, there is nothing to be adopted. For perceiving You, there is nothing to be adopted. You are perceived just, i.e., just without any adoption, just without meditation, just without prayers, just without concentration, just without *dhyāna*, just without maintaining discipline. There is nothing needed in perceiving You.

Actually, in Shaivism, this is the fact that when God is perceived, [He] is perceived, not with the adoption of means.

What are means?

ALEXIS: *Upāya*.

SWAMIJI: *Upāyas*.

Upāyas are just living on that disciplined life, e.g., *brahma-*

carya, *satya*, *asteya*[174], all of these things are to be adopted, then God is revealed. But these are not . . . God is revealed without the adoption of these things. When God is revealed, [He] is revealed. This is the secret.

JOHN: There is no cause and effect relationship . . .

SWAMIJI: No [affirmative].

JOHN: . . . between what you do and God's being revealed.

SWAMIJI: It is not realized with effort. When you do some effort for realizing It, you remain far away from His nature. When you abandon all of your efforts, you remain far away from His nature. God is revealed just when He so likes. It is not in your hands.

ALEXIS: *Śaktipāta.*

SWAMIJI: *Śaktipāta* (grace).

So, *bhavato dṛṣi*, for realizing Thee, *sahakāri na kiñcit iṣyate*, nothing is needed, neither meditation, nor anything, nor discipline, nor *satya*, nor *brahmacarya*, nor *gṛhasthya*[175], nor *asteya*. All of these things are useless there.

DENISE: Then why do anything if it won't help?

SWAMIJI: It is just . . .

DENISE: To keep you busy.

SWAMIJI: . . . to keep you busy.

There is nothing to do. It is not that if you make yourself busy, you are busy with these things, that you are sure to get the realization of God. It may not come at all. It comes when It comes, by Itself.

Bhavato dṛśi sahakāri na kiñcit iṣyate. For realizing You, there is nothing to be adopted, *na pratibandhakaṁ*, and there is no obstruction also for realizing You. You are free to be realized! The path is clear for Your realization. So, there is nothing in-between to stop you from realizing your nature.

Because, *bhavatā eva he sarvamāplutam*, You have pervaded the whole world. You have pervaded the world of *upāyas* and You have pervaded the world of obstacles. Obstacles are also shining because of You because You are shining in obstacles and *upāyas* are also shining because of You because You are shining there.

174 Chastity, truthfulness, and not stealing, respectively. See also appendix 2 for an explanation of the *upāyas*. [*Editor's note*]

175 The householder stage (*gṛhasthya*) is the second stage of an ideal life according to the *Ashrama* system. [*Editor's note*]

ALEXIS: *Aplutam*? Flooded?
SWAMIJI: Flooded.
ALEXIS: The universe is flooded with You.
SWAMIJI: Yes.

Katham, but the problem is, still then, I am kept away from Your realization. This is the problem. There is no problem existing in a real sense because the path is quite clear, but still I don't realize You.

Chapter 12 (04:56)

अपि भावगणादपीन्द्रिय -
प्रचयादप्यवबोधमध्यतः ।
प्रभवन्तमपि स्वतः सदा
परिपश्येयमपोढविश्वकम् ॥२॥

api bhāvagaṇādapīndriya-
pracayādapyavabodhamadhyataḥ /
prabhavantamapi svataḥ sadā
paripaśyeyamapoḍhaviśvakam //2//

O Lord, *bhāvagaṇāt api*, from the objective world, *indriya pracayāt api*, from the collection of the organic world[176], *avabodha madhyataḥ*, and from the center of the cognitive world, *prabhavantamapi svataḥ sadā*, I would like to feel You automatically, always.

And I would like to see You, perceive You, *apoḍhaviśvakam*, where all duality has vanished (*apoḍhaviśvakam*; *viśvakam* means duality), [where] dualistic realization is vanished. I would like to see You that way.

Not in *samādhi* only, *abhāvagaṇāt*; but from the objective world I would like to see You, *indriya pracayāt*, from the organic world I would like to see You, and I would like to see You from the center of cognition also[177]; and automatically, without doing anything. And I would like to see You where all duality has vanished.

---

176 The various sense organs. [*Editor's note*]
177 *Avabodha madhyataḥ*.

ALEXIS: So, he wants to see Him in *rūpātītā*[178] state everywhere.

SWAMIJI: Yes, everywhere.

Chapter 12 (06:31)

कथं ते जायेरन्कथमपि च ते दर्शनपथं
व्रजेयुः केनापि प्रकृतिमहताङ्केन खचिताः ।
तथोत्थायोत्थाय स्थलजलतृणादेरखलितः
पदार्थाद्यान्सृष्टिस्रवदमृतपूरैर्विकिरसि ॥ ३ ॥

katham te jāyerankathamapi ca te darśanapatham
vrajeyuḥ kenāpi prakṛtimahatāṅkena khacitāḥ /
tathotthāyotthāya sthalajalatṛṇāderakhilataḥ
padārthādyānsṛṣṭisravadamṛtapūrairvikirasi //3//

O Lord, how can those fortunate persons again be born in this universe? And how can those fortunate persons be understood by worldly people? Worldly people can never understand them. Beyond understanding, they are beyond understanding to worldly people. Worldly people cannot understand that they are so high, they are so highly elevated. And how can they come again in this birth?

Kenāpi prakṛti mahatāṅkena khacitāḥ. And they have got that unique sign, unique and greatest sign of greatness.[179]

How can they be born in this universe again and how can they be understood by ordinary people?

Who?

tathotthāyotthāya sthalajalatṛṇāderakhilataḥ
padārthādyānsṛṣṭisravadamṛtapūrairvikirasi //3//
[repeated]

To those people whom You do one thing–what?–*tathā utthāya utthāya sthala jala tṛṇāderakhilataḥ padārthā*, You elevate them

178 See appendix 3 for an explanation of *rūpātītā*, viz., *turya*.

179 The "sign" will be described in verse 5. [*Editor's note*]

from the objective world, from all of these worldly pleasures. You elevate them. Those whom You elevate and take out from this mud, that sticky mud of these worldly pleasures–You take out those people–and *sṛṣti sravad amṛta pūrairvikirasi*, and those flows of super-sexual joy or that God consciousness, that *rasa* of God consciousness, You sprinkle on them afterwards, [after] getting [them] out from this lower field of the universal field. when You get those people out. *Yān tathā utthāya utthāya*, *yān*, those people, whom You *utthāya utthāya*, always take out from all of these sticky situations of the worldly state, *utthāya utthāya*, because You elevate them as You elevate Your own nature. You elevate them and elevate, at the same time, Your own nature. You consider this whole universe to be one body of Yours. So, when You elevate them, You elevate Yourself.

So, *utthāya* means *utthāpya* also.[180]

But *tathā*–how [do] You elevate them?–*tathā*, not by their activity, not by their meditating effort, *tathā*, by *nirapekṣa śaktipāta*, by adopting *śaktipāta*, just by Your will. Just by Your independent will, You take them out from all of this objective world and then sprinkle or soak them in Your nectar of God consciousness.

How can they, those [fortunate] people, be born again in this world? How can those people be understood by ordinary people? They are divine. They become divine.

Chapter 12 (11:11)

साक्षात्कृतभवद्रूपप्रसृतामृततर्पिताः ।
उन्मूलिततृषो मत्ताः विचरन्ति यथारुचि ॥४॥

sākṣātkṛtabhavadrūpaprasṛtāmṛtatarpitāḥ /
unmūlitatṛṣo mattāḥ vicaranti yathāruci //4//

In this world, I have found that there are some mad people who enjoy roaming here and there in this world according to their choice–with their choice, with their own independent will, they roam here and there–and *unmūlitatṛśā*, and they have no

180 "Having risen" (*utthāya*) means "to be raised" (*utthāpya*). [*Editor's note*]

thirst for anything, they have no thirst for any object, be it *śabda* (sound), *sparśa* (touch), *rūpa* (form), *rasa* (taste), or *gan-dha* (smell). Without thirst, they enjoy in this universe just like mad people.

Those people are *sākṣātkṛta bhavat rūpa prasṛta amṛta tarpitāḥ*, because they have drunk the nectar, which has flown out by experiencing Your nature–they have drunk that nectar–and by that nectar, by drinking that nectar, they have become satisfied, full.

And so they roam in this world without any object, without any [desires]. They have nothing to do in this world. They just roam.

Chapter 12 (12:41)

न तदा न सदा न चैकदे -
त्यपि सा यत्र न कालधीर्भवेत् ।
तदिदं भवदीयदर्शनं
न च नित्यं न च कथ्यतेऽन्यथा ॥५॥

na tadā na sadā na caikade-
tyapi sā yatra na kāladhīrbhavet /
tadidaṁ bhavadīyadarśanaṁ
na ca nityaṁ na ca kathyate'nyathā //5//

In the real sense, this is the only sign of experiencing Your nature (*tat idaṁ bhavadīya darśanam*).

What?

Yatra, in which nature, in which experience, where there is no [sense of] that time, where there is no [sense of] this time, where there is no simultaneous time, where there is no past time, where there is no present time, where there is no future time, where there is no eternity, where there is no absence of eternity.

So, that really is Your realizing state. *Na ca nityaṁ*, It is not *nityā*, It is not eternal, *na ca kathyate anyathā*, and It is not the absence of eternality. It is always shining. You can't say "always" also.[181]

181 See appendix 20 for explanation of "eternal and not eternal".

Chapter 12 (13:58)

त्वद्विलोकनसमुत्कचेतसो
 योगसिद्धिरिइयती सदास्तु मे ।
यद्विशेयमभिसन्धिमात्रतस्-
 त्वत्सुधासदनमर्चनाय ते ॥६॥

tvadvilokanasamutkacetaso
yogasiddhiriyatī sadāstu me /
yadviśeyamabhisandhimātratas-
tvatsudhāsadanamarcanāya te //6//

O Lord, I want only one *yogic* power. I want to own one *yogic* power and for always. This power I must own for always. Only this much. Only one small thing, which I want to own and that is *yoga siddhi*, only one *yoga siddhi*.

And I am fit for that *yoga siddhi*. I must have that because *tvad vilokana samutkacetasaḥ*, I have only [one] desire in my mind: just to see You. This desire always knocks in the background of my mind.

Which desire?

DENISE: Just to see You.

SWAMIJI: Just to see You.

Bas, this is always the desire knocking in the background of my consciousness. And there is *samutkacetasā*, my mind is trembling, my mind is restless for that. My mind is always restless. My mind wants to see You.

So, I want only one *yoga siddhi*. I don't want those eight great *yogic* powers. I want only one *yoga siddhi*, and that is *yat viśeyaṁ*, I must get entry *yat viśeyaṁ abhisandhimātrataḥ*–not by effort; I must get entry, not by effort, not by adopting effort, any effort–*abhisandhimātrataḥ*, just by my will. Whenever I wish, I must get entry by merely desiring (*abhisandhimātrataḥ* means just by will). *Yad viśeyam*, I must get entry . . .

Where?

. . . *tvat sudhā sadanam*, in the palaces and abode of Your nature. I must get entry there. I have nothing to do. I have not to ask You for anything. I want to worship You, that is all. That is my only desire, which is tickling in the background of my consciousness.

I want to see You. I don't want to see You. I have not to ask You anything.

What then?

DENISE: I just want to worship You.

SWAMIJI: I just want to worship You. You have nothing to worry [about] for me–no worry. I'll worship You and then I am satisfied. I don't ask for anything; no boons, nothing, no *anugraha* (grace), no peace of mind, no *yoga*, nothing. I just want to worship You. This is my joy.

Chapter 12 (17:04)

निर्विकल्पभवदीयदर्शन-
प्राप्तिफुल्लमनसां महात्मनाम् ।
उल्लसन्ति विमलानि हेलया
चेष्टितानि च वचांसि च स्फुटम् ॥७॥

nirvikalpabhavadīyadarśana-
prāptiphullamanasāṁ mahātmanām /
ullasanti vimalāni helayā
ceṣṭitāni ca vacāṁsi ca sphuṭam //7//

And those great souls whose mind has bloomed, whose mind is *phulla manasāṁ*, whose mind has bloomed by attaining, by the achievement, of Your *nirvikalpa darśana* . . .

Nirvikalpa darśana means–when I see you, you are going to ask me something, and there are questions and there are answers, that is *savikalpa*[182] *darśana–nirvikalpa darśana* is just to see you, *bas*, that is all. I don't want to talk–nothing. Just to see you, that is all. That is *nirvikalpa darśana*.[183]

. . . and by that *nirvikalpa darśana* of Thee, whose mind has bloomed–and those are great souls whose mind is like that–and

182 Possessing variety or admitting of distinctions, differentiated. [*Editor's note*]

183 See appendix 9 for more on *nirvikalpa*.

to them, *ullasanti vimalāni helayā ceṣṭitāni ca vacāṁsi ca sphuṭam*, their talks and their activity seem to be divine, all-round divine, filled with divinity. Whatever they do, it is divine. Whatever they talk, it is divine. They may talk nonsense, that is divine. They may talk harsh words, that is divine. They may talk lovely words, compassionate words, that is divine. They may abuse somebody, that is divine. Everything becomes divine to them.

Whom?

Who have achieved that *nirvakalpa darśana* of Thee and whose mind has bloomed.

Teṣāṁ ceṣṭitāni vacāṁsi. Their activities and their words *ullasanti* (shine) in such a way that they become *vimalāni* (*vimālāni* means divine, filled with divinity, pure).

ALEXIS: *Helayā*?

SWAMIJI: *Helayā* [means] automatic, automatic talks. Their automatic talks are divine.

ALEXIS: Spontaneous.

SWAMIJI: Spontaneous.

Chapter 12 (19:50)

भगवन्भवदीयपादयोर्-
निवसन्नन्तर एव निर्भयः ।
भवभूमिषु तासु तास्वहं
प्रभुमर्चेयमनर्गलक्रियः ॥८॥

bhagavanbhavadīyapādayor-
nivasannantara eva nirbhayaḥ /
bhavabhūmiṣu tāsu tāsvahaṁ
prabhumarceyamanargalakriyaḥ //8//

O Lord, there is one problem with me. That is, I want to reside, I want to live, under Your feet, under Your divine feet. I want to live there, under Your divine feet.

And *nirbhaya*, where there is no fear, no fear of anything in this world because you [can live] fearlessly there. There won't be an earthquake, there won't be fire, there won't be anything.

Nothing will happen [to me] there when I am situated under Your feet, under Your divine feet. Then, nothing will happen to me; no bad thing will happen to me. There will be no thief, nothing of that sort, and no [occurrence of] that disease, no trouble.

And, I don't want to remain always like that. The problem is that I want to live there, live under Your feet, but, *bavabhūmiṣu tāsu tāsu*, and I would experience the states of worldly states also. I would like to experience worldly states, worldly enjoyments also, and in those worldly enjoyments, I would like to *prabhum arceyamanargalaḥ*, I would like to adore Thy feet at the same time. Because, for instance, these are [Your] feet, I am living under [Your] feet, and I will come out, just open my eyes and see worldly pleasures. Then, if I get filled with some torture, I will just go again under Your feet. So, I will be happy always and I will adore You always like that.

Chapter 12 (22:16)

भवदङ्घ्रिसरोरूहोदरे परिलीनो गलितापरैषणः
अतिमात्रमधूपयोगतः परितृप्तो विचरेयमिच्छय ॥९॥

bhavadaṅghrisarorūhodare parilīno galitāparaiṣaṇāḥ /
atimātramadhūpayogataḥ paritṛpto vicareyamicchayā / /9

O Lord, *bhavat aṅghri sarorūha udare parilīnāḥ*, I would like to rest under Your lotus feet. I would like to rest under Your lotus feet and where *galitā apara iṣaṇaḥ*, where I will find no other desire in me. No other desire will remain in me. All other desires will vanish altogether.

Atimātra madhu upayogataḥ. And that *madhu*, that pollen, which will fall on me–the pollen of what? Your lotus feet; [on Your] loutus feet, there will be pollen (that is nectar, that is God consciousness)–that *rasa* will drip on me, *atimātra madhu*, and that *rasa* is *atimātra madhu* (intense joy), that will create intense joy. By that, by adopting that intense joy, *paritṛptaḥ*, I would get satisfied, filled. *Vicareyam icchayā*, then I would roam in this world according to my choice.

Chapter 12 (23:51)

यस्य दम्भादिव भवत्पूजासंकल्प उत्थितः
तस्याप्यवश्यमुदितं सन्निधानं तवोचितम ॥१०॥

yasya dambhādiva bhavatpūjāsaṁkalpa utthitaḥ /
tasyāpyavaśyamuditaṁ sannidhānaṁ tavocitam //10//

That person who desires to adore Your nature just for curiosity, just to show people that he is an adorer of Lord Śiva (i.e., just a fraud, fraudulently[184])–*bhavat pūjā saṁkalpaḥ*, and he is worshiping Thee, he worships You, just to show people that he is worshiping You–[nevertheless, the act of] Your worship is so great that to him also, You will become divine.[185] *Tasya api avaśyamuditaṁ sannidhānaṁ tavocitam*, You will appear to him in the state of God consciousness; he will also achieve God consciousness. This is the greatness of Your nature. [Even one] who just touches [Thy worship] with a crooked thought, he will also attain that supreme joy.

[gap in recording]

No, it is very difficult to achieve. I have seen hundreds who have experienced Your state and still I am kept away from You. This is a wonder. And there is no other thought in me except to see You.

Chapter 12 (25:19)

भगवन्नितरानपेक्षिणा
नितरामेकरसेन चेतसा ।
सुलभं सकलोपशायिनं
प्रभुमातृप्ति पिबेयमस्मि किम् ॥११॥

184 *Dambhādiva.*
185 That is, Your divinity will be revealed to him. [*Editor's note*]

bhagavannitarānapekṣiṇā
nitarāmekarasena cetasā /
sulabhaṁ sakalopaśāyinaṁ
prabhumātṛpti pibeyamasmi kim //11//

Bhagavan, O Lord, there is one desire in me and that desire must be fulfilled. That is, I want to swallow You, up to my entire satisfaction. When will that day come, when will that moment come, when I would swallow You in my own nature, up to my entire satisfaction? You who are *sakalopaśāyinam*, You who are found everywhere, You are everywhere found and I want to swallow You at once!

I don't want to swallow You with my mouth. I want to swallow You with my mind, and my mind must be *itara anapekṣiṇā nitarām eka rasena*, my mind must not be diverted to any other point [other] than this point.

Which point?

Just to swallow You.

When that day will come to me?

But, in my mind, there will be no desire other than to swallow You. And You who are *sulabhaṁ*, found everywhere without any effort (*sakalopaśāyinaṁ* means [He] who is everywhere found; *sulabhaṁ* means [He] who is very easy to obtain), I would like to swallow You to my entire satisfaction.

When that day will come?

Chapter 12 (27:19)

त्वया निराकृतं सर्वं हेयमेतत्तदेव तु
त्वन्मयं समुपादेयमित्ययं सारसंग्रह ॥१२॥

tvayā nirākṛtaṁ sarvaṁ heyametattadeva tu /
tvanmayaṁ samupādeyamityayaṁ sārasaṅgrahaḥ //12//

In brief words, the essence of this philosophy is this that *tvayā nirākṛtaṁ sarvaṁ*, everything, where[ever] You are not found, that is to be abandoned. Whatever [it is]–it may be jewelry, it may be gold, it may be a kingdom, it may be sovereignty–it is to be abandoned when You are not [found] there. And when You are there, when You are present–it may be anything absurd–it is worth having.[186] *Ityeyaṁ sāra saṅgrahaḥ*, this is, in brief words, the essence of our philosophy.

This is the meaning of this *śloka*.

Chapter 12 (28:24)

भवतोऽन्तरचारिभावजातं
प्रभुवन्मुख्यतयैव पूजितं तत् ।
भवतो बहिरप्यभावमात्रा
कथमीशान भवेत्समर्च्यते वा ॥१३॥

bhavato'ntaracāri-bhāvajātaṁ[187]
prabhuvanmukhyatayaiva pūjitaṁ tat /
bhavato bahirapyabhāvamātrā
kathamīśāna bhavetsamarcyate vā //13//

"*Īśāna*" is *āmantraṇam*[188].

Īśana, O Lord, *bhavato antaracāri bhāvajātam*, this whole objective world, which is already existing in Your own nature (*bhavataḥ antara cāri bhāva jātam*, this whole universe is entirely existing in Your own nature), and this universe, this whole class of objectivity, is worth adoring because it is one with Your own nature. We must adore everything, whatever we see, just like [we adore] You, in that scale, because *bhavato bahirapi abhāva mātrā*, if there is a non-existent anything, that [object], any object, which is not existing, that non-existent object is also felt in You, in Your nature.[189]

How can that non-existent object exist in that way or how can that [object] be worshiped?

186 Although Lord Śiva wholly pervades and is ultimately observable in all things, whatever object that tends to elicit the awareness of Him is to be possessed, and that which does not is to be abandoned. [*Editor's note*]

187 "*Cāri*" is separate from "*bhāva jātaṁ*". [*Editor's note*]

188 Vocative case.

189 "What is the non-existent universe? The imaginary world." See chapter 3, verse 19 commentary.

[Worshiping] means just to know. When you know anything, it is worship. Just to use these [spectacles], it is the worship of these [spectacles]. Do you understand?

Just to see, this is the worship.

ALEXIS: Because there is unity there.

SWAMIJI: Yes, unity. When you eat food and chew it, that is worship, worship of food; you are worshiping food. When you kiss your beloved, that is worship. All action is worship.

And worship, [everything is] just Your worship, Your direct worship, not any other's worship.

Chapter 12 (30:33)

निःशब्दं निर्विकल्पं च निर्व्याक्षेपमथानिशम्
क्षोभेऽप्यध्यक्षमीक्षेयं त्र्यक्ष त्वामेव सर्वत ॥१४॥

niḥśabdaṁ nirvikalpaṁ ca nirvyākṣepamathāniśam /
kṣobhe'pyadhyakṣamīkṣeyaṁ tryakṣa tvāmeva sarvataḥ / / 14

"*Tryakṣa*" is *āmantraṇam.*[190]

Tryakṣa, O the holder of three eyes, O Lord Śiva, You are *niḥśabdaṁ*, You are soundless; *nirvikalpaṁ*, You are thought-less; *nirvyākṣepaṁ*, You are without any flickering state, without distraction. And, You are like that. So, I want to observe You in the agitated movement of this objective world (*kṣobhe api*, in the agitated state also), i.e., when my mind is absolutely agitated and taken away from God consciousness. In that state also, I would like to observe You, observe Your presence there–everywhere!

Chapter 12 (31:48)

प्रकटय निजधाम देवयस्मिं-
स्त्वमसि सदा परमेश्वरीसमेतः ।
प्रभुचरणरजःसमानकक्ष्याः
किमविश्वासपदं भवन्ति भृत्याः ॥१५॥

190 Vocative case.

prakaṭaya nijadhāma deva yasmiṁ-
stvamasi sadā parameśvarīsametaḥ /
prabhucaraṇarajaḥsamānakakṣyāḥ
kimaviśvāsapadaṁ bhavanti bhṛtyāḥ //15//

Deva, O Lord, *prakaṭaya nija dhāma*, please reveal that abode of Yourself where You are residing along with Your Goddess, along with Pārvatī (*yasmin*, in which residence; *tvaṁ*, You are residing; *parameśvarī sametaḥ*, along with Your better half, Pārvati).

But, in that compartment where Pārvatī is living, that compartment is a private compartment. [Utpaladeva] wants to enjoy that private compartment of Lord Śiva with Pārvati but that is a private compartment; nobody is allowed inside. He wants to get entry into That.

Because, You must trust me. I won't touch any precious things there because I am not a thief. I will just enjoy Your presence, enjoy the presence of You both.

Prabhuḥ caraṇa rajaḥ samāna kakṣyā bhṛtyā. I am Your *bhṛtya*, I am Your slave. Really, I am Your slave. And, have I not even this much ability: am I not equal to that particle, the dust particle, of Your feet? Only one dust particle of Your feet. If that dust particle of Your feet is also admitted in that compartment . . .

Because, His feet are there and there are some dust particles also. They are also allowed [to be there].

. . . if they are also allowed, I should also be allowed in that compartment.

ALEXIS: But they are not allowed. I thought gods were dustless!

DEVOTEES: [laughter]

SWAMIJI: [laughter] It is just imagination. It is just *kāvya* (poetry).

Kiṁ aviśvāsa padaṁ. Don't You . . . ? You should trust me. You should trust me as You trust those dust particles below Your feet.

Chapter 12 (34:27)

दर्शनपथमुपयातोऽप्य-
पसरसि कुतो ममेश भृत्यस्य ।

क्षणमात्रकमिह न भवसि
कस्य न जन्तोर्दृशोर्विषयः ॥१६॥

darśanapathamupayāto'py-
apasarasi kuto mameśa bhṛtyasya /
kṣaṇamātrakamiha na bhavasi
kasya na jantordṛśorviṣayaḥ //16//

Īśa, O Lord, You have come to see me; *darśana patham upayāto api*, You have come to see me today. It is my great fortune that You have come to see me. But, just when You open the door of my *kuṭi* (my hut) to come in, then, from that doorway, You are again returning to Your home. What is the fun in coming to see me in that way?

Have you understood?

Imagine I am here, I am God's devotee, and God is coming [to see me]. He has opened the door just to see me, and just after opening the door, He closes the door and returns.

Darśanapatham, You have come to see me–that is good, that is fine, that is my fortune–but [as soon as] You have come to see me, You are returning at once. What is the fun in seeing me this way?

Now, You will say that, "This was the only point: I had to show you My face and I have returned". But this way, everybody perceives You; this way, everybody perceives You.

For instance, when you sneeze, at this just first start of sneezing, there is God consciousness. So, you perceive that God consciousness that way.[191]

DENISE: Because there is joy?

SWAMIJI: There is some joy. When there is yawning, at the first start of yawning, there is God consciousness.

ALEXIS: *Nirvikalpa*.[192]

SWAMIJI: This is the meeting of God consciousness in this way.

And, in the same way, You have come to see me and You return at once; just a spark of [Your] *darśana* and finished.

---

191 *Vijñāna Bhairava–The Manual for Self Realization,* Dhāraṇā 92.

192 See appendix 9 for an explanation of *nirvikalpa*.

Really, there are many *yogīs* who experience God consciousness like this; just in a flash and *bas*, It is no more. But he is not satisfied with this flash way of meeting of God.

He says, *darśanapatham upayāto'pi*, You have come to see me, [so] just come in and we'll talk. We'll talk [about] some subjects, we'll discuss some things, e.g., how we live, how we . . . [laughter]

I am Your slave (that is *bhṛtyasya*). Why should You get afraid from me? I am your slave. What can I do [to You]? I can't . . . there is no offence, i.e., I am not this aggressive [person]. I am just Your slave. You should come and sit and give me some joy.

Kṣaṇamātrakamīha na bhavasi. Now, You will say, "No, that was the joy I had to bestow [upon] you. I have bestowed [it upon] you already by just opening your door and returning". But this way, i.e., the joy of Your meeting, is held by everybody in this world. Those who are not Your slaves, they also perceive you like that. At the time of sneezing, at the time of yawning, at the time of going to sleep (from wakefulness to sleep), there is a point where God consciousness is shining. This way of meeting [You] is not satisfying me. I have not recognized this meeting. You have not come at all, so there is no [justification] that You will say that, "I have done this help to you". There is nothing. You have done nothing for me!

ALEXIS: It is commonplace.

SWAMIJI: Yes.

Chapter 12 (38:50)

ऐक्यसंविदमृताच्छधारया
सन्ततप्रसृतया कदा विभो ।
प्लावनात् परमभेदमानयं-
स्त्वां निजं च वपुराप्नुयां मुदम् ॥ १७॥

aikyasaṁvidamṛtācchadhārayā
santataprasṛtayā kadā vibho /
plāvanāt paramabhedamānayaṁ-
stvāṁ nijaṁ ca vapurāpnuyāṁ mudam //17//

In fact, in my mind, this desire is knocking in the background of my mind. That is, O Lord, *aikyasaṁvit amṛta acchadhārayā santata prasṛtayā kadā vibho plāvanāt*, I want to be over-flooded by that flood, great flood, which is *aikyasaṁvid amṛtācchad-hārayā*, which is flowing the stream of the nectar of oneness, non-dualism; that is, flowing the stream of the nectar of non-dualism. I want to get flooded by that.

You understand?

And *santata prasṛtayā*, and that stream must flow without . . . in continuity, without any break. And *plāvanāt*, it must flood me. I will be flooded by that stream.

Then, what will happen to me? I will tell you what would happen to me.

That is, *paramabhedamānayaṁ*, there will be one great union of me with You and with bliss. *Mudam* (*mudam* means that highest beatitude of God consciousness), that will be there, and with that beatitude of God Consciousness, You will be united, and with You, I will be united, and we will become one. This is my desire.

Chapter 12 (41:10)

अहमित्यमुतोऽवरुद्धलोकाद्-
भवदीयात्प्रातिपत्तिसारतो मे ।
अणुमात्रकमेव विश्वनिष्ठं
घटतां येन भवेयमर्चिता ते ॥१८॥

ahamityamuto'varuddhalokād-
bhavadīyātprātipattisārato me /
aṇumātrakameva viśvaniṣṭhaṁ
ghaṭatāṁ yena bhaveyamarcitā te //18//

O Lord, *aham iti amuto avaruddhalokāt bhavadīyāt prātipat-tisārato me*, there is one desire in me and that is, I would like to have just one particle–one tiny, smallest, particle–from the essence of Your God consciousness, from the essence of Your knowl-edge, unity of knowledge. From that unity of knowledge, I would like to have just a minute particle of that knowledge. And that knowledge is perfect universal I-consciousness (*ahamiti*). And where *avaruddhalokāt*, where all differentiated perceptions are vanished, have vanished. I would like to have one particle from That; *aṇumātrakam*, only just a minute one, just the smallest particle from That consciousness, God consciousness. And that particle must not [exclude] universal consciousness. Universal consciousness also must be united with that God consciousness.

So, he wants that the union of God consciousness must take place with universal consciousness.

The universe and God consciousness must appear to me as one. I am not selfish to have it. I just want to adore You in that way. In that position, I want to adore You. For instance, I would perceive an object and that perception of the object would be worship of You. I would perceive You and that would be the worship of the object.

Perceiving God is worshiping the object, the objective world. Perceiving the objective world is, in other words, worshiping God. Worshiping God is the perception of the objective world and the perception of the objective world is the worship of God.

That way I would worship You, in and out.

Chapter 12 (43:59)

अपरिमितरूपमहं
तं तं भावं प्रतिक्षणम् पश्यन् ।
त्वामेव विश्वरूपं
निजनाथं साधु पश्येयम् ॥१९॥

aparimitarūpamahaṁ
taṁ taṁ bhāvaṁ pratikṣaṇam paśyan /
tvāmeva viśvarūpaṁ
nijanāthaṁ sādhu paśyeyam //19//

The same thing he clarifies in this next *śloka*.

This is the desire . . . in other words, this is the desire in me: *aparimita rūpam aham*, *aparimita rūpam taṁ taṁ bhāvam*, I would perceive all of these worldly objects *aparimitarūpam*, just infinite, in an infinite way. I must feel that these [spectacles], when I perceive these [spectacles, I must perceive that] this is infinite, that there is everything lying in it. There is everything, there are one hundred and eighteen worlds, in this perception, in perceiving these [spectacles].[193] *Tvāmeva nijarūpam*, and when I perceive You, then I must feel that I perceive one hundred and eighteen worlds. In this way, perception becomes tasty (*sādhu*). The perception becomes tasty. I would like to have that taste.

ALEXIS: From Śiva to earth.

SWAMIJI: From Śiva to earth [and from] earth to Śiva. This is tasty perception!

Chapter 12 (45:31)

भवदङ्गगतं तमेव कस्मान्-
न ममः पर्यटतीष्टमर्थमर्थम् ।
प्रकृतिक्षतिरस्ति नो तथास्य
मम चेच्छा परिपूर्यते परैव ॥२०॥

bhavadaṅgagataṁ tameva kasmān-
na manaḥ paryaṭatīṣṭamarthamartham /
prakṛtikṣatirasti no tathāsya
mama cecchā paripūryate paraiva //20//

Why should I delete[194] objective perception? I would never like to delete objective perception. I would never abandon objective perception because worldly objects are actually Your own private limbs of Your body. *Bhavat aṅgagatam*, this is Your *aṅga*, it is the limbs of Your body.

What?

This whole objective perception–e.g., the perceiving this is a frame, this is a box, this is a [microphone], this is Denise, Ernie–this is only perceiving His limbs.

Why should I abandon this kind of perception? I will never abandon this kind of perception. Why my mind should not *paryaṭati*, why my mind should not roam in each and every [perception of the] objective world? Let it roam, let it be scattered, let it go astray, everywhere. But everywhere, there will be Your presence.

193 See appendix 21 for the perception of "everything in everything".
194 *Kṣati*: destruction, the removal of.

In this way . . . what is meant by "in this way" by me?

The meaning is, *prakṛti kṣatir asti no tathāsya*, this way, my mind won't be controlled. There is no question of controlling my mind because I [will] leave my mind as it is. [My mind] goes there, he goes there, he goes there–let it go.

But you must feel that these [perceptions], wherever [your mind] reaches, there are the limbs of God, those are the limbs of God. They are not away from That place.

DENISE: So, all wanderings of the mind are just . . .

SWAMIJI: . . . is just wandering in You.

Prakṛti kṣatir asti no tathāsya. The nature of the mind won't be controlled. In this way, the nature of the mind will be at ease. Wherever my mind wants to go, let it go.

And *mama ceccha paripūryate*, *mama paraiva iccha*, my supreme desire of meeting, realizing, God consciousness, is also complete, is also there.

ALEXIS: Because otherwise it would not be in continuity.

SWAMIJI: No, it won't be. How could he? He would come out of *samādhi* and then again finished.

Now, You will say, "No, it is very difficult to have". Now, You will argue, I know that [You] will argue with me and You will say that, "it is very difficult to have this kind of state"–*jagadānanda*, this is *jagadānanda*–"this kind of state is very difficult to possess", but I have seen . . .

Chapter 12 (48:50)

शतशः किल ते तवानुभावाद् -
भगवन्केऽप्यमुनैव चक्षुषा ये ।
अपि हालिकचेष्टया चरन्तः
परिपश्यन्ति भवद्वपुः सदाग्रे ॥२१॥

śataśaḥ kila te tavānubhāvād-
bhagavanke'pyamunaiva cakṣuṣā ye /
api hālikaceṣṭayā carantaḥ
paripaśyanti bhavadvapuḥ sadāgre //21//

[not recited]

. . . *śataśaḥ kila te tavānubhāvāt*, by Your grace (*tavānubhāvāt*, by Your grace), I have seen hundreds of [Your] devotees like that, *bhagavan*, O Lord, *ke'pi*, and they are very unique. Those hundreds of devotees I have seen, I have come across, and they are Your devotees and they feel *amunā eva cakṣuṣā*, with these very eyes, with these, their own eyes, they see *api hālikaceṣṭayā carantaḥ*, while doing activities, while doing degraded activities of the world, . . .

Hālika ceṣta is not knowing God. Those who have no inclination of knowing God, they do . . . what do they do from morning to evening? They eat, they drink, they have sex, they enjoy, they plough, they dig, they sleep. This is *hālika ceṣṭā*.

. . . and those people [i.e., Your devotees], they are doing the same actions. I have seen with my own eyes hundreds of such people who are [engaged] in this very activity, *paripaśyanti bhavadvapuḥ sadāgre*, and they feel Your presence just near to them. I have seen such people, hundreds of such people.

And You will say, "This is very difficult!" How is it very difficult for You? You can bestow this kind of state to me also. What have I done? I have no fault because I am always . . . I have been longing for You. There is only desire always in the background [of my mind] just to see You. Why should I not have this? I have seen hundreds of people like that in this universe.

Chapter 12 (50:40)

न सा मतिरुदेति या न भवति त्वदिच्छामयी
सदा शुभमथेतरद्भगवतैवमाचर्यते ।
अतोऽस्मि भवदात्मको भुवि यथा तथा सञ्चरन्
स्थितोऽनिशमबाधितत्वदमलाङ्घ्रिपूजोत्सवः ॥२२॥

na sā matirudeti yā na bhavati tvadicchāmayī
sadā śubhamathetaradbhagavataivamācaryate /
ato'smi bhavadātmako bhuvi yathā tathā sañcaran
sthito'niśamabādhitatvadamalāṅghripūjotsavaḥ //22//

Alright, don't give [it to] me! I have already achieved this kind of state. If you don't give [it to] me, I have still achieved this state.

He is very rude to the Lord [laughter]. Because *na sam,* from, from

Logically I will prove to You how I have achieved this state. *Na sā matirudeti yā*, that intellectual perception will not rise, which is not one with You. It will never rise! *Sadā śubham*, and the bad desires and good desires are handled by You, in the real way. In the real way of thinking, good desires and bad desires, which come in [the minds of] individuals, they are handled by You. *Ato'smi bhavadātmako*, so, I am always with You. *Bhuvi yathā tathā sañcaran*, wherever I am going, or to which place I am going, or wherever I am seated, I am with You. So, *sthito'niśam-abādhita tvadamalāṅghri pūjotsavaḥ*, my worshiping You is continuing. Don't give me anything; I am there! [laughter]

Chapter 12 (52:24)

भवदीयगभीरभाषितेषु
प्रतिभा सम्यगुदेतु मे पुरोऽतः ।
तदनुष्ठितशक्तिरप्यतस्तद्-
भवदर्चाव्यसनं च निर्विरामम् ॥२३॥

bhavadīyagabhīrabhāṣiteṣu
pratibhā samyagudetu me puro'taḥ /
tadanuṣṭhitaśaktirapyatastad-
bhavadarcāvyasanaṁ ca nirvirāmam //23//

Now, there is a problem in me. There is another . . .

He is again [feeling] down.

. . . there is one desire in me. First, *bhavadīyagabhīrabhāṣiteṣu*, Your *gabhīrabhāṣita* is Your secret philosophy, secret non-dualistic philosophy, in those *śāstras* which explain Your non-dualistic philosophy. In those *śāstras,* let my intellect work; let me digest that understanding.

ALEXIS: So, *pratibhā* is intuitive understanding, grasping.

SWAMIJI: Yes, grasping.

I must grasp those *śāstras*. This is my one desire. Not only this much. *Bhavadīya gabhīrabhāṣiteṣu pratibhā samyagudetu*, I must understand it fully well, first. Then, there is another problem. And afterwards, after understanding it, *me ataḥ tvadanuṣṭhita śakti*, I must tread on that philosophy; I must have practical shape on that philosophy.[195] And third, the third point is, *bhavat arcāvyasanaṁ ca nirvirāmam*, and that exertion just to worship You day and night–day and night without any break–that must also be there. You are [to be worshiped] day and night without any break. Exertion! I must get exerted [to the point of] exhaustion. I must exert myself in worshiping You. And these three things, I would like to have.

What three things?

Knowledge of *śāstras* (first), and its practice (this is second) . . .

ALEXIS: Third, devotion.

SWAMIJI: Third, devotion.

DEVOTEE: Unbroken devotion.

SWAMIJI: Unbreakable devotion, no. Exertion! I must get exhausted. I must have no . . .

ALEXIS: Without rest.

SWAMIJI: . . . I must have no rest.

ALEXIS: So, the second one, *anuṣṭhita śakti* . . .

SWAMIJI: The power of treading on that theory.

ALEXIS: First is knowledge, second is capacity, and third is devotion.

SWAMIJI: . . . devotion.

Chapter 12 (55:03)

व्यवहारपदेऽपि सर्वदा
प्रतिभात्वर्थकलाप एष माम् ।
भवतोऽवयवो यथा न तु
स्वत एवादरणीयतां गतः ॥२४॥

195 That is, I must put that philosophical understanding to practice. [*Editor's note*]

vyavahārapade'pi sarvadā
pratibhātvarthakalāpa eṣa mām /
bhavato'vayavo yathā na tu
svata evādaraṇīyatāṁ gataḥ //24//

O Lord, in this worldly activity, let all of these worldly objects appear to me as they appear to others, i.e., those who are not realized, unrealized people also. Like that, let these worldly objects appear to me.

But, there must be one restriction. That restriction is, *bhavato avayavo*, they must appear to me as Your own limbs, as the limbs of Your body. *Na tu svata evādaraṇīya*, they must not appear to me [as if] separate from God consciousness.

Chapter 12 (56:13)

मनसि स्वरसेन यत्र तत्र
प्रचरत्यप्यहमस्य गोचरेषु ।
प्रसृतोऽप्यविलोल एव युष्मत्-
परिचर्याचतुरः सदा भवेयम् ॥२५॥

manasi svarasena yatra tatra
pracaratyapyahamasya gocareṣu /
prasṛto'pyavilola eva yuṣmat-
paricaryācaturaḥ sadā bhaveyam //25//

There is one problem: I don't want to control my mind because the mind is so swift, you cannot control it. It can't be controlled by even the gods, i.e., the mind.

DENISE: Really?

SWAMIJI: Really. It is very swift. If you watch your breath, you are watching your breath, and you won't feel that point where your mind has escaped.

DENISE: Your mind is still going on.

SWAMIJI: [Your mind] is escaping. He escapes when you are not aware. If there will be unawareness for only one hundredth part of a second, and you will see that it has escaped one hundred miles away from that [first thought]. You can't watch [the mind easily]. So, it is very difficult to handle.

DENISE: Control.

SWAMIJI: Control it.

So, I don't want to control it. It is beyond my power. Let it go, let it go; *manasi svarasena yatra yatra pracarati*, *asya gocareṣu*, let it go to objects, to worldly objects.

It is very difficult. The difficulty is felt only by those who watch. Those who do not watch, they don't find any difficulty in controlling the mind.

I would like to have this kind of mind–it is [admitted]–but *avilola eva*, I must not be disturbed by its being astray always. Wherever my mind goes, I must adjust worship of God consciousness (God) there. Let it go. Let it go and I will worship God [wherever it goes]. I will worship God because God is everywhere. God is everywhere. If [my mind] goes to sex, I will worship God. If he goes to taste, I will worship God. If he goes to Amirakadal[196], I will worship God. This strength must be maintained by me, possessed by me, *avilola eva*, without any worry, without worry. And *yuṣmat paricaryā caturaḥ*, and clever and aware in worshiping You, I must remain clever in worshiping You in each and every act of my mind, because it is not controllable, you can't control it.

Chapter 12 (58:58)

भगवन्भवदिच्छयैव दास -
स्तव जातोऽस्मि परस्य नात्र शक्तिः ।
कथमेष तथापि वक्त्रबिम्बं
तव पश्यामि न जातु चित्रमेतत् ॥२६॥

bhagavanbhavadicchayaiva dāsa-
stava jāto'smi parasya nātra śaktiḥ /
kathameṣa tathāpi vaktrabimbaṁ
tava paśyāmi na jātu citrametat //26//

196 A place in Srinagar, Kashmir.

O Lord, by Your own will, You have made me Your slave. I didn't ask You to put me on Your path. I never wished [for that]. It was Your own free will that You have kept me on Your path and You have made me Your slave.

Well and good. If you have made me Your slave, that is alright. But I must see my master. If I am a slave of somebody, I must see that master. *Katham*, then how . . .

Because, *parasya nātra śakti*, no other power could do it.

What?

DENISE: Make me Your slave.

SWAMIJI: Make me Your slave. It is Your own will that I have become Your slave.

. . . *kathameṣa tathāpi vaktra bimbaṁ tava*. And this, Your face, this beautiful face, why Your beautiful face is not shown to me? *Na jātu paśyāmi*, I never see Your face. So, when I am asked by the public, "whom you are serving?" what will I say? I have not seen my master. I've never seen You. *Citrametat*, this is a surprise; this is a surprising action.

Because, when you want to engage some servant for your [service], you are always with him, just coaching him, just ordering him, "do this, do this, do this".

Bas, I am only a servant and there is no master to be seen. This is a wonder to me.

Chapter 12 (01:01:17)

समुत्सुकास्त्वां प्रति ये भवन्तं
प्रत्यर्थरूपादवलोकयन्ति ।
तेषामहो किं तदुपस्थितं स्यात्
किं साधनं वा फलितं भवेत्तत् ॥२७॥

samutsukāstvāṁ prati ye bhavantaṁ
pratyartharūpādavalokayanti /
teṣāmaho kiṁ tadupasthitaṁ syāt
kiṁ sādhanaṁ vā phalitaṁ bhavettat //27//

This is a wonder to me. This thing is a wonder to me. In this matter, I am lost. I can't understand how it happens.

Samutasukāstvāṁ prati ye bhavantaṁ. Ye samutsukāstvāṁ, those who are intensely attached to You, who have got an intense desire to meet You, those people, *bhavantam*, perceive You, *bhavantam avalokayanti*, perceive you *pratyartharūpāt*, from each and every object. From each and every object, they [perceive] Your presence.

Who?

Those who have got an intense desire to meet You, they perceive Your presence from each and every object. How [do] they perceive? What is the way, what is the technique, [by which] they perceive? *Teṣāṁ aho kiṁ tadupasthitam syāt*, what have they got, what have they achieved, what technique they have achieved? There, I am lost. What technique [do] they possess to perceive You in each and every object?

I perceive and even [strain] my eyes, still I can't perceive Your presence in any object. And they perceive Your presence in each and every object. What technique have they possessed? *Teṣām aho kiṁ tadupasthitaṁ syāt*, what is there, which is present to them? *Kiṁ sādhanam*, what means have they achieved? And what fruit [do] they get, what tremendous fruit [do] they get, from that achievement? This is beyond my imagination. I cannot imagine.

ALEXIS: It's a miracle.

SWAMIJI: This is a miracle. What happens to them? What is achieved by them? What unique technique is possessed by them? I can't understand because they only have an intense desire and by that intense [desire, by] possessing that intense desire for meeting You, they perceive You in each and every object, face to face. This is a wonder to me.

And I, I am lost, I am ruined. There is no sign of Your presence to me and they perceive You in each and every object. That is a wonder to me.

Chapter 12 (01:04:39)

भावा भावतया सन्तु भवद्भावेन मे भव ।
तथा न किञ्चिदप्यस्तु न किञ्चिद्भवतोऽन्यथ ॥२८॥

bhāvā bhāvatayā santu bhavadbhāvena me bhava /
tathā na kiñcidapyastu na kiñcidbhavato'nyathā //28//

There is one desire in me. Let the objective world be perceived by me in its existent way (*bhāvatayā*). Let the non-existent world remain non-existent to me because it is not existing. That world, which is not one with You, is not-existing. That world, which is one with You, is existing.

It is philosophy.

That world, which is existing, is one with You. That world, which is not existing, is away from Your God consciousness. Let these two kinds of worlds remain as they are.

Bhāvā bhāvatayā, let the existent world be perceived by me just . . .

ALEXIS: As it is.

SWAMIJI: . . . as it is. Let the non-existent world [remain] as non-existing. *Na kiñcit*, *na kiñcidastu*, the non-existent world, let the non-existent world be perceived by me as non-existent because *bhavato anyathā*, it is away from You. Let the existent world remain as the existent world to me because it is one with You.

JOHN: I thought also non-existent world was one with You.

SWAMIJI: Yes, if you go into the depth of that understanding, then that non-existent world is also one with You.

But that which is not one with You, it is not there. The non-existent world means, e.g., not the milk of a bird.

ALEXIS: Son of a barren woman.

SWAMIJI: That is also existing.

ALEXIS: As an idea.

SWAMIJI: Yes. In *mahāvyāpti*, that is also existing.[197]

Non-existing is that world, which is not that way also, i.e., which you cannot imagine. That which you cannot imagine, that is non-existent.

JOHN: In other words, what really is non-existent.

---

197 "And it is *mahāvyāpti*, the great pervasion. The great pervasion is that pervasion [of consciousness] where you pervade this whole universe. . . . Not only the existence of the universe is pervaded, but also the negation of the universe is also pervaded there." *Tantrāloka*, 5.49 (USF archives).

SWAMIJI: As long as it is said, as long as it is imagined, it is existing. That thing that is not imagined is not existing. Even that non-existing thing [that is imagined] is also existing in God consciousness. So, It is beyond that.

This is discussed in Pratyabhijñā in *mahāvyāpti*.[198]

Chapter 12 (01:07:38)

यन्न किञ्चिदपि तन्न किञ्चिद् -
    प्यस्तु किञ्चिदपि किञ्चिदेव मे ।
सर्वथा भवतु तावता भवान्
    सर्वतो भवति लब्धपूजितः ॥२९॥

yanna kiñcidapi tanna kiñcid-
apyastu kiñcidapi kiñcideva me /
sarvathā bhavatu tāvatā bhavān
sarvato bhavati labdhapūjitaḥ //29//

Whatever is not existing, that is not existing; whatever is existing, that is existing. So, in this way, let me perceive this objective world. Let me perceive the objective world in this way: that object, which is not existing, is not existing; that object, which is existing, is existing.

In this way, when I come to this [conclusive] perception, by

198 "Those of limited vision, however, in various parts are caused to identify themselves with the various [limited] stages by His will on account of which, even though when it is made clear that the essential reason of the erroneous concepts of the preceding experients lies in their identification with the body, etc., they are unable to comprehend the great pervasion [*mahāvyāpti*] (of the Ātman) described above (by Trika philosophy, viz., that the *ātman* is both immanent in the universe and transcends it) unless the Śakti of the Highest descend upon them (i.e. without the grace of the Highest Śakti)." *Pratyabhijñāhṛdayam, The Secret of Self-Recognition*, Sanskrit Text with English Translation, Notes and Introduction by Jaideva Singh (Motilal Banarsidass, Delhi, 1963-2011). Note: Jaideva Singh studied this text word-by-word with Swami Lakshmanjoo. The above quote on '*mahāvyāpti*' appears in Kṣemarāja's commentary of *sūtra* 8, p56.

that way, I would achieve You and I would worship You. This is my only desire. *Sarvathā bhavatu, tāvatā*, by that way (after *bhavatu*, you must put a comma), *tāvatā*, by this kind of perception, *bhavān sarvato bhavati labdha pūjitaḥ*[199], I will find You everywhere and I will worship You everywhere.

199 *Pūjita* (he is worshiped) *bhāvaikataḥ* (by the oneness of our Being). [*Editor's note*]

Chapter Thirteen
In Summary . . .
Saṅgrahastotranāma trayodaśaṁ stotram

SWAMIJI: *Saṅgrahastotranāma trayodaśaṁ stotram.* These *ślokas* he has composed when he was in [his] senses. These [previous] *ślokas* composed by him [were sung] when he was gone.

JOHN: The rest of these *ślokas* in this book are when he was sane?

SWAMIJI: No, this, only the 13th chapter and 14th chapter. He was in his senses. Here [i.e., other chapters], he was not in senses.

Chapter 13 (00:29)

संग्रहेण सुखदुःखलक्षणं
मां प्रति स्थितमिदं शृणु प्रभो ।
सौख्यमेष भवता समागमः
स्वामिना विरह एव दुःखिता ॥१॥

saṅgraheṇa sukhaduḥkhalakṣaṇaṁ
māṁ prati sthitamidaṁ śṛṇu prabho /
saukhyameṣa bhavatā samāgamaḥ
svāminā viraha eva duḥkhitā //1//

Prabho, O Lord, in brief words, I will give you the definition of my pain and pleasure.

Just the meeting of Thee, just to meet You, is pleasure for me. Just to be away from You is pain for me. In brief words, it is the definition of pain and pleasure for me.

In brief words (*saṅgraheṇa* means in brief words), *sukha-duḥkhalakṣaṇam*, the definition of pain and pleasure for me, *māṁ prati sthitam*, for me, please hear, please note, that this is the definition of pain and pleasure for me.

And that definition [of my pleasure] is *saukhyameṣa bhavatā samāgamaḥ*, just to meet You, Thy meeting is pleasure for me and *svāminā viraha eva*, and being carried away from Thy presence is pain for me.

Chapter 13 (01:54)

अन्तरप्यतितरामणीयसी
या त्वदप्रथनकालिकास्ति मे ।
तामपीश परिमृज्य सर्वतः
स्वं स्वरूपममलं प्रकाशय ॥२॥

antarapyatitarāmaṇīyasī
yā tvadaprathanakālikāsti me /
tāmapīśa parimṛjya sarvataḥ
svaṁ svarūpamamalaṁ prakāśaya //2//

Īśa, O Lord, *antarapi atitarāmaṇīyasī yā tvad aprathana kālikāsti me*, I have that impurity in my mind, by which impurity, *tvad aprathana kālikā*; *tvad aprathana*, You are not appearing to me. I can't perceive You by that impurity of mine.

ALEXIS: *Kālikā* is . . .

SWAMIJI: *Kālikā* means blackness.

ALEXIS: [For example], in gold, some *kālikā* is there, some impurity.

SWAMIJI: Impurity, yes. *Kālikā* means blackness (*malinatā*, dirt).

And that dirt is residing in my internal state of mind. The outside states of my mind are quite clear, quite pure, but inside there is some dirt in my mind.

ALEXIS: Minute.

SWAMIJI: Minute. *Aṇīyasī* means minute.

ALEXIS: *Atitarāmaṇī.*

SWAMIJI: *Atitarām*, very minute and [existing] internally. That is *āṇavamala*. That is . . .

ALEXIS: *Aṇavamala.*[200]
SWAMIJI: *Āṇavamala.*
ALEXIS: *Māyīyamala* he has got rid of.
SWAMIJI: *Māyīyamala*, I have got rid of *māyīyamala* and I have got rid of *kārmamala*. But there is inside that impurity, which is *aprathana kālikā*, which disturbs me by keeping away Your perception.
ALEXIS: Because he can't rest completely in Śiva *bhāva*. Is that right?
SWAMIJI: Yes.
ALEXIS: Because there is always some *āṇavamala*.[201]
SWAMIJI: O Lord Śiva, *tvamapi parimṛjya sarvataḥ*, please remove that impurity also from all sides in my mind. And *svaṁ svarūpaṁ amalam*, and let Your pure form, pure presence, be revealed to me.

Chapter 13 (04:32)

तावके वपुषि विश्वनिर्भरे
चित्सुधारसमये निरत्यये ।
तिष्ठतः सततमर्चतः प्रभुं
जीवितं मृतमथान्यदस्तु मे ॥३॥

tāvake vapuṣi viśvanirbhare
citsudhārasamaye niratyaye /
tiṣṭhataḥ satatamarcataḥ prabhuṁ
jīvitaṁ mṛtamathānyadastu me //3//

O Lord, there is one desire in me, there is one longing in me. That is, *tāvake vapuṣi viśvanirbhare citsudhārasamaye nirat-*

200 See appendix 15 for an explanation of the *malas*.
201 "In the first state [of *sakala pramatṛ*], there are all the three *malas* (*āṇavamala*, *māyīyamala*, and *kārmamala*). And in the next, *pralayākala pramātṛ*, *kārmamala* is gone; only two *malas* remain there: *āṇavamala* and *māyīyamala*. But in this state of *vijñānākala pramātṛ*, in this third state of *vijñānākala pramātṛ*, only one *mala* remains, the other two are gone. *Āṇava* remains, *māyīya* and *kārma malas* are finished." *Kashmir Shaivism–The Secret Supreme*, 7.47-49. See appendix 14 for an explanation of the 'Seven Perceivers' (*pramātṛs*).

yaye, Thy body, which is *viśvanirbhare*, filled with universal consciousness, *citsudhārasa maye*, filled with the nectar of God consciousness, and everlasting (*niratyaye*, everlasting, *niratyaye*), where there is no end (*atyaya* means "unending"), unending state of Your body, which is filled with universal consciousness and also filled with absolute God consciousness . . .

ALEXIS: So, *cit*, here, means transcendental consciousness.

SWAMIJI: Transcendental consciousness.

. . . I would like to reside in That body of Yours (*tiṣṭhataḥ*). I don't want to reside in That body just to relax. No. Let me be in exhaustion there. I have to work there. And that work is *satatamarcatā*, I want to worship You day and night without any rest. This is my desire, *bas*.

Jīvitam, let me have life then afterwards. Let me live in this universe [or] *mṛtaṁ*, let me die in this universe, [or] let me have this liberation from repeated births and deaths.[202] I have not thought about it. Let me die, that is alright. If I die, that is alright. If I live, that is alright. Let me live afterwards if I do this kind of exertion, i.e., exerting myself in worshiping You constantly.

Who? Whom [am I] worshiping? You who are filled with universal consciousness and You who are filled with the nectar of transcendental bliss (both universal consciousness and transcendental bliss).

And That body, I would like to remain in That body, live in That body, reside in That body, and just to worship You. I would like to worship You constantly!

Afterwards, when I do this, when I have this kind of position, let me then live in the universe [or] let me not live in this universe; let me die, let me go to hell, let me go to heaven, let me go to *mokṣa dhāma*[203]–I don't care. *Bas*, there must only be this worship [of You].

Chapter 13 (07:53)

ईश्वरोऽहमहमेव रूपवान्
पण्दितोऽस्मि सुभगोऽस्मि कोऽपरः ।

202 *Anyat* means *mokṣa*. [*Editor's note*]

203 Abode of liberation.

मत्समोऽस्ति जगतीति शोभते
मानिता त्वदनुरागिणः परम् ॥४॥

īśvaro'hamahameva rūpavān
paṇḍito'smi subhago'smi ko'paraḥ /
matsamo'sti jagatīti śobhate
mānitā tvadanurāgiṇaḥ param //4//

"I am the Lord." "I am beautiful." "I am charming." "I am learned." "I am a scholar." "*Subhaga asmi*, I am liked by everybody." "Who else is parallel to me in this world?" This kind of *mānitā*, this kind of ego, in the real sense, shines and is appropriate in those who have got love for Thee, *bas*.

Those who love You, if they say, "I am Īśvara, I am the Lord myself", "I am charming", "I am handsome", and "I am liked by everybody", "there is no other person equal to me in this world"–this is ego–this kind of ego is appropriate, shines beautifully, in those who have got Your attachment.

[For those] who are detached from You, if they will say, "I am the Lord", let them go to the dogs. [If he] will say, "I am beautiful", [actually] he is not beautiful, he is ugly. If he has make-up and everything, still he is ugly. And that person who has got Your devotion, and he is not beautiful, he is ugly, still he is beautiful. He is beautiful. Everything is beautiful in him. *Tvat anurāgiṇaḥ*, those who have got love for Thee, *paraṁ śobhate*, this shines only in them.

[He] who is attached to God, he is beautiful because there is love for God. Love for God is charming.

Chapter 13 (10:07)

देवदेव भवदद्वयामृता-
ख्यातिसंहरण लब्धजन्मना ।
तद्यथास्थितपदार्थसंविदा
मां कुरुष्व चरणार्चनोचितम् ॥५॥

devadeva bhavadadvayāmṛtā-
khyātisaṁharaṇa labdhajanmanā /
tadyathāsthitapadārthasaṁvidā
māṁ kuruṣva caraṇārcanocitam //5//

O Lord of lords, *yathāsthita padārtha saṁvidā*, whatever is seen, whatever is perceived (*śabda*, *sparśa*, *rūpa*, *rasa*, and *gandha*, all of these five kinds of perceptions), whatever perception is there–it may be touch, it may be taste, it may be smell, it may be something [else]–this perception should be born to me anew. This perception is old perception, e.g., eating, drinking, cheese, everyday cheese. It is boring perception. But this perception must be born afresh.

How?

Bhavat advaya amṛta akhyāti saṁharaṇa labdha janmanā. Bhavat advaya amṛta, the nectar of Your oneness, the nectar of Your oneness of perception–that is nectar–and by that nectar, when this perception of *śabda*, *sparśa*, *rūpa*, *rasa*, and *gandha* will be born anew by that nectar, . . .

Nectar of what?

GANJOO: Non-duality.

SWAMIJI: Nectar of non-duality. And that perception will be born anew, in a new way.

. . . and, that way, let me be worthy, let me become worthy, in that way of perception.

He wants to become worthy of that kind of perception, i.e., that perception, which has been born anew, afresh.

ALEXIS: By winding up that old non-appearance of God consciousness, *akhyāti samāhāraṇa*.

SWAMIJI: Yes, *akhyāti samāhāraṇa*. Winding up . . .

ALEXIS: Winding that up and revealing that.

SWAMIJI: . . . and revealing that direct God consciousness in *śabda*, *sparśa*, *rūpa*, *rasa*, and *gandha*.

And when that *janma*, that new life, will be possessed by me, let me be worthy then of worshiping You. Let me worship You for always afterwards. Let me be capable of worshiping You (*māṁ kuruṣva bhavat caraṇa arcana ucitam*).

ALEXIS: *Yogyam*.

SWAMIJI: *Yogyam*.

Let me be capable of worshiping You afterwards. Because, I am not capable of worshiping You unless there is *śabda*, *sparśa*, *rūpa*, *rasa,* and *gandha.*[204] [With] these *śabda*, *sparśa*, *rūpa*, *rasa*, and *gandha*, as they are at present, I can't be capable of worshiping You. They must get a new life. These *śabda*, *sparśa*, *rūpa*, etc.–these perceptions, organic[205] perceptions–must get a new life, and that new life will [occur] only when they are 'nectarized' by Your God consciousness. Then, let me be worthy of worshiping You afterwards. I would worship You. I have nothing [else] to do here [except] just to worship You.

ALEXIS: Swamiji, when Utpaladeva says, "worshiping Your feet", is he just being poetical? [Is it] the same as "worshiping You", or does he mean for us to understand by "feet" the energies of the Lord?

SWAMIJI: Energies.

ALEXIS: Worshiping Your outward energy of manifestation.

SWAMIJI: *Cit śakti*, *ānanda śakti*, *icchā śakti*, *jñāna śakti*, *kriyā śakti*–they are [His] feet.

ALEXIS: Or, otherwise, *jñāna* and *kriyā*?

SWAMIJI: *Jñāna* and *kriyā*, two feet. If you say "two feet", yes.

Chapter 13 (14:06)

ध्यायते तदनु दृश्यते ततः
स्पृश्यते च परमेश्वरः स्वयम् ।
यत्र पूजनमहोत्सवः स मे
सर्वदास्तु भवतोऽनुभावतः ॥६॥

dhyāyate tadanu dṛśyate tataḥ
spṛśyate ca parameśvaraḥ svayam /
yatra pūjanamahotsavaḥ sa me
sarvadāstu bhavato'nubhāvataḥ //6//

204 "So, it means all your senses, these are the energies of Lord Śiva. All the five senses are the energies of Lord Śiva. And they are bent upon carrying all these beautiful things inside and offering them to Lord Śiva who is residing in one's own heart." See chapter 2, verse 23.

205 Pertaining to the organs. [*Editor's note*]

There is a point where Parameśvara (Lord Śiva) is being concentrated [upon]–not by effort, not with effort–automatically. There is a state . . . that state comes when you automatically meditate on Lord Śiva. And automatically when you meditate on Lord Śiva, automatically you perceive Lord Śiva, because that is from *anugraha*[206], it is not from your effort. Your effort is useless. I told you once.[207]

ALEXIS: So, anything you do, e.g., you scratch your ear and you will feel God consciousness.

SWAMIJI: That effort is complete. If you don't feel [God consciousness], that is useless. Just to scratch your ear tip, it is useless.

Dhyāyate, when that Parameśvara (Lord Śiva) is meditated [upon] automatically, is perceived automatically, is embraced automatically, [where that takes place], that is the state. That [is the] state where Parameśvara is automatically meditated upon, where Parameśvara is then, after meditation, perceived, and after perception, is embraced.

There, that *pūjana mahotsava*, that greatest festival of worshiping Thee, let that greatest festival of worshiping Thee be attained by me everyday, in each moment. This festival, I want to remain in this festival for always (*sarvadāstu*).

I have no claim for this festival. If You say, "No, you are not worthy", I know that. I am not worthy for having this, remaining in this festival. By Your grace (*bhavataḥ anubhāvataḥ*, by Your grace), let this [festival] take place to me by Your grace. What is there in it? Just think [of it] and it will happen.

ALEXIS: By "*sarvadā*", he means that usually a festival is on a fixed point in the calendar.

SWAMIJI: Fixed point, e.g., only in April, my festival, birthday festival. No, he wants this kind of festival for always.

Chapter 13 (16:36)

यद्यथास्थितपदार्थदर्शनं
युष्मदर्चनमहोत्सवश्च यः ।

206 Grace.

207 See chapter 4, verse 12.

युग्ममेतदितरेतराश्रयं
भक्तिशालिषु सदा विजृम्भते ॥७॥

yadyathāsthitapadārthadarśanaṁ
yuṣmadarcanamahotsavaśca yaḥ /
yugmametaditaretarāśrayaṁ
bhaktiśāliṣu sadā vijṛmbhate //7//

There are two moments of that great festival. One is *yathā sthita padārtha darśanam*, just *śabda*, *sparśa*, *rūpa*, *rasa*, and *gandha*; to feel this object as [being] in the shape of a [microphone], to feel this as [spectacles], to feel this as a book, or to touch, to taste, to hear, to smell . . . all of these organic perceptions. This is one way of the world of perception. This is the perception of the organic world. The organs perceive like that. And there is another world. That is, *yuṣmat arcana mahotsavaḥ*, that great festival of worshiping You.

Now, there is a problem in me. This is a problem that there are devotees who, as soon as they perceive this, as soon as they get entry in that . . .

In what? In this worldly perception.

. . . there are some devotees who *itaretarāśrayam*, no sooner [than] they perceive these worldly activities, they get entry in God consciousness. As soon as they get entry in God consciousness, they perceive this universal activity. So, [for them], this universal activity and God consciousness remain one, dependent to each other (*itaretarāśrayam*).

ALEXIS: Mutually dependent.

SWAMIJI: Mutually dependent. It is not that I will perceive Bruce Hughes and I will be carried away from God consciousness. This way of perception is ordinary perception. But he wants to perceive Bruce Hughes and, at the same time, get entry in God consciousness. That is what he says.

And that is shining in only Your devotees. And this takes place every now and then in [Your] devotees.

Chapter 13 (19:28)

तत्तदिन्द्रियमुखेन सन्ततं
युष्मदर्चनरसायनासवम् ।
सर्वभावचसकेषु पूरिते-
ष्वापिबन्नपि भवेयमुन्मदः ॥८॥

tattadindriyamukhena santataṁ
yuṣmadarcanarasāyanāsavam /
sarvabhāvacasakeṣu pūrite-
ṣvāpibannapi bhaveyamunmadaḥ //8//

There is one desire in me, O Lord. That desire is, I want to get drunk, I want to get drunk always. Always drunk!

ALEXIS: *Unmada.*

SWAMIJI: *Unmada*. By what?

By drinking some alcohol and that alcohol is *yuṣmad arcane rasāyanāsavam*, the alcohol of the nectar of Your worship, Thy worship. I would like to worship You and that worshiping is nectar, and that nectar is alcohol, wine, and that is Scotch-wine from Scotland. It is not Canadian wine.

DEVOTEES: [laughter]

ALEXIS: So, this *rasāyana*, that *rasāyana* is that drink, which, when you take it, destroys old age and death; gives you eternal life.

SWAMIJI: Yes.

ALEXIS: In the outward sense, *rasāyana*.

SWAMIJI: Yes.

ALEXIS: Its like some alchemical preparation.

SWAMIJI: Yes.

And *santataṁ yuṣmadarcana rasāyanam. Santatam*, [it is] always [served] by organic perceptions; organic perceptions have [served] this *rasāyana* (*tat tat indriya mukhena*).

Mukhena means those boys in a bar. They place these glasses of wine on the tables. [The] boys are *śabda*, *sparśa*, *rūpa*, *rasa*, and *gandha*, and these organs. These organs are the boys, i.e., those who keep this *rasāyana* in front of devotees, *tat tat indriya mukhena santatam*, by perceiving *rūpa*, *śabda*, *sparśa*, *rūpa*, *rasa*, and *gandha*.

ALEXIS: Bring me one more drink!

SWAMIJI: Yes, one more *gandha* (smell), one more *rūpa* (form).

Tat tat indriya mukhena santatam yuṣmat arcana rasāyanāsavam. And it is filled in glasses, in wine glasses, and those wine glasses are *sarva bhāva caṣakeṣu*; *sarva bhāva*, all of this objective world. All of this collection of objectivity is this.

What?

Pots, wine pots, wine glasses.

ALEXIS: So, every object that you perceive or sense is a glass to drink from.

SWAMIJI: And, in it, *āpiban*, I would like–there is one desire in me–I would *āpiban* (*āpiban* means just drink), go on drinking and *unmadaḥ bhavet*, I would get drunk (*ākaṇṭhataḥ pibet madya*).

Chapter 13 (22:26)

अन्यवेद्यमणुमात्रमस्ति न
स्वप्रकाशमखिलं विजृम्भते ।
यत्र नाथ भवतः पुरे स्थितिं
तत्र मे कुरु सदा तवार्चितुः ॥९॥

anyavedyamaṇumātramasti na
svaprakāśamakhilaṁ vijṛmbhate /
yatra nātha bhavataḥ pure sthitiṁ
tatra me kuru sadā tavārcituḥ //9//

O Lord, there is a place, there is one place, one country–in this universe there is one country–where *anyavedyam aṇumātram asti*, where no other object is felt [as other] than Your God consciousness. That country, in that country where no object is found as other than God consciousness, *svaprakāśam akhilaṁ vijṛmbhate*, where everything is understood as *svaprakāśa*, of just transcendental God consciousness and nothing else, in that country, in that *bhavataḥ pure*, in that country of Thine, in Thine world, let me reside. Let me be . . . let me get the capacity of residence.

ALEXIS: Visa.

SWAMIJI: Visa [laughter]. I would like a visa to go in that country.

Now, you will say, "Why should I give you that visa?" *Tavārcituḥ*, because there is only one desire in me, just to worship You [Swamiji weeps]. That is the desire in me . . . that is the desire. *Bas*.

Chapter 13 (24:03)

दासधाम्नि विनियोजितोऽप्यहं
स्वेच्छयैव परमेश्वर त्वया ।
दर्शनेन न किमस्मि पात्रितः
पादसंवाहनकर्मणापि वा ॥१०॥

dāsadhāmni viniyojito'pyahaṁ
svecchayaiva parameśvara tvayā /
darśanena na kimasmi pātritaḥ
pādasaṁvāhanakarmaṇāpi vā //10//

Parameśvara, O Lord, ("O Lord", it is *āmantraṇam*[208]), *Parameśvara*, *aham tvayā dāsa dhāmani svecchayaiva viniyojitaḥ*, I have been kept as, I have been made as Your slave by You by Your own will. I didn't insist that I would like to be Your slave–I never said that–but You have made me Your slave by Your own will.

Now, *darśanena na kimasmi pātritaḥ*, why am I not fit to see You at all? I don't see You now. I have [been] made by You as Your slave, but I am not worthy, I am not supposed to be worthy, of seeing You.

Or, if You don't like me, if You hate me, if You hate my presence, then still, stretch Your legs [out and] I will just massage Your feet. But give me something to do [because] I am Your slave, I am your *dāsa*.

208 Vocative case.

Chapter 13 (25:43)

शक्तिपातसमये विचारणं
प्राप्तमीश न करोषि कर्हिचित् ।
अद्य मां प्रति किंमागतं यतः
स्वप्रकाशनविधौ विलम्बसे ॥ ११ ॥

śaktipātasamaye vicāraṇaṁ
prāptamīśa na karoṣi karhicit /
adya māṁ prati kiṁāgataṁ yataḥ
svaprakāśanavidhau vilambase //11//

Īśa, O Lord, at the time of showering grace, when You bestow grace on Your devotees, at that time, it was necessary for You to think over it first, i.e., if the person whom You shower grace [upon] is worthy to receive it, is capable to receive that grace from You. *Na karoṣi karhicit*, You never think that way. You never think that way. *Bas*, You shower grace without thinking if he is fit or capable or not.

If I am capable, if Your grace has made me capable, why *adya māṁ prati kimāgataṁ yataḥ*, now, what has become of me? What has happened to me? *Svaprakāśanavidhau*, then, You don't come to me. You are not perceived by me at all. *Svaprakāśanavidhau*, by revealing Your nature, in revealing Your nature, You hesitate. You hesitate [and say], "No, I will come to your place just after a few days", and [after] those few days are also gone, still, still [You say] "*paga*"[209], and tomorrow never [comes].

This is the way of His bestowing grace.

This *śloka* is commentated upon by Abhinavagupta in the *Tantrāloka*:

śrimānutpaladevaścāpyasmākaṁ paramo guruḥ
śaktipātasamaye vicāraṇaṁ
prāptamīśa na karoṣi karhicit /[210]

209 Tomorrow.
210 *Tantrāloka*, 13.290 (USF archives).

Utpaladeva also, who is our great grand master[211], he has also said in his book that *śaktipāta samaye vicāraṇaṁ prāptam īśa na kuryāt*, at the time of showering grace, You ought to have thought if the person whom You shower grace [upon] is worthy, is capable to receive it. But You never do it! Now, what has happened to me that I never see You? I have been made Your slave and still I don't see You.

Now, Abhinavagupta commentates [on] this *śloka*:

> *karhicitprāptaśabdābhyāmanapekṣitvamūcivān* //[212]
> *durlabhatvamarāgitvaṁ śaktipātavidhau vibhoḥ* /[213]

There are two words–they are very important words–that Utpaladeva has put in this verse. That is, "*karhicit*" and "*prāpta*". *Prāpta* means it was due for You to think over it first and You never do it (*karhicit*)![214] *Karhicit* means You never do it, You never think over it. Lord Śiva never thinks first before showering grace. He never thinks if [one] is worthy or not.

But, sometimes there is the possibility [that You may think], "Before showering grace, I have thought over it. Today, by mistake, I have thought [over it]." But, by mistake also, You never think [over it]. So, it is always spontaneous and that You never think [over it]. So, *durlabhatvam*; so, it is *durlabha*; so, it is very difficult to receive. The conclusion of this not-thinking is, it has become very rare (*durlabha*), it has become very difficult to achieve.

Because, that [thing] is very easy to achieve when there is some way, when you [can] adopt some means and achieve it. If you adopt some means [to achieve grace], you won't [necessarily] achieve it. It is only by His grace that you achieve it. So, it is *durlabhatvam.*

And *arāgitvam* (*arāgitvam* means You have no attachment for anybody). For instance, if somebody prays to You for twenty-four

211 The great grand-master of Kṣemaraja. Utpaladeva was the master of Lakṣmanagupta, who in turn was Abhinavagupta's master in the Pratyabhijñā system. Kṣemaraja was Abhinavagupta's principal disciple. [*Editor's note*]

212 *Tantrāloka*, 13.291 (USF archives) .

213 Ibid., 13.292a.

214 See appendix 22 for "no qualifications for receiving grace".

hours a day, for months and months, years and years, for his whole life, still You don't have any attachment for him.

DENISE: So, You don't hear him actually?

SWAMIJI: No. You hear him but You are not attached to him.

At his place, You have ought to have showered grace on him, i.e., in that place [of continual worship]. On the contrary, You shower grace on him who has never thought of You.[215] So, it is *arāgitva*, You have no attachment for Your devotees.

> *aparārdhena tasyaiva śaktipātasya citratām /*
> *vyavadhānacirakṣiprabhedādyairūpavarṇitaiḥ //*[216]

The next two lines of this *śloka* indicate *adya māṁ prati kimāgataṁ*: now, what has happened to me that You don't come to me? You came to me at that point.

When?

When You showered grace, You had revealed [Yourself] to me and I was overjoyed, I was intoxicated, and then it stopped, no sign of [Your grace] coming to me.[217]

---

215 "At the point of *śaktipāta*, at the point of showering grace, You ought to have thought first before showering grace on some individual. You ought to have thought if he has the capacity, if that person has the capacity to contain that *śaktipāta*. That, You never do! That, You have never done beforehand and You [will] never do. Intentionally, You don't think about it at the time of showering grace. You just shower grace, that is all. Thinking of good or bad, You avoid that. If You want to shower grace on some bloody fool, then You shower grace, not thinking if he will contain it, maintain it, or not." *Tantrāloka*, 13.291 (USF archives).

216 *Tantrāloka*, 13.292 (USF archives).

217 "Now, You have showered grace on me, but I couldn't contain it, because it moves out again and again. This grace of Yours moves out from my consciousness. I can't maintain this consciousness of this joy. *Adya māṁ prati kimāgataṁ*, what has become of me now? *Sva prakāśana vidhau*, You delay now in showering grace. I am stuck. Why am I stuck? Why did You shower grace beforehand? Why didn't You think if I was fit for that grace? Why do You hesitate now? Now, You have felt that [I cannot] maintain it, so You withdraw it. For the time being, You withdraw it, but it can't be withdrawn because I have experienced that grace. It can't be withdrawn at any cost. And [yet] You withdraw again!

Aparārdhena tasyaiva śaktipātasya. In this, in the other two lines, Utpaladeva indicates that the *śaktipāta* He showers–the grace, whatever He showers–He showers in many ways. He will appear to you today and then He will never appear to you [again] until you die, [or] He will appear to you today, then He will appear to you after one month, then after two months, then after three months. This way also. [Or] He will appear to you and [continue to] be appearing to you, *bas*, and you can't do any other thing. These are the ways of *śaktipāta*. You have to receive it, receive it again and again, again and again. [Lord Śiva bestows grace] without thinking if you are fit or not, but it makes you fit.[218] This is the *citratā*, varieties of *śaktipāta*, and it is indicated by the next two lines in Utpaladeva's *śloka*.

ALEXIS: In other words, sometimes there is a gap, sometimes it comes again and again, *cira*?

SWAMIJI: Yes. *Cira* (*cira* means long delay). For instance, He appears to me today [and then] He will appear to me not at all in this life; at the time of death, He will appear to me. It is essential. When once you have realized His joy, only once, only for one second, you are supposed to be *jīvan mukta*, you are supposed to get liberation, in the end.

ALEXIS: At death.

SWAMIJI: At death.

JOHN: Why is that? You mean, if somebody has one experience of God at any time of their life–e.g., twelve years old, fifteen years old–the idea is that when he dies, he will also become liberated?

SWAMIJI: No. God consciousness will be revealed to him automatically, because, at the time of experiencing God consciousness, It penetrates you everywhere! It destroys all of your bondages. It is such joy! And that joy is stopped, but the spot, the print, the imprint in his brain is there for his whole life. And that [impression], when he leaves this body, that will expand;

Why did You shower it at all in the first [place]? Why didn't You think over it first, i.e., if I had the capacity of maintaining this grace?" Ibid., 13.291.

218 "If it is not maintained, He withdraws it for sometime. . . . It creates more capacity. Withdrawing and showering, withdrawing and showering, withdrawing and showering, until he becomes one with Him. Because He wants him to be liberated." Ibid., 13.291.

that will expand and there will be God consciousness.

DENISE: Because, at the time of death . . .

SWAMIJI: So, at the time of death . . .

DENISE: . . . the strongest impression in your mind comes.

SWAMIJI: Yes, comes.

ALEXIS: The deepest.

DENISE: The deepest, and that would be God consciousness.

SWAMIJI: So, there is no worry. Only once you must realize It.

ALEXIS: So, because at death, you lose your body, identification with the body is going, you will go back in your awareness to the deepest point of which you have ever realized [during your lifetime], and that will be God consciousness.

SWAMIJI: That will be revealed and that will be God consciousness. It is what happens at the time of death. You need this experience only once. God is so great that whenever He reveals His nature, sometimes He reveals [It continuously], without a break. So, he cannot maintain it. He is just . . . he is mad for it.

ALEXIS: So, there is absolutely no consideration of suitability . . .

SWAMIJI: Suitability, there is no consideration. It can happen to anybody.

ALEXIS: . . . of creed or caste.

SWAMIJI: It can happen to anybody. It can happen to anybody.

Chapter 13 (34:51)

तत्र तत्र विषये बहिर्विभा -
त्यन्तरे च परमेश्वरीयुतम् ।
त्वं जगत्त्रितयनिर्भरं सदा
लोकयेय निजपाणिपूजितम् ॥ १२॥

tatra tatra viṣaye bahirvibhā-
tyantare ca parameśvarīyutam /
tvaṁ jagattritayanirbharaṁ sadā
lokayeya nijapāṇipūjitam //12//

There is one desire in me, O Lord! *Tatra tatra viṣaye bahir vibhāti antare ca*, whenever I perceive, when I join in the organs of the senses, when I utilize enjoyment in the organs of the senses, it may be outside or inside (outside enjoyment is just *śabda*, *sparśa*, *rūpa*, *rasa,* and *gandha*; inside enjoyment is in impressions, in thoughts)–I do this, it is the automatic way of life, of everybody's life–but my desire is that I would *parameśvar-īyutam tvāṁ jagat tritaya nirbharaṁ sadā lokayeya*, this is my desire, the only desire, that I want to perceive You along with Pārvatī in those actions, i.e., outward actions and internal actions of sensual enjoyments.

I want to see You in all of these sensual enjoyments, outside and inside, not because I want to see You. There is only one desire in me: *lokayeya nijapāṇipūjitam*, I would like to feel myself as doing Your worship, always. When I hear sound, at that time, You must appear to me and I will worship You, and that hearing of sound will be Your worship. The sensation of touch will be Your worship. The sensation of perceiving form will be Your worship. Worship will be the worship of You both, Pārvatī and You.

ALEXIS: What does that mean in non-figurative terms? Directly? What does it mean to perceive Lord Śiva and Pārvati in all actions? Transcendental and universal consciousness?

SWAMIJI: Yes, universal and transcendental. Transcendental is Śiva's position and universal is Pārvati's position.

ALEXIS: "*Nijapāṇipūjitam.*" What is the exact meaning?

SWAMIJI: *Nijapāṇipūjitam tvaṁ loke.*

ALEXIS: By my own hands, *svaśaktyā.*

SWAMIJI: I would like to perceive You [in such a way] that I [will] have worshiped You, that I am already worshiping You with my own hands.

Jagat tṛtaya nirbharaṁ, and because Your fullness would appear to me in all of the three worlds; not only in all of the three worlds, but in all of the three states of *jāgrat*, *svapna*, and *suṣupti* also.[219] These states are also three worlds.

ALEXIS: So, when we find "three worlds", we should understand that in those terms, always.

SWAMIJI: Yes.

ALEXIS: Sometimes it is commentated, the commentators say

219 Waking, dreaming, and deep sleep, respectively. [*Editor's note*]

[that "three worlds"] means *bhāva*, *abhāva*, and *atibhāva*.

SWAMIJI: That is *jāgrat*, *svapna*, and *suṣupti*.

ALEXIS: We should understand in that way?

SWAMIJI: Yes.

ALEXIS: Not from earth to *prakṛti*, not to *kalā*, and then to Śiva?

SWAMIJI: No, no.

Chapter 13 (38:51)

स्वामिसौधमभिसन्धिमात्रतो
निर्विबन्धमधिरूह्य सर्वदा ।
स्यां प्रसादपरमामृतासवा -
पानकेलिपरिलब्धनिर्वृतिः ॥ १३ ॥

svāmisaudhamabhisandhimātrato
nirvibandhamadhirūhya sarvadā /
syāṁ prasādaparamāmṛtāsavā-
pānakeliparilabdhanirvṛtiḥ //13//

The throne of my Master, my Lord Śiva, I would like to ascend on that throne, not by effort, not with effort, but *abhisandhimātrataḥ*, whenever I wish, whenever I desire. Whenever I will it, I must ascend to that throne of my Master, *nirvibandham*, without any obstacles, without any halts (*nirvibandham*).

ALEXIS: Directly.

SWAMIJI: Directly.

I must ascend to that throne with my own will, by my own will, and directly, without any obstacles. And I must ascend–not tomorrow or weekly or monthly or fortnightly–daily (*sarvadā*, daily)! I must ascend to that throne daily.

And then, *prasāda parama amṛta āsava*, and then You will pat my back. With Your divine hands, You will pat my back, You will be patting my back. That is *prasāda* (*prasāda* means grace). And that patting of grace will create intoxication in me; intoxication, that will be liquor for me. That will be as good as Scotland liquor, best liquor!

ALEXIS: Scotch whisky.

SWAMIJI: Scotch whisky.

Prasāda paramāmṛta, and that will be absolutely nectar. When I will be 'nectarized' by that and *pāna keli parilabdha nivṛttiḥ*, then I would dance with You. This is my desire. I would dance with You [while] holding that bottle of whisky.

ALEXIS: *Pāna keli prasāda parama amṛta, apāna ākaṇṭhatah, āsavanta.*

SWAMIJI: [laughter] Yes, *apāna keli* (*keli* means dancing).

And by that dancing, *parilabdha nirvṛti syām*, I will get absolute satisfaction, absolute peace. This is my desire.

ALEXIS: Beautiful verse.

Chapter 13 (41:33)

यत्समस्तसुभगार्थवस्तुषु
स्पर्शमात्रविधिना चमत्कृतिम्
तां समर्पयति तेन ते वपुः
पूजयन्त्यचलभक्तिशालिनः ॥१४॥

yatsamastasubhagārthavastuṣu
sparśamātravidhinā camatkṛtim /
tāṁ samarpayati tena te vapuḥ
pūjayantyacalabhaktiśālinaḥ //14//

Samasta subhagārthavastuṣu sparśamātra vidhinā camatkṛtiṁ. Whenever we hear sound (not ordinary sound; very beautiful sound, penetrating sound, soft sound), and touch (very intoxicative touch), beautiful form (you perceive beautiful form)–*samasta subhagārtha vastuṣu* (*śubhagārtha* means those who are very beautiful), very beautiful *śabda*, *sparśa*, *rūpa*, *rasa*, and taste [that is] also very beautiful, and *gandha*, smell also–and in tasting all of these five senses, five beautiful senses, you should avoid those which are not beautiful because [these senses are] meant for worshiping You. We have to worship You. We must not worship You with bad things. We must worship You with good things, with beautiful things.

ALEXIS: While we still have the impression of that distinction, we must adopt beautiful things.

SWAMIJI: Yes, beautiful things.

ALEXIS: When that distinction is uprooted?

SWAMIJI: Then that is Shaivism. Then that is Shaivism, that is not devotion. In devotion, there are two: master and devotee. In devotion, you find two things: one master [who is] high and the devotee [who is residing] on a lower level. The devotee has to weep, the devotee has to cry. When the crying stops, that is Shaivism. We have nothing to do with that here.[220] [Here], we want to perceive the Master at the stage of His being a Master and we have to imagine ourselves as His slaves.

Yatsamastasubhagārthavastuṣu sparśa mātra vidhinācamatkṛtim. Just by touching that, by touching those things ("touching" means sensation), at the time of sensation of those things (*śabda*, *sparśa*, *rūpa*, *rasa*, and *gandha*), . . .

[Do] you understand these *śabda*, *sparśa*, *rūpa*, *rasa*, and *gandha*? These five senses.

. . . there are some devotees of Thee, *acala bhaktiśālinaḥ*, whose devotion is stationary, *acala bhakti*, whose devotion is . . .

ALEXIS: Un-swerving.

SWAMIJI: . . . unmoving, always stable devotion . . .

DENISE: Unwavering devotion.

SWAMIJI: Unwavering devotion.

. . . those devotees, *tāṁ samarpayati*, they adore You with that. Those devotees of Thee, those who are perfectly devotees, they adore You with that, i.e., whenever they hear some beautiful sound, they carry that sound to You and worship You with that sound. Whenever they [see] some beautiful body of some most beautiful girl, that sensation they carry and offer it [to You].

JOHN: Is that [like] when your master saw that beautiful girl sitting in front of him?[221] That time you told us that story that your master . . .

SWAMIJI: He got entry in God consciousness.

JOHN: He didn't go to her, he went to God. That carried him [to God]. That's what is meant by these, here.

SWAMIJI: Yes, that is . . .

ALEXIS: This is real *śākta pūjā*.

---

220 That is, in this devotional treatise. [*Editor's note*]

221 She was a beautiful young girl adorned with beautiful ornaments who was serving tea to Swamiji's master, Swami Mahatabkak. [*Editor's note*]

SWAMIJI: Yes.

Tena te vapuḥ pūjayanti acala bhaktiśāliṅaḥ. So, they adore Your body that way, i.e., those who are such devotees.

Chapter 13 (45:32)

स्फारयस्यखिलमात्मना स्फुरन्
विष्वमामृशसि रूपमामृशन् ।
यत्स्वयं निजरसेन घूर्णसे
तत्समुल्लसति भावमण्डलम् ॥ १५ ॥

sphārayasyakhilamātmanā sphuran
viṣvamāmṛśasi rūpamāmṛśan /
yatsvayaṁ nijarasena ghūrṇase
tatsamullasati bhāvamaṇḍalam //15//

O Lord, when You *ātmanā sphuran*, when Your joy knows no bounds, when You are joyously shining, then the whole universe shines joyously.

Viśvamāmṛśasi, when You perceive Your own nature, the whole universe is perceived.

Yat svayaṁ nijarasena ghūrṇase, when You are intoxicated by Your own nectar of God consciousness, of Your nature of God consciousness, *tat samullasati bhāva maṇḍalam*, this whole universe comes into its being.

So, there is no difference between the universe and Your Self, Your nature.

Whenever You are shining, that means the whole world is shining. Whenever You perceive Your nature, that means the whole universe is being perceived. Whenever You are intoxicated by Your nectar of God consciousness, it means this whole universe is intoxicated.

ALEXIS: So, this transcendental consciousness is just our imagination from the point of view of rising. Withdrawing the world. From Śiva's point of view, Self-awareness is universal awareness–same thing.

SWAMIJI: The same thing. It is *śakti vikāsa* and *śiva vikāsa*, the expansion of [His] energy and the expansion of His nature. The expansion of [His] nature is God consciousness and the expansion of His energy is consciousness of energy, universal energy.

ALEXIS: So, this is an absolute point, which is both transcendent . . .

SWAMIJI: Yes, it is not imagination only.

ALEXIS: *Śāntoditaṁ parama dhāma.*

SWAMIJI: *Śāntā* and *uditā*. It is *śāntā* also and it is *uditā* also, both simultaneously.

ALEXIS: Withdrawn and emergent.

SWAMIJI: From one point of view, when you perceive as God consciousness, it is *śāntā*, appeased. From another point of view, if you perceive [God consciousness], you'll feel It is bubbling, It is flowing, It is just like a fountain.

Chapter 13 (48:06)

योऽविकल्पमिदमर्थमण्डलं
पश्यतीश निखिलं भवद्वपुः ।
स्वात्मपक्षपरिपूरिते जग-
त्यस्य नित्यसुखिनः कुतो भयम् ॥१६॥

yo'vikalpamidamarthamaṇḍalaṁ
paśyatīśa nikhilaṁ bhavadvapuḥ /
svātmapakṣaparipūrite jaga-
tyasya nityasukhinaḥ kuto bhayam //16//

Īśa, O Lord, any person who perceives this whole universe, this whole objective world, as one with Your nature–*paśyatīśa nikhilaṁ bhavadvapuḥ*, he feels that this whole objective world is Your own body–and for him, *svātma pakṣa paripūrite jagati*, for him, this whole universe is filled with God consciousness everywhere. *Asya nitya sukhinaḥ*, he is always blissful. *Kuto bhayam*, where there is fear for him? There is no fear for such a person.

ALEXIS: *Akutobhayam* state.

SWAMIJI: *Akutobhayam* state.[222]

Chapter 13 (49:11)

कण्ठकोणविनिविष्टमीश ते
कालकूटमपि मे महामृतम् ।
अप्युपात्तममृतं भवद्वपुर्-
भेदवृत्ति यदि रोचते न मे ॥१७॥

kaṇṭhakoṇaviniviṣṭamīśa te
kālakūṭamapi me mahāmṛtam /
apyupāttamamṛtaṁ bhavadvapur-
bhedavṛtti yadi rocate na me //17//

O Lord, there is one tremendous poison in Your neck of *kālakūṭa* [from the time] when You swallowed that *kālakūṭa viṣa* (poison) at the time of churning this *kṣīrasāgara* (the ocean of milk, milky ocean[223]), and that *kālakūṭa viṣa* appeared from that [ocean] while churning it, and it was tolerated by nobody! Everybody cried and it created a crisis from all sides in heaven. Who could touch it?

DEVOTEES: What was it?

SWAMIJI: It was poison. It was one bowl of poison that came out from that ocean.[224]

DENISE: When it was churned.

SWAMIJI: When it was churned.

And then You consoled all of the *devās*, all of the gods, [by saying], "there is no fear, I will drink it". And You drank it and what happened? You kept it, You swallowed it, and You digested it only in Your throat.

It was not sentenced to the heart of Lord Śiva, otherwise Lord

222 Having no fear from any quarter, secure.

223 See chapter 14, verse 17.

224 "Differentiated perception is poison, i.e., to perceive everybody different from your nature, that is real *kālakūṭa* poison." *Janmamaraṇavicāragranthaḥ*, *Janma Maraṇa Vicāra* of Bhaṭṭa Vāmadeva, translation and commentary by Swami Lakshmanjoo (original audio recordings, USF archives, Los Angeles, 1980).

Siva would [have] also disappeared. So, it spread only on the surface of His neck and His neck became absolutely black because of that poison. So, from that day, He [was] nominated, Lord Śiva is nominated, as Nīlakaṇṭha. His black neck is also adored by people.

ALEXIS: So, "*nīlakaṇṭha*" means having a black neck; Nīlakaṇṭha, He of the black neck.

SWAMIJI: Black neck due to that poison.

And *kaṇṭhakoṇa viniviṣṭam*, that *kālakūṭam*, *kālakūta* poison, which is residing at the place of Your throat, that is only for me, that is a great nectar for me. Keep me there!

Apyupāttam amṛtaṁ bhavadvapur bhedavṛtti. If I receive that nectar from the gods–nectar also came from that ocean of *kṣīra* (milk) and the nectar was utilized by the gods because they became immortal by that–I don't want that nectar. If You are away from me, I don't want [that nectar], I want that poison. Keep me in that poison! *Apyupāttam amṛtam*, if I have received that *amṛta*, that nectar, but *bhavat vapur bhedavṛtti*, You are away from me, I don't like that. Give me that poison, that great poison, and keep me there. I don't mind if I die there. I want to die in You.

This is his desire.

Chapter 13 (52:46)

त्वत्प्रलापमयरक्तगीतिका
नित्ययुक्तवदनोपशोभितः ।
स्यामथापि भवदर्चनक्रिया-
प्रेयसीपरिगताशयः सदा ॥१८॥

tvatpralāpamayaraktagītikā
nityayuktavadanopaśobhitaḥ /
syāmathāpi bhavadarcanakriyā-
preyasīparigatāśayaḥ sadā //18//

Everybody wants songs and a beautiful girl. Songs and a beautiful girl are liked by everybody. Everybody wants a girl and songs, various songs. I too also want the same thing, but in another way.

Tvat pralāpamaya raktagītikā. [I want] songs connected with Thy devotion. *Nitya yuktavadanopaśobhitaḥ*, I would like to have my mouth beautified and 'nectarized' by those songs, always.

Which songs?

ALEXIS: Songs of love.

SWAMIJI: Songs of Your devotion. This way of songs.

And *athāpi*, and next I would like to have *bhavat arcana kriyā-preyasī*, just Your worship, and just worshiping You, always. And that worshiping You always is a beautiful girl. I want to *parigatāśayaḥ*, I want to embrace that beautiful girl always; be embraced, be married to that beautiful girl!

You know married?

ALEXIS: Yeah, yeah.

SWAMIJI: What? Not sexual intercourse. Married means always . . .

DENISE: United.

SWAMIJI: United.

ALEXIS: United, *parigatāśaya*, my heart filled with, pervaded, *prāptā*.

SWAMIJI: With that beautiful girl. Which beautiful girl?

ALEXIS: Devotion.

SWAMIJI: Just with Your worship.

These two things I want. And these two things are longed for by everybody, desired by everybody. Everybody wants to hear beautiful songs, beautiful music, and [have a] beautiful girl in their lap. I want the same thing but in another way [laughter].

Chapter 13 (54:54)

ईहितं न बत पारमेश्वरं
शक्यते गणयितुं तथा च मे ।
दत्तमप्यमृतनिर्भरं वपुः
स्वं न पातुमनुमन्यते तथा ॥ १९ ॥

īhitaṁ na bata pārameśvaraṁ
śakyate gaṇayituṁ tathā ca me /
dattamapyamṛtanirbharaṁ vapuḥ
svaṁ na pātumanumanyate tathā //19//

[These are] the tricks of Lord Śiva, O people!

He addresses now this to people, to His devotees. Amongst his devotees, he addresses.

O devotees, O you devotees, come and hear from me the latest news. *Īhitaṁ na*, I have found Lord Śiva [to be] a first class hypocrite, first-class . . ."

ALEXIS: Fraud.

SWAMIJI: ". . . fraud. You can't imagine, you can't calculate [the extent of] His fraudness. This expanded fraudness, you can't imagine, i.e., how [much of a] fraud He is! *Tathā ca*, I'll just prove that before you."

ALEXIS: *Īhitam*?

SWAMIJI: *Īhitam* means "fraud".

Īhitaṁ pārameśvaram, the fraudness of Pārameśvarah, *na bata śakyate gaṇayituṁ*, cannot be understood by anybody! You can't understand and I have not understood His fraudness. And I have come to know that He is a first-class fraud. *Tathā ca*, I will prove it to you. Before you, I will prove how He is a fraud.

Dattamapi amṛta nirbharaṁ. He has bestowed [upon] me His nature of God consciousness. That supreme nectar of God consciousness, He has handed this over to me, but *na pātum anumanyate*, He does not allow me to eat or drink It. Is this not [the behavior of a] fraud? He has bestowed [It to] me, He has presented That nectar before me, but He does not allow me to drink It. What kind of fraud [is this]? Is it not fraud?

DENISE: It's cruel.

SWAMIJI: To give and *bas* . . .

DENISE: You can't drink.

SWAMIJI: . . . you can't [drink it].

DENISE: You're dying of thirst but you can't drink.

SWAMIJI: *Dattamapi amṛta nirbharaṁ vapuḥ*. He has given me, bestowed [upon] me, that *svarūpa*, which is filled with nectar, but *na pātum anumanyate tathā*, He does not permit me to drink It according to my choice. He says, "I will let you know when you can drink it".

JOHN: This means he has had a taste.

SWAMIJI: He has not given It at all. It is just giving nothing. It is just equal to giving nothing.

JOHN: So, here he means that He has put before him this God consciousness only in intellect, or he has had some taste of It but has not been given It fully?

SWAMIJI: No [affirmative].

JOHN: It's like its a tease. Is that what it is, like a tease for him?

SWAMIJI: Yes, it is teasing, yes.

Chapter 13 (57:41)

त्वमगाधमविकल्पमद्वयं
स्वं स्वरूपमखिलार्थघस्मरम् ।
आविशन्नहमुमेश सर्वदा
पूजयेयमभिसंस्तुवीय च ॥२०॥

tvamagādhamavikalpamadvayaṁ
svaṁ svarūpamakhilārthaghasmaram /
āviśannahamumeśa sarvadā
pūjayeyamabhisaṁstuvīya ca //20//

O Lord, leave that [issue of] Your fraudness aside. I don't say that! I didn't mean that! It was just because I was perturbed [laughter].

Still, where will he go? Where this devotee will go? If he will abuse Lord Śiva, he is finished. So, he again comes for apology.

Agādham, You are *agādha*, You are infinite; *avikalpam*, You are thoughtless; *advayaṁ*, *advaita* means You are always *advaita*, without duality; and You are the nature of everybody[225]; *akhilārtha ghasmaram*, and You are fond of taking all cognitions, all dualistic cognitions, in Your own nature. You are fond of that. You are fond of taking all of this cognitive consciousness, dualistic cognitive consciousness, in Your own nature.

There is one desire in me. I would like to enter in You (*āviśan*). *Umeśa*, O Pārvatī's husband, *āviśan aham*, when I enter in You, I don't want . . . this is not my way of desire that I will enter in You and be one with that God consciousness, that blissful state. That is not my only desire. My chief, main desire, is *pūjayeyam*

225 *Svaṁ svarūpam.*

abhisaṁ stuvīyaca, I would adore You always there because it would be very easy to adore You. Not only adore You! I would adore You and I would sing the glory of You.

Chapter Fourteen
Singing the Glory of Lord Śiva
Jayastotranāma caturdaśaṁ stotram

SWAMIJI: *Jayastotranāma caturdaśaṁ stotram.*

Chapter 14 (00:03)

जयलक्ष्मीनिधानस्य निजस्य स्वामिनः पुरः ।
जयोद्घोषणपीयूषरसमास्वादये क्षणम ॥ १ ॥

jayalakṣmīnidhānasya nijasya svāminaḥ puraḥ /
jayodghoṣaṇa pīyūṣarasamāsvādaye kṣaṇam //1//

My own master is the treasure of all glory. My master is the treasure . . .

ALEXIS: Treasure-house.

SWAMIJI: *Jaya lakṣmī nidhānasya.*

ALEXIS: Receptacle of all, treasure-house.

SWAMIJI: Treasure-house of glory. My master is the only treasure-house of glory.

ALEXIS: The Bank.

SWAMIJI: There is one desire in me. That desire is that, before Him, before my master, *nijasya svāminaḥ*, before my own master, . . .

[Utpaladeva] says, He is not [just] anybody's master. He is my master! He is not anybody's . . . He is not owned by anybody [else]. He is owned by me only (*nijasya svāminaḥ puraḥ*).

. . . before Him, *jaya udghoṣaṇa pīyūṣarasam āsvādaye kṣaṇam*, I would like to taste the nectar of this announcement before Him. Before God, I would like to taste the nectar of this announcement: "O Lord, glory be to Thee, glory be to You, glory be to You, glory be to You, *jaya*, *jaya*!"

I don't want glory for myself, just for Yourself. You will be glorified. I will pray, I will pray for You that You'll live a long life.

I don't want my life. I want to shorten my life. I want to give my span of life also for You. You will be glorified everywhere, always.

[Utpaladeva] doesn't want his life. He wants Him to live. This is real love.

Chapter 14a (02:28)

जयैकरुद्रैकशिव महादेव महेश्वर ।
पार्वतीप्रणयिञ्शर्व सर्वगीर्वाणपूर्वज ॥२॥

jayaikarūdraikaśiva mahādeva maheśvara /
pārvatīpraṇayiñśarva sarvagīrvāṇapūrvaja //2//

These are only *āmantraṇas* (*āmantraṇa* means calling).

Eka rūdra, O Lord, You are *eka rūdra*, You are the only Rūdra! *Eka Śiva*, O Lord, You are the only Śiva! *Mahādeva*, You are the only Mahādeva! *Maheśvara*, You are Maheśvara! *Pārvatī praṇayin*, You are the beloved of Pārvatī! *Śarva*, You are the destroyer of the dualistic world (*śarva* means *hiṁsaka*, *śarva hiṁsāyām*[226]). *Sarva gīrvāṇa pūrvaja*, You are the source of all gods! Glory be to Thee. Let You live one hundred million years, for me. I will die and be born again. I will die and see You [again] as my Master. You must live!

Jaya means, in another sense, that he wants Him to live. He doesn't want himself to live. He wants His glory.[227]

Chapter 14a (04:00)

जय त्रैलोक्यनाथैकलाञ्छनालिकलोचन ।
जय पीतार्तलोकार्तिकालकूटाङ्ककन्धर ॥३॥

jaya trailokyanāthaikalāñcchanālikalocana /
jaya pītārtalokārtikālakūṭāṅkakandhara //3//

226 Swamiji is using "*hiṁsaka*" in the sense of one who gives trouble to the dualistic world. "*Śarva*" is an appelation of Lord Śiva as Rūdra, the destroyer. [*Editor's note*]

227 That is, Utpaladeva wants Lord Śiva to be glorified.

Trailokyanāthaikalāñcchanā alikalocana. You know, O Lord, why You have kept this third eye on Your forehead? This is the indication that You have made, in this respect, that, "I, [Lord Śiva], am the only master of all the three worlds". This is the indication of being the master of the three worlds. This [third eye] You have kept as a sign of that indication. Glory be to Thee! You just live long, for always!

Pītārta lokārti kāla kūṭāṅka kandhara. Ārta loka ārti, ārta loka, those people, those gods, who were kept in crisis at the time of churning that milky ocean . . .*

How the crisis happened to them?

JOHN: By that poison.

SWAMIJI: By the poison that came out from that churning. And this was not poison. This was just torture for all of the gods. This was the appearance of torture and crisis for all of the gods. They just began to die.

DENISE: From fright?

SWAMIJI: Not from fright; from that smell, from that poisonous smell.

*. . . *pītārtaloka*, and that crisis of all of the gods, You have drunk. Glory be to Thee. Let You live for a billion thousand years [laughter]!

Chapter 14a (06:08)

जयमूर्तत्रिशक्त्यात्मशितशूलोल्लसत्कर ।
जयेच्छामात्रसिद्धार्थपूजार्हचरणाम्बुज ॥४॥

jayamūrtatriśaktyātmaśitaśūlollasatkara /
jayecchāmātrasiddhārthapūjārhacaraṇāmbujaḥ / /4/ /

[Utpaladeva] reveals His history also in this *Jayastotra* and, at the same time, glorifies Him with long life and prosperity.

I don't want to become prosperous. You must remain prosperous. You must remain shining, beautiful, healthy. All bad things must come to me. I don't mind. This is the only consolation for me that if You live, if You live happily.

He [laughter], this bloody fool, Utpaladeva, doesn't know that He is always living. It is just out of his love [for Him].

DENISE: And feeling selfless.

SWAMIJI: Yes.

Jaya mūrta triśakti ātma śita śūla ullasatkara. You have held the *triśūla* in Your hand. You have held the *triśūla*, sharp *triśūla*, in Your hand. You have held . . .

Triśūla, you know?

With three prongs. That weapon of *triśūla*.

. . . *śitaśūla ullasatakara*, You have held this sharp *triśūla* in Your hand, *mūrtatriśakyāt*, and that is the indication of Your three great energies. That indicates that You possess the three great energies (*parā*, *parāparā*, and *aparā*).[228] Glory be to Thee.

Icchā mātra siddhārtha pūjārha caraṇāmbuja. And You have got lotus feet. You have got lotus feet and those lotus feet are worthy of being worshiped (*pūjārha caraṇāmbuja*). *Icchāmātra siddhārtha*, and these lotus feet, which are worthy of being worshiped by devotees, these lotus feet of Thee, *icchāmātra siddhārtha*, they bestow the *siddhis*, the fulfillment of all ambitions. They bestow the fulfillment of all ambitions, not by some effort, without effort, but by will only (*icchāmātrataḥ*)! By *icchayā*, only with will, these lotus feet of Thee, [which] are worthy of being worshiped by everybody, they bestow all of the powers and all of the fulfillments of worldly enjoyments and spiritual enjoyments by will, by only desire. Glory be to Thee. Let You live for one thousand billion years!

---

228 "The supreme Energy (*parā śakti*) is that Energy beyond limitation. It is non-dual (*advaita*), monistic. Medium (*parāparā*) energy is both non-dual (*advaita*) and dual (*dvaita*). Inferior (*aparā*) energy is only dual (*dvaita*). These three energies correspond to subjective consciousness, conceptual consciousness, and objective consciousness. I bow to that Consciousness which shines in these three ways. That Consciousness is the heart of Lord Śiva. It is both one with the universe and above the universe.

"These three states of consciousness are the three aspects that make up any perception. There is the perceiver, which is subjective consciousness; the means of perceiving that object, which is cognitive consciousness; and the object being perceived, which is objective consciousness." *Self Realization in Kashmir Shaivism*, 3.55-56.

Chapter 14a (09:53)

जय शोभाशतस्यन्दिलोकोत्तरवपुर्धर ।
जयैकजटिकाक्षीणगङ्गाकृत्यात्तभस्मक ॥५॥

jaya śobhāśatasyandilokottaravapurdhara /
jayaikajaṭikākṣīṇagaṅgākṛtyāttabhasmaka //5//

All of these are *āmantraṇa* words. They are all *āmantraṇas*.

ALEXIS: Vocatives.

SWAMIJI: Vocatives.

Śobhāśata syandi lokottara vapurdhara. You have possessed that body, which is *lokottara* (*lokottara vapuḥ* means "a supernatural body and form"). Your form is also supernatural. There is no comparison with [Your] body anywhere.

The only beautiful and the best body is possessed by Lord Śiva. You can't imagine how beautiful and how great and how shining and how glorious He is.

Śobhā śata syandi. It flows out with glory and beautifies everybody near Him, near His body. When you are placed before [His] body, you will also shine. All of your ugliness will vanish; it will be shattered to pieces and you will become divine, divinely beautiful. That is *śobhā śata syandi lokottara vapurdhara.* You have possessed that kind of body, that kind of *rūpa* (form). Glory be to Thee! Let You live for one *lakh* billion years. More than that!

Jaya eka jaṭikā kṣīṇa gaṅgā kṛtyātta bhasmaka. Eka jaṭikā kṣīṇa gaṅgā kṛti (*jaṭikā* means "matted locks"), by one twisted, matted lock, this whole Ganges, the Gaṅgā, has flown out (from one lock of His matted hair). *Ātta bhasmaka*–and, at the same time, it is not only the water that is white on Your head–*ātta bhasmaka*, You have applied these ashes also on Your face just to conceal Your beauty, because You are too much beautiful! Just to conceal it, You have put that. Glory be to Thee. Let You live for always.

Chapter 14a (12:40)

जय क्षीरोदपर्यस्तज्योत्स्नाच्छायानुलेपन
जयेश्वराङ्गसङ्गोत्थरत्नकान्ताहिमण्डन ॥६॥

jaya kṣīrodaparyastajyotsnācchāyānulepana /
jayeśvarāṅgasaṅgottharatnakāntāhimaṇḍana //6//

These are all *āmantraṇas*, calling.

Kṣiroda paryasta jyotsnāt chāyā anulepana (*kṣīroda* means *kṣīrasāgara*, the milky ocean). From the milky ocean, *paryasta jyotsnācchāya*, the *pratibimba*, the reflection of the moon, which has come out from that–*jyotsnā*, the moon also came out from that [milky ocean]–that *chāyā anulepana*[229], that is equivalent to Your shining, i.e., that *chāyā anulepana*, that *chāyā* (reflection) has reflected on Your face. Glory be to Thee.

Īśvara aṅga saṅgottha ratna kāntāhi maṇḍana. And those great big snakes, which You have . . .

DENISE: Wrapped around your neck?

SWAMIJI: . . . wrapped under Your neck and arms, *īśvarāṅga saṅgottha*, . . .

It is said in the history of the *Purāṇas* that those cobras have developed stars [on the top of their heads] because of the touch of Lord Śiva.

. . . *īśvara aṅga saṅga ratnotkānta ahi maṇḍalam*, O, You have decorated Your body with those great snakes, glory be to Thee!

ALEXIS: And *they* have become beautiful by Your touch.

SWAMIJI: Yes.

Glory be to Thee. Let You live for always!

Chapter 14a (14:44)

जयाक्षयैकशीतांशुकलासदृशसंश्रय ।
जय गङ्गासदारब्धविश्वैश्वर्याभिसेचन ॥७॥

jayākṣayaikaśītāṁśukalāsadṛśasaṁśraya /
jaya gaṅgāsadārabdhaviśvaiśvaryābhisecana //7//

Akṣa eka śītāṁśu kalā. There is one *kalā*[230] of the moon, which does not decrease, which does not vanish. That is *amākalā*, the

229 Lit., the anointing or besmearing (*anulepana*) of the moon's reflection (*chāyā*).

230 *Kalā* means "a digit or segment of the moon". [*Editor's note*]

sixteenth *kalā*, the sixteenth part of the moon that is the outline of that [new] moon.

You have seen that outline of that moon. It does not vanish [completely]. All of those internal parts [of the moon] vanish in fifteen days, but that *amākalā* does not vanish. And that *amākalā* He has kept on His forehead. That *amākalā*, He has placed on His forehead.

Sadṛśa saṁśraya, it is exactly like You! *Sadṛśa saṁśraya*, You are *samāna bhāva*[231]—immortal and this *kalā* is also immortal, imperishable. So, You are *sadṛśa saṁśraya*, You are the *saṁśraya*, the *ādhāra* (the basis) of that–the basis of *amākalā* is divine; *amākalā* is immortal–the basis that is [on] Your forehead, that is also immortal. Glory be to Thee! You have kept it like that; You have decorated Your forehead.

ALEXIS: So, He is *saptadaśī kalā*[232] in the background of that.

SWAMIJI: Yes [laughter].

Gaṅgā sadārabdha viśvaiśvarya ābhiṣecana. And You are bestowing glory and prosperity to the whole universe; prosperity to the whole universe through the Ganges, through the Ganges, which You have on Your head. Glory be to Thee. Let You live long.

Chapter 14a (16:55)

जयाधराङ्गसंस्पर्शपावनीकृतगोकुल ।
जय भक्तिमदाबद्धगोष्ठी नियतसन्निधे ॥८॥

jayādharāṅgasaṁsparśapāvanīkṛtagokula /
jaya bhaktimadābaddhagoṣṭhī niyatasannidhe //8//

Adharāṅga saṁsparśa pāvanīkṛta gokula.

Do you know what You have done?

You have Your transport, You have made Your transport a bull, and You have kept Your lower portion of Your body on that bull. It is why all of the bull class and all cows are supposed to be pure. Everybody respects this dynasty of bulls and cows.

They say they are divine; they are mothers for our lifetime.

231 *Samāna bhāva*: the state or appearance of similarity. That is, the *kalā* of the moon is just like Lord Śiva.

232 See appendix 23 for an explanation of *saptadaśī kalā*.

Our mother is, actual mother is, only up to that time when we have grown [up]. Up to that point, our mother is serving us but the cow-mother is serving us for all of our life.

Adharāṅga saṁsparśa, it is why You have touched Your lower portion of [Your] body on the bull for going, moving here and there. *Pāvanī kṛta gokula*, You have made the dynasty of bulls and cows pure by that. Glory be to Thee!

Jaya bhaktimadābaddha goṣṭhī niyatasannidhe. When Your devotees gather (*bhaktimat* means "devotees"), when they gather at a certain place and they talk and they think of You and discuss matters regarding You, when they discuss [matters] regarding Your position and Your thinking and Your everything, when they discuss these things, there, *niyata sannidhe*, You are hearing those things there in disguise. You are always there. When they have gathered, i.e., Your devotees, wherever they have gathered–maybe in London or in America or in Kashmir or in India–wherever they gather and talk of You, You are there hearing all of those talks. *Niyata sannidhe*, it is essential (*niyata* means it is . . . definitely You are there in disguise hearing those talks). Glory be to Thee [laughter]! *Bhakti mat ābaddha goṣṭhī* (*goṣṭhī* means gathering), *niyata sannidhe*, You are there, You are present always there in disguise.

Chapter 14a (19:57)

जय स्वेच्छातपोवेशविप्रलम्भितबालिश ।
जय गौरीपरिष्वङ्गयोग्यसौभाग्यभाजन ॥९॥

jaya svecchātapoveśavipralambhitabāliśa /
jaya gaurīpariṣvaṅgayogyasaubhāgyabhājana //9//

Svecchātapoveśa vipralambhitabāliśa . . .

You know, he relates His history, all of His history, in this *stotra*.

Svecchātapa, by Your own will, You have made Yourself as in the disguise of [one who is] performing penance.

Is there any such picture of Lord Śiva [here]? No, not here. Somewhere you will see that picture of Lord Śiva in *padmāsana*, eyes closed, and with beads, eyes closed, and keeping those [beads in His hand], *bas*, meditating. Meditating on whom? That is yet to be known [laughter]! Because, He is the object of meditation, but He is meditating.

ALEXIS: He is meditator and meditated upon.

SWAMIJI: *Svecchātapoveśa*, this *veśa*, this *rūpa* (form) of His being the devotee of some other Lord, *vipralambhitabāliśa*, by that position of Yours, You have [misled] those fools who don't understand Your trick. This is only a trick. Just, this is a trick, just to carry away those fools from the real point. They [mistakenly] understand that, for Lord Śiva, there is some other god, some important god, because He is reciting *mantra*. *Vipralambhitabāliśa*, You have *vipralambhita* (*vipralambhita* means "You have misdirected them"), misdirected those people.

ALEXIS: Fooled the fools.

DENISE: Purposely misdirected them.

SWAMIJI: Yes.

Glory be to Thee for this trick [laughter]!

Jaya gauripariṣvaṅga yogyasaubhāgyabhājana. And You have embraced Pārvatī. You are always . . . Your Pārvatī is always in Your arms. You don't know how much joy and how much fortunate You are! You are so much fortunate to have Her in Your arms (*gaurīpariṣvaṅga*). This fortune was only befitting You because You are also fortunate. *Yogya saubhāgya bhājana* (*yogya saubhāgya* means "She is fortunate because of You and You are fortunate because of Her"), You are both fortunate. And this is *yogyatā*, this combination is the best combination for You both. Pārvatī's being in Your arms is befitting and Your embracing Pārvatī is befitting. Glory be to Thee.

Chapter 14a (23:33)

जय भक्तिरसार्द्रार्द्रभावोपायनलम्पट ।
जय भक्तिमदोद्दामभक्तवाङ्नृत्ततोषित ॥१०॥

jaya bhaktirasārdrārdrabhāvopāyanalampaṭa /
jaya bhaktimadoddāmabhaktavāṅnṛttatoṣita //10//

Bhakti rasārdrārdra bhāvopāyanalampaṭa. You are fond of those presents, which are kept before You by Your devotees with *ārdrārdra bhāva* (*ārdrārdra bhāva* means “with moist point of view”), they are with [moisture]. Devotedly, with great love, they place before [You], they offer those offerings, whatever they like. Some flowers, good flowers, they offer, [or] some fruits they offer to You, before Your image, with great love and devotion. You are fond of those offerings! *Bhakti rasārdrārdra bhāva* (*upāyana* means offering) *lampaṭa*, You crave for those offerings, always. You search for those offerings. You are in search for those offerings, always. You dream . . . Your dream comes true when You get those offerings from those devotees (*lampaṭa* means You are “craving” for that). Glory be to Thee! Glory be to Thee! Let You live for long!

Bhaktimada uddāma bhakta vāk nṛttatoṣita. When there is a devotee filled with the intoxication of Your devotion, Your attachment, and he cries only one word and calls You, “O Lord Śiva”, by that, by hearing that [cry of] “Lord Śiva, O Lord Śiva” from those lips, those . . .

Whose lips?

DENISE: Those who are craving for You, who love You so dearly.

SWAMIJI: Yes.

. . . *nṛttatoṣita*, You dance and You are satisfied by hearing those things. You just dance there, whenever You hear those calls from Your devotees. Glory be to Thee.

Chapter 14a (25:57)

जय ब्रह्मादिदेवेशप्रभावप्रभवव्यय ।
जयलोकेश्वरश्रेणीशिरोविधृतशासन ॥११॥

jaya brahmādideveśaprabhāvaprabhavavyaya /
jayalokeśvaraśreṇīśirovidhṛtaśāsana //11//

Brahmādi deveśa: Brahma (the creator), Viṣṇu (the protector), and Rūdra (the destroyer) of this universe. The *prabhāva* (the glory) of Brahma is to create the world, and the glory of Viṣṇu is to protect it, and the glory of the Rūdra is to destroy this universe.

You are *prabhavavyaya*, You are the creator of that glory and withdrawer of that glory. You create that glory in them and You withdraw that glory from them. You have got that power. You have bestowed this glory to them, O Lord Śiva. Glory be to Thee. Let You be glorious!

Jayalokeśvara śreṇī śirovidhṛtaśāsana. Lokeśvara means "*lokapāla*", those who are bent upon governing all of the ten sides of this universe. The eastern side is governed by Indra, this [South-East] corner is governed by god Agni, this [south] corner is ruled by Yama, and that [South-West] corner is ruled by Nairitti, and this West side is ruled by Varuṇa, and this [North-West] corner is ruled by Vāyu (the god of wind), and this [North] side is ruled by Kubera, and this [North-East] corner is ruled by Īśvara. And this is the *lokeśvara śreṇī*, the class of *lokapālas*, the protectors of these sides of this whole universe. Brahma is up, and down is Viṣṇu. So, there are ten *lokapālas*, ten [gods] who look after, govern, this whole universe, and those *lokapālas* have *śiro vidhṛta śāsana*, have accepted Your order, Your kingdom, on their foreheads.

Whose kingdom?

Kingdom of Lord Śiva. The kingdom of Lord Śiva is accepted by each *lokapāla* on their foreheads. Glory be to Thee.

JOHN: "Accepted by them on their foreheads" means?

SWAMIJI: They have accepted whatever . . . they bow to His order, they accept His order. It may be anything, bad or good, they have to accept it!

GANJOO: They accept His sovereignty.

SWAMIJI: Yes.

Glory be to Thee!

Chapter 14a (29:13)

जयसर्वजगन्न्यस्तस्वमुद्राव्यक्तवैभव ।
जयात्मदानपर्यन्तविश्वेश्वर महेश्वर ॥१२॥

jayasarvajagannyastasvamudrāvyaktavaibhava /
jayātmadānaparyantaviśveśvara maheśvara //12//

It is not "*vyaktavaibhava*" as it is commentated upon by Kṣemarāja, i.e. "Your glory is found . . .

ALEXIS: Manifested (*vyakta*).

SWAMIJI: . . . your glory is already vividly existing in this whole universe". That is not the meaning of this *śloka*.

Sarvajagat nyasta svamudrāvyaktavaibhava. Your glory is vividly found in all of this universe. In all of this universe, Your glory is vividly found because You have put Your own stamp everywhere!

That [word] "stamp" (*svamudrā*), I would like to translate in my own way, not as the commentator of this *Śivastotrāvalī* [i.e., Kṣemarāja] has translated it. It is also in one way correct but it looks rather mean, i.e., this kind of explanation. "*Svamudrā*" he has [commentated as]: Lord Śiva's stamp is *yoni* (that *praṇālī*) and *liṅga*. *Praṇālī* is concerned with a woman and *liṅga* is concerned with a man. So, You have put these two signs everywhere in this world. That is Your own stamp. You have put [Your] stamp everywhere. This is how Kṣemarāja translates this [word] "*svamudrā*".

But, from my viewpoint, *svamudrā* means "all-knowledge" and "all-activity". [Your powers of] all-knowledge and all-activity, You have put everywhere. Partly, everybody has knowledge and partly, everybody has action. So, this is His stamp. Not [*yoni* and *liṅga*] only.

Sarva jagat nyasta. You have put Your spiritual stamp on each and every act of this universe. It may be a creative act, it may be a protective act, it may be a destructive act, on all of these acts, You have kept Your stamp. So, it won't be touched by anybody; it won't be owned, it won't be utilized by anybody except when this seal, when You will break this seal. You have kept that seal, stamped it, so [there can be] no other further handling [of it] except only when You handle it. When You order [someone] to handle it, then it will be handled.

So, Your *aiśvarya* (Your glory) is *avyakta*, Your glory is not revealed to anybody! Nobody has perceived Your glory, what Your glory is. On That glory, You have kept that stamp. It is absolutely stamped [i.e., sealed].

ALEXIS: But surely a "stamp" means a seal of recognition.

SWAMIJI: Sealed! But no, not a seal of recognition. That is what Kṣemarāja has commentated.

I believe this whole universe is handled by Lord Śiva Himself. There is no authority of anybody [else] to handle it. The only handler of this universe is Lord Siva. Only by His. . . with His orders, Brahma will create; with His orders, Viṣṇu will protect; with His orders, Rūdra will destroy it. So, You have kept Your glory absolutely under [Your] stamp. Glory be to Thee!

And, at the same time, on the contrary, what do You do? *Jayātmadāna paryantaviśveśvara*, You are so generous that You bestow Your own Self to Your devotees! You become the slave of Your devotees! This is Your greatness! You don't become the master of Your devotees. You [give] Your everything to them.[233] This is Your greatness! *Ātmadānaparyantaviśveśvara*, this *viśveśvara*, this generosity of Yours, is so great that You bestow Your own everything, Your own Self also, to Your devotees.[234] And Your devotees handle You and You are their slave. Glory be to Thee!

Chapter 14a (34:10)

जय त्रैलोक्यसर्गेच्छावसरासद्वितीयक ।
जयैश्वर्यभरोद्वाहदेवीमात्रसहाय ॥१३॥

jaya trailokyasargecchāvasarāsadvitīyaka /
jayaiśvaryabharodvāhadevīmātrasahāyaka //13//

Trailokya sarga icchāvasare. At the time when You create this universe, at the time of creating this universe, *asad dvitīyaka*, You don't take anybody's help. You don't need anybody's help to assist You. Nobody assists You at that moment when You create this whole universe. There is no assistance needed by You. You create, *bas*, according to Your own will.

Jaya aiśvarya bharodvāha devī mātra sahāyaka. Glory be to Thee, and, at the same time, *aiśvarya bhara udvāha* (*aiśvarya bhara* means the intensity of glory is found in You), and the intensity of glory, which You have accomplished, which You have gained [when You create the universe], at that time, You have taken the help of Pārvatī because Pārvatī is the only instrument to glorify You.

233 "You have got the authority and You have got the power to give, to bestow, whatever You have." *Śivastotrāvalī* (additional audio, USF archives).

234 "*Ātmadāna*, He gives His own Self in alms." Ibid.

Nobody knew Lord Siva when He was not married to Pārvatī.

DENISE: He was transcendental.

SWAMIJI: He was transcendental and nobody knew Him. He was known only when Pārvatī shook hands with Him; then He was known to the whole universe. Pārvatī means the world of means, *upāyas* (*śaivī mukhamihocyate*[235]). So, Pārvatī is the revealer of Lord Śiva.

Glory be to Thee!

> *jaya trailokyasargecchāvasarāsadvitīyaka /*
> *jayaiśvaryabharodvāhadevīmātrasahāyaka / / 13 / /*
> [repeated]

Whenever You have the desire to create this triple universe, . . .

The triple universe is *trailokya*, the three worlds. Actually, there are one hundred and eighteen worlds, but [these] one hundred and eighteen worlds, they are consumed in three worlds only–*bhūḥ*, *bhuvaḥ*, and *svaḥ*.[236]

. . . at the time when You desire, when You have got the desire, to create this triple universe, at that time, at that moment, *asat dvitīyaka*, nobody helped You at that time, because there was nobody who was capable to help You to create this triple universe. You created it by Your own self. O such a Lord, victory be to Thee.

Jayaiśvaryabharodvāha devī mātra sahāyaka. Aiśvarya bhara udvāha, when You have carried Your own glory of Your consciousness [into manifestation], at the time of carrying the glory of Your consciousness, there was nobody to help You except for Your better half, Pārvatī. O such a Lord, victory be to Thee!

---

235 "*Śakti* is, first, the means. *Śakti* is the pathway on which you have to tread. Because later on he will say, "*Śaivī mukham ihocyate*". *Śaivī* means *śakti*; *mukham* is the pathway. It is said that the pathway is *śakti*. You have to sentence your mind to Lord Śiva through that pathway–Pārvatī Śakti (not the Pārvatī who is residing in Kailash)." *Vijñāna Bhairava–The Manual for Self Realization*, verse 4, p7. See appendix 2 for an explanation of the *upāyas*.

236 See chapter 4, verse 23.

Chapter 14a (37:45)

जयाक्रमसमाक्रान्तसमस्तभुवनत्रय ।
जयाविगीतमाबालगीयमानेश्वरध्वने ॥ १४ ॥

jayākramasamākrāntasamastabhuvanatraya /
jayāvigītamābālagīyamāneśvaradhvane / / 14 / /

These, all the compound words, are *āmantraṇa padas*, only calling of Lord Śiva.

Akrama samākrānta samasta bhuvana traya. O Lord Śiva, all of these three worlds You have pervaded simultaneously; simultaneously You pervade all of these three worlds. The pervasion of the three worlds by You takes place . . .

ALEXIS: Without succession.

SWAMIJI: . . . without any succession.[237]

Glory be to Thee!

Avigītam ābāla gīyamāna īśvara dhvane. Just from Lord Rūdra to just an innocent child–right up to the innocent child–*gīyamāna īśvara adhvane*, everybody sings Your glory, everybody knows Your glory. Whenever there is an earthquake, whenever there is some crisis, automatically this sound comes [from the mouths of people]: "*namaḥ śivāya, namaḥ śivāya*!"

DENISE: "O God!" "O Jesus!"

SWAMIJI: "O God! O God!"

Jayāvigītamābāla gīyamaneśvardhvane. Your glory of being the Master of the three worlds is sung by all. From ignorant beings up to the elevated souls, everybody sings Your glory.

JAGDISH: *Ābāla* means there "ignorant persons".

SWAMIJI: Yes, *ābāla*. *Ābāla* there means "ignorant people". *Bāla* does not mean "boys" [or] "children".

Ābāla, right from ignorant persons up to the elevated souls, all sing Your glory, knowingly or unknowingly.

Mahatma Gandhi, on his tour to Mysore, in some village, he visited that place and asked them who was ruling them; he

237 "O Lord, You have possessed all of the three worlds, not one by one, but simultaneously, in one push. You have–*samākrānta* means "possessed"–You have possessed these three worlds just simultaneously, instantaneously." *Śivastotrāvalī* (additional audio, USF archives).

asked those guys who were digging the grounds there, [he] asked them, "who [is ruling you]?" They replied, "some God must be ruling us!" That is all [laughter]. They didn't know who but they admitted that there was a ruler.

So, right from ignorant persons to elevated souls, [they] all sing Your glory. O such a Lord, victory be to Thee!

Chapter 14a (40:37)

जयानुकम्पादिगुणानपेक्षसहजोन्नते ।
जय भीष्ममहामृत्युघटनापूर्वभैर ॥१५॥

jayānukampādiguṇānapekṣasahajonnate /
jaya bhīṣmamahāmṛtyughaṭanāpūrvabhairava //15//

Anukampādi guṇa anapekṣa sahajonnate. A man possessing all [good] qualifications is worthy of receiving grace from the gods. If you have [good] qualifications, you will receive grace from Brahma, you will receive grace from Nārāyaṇa, you will receive grace from Rūdra, you will receive grace from your master, when you are qualified, when you are devoted to him. But this case is not attributed to You, Sir!

Anukampādi guṇa anapekṣa sahajonnate. Your *unnate*, Your greatness of bestowing grace is not dependable to all of these qualifications. Without qualifications, You bestow grace to people! That is *śaktipāta*.[238]

Anukampādi guṇa anapekṣa sahaja unnate. O Lord, Your greatness (*unnate* means Your greatness) is *sahaja*, unartificial. Your greatness is not developed by Your maintaining discipline and *dharma* and virtue and purity and good qualities.

[Generally], if you have developed good qualities, if you develop good qualities, purity and everything, then you are great, you are supposed to be great.

But Your greatness is unartificial. Your greatness is not developed by You. You have got natural greatness, without maintaining this discipline of *anukampā*.[239]

You must love your fellow men. You must not hate. You must

238 Grace, which is spontaneous (*sahaja unnate*). [*Editor's note*]
239 *Dharma*, virtue, purity, etc.

not be rude to anybody. You must be pious. You must not tell lies. All of these qualities, when you develop [them], then you become great. This is the general case. But for You, this is not the case. You are naturally great. Glory be to Thee! Let You live for one hundred billion years!

Jaya bhīṣma mahā mṛtyu ghaṭanā pūrva bhairava. Bhīṣma mahā mṛtyu (*bhīṣma* means frightful; *mahā mṛtyu* means the great lord of death), the frightful great lord of death who is not conquered by anybody in this world . . . but that frightful lord of death also You have conquered, You have destroyed (*ghaṭana*; *ghaṭana* means "destroyer").

O Lord, *bhīṣma mahāmṛtyu*, that great god of death who is *bhīṣma* (*bhīṣma* means furious), the lord of death, when he comes, he will meet us one by one–it is definite. But, at that time, when he comes to shake hands with us, just only shaking hands [with him] will terrify [us and that] will be our death time. We will suffocate at that very moment when he just touches us. Just by his slight touch, we'll grumble at that moment. We will say, "*ahhh*, we are gone!" It is so furious. And that is *bhīṣma māha mṛtyu*, that lord of death is *bhīṣma*. So, he is furious!

O Lord, You *ghatanā* (*ghaṭanā* means You destroy), by destroying that lord of death also, You are *apūrva bhairava*, You are really the supreme Bhairava! You finish him also!

Whom?

DEVOTEES: Lord of Death.

SWAMIJI: Lord of Death.

O destroyer of that frightful lord of death, O Lord Śiva, glory be to Thee! You have destroyed that god of death also.

So, there is no worry of His dying. We just [pray for Him] for our satisfaction; [we] pray for His long life. Otherwise, He is always there.

Chapter 14b (00:00) start.

जय विशक्षयोच्चण्डक्रियानिष्परिपन्थिक
जय श्रेयःशतगुणानुगनामानुकीर्त ॥ १६ ॥

jaya viśakṣayoccaṇḍakriyāniṣparipanthika /
jaya śreyaḥśataguṇānuganāmānukīrtana //16//

Viśva kṣaya uccaṇḍa kriyā. At the time of the destruction of this universe, when You destroy this whole universe (that is *uccaṇḍa kriyā*; *uccaṇḍa kriyā* means frightful action), when You adopt that frightful action, fearful action, of destroying this whole universe (*uccaṇḍa kriyā*)–this frightful action is not a joke–You just destroy everything! O Lord, *viśvakṣaya uccaṇḍa kriyā*, at the time of destroying this whole universe (one hundred and eighteen worlds), *uccaṇḍa kriyā*, when you possess *uccaṇḍa kriyā*, this furious activity of dancing (that *tāṇḍava nṛtya*[240], not *lasya nṛtya*[241]) . . .

He dances at the time of destroying [this universe]. When He has to destroy this whole universe, He just dances, and that dance is called *tāṇḍava nṛtya*, *tāṇḍava* dance. When He just dances, what happens? This whole universe comes to an end; this whole universe is destroyed. [The universe comprised] of one hundred and eighteen worlds, it is destroyed. At that time, nobody puts Him to task, "why have You [caused] so much loss in this universe?" *Niṣpari-panthika*, that is *niṣparipanthika*.

. . . there is nobody to put opposition, to put You to task, "why have you caused this great loss of this universe?" O such a Lord, victory be to Thee! Because, there is nobody to ask You, to put You to task, "why have You caused so much loss?"

As He has done it, finished!

Glory be to Thee! Let You live for one thousand years, one thousand and one years!

Jāya śreya śataguṇānuganām ānukīrtana. When anybody remembers You, when anybody recites Your name, "*namaḥ śivāya*, *namaḥ śivāya*, *namaḥ śivāya*" (*nāma anukīrtana*, that is *nāma anukīrtana*, i.e., taking Your name), *śreya śataguṇānuga*, by taking Your name, wherever it may take place, this reciting of Your name, *śreya śataguṇa anugamāt*, hundreds and thousands of glories are followed by that recitation.

So, as soon as anybody recites the name of Lord Śiva, you must understand that this name is followed by hundreds and

240 A furious dance.

241 A dance representing the emotions of love.

thousands of these glories; hundreds and thousands of glories are coming soon.[242]

Glory be to Thee!

Chapter 14b (03:17)

जय हेलावितीर्णैतदमृताकरसागर ।
जय विश्वक्षयाक्षेपिक्षणकोपाशुशुक्षणे ॥ १७ ॥

jaya helāvitīrṇaitadamṛtākarasāgara /
jaya viśvakṣayākṣepikṣaṇakopāśuśukṣaṇe //17//

When, at the time when the gods and *asuras* (demons) went to Lord Śiva–you know this *kṣīrasāgara* (the milky ocean), the owner of the milky ocean is Lord Śiva–and all of the gods and *asuras* went to Him and requested Him that they would like to churn this [milky ocean] and whatever comes from it, they would [like to] have it. First, He denied [their request]. He said, "No, there is no one [allowed] to touch it. I am not going to [let] you touch it. Get away!" So, all of the gods and goddesses flew back. And then, Nārāyaṇa–they kept Nārāyaṇa as the medium for [their] request–and Nārāyaṇa was in front and he bowed before Lord Śiva and he said, "Only we will churn it because we want some nectar from it so that we will [become] immortal. Please, allow us to churn it". Then, He allowed them to churn it. With great difficulty, He allowed them to churn it.

And *helā vitīrṇaikad amṛtākara sāgara*, Upamanyu was a devotee of Lord Śiva. He was so pleased with Upamanyu that He bestowed the whole milky ocean to him. [Lord Shiva] said, "No, I won't [keep it for Myself]. It is yours! From this day, the milky ocean will belong to you. I have nothing to do with the milky ocean." This is the greatness of Lord Śiva. Glory be to Thee!

Viśva kṣaya ākṣepakṣaṇa kopāśuśukṣaṇe. Kṣaṇa kopa āsuśukṣaṇe (*āśuśukṣaṇe* means "fire"; *kopa āśuśukṣane* means "fire of wrath", *krodhāgni*), that wrath, when that wrath comes in Lord Śiva, only for one second (*kṣaṇa* means only for one second), that

242 "At that very moment, all joy [chases] after you, all victory is after you, everything good is after you." *Śivastotrāvalī* (additional audio, USF archives).

is *viśva kṣaya ākṣepa*; *viśva kṣaya ākṣepa*, you must understand that this is the end of universe!

When there is wrath in Lord Śiva, it means this whole universe is to be destroyed; it will be destroyed in the next second–finished! We are all gone! This is *viśva kṣaya ākṣepi* (*ākṣepi* means this is the indication of the destruction of the whole universe). What is the indication of the destruction of the whole universe?

DENISE: Lord Śiva's wrath.

SWAMIJI: Lord Śiva's wrath for even for one second–finished! O such a Lord, victory be to Thee!

Chapter 14b (06:42)

जय मोहान्धकारान्धजीवलोकैकदीपक ।
जय प्रसुप्तजगतीजागरूकाधिपूरुष ॥१८॥

jaya mohāndhakārāndhajīvalokaikadīpaka /
jaya prasuptajagatījāgarūkādhipūruṣa //18//

Mohāndha kārāndha jīvaloka. *Jīvaloka*, this world of mortality, this mortal world, is absolutely blind with illusion, blind with being away from God consciousness. This *jīvaloka*, this *martya loka* (*martya loka* means "mortal world"), the mortal world is blind because of its ignorance. And, in this mortal world, which is a blind mortal world, in this blind mortal world, You are the only candle to show light. Glory be to Thee! You are the only candle, torch, in this blind mortal world.[243] Glory be to Thee!

Jaya prasuptajagatī jāgarūkādhipūruṣa. *Prasupta jagatī*, this whole universe is just under chloroform. They don't know what they are doing.

They are just snoring–not outwardly–internally they are snoring because they do not find that gap [between] the in-going and out-coming breath. They are unaware of pointing that [out]. Otherwise, there is no cause why you don't [wake up]. You are . . . He gives you a trial [i.e., an opportunity], Lord Śiva gives

243 "This whole universe is just sunk in that darkness, and for them, You are *eka dīpaka*, one torch, torch light, just to make them enlightened." *Śivastotrāvalī* (additional audio, USF archives).

you a trial, twenty-one thousand and six hundred times, day and night. He gives you a trial. Doesn't He give you a trial? You breathe in and breathe out, then you breathe in again and another trial, another trial, another trial . . . twenty-one thousand and six hundred trials are bestowed to you, day and night. And all of those trials we ignore.[244]

Do you understand what I mean?

So, it is *moha andhakāra. Moha andhakāra* means we are sunk in that illusion, the darkness of illusion.

You are the only torch! O such a Lord, victory be to Thee! *Jaya mohāndhakāra andha jīvalokaikadīpaka, jaya*!

Jaya prasupta jagatījāgarūkādhipūruṣa. And this *prasupta jagatī*, this whole universe, [which] is *prasupta* (*prasupta* means "asleep", [one] who is snoring, unconscious; this whole universe is unconscious), in that unconscious world, You are the only one person who is conscious! O such a Lord, victory be to Thee! You are the only [one who is] aware, You are the only [one who is] wakeful, all [others] have slept. *Prasupta jagatī jāgarūkādhipurūṣa*, so, You are a great person (*adhipurūrṣa* means [Lord Śiva is the only] super-being in all of this universe).

Chapter 14b (10:20)

जय देहाद्रिकुञ्जान्तर्निकूजञ्जीवजीवक ।
जय सन्मानसव्योमविलासिवरसारस ॥१९॥

jaya dehādrikuñjāntarnikūjañjīvajīvaka /
jaya sanmānasavyomavilāsivarasārasa //19//

Dehādri, this body is just like a mountain; *deha* (the body) is

244 "On the pathway of your breath, maintain continuously refreshed and full awareness on, and in the center of, the breathing in and breathing out. This is force and this is internal *āsana*.

"You should not only concentrate on the center when the center is reached at the end point of exhaling, but from the beginning of the breath until the end point of exhaling, the effort is to be one-pointed in the center. You must meditate in this way for your efforts not to be wasted." *Self Realization in Kashmir Shaivism*, *Talks on Practice*, 2.38. See appendix 9 for an explanation of *nirvikalpa*.

just like a mountain. In this body, *kuñjāntaḥ*, there is one cave[245], cave in the heart. There is a cave in the heart. In the mountain of the body, there is a cave where there is *nikūjat jīva jīvaka* (*jīva* means individual). The individual is a bird[246] and that individual is [actually] universal, universal Lord Śiva. Universal Lord Śiva has become the individual bird there, in each and everybody, in the heart. *Nikūjat*[247], and that bird is making the sound, "*koo, koo, koo, koo, koo, koo, koo*", all by *śabda*, *sparśa*, *rūpa*, *rasa*, and *gandha*. By all of these five senses, he talks, he produces, sound. You are that bird! O Lord Śiva, You are that bird who has become that individual in that cave of the heart in each and every mountain of the body.[248] Glory be to Thee!

Jaya sanmāna savyomavilāsivarasārasa. And You are that glorified swan (*haṁsa*). And You are that swan who is *vilāsi*, who is playing in the *sarovara* (*sarovara* means the lake of *sanmānasa*; *sanmānasa* means "in the mind"; the mind is the lake).

Whose mind?

The mind of Your devotees. The mind of Your devotees is a lake and in that mind of Your devotees (that mind is a lake), in that lake, You are playing. You just play always. So, it means, in the mind of all of Your devotees, You are shining, You are playing.[249] You are that swan always [playing] in *sarovara* lake, Mānasarovara.[250] Glory be to Thee!

---

245 "*Kuñja* means *guhā*, a cave." *Śivastotrāvalī* (additional audio, USF archives).

246 *Haṁsa*, a swan. [*Editor's note*]

247 *Nikūj*: to warble, moan, groan.

248 That is, in each and every mountain-like body. [*Editor's note*]

249 "*Sanmānasa* (*san* means "those who are saints"; *sanmānasa* means "in the mind of saints"; not only in mind of saints, in the *mānasarovara* of saints). That is, the mind is just [like] a lake; the mind, he has given the similarity of a lake. . . . You are a supreme swan who likes to walk and travel and play in that *sarovara*, in that lake. What is that lake? The mind of saints. *Bas*, You want to play in the mind of saints. So He is always residing in the minds of saints. It seems like that." *Śivastotrāvalī* (additional audio, USF archives).

250 A lake near Mount Kailash in Tibet, which literally means "the lake of the mind". [*Editor's note*]

Chapter 14b (12:53)

जय जाम्बूनदोदग्रधातूद्भवगिरीश्वर ।
जय पापिषु निन्दोल्कापातनोत्पातचन्द्रम ॥२०॥

jaya jāmbūnadodagradhātūdbhavagirīśvara /
jaya pāpiṣu nindolkāpātanotpātacandramaḥ //20//

Jāmbūnada udagra (*jāmbūnada* means "gold"), *jāmbūnada udagra dhātu*, just like gold (*udagra dhātu* means "very precious *dhātu's*", precious minerals, just like gold), and by these precious minerals is [formed] this Sumerū mount, the great Sumerū mount.[251] The Sumerū mount is filled with those [precious] minerals, pearls, gold, etc. There is no ordinary stone found there. It is only of gold. It is a golden mount. It is nominated as Sumerū *parvata*.[252]

You [Lord Śiva] have become that Sumerū *parvata* [among] all of these mounts. In all of these mounts, You are Sumerū *parvata*, possessing all those valuable and precious minerals.[253] Glory be to Thee!

Pāpiṣu nindolkāpātanotpāta candramaḥ. You are that moon of crisis; You have become that moon of crisis.

When that moon comes, this whole destruction of the world is to take place, the crisis is to take place. Then the moon shines in the sky and blood flows out of the moon, and it falls on the ground; fire flows out of the moon, flows out, and it falls on the ground. At that moment, that moon is nominated as "*utpāta candramaḥ*", that *candramā* which is the indication of destruc-

251 "We have not seen that [mountain] but we have to believe that there is a golden mount in this universe, somewhere in the northern side. In the northern side, there is a golden mount, big golden mount, and it is a very high mount. And in that mount is supposd to be the place of the heavens also; and above the heavens also, that mount has gone so high. That mount is called Sumerū *parvata*." *Śivastotrāvalī* (additional audio, USF archives).

252 Sumerū mountain.

253 "O Lord, You are the master of Sumerū (*girīśvara*). You have become the master of that Sumerū *parvata* where *udagradhātū*, where valuable metals are found." *Śivastotrāvalī* (additional audio, USF archives).

tion.[254]

You have become that moon.

For whom?

For those who are sinners. For sinners, You have become the moon, that [*utpāta*] moon, just to destroy them totally for good.

JOHN: "Sinner" means here?

SWAMIJI: Who are away from Your God consciousness, who don't love You, who are away from You, who are detached from You–those are sinners. Those are not sinners who do sins. Who neglect His presence, those are sinners, and those people are liable to be destroyed. They must be destroyed because they are actually sinners.[255]

For that sinner, what reward [does] he get? He gets that punishment (it is not a reward; it is a punishment)–what is that punishment?–he gets that punishment of disbelieving in the Lord. He disbelieves more and more. The more he disbelieves in Him, the more he becomes a sinner. The more he becomes a sinner, the more he disbelieves in Him. So, *nindā*, and that *nindā* (that disbelief) is a thunderbolt, thunder for him! Disbelieving in Lord Śiva is just . . . it has taken the shape of thunder for him.

For whom?

DENISE: That disbeliever.

SWAMIJI: Disbeliever.

Nindā ulkāpāta, and that thunder takes place only when you see sometime–God forbid, we never see him, we should never see that kind of moon–when you see the moon at that moment when there is *utpāta*–*utpāta* [signifies that] some disaster is to happen next, in the [near] future–you [will] see blood shed, blood oozing, blood dripping, from that moonlight. It is the sign that somebody has . . . some great sin has taken place in this world and something unnatural will happen now in the next moment. That is *utpāta candrama*. *Utpāta candrama* is that *candrama* that gives you a sign of *utpāta* (*utpāta* is disaster, torture, destruction).

254 "'*Candrama*' is *saṁbodhana* (vocative case); otherwise, it would have been '*candramā*'." *Śivastotrāvalī* (additional audio, USF archives).

255 "Only there is one sin for Shaivites: to be separated from [God] consciousness." *Interview on Kashmir Shaivism*, Swami Lakshmanjoo with Alexis Sanderson and John Hughes (original audio recordings, USF archives, Los Angeles 1980).

> When there was a riot between Muslims and Hindus–Hindus killed Muslims and Muslims killed Hindus in 1932 when I was alive–Muslims put Hindus in bags, tied it, and then threw it with stones inside, and threw it into the Jehlum river.[256] And the same thing Hindus [did] to Muslims in their territory. And it was disaster everywhere! And before that, you know what I had seen? I had seen . . . four days before, I went to Kṣīrabhavānī[257] and I saw Kṣīrabhavānī's water, just this color of water was blood red. I have seen it with my own eyes. It was blood red; even more rich than this red. So, I thought something bad [was going to happen] and that happened. So, in the same way, when you see that kind of moon dripping this blood and all of these furious things, that moon is called "*utpāta candrama*", *utpāta*.

You, [Lord Śiva], have become *utpāta candrama* for those, for those sinners. You become *utpāta candrama* for those sinners who disbelieve in You. Victory be to Thee!

Chapter 14b (19:32)

जय कष्टतपःक्लिष्टमुनिदेवदुरासद ।
जय सर्वदशारूढभक्तिमल्लोकलोकि ॥२१॥

jaya kaṣṭatapaḥkliṣṭamunidevadurāsada /
jaya sarvadaśārūḍhabhaktimallokalokita //21//

All *munis*, all *ṛṣis*, all gods, adopt severe penance, severe penance for thousands and thousands of years to attain You, but they don't find You. After adopting that severe penance, severe *japa* (severe recitation), they don't find You.[258] Glory be to Thee!

And those people who enjoy worldly actions and who are attached to You internally–internally they love You!–they find

256 A river in Kashmir that runs through Srinagar. [*Editor's note*]

257 A Shrine in Kashmir dedicated to Mother Divine. [*Editor's note*]

258 "When sages and gods conduct severe penance, troublesome penance, for those, O Lord, You are unfound, You are not found at all. Or, if You are found, You are found with the greatest difficulty!" *Śivastotrāvalī* (additional audio, USF archives).

You there! And *sarva daśā rūḍha bhaktimat*, and Your devotees who are gardening, who are talking, who are going to the pictures, etc., those devotees, *sarva daśā* (*sarva daśā* means "in all circumstances"), in all circumstances, You are found by them. You are found by them in cinema halls. You are found by them while [they are] gardening. You are found by them [in all worldly activities]. O such a Lord, victory be to Thee!

Sarvadaśārūḍha bhaktimat loka. Bhaktimat loka, those who are *bhaktimat loka*, who are too much devoted to You, *lokita*, they have found You, they have talked to You. They talk to You! They have not found Him, i.e., those who have undergone that penance and difficulty.[259] And they [i.e., Your devotees] have talked to You, they are talking to You, just as I talk to you, they talk to Him, they shake hands with Him–*sarvadaśārūḍha bhaktimat loka lokitaḥ.*[260] O such a Lord, victory be to Thee!

Chapter 14b (21:35)

जय स्वसम्पत्प्रसरपात्रीकृतनिजाश्रित ।
जय प्रपन्नजनतालालनैकप्रयोज ॥२२॥

jaya svasampatprasarapātrīkṛtanijāśrita /
jaya prapannajanatālālanaikaprayojana //22//

Svasampat prasara pātrīkṛta nijāśrita. Anybody who has taken refuge in Thee, anybody who takes refuge in Thee, You make him capable of receiving all of the glories of Yours. All glories are . . . he becomes capable, worthy, of receiving all glories from You. All glories are digested in him. He gets that capacity.

259 "You are such a Lord who is not found by those who observe that great severe penance. [Those who only observe] fasting, penance, and doing nothing, only recitation of the Lord's *mantra*, You are not found by them." *Śivastotrāvalī* (additional audio, USF archives).

260 "*Bhaktimat loka*, those devotees of Thee who are *sarvadaśārūḍha*, who do everything, all activities of worldly things, still they are with You, still You are present to them. And You are absolutely absent to those who are adopting severe penance and *tapas*, etc." Ibid.

The capacity grows in him by that.[261]

By which act?

Just taking refuge in Him.

Anybody who takes refuge in Thee, he becomes capable of receiving all of the glories from Thee (*svasampata prasara pātrīkṛta nijāśrita*; *nijāśrita* means "the one who takes refuge in Thee").[262]

DENISE: That means to totally surrender?

SWAMIJI: Surrender!

Jayaprapannajanatā, and that person, those persons, who have surrendered in You, taken refuge in You, and just bow down before You, Your only daily work, day and night work, is just to fondle them, just to fondle them richly! *Ho*, *ho*, *ho*, *ho*, *ho*–You fondle them.

Whom?

DENISE: Those devotees who have taken refuge in You.

SWAMIJI: Refuge in You, yes.

You have only that *prayojana*, You have only that work. You have accepted only that kind of work. You forget all of the other works. You are fond of doing that fondling to Your devotees.[263] Glory be to Thee!

Chapter 14b (23:33)

जय सर्गस्थितिध्वंस कारणैकावदानक ।
जय भक्तिमदालोललीलोत्पलमहोत्स ॥२३॥

jayasargasthitidhvaṁsa kāraṇaikāvadānaka /
jaya bhaktimadālolalīlotpala mahotsava //23//

Sarga sthiti dhvaṁsa kāraṇa. In the act of creating this uni-

261 "*Svasampat prasara pātrī kṛta*, You make him worthy of holding, possessing, Your internal glory of God consciousness. He becomes worthy of possessing the internal glory of God consciousness." *Śivastotrāvalī* (additional audio, USF archives).

262 "[One] who has just bowed before You internally–with mind, body, and soul–who has bowed, who has fallen at Thy feet." Ibid.

263 "It is *eka prayojana*, it is Your only ambition. The only ambition of Yours is just to pat him, always, day and night." Ibid.

verse, in the act of protecting this universe, and in the act of destroying this universe, *eka avadānaka*, You are the only glorified actor.[264]

Brahma is not the glorified actor in creating. You are the glorified actor. Brahma is the ordinary actor to create this universe. If he acts not according to Your wishes, he (Brahma) will be Brahma no more. His seat will be snatched away. And when Nārāyaṇa is the actor in protecting this universe, [actually] You are the glorified actor in protecting this universe. That is, when Nārāyaṇa does not protect it according to Your choice, his seat will be [removed] and You will take his seat. You are the only glorified actor in creating this universe, protecting, and destroying this universe. Glory be to Thee!

You know, O Lord, who is Utpala?[265]

For Utpala is *bhaktimada ālola līlā*. *Bhakti*, the devotion of Utpala is just a kind of intoxication (*bhaktimada*; *mada* means "intoxication"). Utpala is intoxicated by Your devotion. So, by this intoxication, Utpaladeva is always found in *ālola līlā*, in a swinging way (*ālola* means "swinging way"[266]). "I am swinging!" Utpaladeva says that, "I am always swinging with Your devotion. O Lord, You are my festival! You are my festival, O Lord!"

Whose festival?

Festival of Utpaladeva.

Victory be to Thee! You are my festival. I have no other festivals in this world, only You.

Chapter 14b (26:26)

जय जयभाजन जय जितजन्म -
जरामरण जय जगज्ज्येष्ठ ।

264 "*Sarga* means "to create this universe"; *sthiti* means "to protect this universe"; *dhvaṁsa* means "to destroy this universe". These three things are Your signboards. . . . Through this signboard, You will be recognized, O Lord! *Ekavadānaka*, this is the only signboard of You." *Śivastotrāvalī* (additional audio, USF archives).

265 Utpaladeva, the author of the *Śivastotrāvalī*, is speaking of himself. [*Editor's note*]

266 "A swinging play intoxicated by devotion." *Śivastotrāvalī* (additional audio, USF archives).

जय जय जय जय जय जय जय
जय जय जय जय जय जय त्र्यक्ष ॥२४॥

jaya jayabhājana jaya jitajanma-
jarāmaraṇa jaya jagajjyeṣṭha /
jaya jaya jaya jaya jaya jaya jaya
jaya jaya jaya jaya jaya jaya tryakṣa //24//

Jaya bhājana, You are worthy of glory.[267] *Jita janma jarāmaraṇa*, You have conquered birth and death.[268] *Jagat jyeṣṭha*, You are the elder of the whole universe. You are superior (*jagat jyeṣṭha*; *jyeṣṭha* means "elder", elderly to the whole universe). Glory be to Thee! Glory be to Thee! Glory be to Thee! Glory be to Thee! Glory be to Thee! Glory be to Thee! Endless glory be to Thee![269]

Here ends this *Jaya stotra*.

267 "You are *bhājana*, You are capable of victory." *Śivastotrāvalī* (additional audio, USF archives).
268 "You have conquered the cycle of repeated old age. You have conquered the cycle of repeated deaths." Ibid.
269 "*Tryakṣa*, O possessor of the third eye, glory be to Thee!" Ibid.

Chapter Fifteen
Singing the Glory of Devotion
Bhaktistotranāma pañcadaśaṁ stotram

SWAMIJI: *Bhakti stotra*, fifteenth.[270]

Chapter 15 (00:04)

त्रिमलक्षालिनो ग्रन्थाः सन्ति तत्पारगास्तथा ।
योगिनः पण्डिताः स्वस्थास्त्वद्भक्ता एव तत्त्वतः ॥ १ ॥

trimalakṣālino granthāḥ santi tatpāragāstathā /
yoginaḥ paṇḍitāḥ svasthāstvadbhaktā eva tattvataḥ //1//

You will find books also in this world [that describe how to] remove all of your *malas*, all of the three *malas* (*āṇava mala*, *māyīya mala*, and *kārma mala*).[271] These three-fold impurities are removed by these *śāstras*. Those *śāstras* are also available. *Tat pāragās*, and those who are absolutely informed in those *śāstras*, they are also found in this world, i.e., those *paṇḍits*, those scholars. *Yoginaḥ*, *yogīs* are also found in this world. *Paṇḍitāḥ*, learned scholars are also found in this world. But only Your devotees are appeased. They are really appeased in their mind. Their mind is calm.

These books that remove all of the three *malas* are already agitated and those who are informed in those books, they are also agitated. *Yogīs* are also agitated and those *paṇḍits* (scholars) are agitated as you[272] are agitated with those books.[273] But the

---

270 "The thirteenth, fourteenth, and fifteenth [*stotra's*] he has composed when he was aware [i.e., sane]. Otherwise, he was just crying: "I wish I was . . . !" *Śivastotrāvalī* (additional audio, USF archives).

271 See appendix 15 for an explanation of the *malas*.

272 Referring to one of the scholars present. [*Editor's note*]

273 "That philosophy, the philosophers, all of those others, are nonsense." *Śivastotrāvalī* (additional audio, USF archives).

unagitated position is held only by Your devotees.[274]

Chapter 15 (02:00)

मायीयकालनियतिरागाद्याहारतर्पिताः ।
भवन्ति सुखिनो नाथ भक्तिमन्तो जगत्तटे ॥ २ ॥

māyīyakālaniyatirāgādyāhāratarpitāḥ /
bhavanti[275] *sukhino nātha bhaktimanto jagattaṭe //2//*

Nātha, O Lord, Your devotees, *bhaktimantāḥ*, Your devotees who are absolutely filled and satisfied by consuming–what?–consuming *māyīya*, *kāla*, *niyati*, *rāgādi* (i.e., *māyā*, *kāla*, *niyati*, and *raga*[276]), all of these elementary worlds, they have consumed those elementary worlds in their own nature, . . .

ALEXIS: Differentiated perception, time, attachment, etc.

SWAMIJI: Yes.

. . . and those, Your devotees, on the shores of this universe, they are not drowned in the ocean of the universe, they just walk and roam and [live] happily. *Nātha*, O Lord, they happily are found on the shores of the universe, not being drowned in the ocean of the universe.

Chapter 15 (03:19)

रुदन्तो वा हसन्तो वा त्वामुच्चैः प्रलपन्त्यमी ।
भक्ताः स्तुतिपदोच्चारोपचाराः पृथगेव ते ॥ ३ ॥

rudanto vā hasanto vā tvāmuccaiḥ pralapantyamī /
bhaktāḥ stutipadoccāropacārāḥ pṛthageva te //3//

274 "*Tvad bhaktāḥ eva kevalā tattvataḥ*, in reality, only Your devotees are *svasthā*, peacefully situated, peacefully appeased." *Śivastotrāvalī* (additional audio, USF archives).

275 Swamiji said that he preferred the reading of "*bhavanti*" rather than "*caranti*" although he accepted "*caranti*" as a valid reading. [*Editor's note*]

276 For *kañcukas* see *Kashmir Shaivism–The Secret Supreme*, 1.7-8.

Your devotees, although they are weeping, crying for You, *hasanto vā*, they laugh also at the same time. While weeping, they laugh. *Tvāmuccaiḥ pralapanti*, and they cry for You with loud words. And those devotees are actually *stuti pada upacāraḥ*, they are actually worthy of being adored by people; *pṛthageva te, stuti pada upacārāḥ*, they are worthy of being adored by everybody. You should adore them because they are *pṛthak eva*, they are absolutely unique. There is no parallel to them.

Chapter 15 (04:27)

न विरक्तो न चापीशो मोक्षाकाङ्क्षी त्वदर्चकः ।
भवेयमपि तूद्रिक्तभक्त्यासवरसोन्मद ॥४॥

na virakto na cāpīśo mokṣākāṅkṣī tvadarcakaḥ /
bhaveyamapi tūdrikta bhaktyāsavarasonmadaḥ //4//

I don't want to become the governing agent for this universe. I don't want to govern this universe. I don't want to become detached from the universe. *Mokṣākāṅkṣī*, I don't want liberation even. *Tvadarcaka*, I don't want to become Your worshiper. I don't want to worship You. But, I want to become *udrikta bhaktyāsava rasa*, I want to become mad by the intensity of Thy devotion. I want that madness.

I don't want to become detached or [become] the governor of this universe. I don't want to desire for liberation. I don't want to become Your worshiper. I don't want to become Your worshiper! I want to get that madness! I want to be mad by the intensity of Your love!

ALEXIS: Why does he say, "I don't want to be Your devotee"?

SWAMIJI: *Bas*, he [just] wants to get madness after [Him].

ALEXIS: Because, in *arcana*[277] also, there is some distance . . .

SWAMIJI: Yes, there is distance.

ALEXIS: . . . between worshiped and worshiper. He wants complete intoxication.

SWAMIJI: Yes.

---

277 The act of honoring or praising, i.e., devotion. [*Editor's note*]

Chapter 15 (06:00)

बाह्यं हृदय एवान्तराभिहृत्यैव योऽर्चति ।
त्वामीश भक्तिपीयूषरसपूरैर्नमामि तम् ॥५॥

bāhyaṁ hṛdaya evāntarābhihṛtyaiva yo'rcati /
tvāmīśa bhaktipīyūṣa rasapūrairnamāmi tam //5//

Īśa, O Lord, that person who is capable of worshiping You, worshiping You by all of this objective world, by all of this outward objective world, by diverting it in one's own heart, . . .

He wants to divert, to gather, all of this objective world in [his] own heart and then worship You with this objective world.

ALEXIS: *Abhītaḥ.*

SWAMIJI: *Abhītaḥ saṁhṛtya.*

ALEXIS: Heart.

SWAMIJI: . . . and who worships Thee by *bhaktipīyūṣa rasa-pūrair*, by the floods of the streams of the nectar of devotion, . . .

You understand?

ALEXIS: Yes.

SWAMIJI: . . . when that stream flows of the nectar of Thy devotion, by that stream, by that *rasa*, the person who wants to worship You with that *rasa* of supreme devotion of Thee with this objective world after gathering it from the outside world and putting it in his own heart, and then, from the heart, he offers this objectivity to You along with the stream of *rasa*, the stream of that *rasa*, . . .

Rasa means . . .

ALEXIS: Relish.

SWAMIJI: *Rasa* means the substance of that taste, water.

ALEXIS: The essence.

SWAMIJI: Essence, essence of . . .

ALEXIS: Liquid essence.

SWAMIJI: The liquid essence of the nectar of devotion, Thy devotion.

. . . the one who is capable of doing this, this kind of worship for You, *namāmi tam*, I bow to him.

ALEXIS: This is real worship.

SWAMIJI: Real worship of [Thee].

Chapter 15 (08:20)

धर्माधर्मात्मनोरन्तः क्रिययोर्ज्ञानयोस्तथा ।
सुखदुःखात्मनोर्भक्ताः किमप्यास्वादयन्त्यहो ॥६॥

dharmādharmātmanorantaḥ kriyayorjñānayostathā /
sukhaduḥkhātmanorbhaktāḥ kimapyāsvādayantyaho //6

There are such devotees of Thee who, not only in the ecstasy of God consciousness [do] they enjoy that absolute joy, but even also in the center of right and wrong, in two actions, in two knowledges, in two cognitions, in pleasure and pain, etc., they also taste that divine nectar of God consciousness.

ALEXIS: *Ke'pi camatkārāḥ.*

SWAMIJI: Yes.

ALEXIS: When he says "it", does he mean "between"?

SWAMIJI: Between, between.

Chapter 15 (09:16)

चराचरपितः स्वामिन् अप्यन्धा अपि कुष्ठिनः ।
शोभन्ते परमुद्दामभवद्भक्तिविभूषणाः ॥७॥

carācarapitaḥ svāmin apyandhā api kuṣṭhinaḥ /
śobhante paramuddāma bhavadbhaktivibhūṣaṇāḥ //7//

O Lord of inert objects and living objects, *carācara pitaḥ*, O Father of inert objects and moving objects, *apyandhā*, although they are blind and although they are *kuṣṭhinaḥ*, they have got that incurable disease–Your devotees, although they are first blind and then caught by this leprosy[-like] disease and nobody wants to touch them–*śobhante*, they are glorified in their own way. They are still glorified, *paramuddāma bhavad bhakti vibhūṣaṇāḥ*, because they are ornamented with supreme devotion of Thee; *uddāma bhavad bhakti*, Your devotion is their ornament. They are glorified with that! They are divine! They are filled with that divinity although they have got these diseases. *Loke atyantaṁ garhitā api*, nobody cares to look after them, nobody wants to go near to them, but still, in their own way, they are shining, in their own way.

Chapter 15 (10:58)

शिलोञ्छपिच्छकशिपुविच्छायाङ्गा अपि प्रभो ।
भवद्भक्तिमहोष्माणो राजराजमपीशते ॥८॥

śiloñchapicchakaśipu vicchāyāṅgā api prabho /
bhavadbhaktimahoṣmāṇo rājarājamapīśate //8//

Prabho, O my Master, *śiloñchapicchakaśipu vicchāyāṅgā api*, although their body is covered by banana leaves and their eating substance is *śiloñcha*.

Śiloñcha vṛtti is when this [rice] paddy is cut in the fields and afterwards some [grain] particles remain on the ground, and they collect those. That is *śiloñcha vṛtti*, to collect those grains, individual grains, and grind them and eat them afterwards. . . .

ALEXIS: Chaff, is it chaff?

SWAMIJI: Yes.

ALEXIS: No it's not chaff, it is not what comes of the grain. It is the grains that are left.

SWAMIJI: Grains are left.

ALEXIS: There is a word for that.

SWAMIJI: It is called *śiloñchavṛitti.*

ALEXIS: There is a word for that in English.

Śiloñccha picchakaśipu.

SWAMIJI: Piccha means "leaves" *Śiloñccha means. . .*

ALEXIS: Gleanings.

SWAMIJI: . . . those collected grains from the ground.

Piccha means "leaves", the leaves of banana trees that are [used] for covering the body. *Śiloñchā* is for eating purposes. So, it is a very degraded state, position, of Your devotees. *Vicchāyāṅgā kaśipu. Kaśipu* means *bhojana* and *ācchādana*, both. *Kaśipu* means for eating and covering. *Kaśipu* is both. *Kaśipu* means *bhojana* and *ācchādana. Bhojana* means for eating purpose (*śiloñchana*); *piccha* is for *ācchādana*, for covering their bodies.

Vicchāyāṅgā api, although they are protected like that, their body and their belly is protected in this way, but still, *bhavat bhakti mahoṣmāṇo*, there is warmth in their heart of Your devotion. *Bhavad bhakti mahoṣmāṇo rājarājamapi*, they rule the king of kings; they rule the kings of kings. They rule [over] the kings of kings even then, i.e., in this [degraded] position.

They say, "O get out, bloody king [laughter]! I don't want . . . I have no time to see you!" They don't care.[278]

Chapter 15 (13:47)

सुधार्द्रायां भवद्भक्तौ लुठताप्यारुरुक्षुणा ।
चेतसैव विभोऽर्चन्ति केचित्त्वामभितः स्थिताः ॥९॥

sudhārdrāyāṁ bhavadbhaktau luṭhatāpyārurukṣuṇā /
cetasaiva vibho'rcanti kecittvāmabhitaḥ sthitāḥ //9//

There are two classes of Your devotees. One class of devotees is *ārurukṣu*, those who want to get liberated from repeated births and deaths. This is one class of Your devotees. Another class of devotees are those who see You, perceive You, and worship You everywhere! Those are another class of devotees.

Sudhārdrāyāṁ bhavadbhakau luṭhatāpyārūrūkṣūṇā, but the first class, those devotees who want *mumūkaṣu*, who want to get released from repeated births and deaths–those are *ārurukṣu*–they are *sūdhārdrāyāṁ bhavadbhaktau luṭhatā*, they don't get a firm establishment in the nectar of Your devotion. In the nectar of devotion, they slip off, they slip off every now and then.

ALEXIS: They stumble.

SWAMIJI: They stumble. They don't remain established in the nectar of that devotion of Thee. But, *cetasaiva vibho'rcanti*, with their own minds, there are other classes of Your devotees who worship You in their own hearts and perceive You everywhere in this universe.

278 Swamiji gave the example of the Shaivite Rajanaka Gopala Razdan, who addressed the King of Kashmir as a poor beggar by saying, "*Garība warachama*, are you all right, O poor, poor, poor, O poor man? Are you alright?" [*Editor's note*]

Chapter 15 (15:27)

रक्षणीयं वर्धनीयं बहुमान्यमिदं प्रभो ।
संसारदुर्गतिहरं भवद्भक्तिमहाधनम ॥१०॥

rakṣaṇīyaṁ vardhanīyaṁ bahumānyamidaṁ prabho /
saṁsāra durgati haraṁ bhavad bhakti mahādhanam //10

This bank balance is not to be protected. Let it go to the dogs! Only the supreme treasure of Your devotion is to be protected all-round. So, it is *rakṣaṇīyam*, it is worth protecting, it is worth increasing (*vardhanīyaṁ*), *bahumānyam*, it is worth respecting, O Lord, *saṁsāra durgatiharaṁ*, because it removes away the poverty of differentiated perception. The poverty of differentiated perception is removed by this supreme treasure. And this supreme treasure is the treasure of Thy devotion. So, it is to be protected, it is to be kept, it is to be owned; not this bank balance–let it go to the dogs!

Chapter 15 (16:37)

नाथ ते भक्तजनता यद्यपि त्वयि रागिणी ।
तथापीर्ष्यां विहायास्यास्तुष्टास्तु स्वामिनी सदा ॥११॥

nātha te bhaktajanatā yadyapi tvayi rāgiṇī /
tathāpīrṣyāṁ vihāyāsyās tuṣṭāstu svāminī sadā //11//

O *nātha*, O my dear Lord, *bhakta janatā*, there are two wives who have owned You, two girls have owned You. One girl is Pārvati and another girl is my devotion for You. I want to be devoted to You. That devotion is another girl who is fond of You. Although *yadyapi tvayi rāgiṇī*, although she is attached to You, . . .

Who?

DENISE: That wife of devotion.

SWAMIJI: My devotion, my devotion towards You, and that, my devotion, is one girl who wants to have You, but that Pārvatī hates her because it is obvious, it is clear.

When there is a first wife and another wife comes, the first wife is jealous of that second wife.

Now, it can't be . . . You can't disown her, i.e., my devotion towards You. You can't disown her. She wants to have You and there is already Pārvatī with You. So, I [have] one request. I would like to request You in such a way that Pārvatī, Your first wife, *īrṣyāṁ vihāya*, She should not hate her. She should not develop hatred for that other girl [i.e., my devotion], jealousy for that other girl, and She should give her an occasion to meet with You.

For instance, here is Pārvatī, here is Śiva, and you are [His] devotion, you have come [to see Him]. When you have come to see Him, you have nothing to do with [Pārvatī]. So, you want to have Him. Pārvatī must go, at that time, outside to give her an occasion to meet Him. Let it be done. This is my request. *Īrṣyāṁ vihāyāsyā*, Pārvatī should not hate her altogether and *tuṣṭāstu svāminī sadā*, and Pārvati should be helpful to that other girl in meeting [You].

ALEXIS: *Śaivī mukham.*

SWAMIJI: *Śaivī mukham.*

This is one request.

DENISE: What is *śaivī mukham*?

SWAMIJI: *Śaivī* means *śakti*. *Śakti* is the source.[279] You see, he says, *īrṣyātyāgah avakāśadānam* (*avakāśa dānam* means "to give her occasion"), give her also a chance to see Him.

No, [there is] not a chance in the presence of Pārvatī. She must leave, She must leave for some time. What is there wrong in that?

ALEXIS: Give me a chance.

SWAMIJI: Yes, She must give her a chance.

ALEXIS: *Avakāśa.*[280]

SWAMIJI: Yes.

Chapter 15 (19:59)

भवद्भावः पुरो भावी प्राप्ते त्वद्भक्तिसम्भवे ।
लब्धे दुग्धमहाकुम्भे हता दधनि गृध्नुता ॥१२॥

279 See footnote 235.

280 Room, occasion, opportunity.

bhavadbhāvaḥ puro bhāvī prāpte tvadbhaktisambhave /
labdhe dugdhamahākumbhe hatā dadhani gṛdhnutā / / 12

Tvadbhakti sambhave prāpte. O Lord, if there is devotion, if Thy devotion is available, if Thy devotion is owned, *bhavad bhāva puro bhāvī*, then You are owned. In other words, You are owned altogether if Thy devotion is there. If Thy devotion is there, You are there. Because, *labdhe dugdha mahā kumbhe*, when a big jar of milk is available, then the greed for curds is finished [because] curds will come out of that jar [of milk]. So, if there is devotion for You, [it means] You are there.

ALEXIS: It only needs to be churned.

SWAMIJI: Yes.

Chapter 15 (21:01)

किमियं न सिद्धिरतुला
किं वा मुख्यं न सौख्यमास्रवति ।
भक्तिरुपचीयमाना
येयं शम्भोः सदातनी भवति ॥ १३ ॥

kimiyaṁ na sidhiratulā
kiṁ vā mukhyaṁ na saukhyamāsravati /
bhaktīrupacīyamānā
yeyaṁ śambhoḥ sadātanī bhavati / / 13 / /

Is it not that unparalleled power, *yogic* power? Is it not called obtaining that unparalleled *yogic* power? *Kiṁ vā mukhyaṁ na saukhyamāsravati*, is it not that state wherefrom this predominant beatitude of the ultimate reality [flows]? This *is* that predominant source of ultimate beatitude.

ALEXIS: Is it not that?

SWAMIJI: Is it not that? It is that!

What?

Bhakti rupacīyamānā yeyaṁ śambhoḥ sadātanī bhavati. [It is] if there is increasing [devotion], if there is eternal devotion for Thee in the form of the increasing state, in the form of increasing movement, accumulation.

Chapter 15 (22:14)

मनसि मलिने मदीये
मग्ना त्वद्भक्तिमणिलता कष्टम् ।
न निजानपि तनुते तान्
अपौरुषेयान्स्वसम्पदुल्लासान् ॥१४॥

manasi maline madīye
magnā tvadbhaktimaṇilatā kaṣṭam /
na nijānapi tanute tān
apauruṣeyānsvasampadullāsān //14//

O Lord, my mind is absolutely impure–*madīye manasi maline*, my mind is absolutely impure, it is all-round impure, my mind–and in my mind, in the mud of my mind, *tvad bhakti maṇilatā*, the creeper of the pearls of Thy devotion, the pearl-creeper of Thy devotion, has sunk. It has submerged in that, in that mud of my impure mind. In my mind, it ought to have grown and beared [born] those fruits of jewelry, jewelry-fruits [of Thy devotion]. But, the problem is, this creeper of the jewelry-fruits of Thy devotion is sunk in that mud of my impure mind.

ALEXIS: Like a lotus.

SWAMIJI: Like a lotus.

And [*na*] *nijānapi tanute tān apauruṣeyān svasampadullāsān. Na tanute*, and it [i.e., my devotion for Thee] does not expand the fruits and flowers and branches as it ought to be. It does not grow. This is a great problem in me. My mind is very impure and in my impure mind, it has sunk altogether. This is a problem in me.

ALEXIS: *Apauruṣeyān*?

SWAMIJI: *Apauruṣeyān*, beyond [i.e., out of reach of] those divine flows of *svasampat*[281].

Ātmasampati, the reality of that glory of that God consciousness is not expanded in [my impure mind]. It is stuck, it has [become] stuck.

281 Lit., self-encounter.

Chapter 15 (24:27)

भक्तिर्भगवति भवति त्रिलोकनाथे ननूत्तमा सिद्धिः ।
किन्त्वणिमादिकविरहात् सैव न पूर्णेति चिन्ता मे ॥१५॥

bhaktirbhagavati bhavati trilokanāthe nanūttamā siddhiḥ /
kintvāṇimādikavirahāt saiva na pūrṇeti cintā me //15//

It is a fact, it is absolutely quite cent-percent correct, that *bhaktirbhagavati bhavati*, if there is devotion for Thee, O Lord, if there is devotion and attachment for Thee, that is the real and the supreme, the highest, *yogic* power already attained. The highest and supreme *yogic* power is already attained.

But still, *aṇīmādika virahāt*, those eight *yogic* internal powers are not found in that, in that devotion. And that devotion is not complete; hence, that devotion is not complete. This is a worry in me. This is a worry that knocks in the background of my mind.

Chapter 15 (25:32)

बाह्यतोऽन्तरपि चोत्कटोन्मिषत्-
त्र्यम्बकस्तवकसौरभाः शुभाः ।
वासयन्त्यपि विरुद्धवासनान्
योगिनो निकटवासिनोऽखिलान् ॥१६॥

bāhyato'ntarapi cotkaṭonmiṣat-
tryambakastavakasaurabhāḥ śubhāḥ /
vāsayantyapi viruddhavāsanān
yogino nikaṭavāsino'khilān //16//

There are *tryambaka stavaka saurabhāḥ* (*tryambaka stavaka* means, *bas*, “singing the glory of Lord Śiva”), singing the glory of Lord Śiva is actually a bunch of fragrant flowers.

ALEXIS: *Stavaka.*

SWAMIJI: *Stavaka.*

And that fragrant bunch of flowers, . . .

What is that bunch of fragrant flowers?

DENISE: Singing the glory of Lord Siva.

SWAMIJI: Singing the glory of Lord Śiva.

. . . *bāhyatā antarapi ca utkaṭa unmiṣat*, and this fragrance is so intense, so densely found in that bunch of flowers, that it is circulated outside and inside, everywhere. And this bunch of flowers, [the person] who holds this bunch of flowers, those *yogīs* who hold this bunch of flowers in their hands, in their divine hands, . . .

What is that bunch of flowers? Singing the glory of the Lord.

. . . they *vāsayanti*, they make fragrant all of those [people] who are near him, who are living near him, near that *yogi's* hermitage. *Viruddha vāsino akhilān*, everybody, whomever comes near that *yogi*, he is also flooded by that fragrance. That fragrance passes through their minds also. This is the greatness of this bunch of flowers of Thy devotion.

Chapter 15 (27:47)

ज्योतिरस्ति कथयापि न किंचिद्-
विश्वमप्यतिसुषुप्तमशेषम् ।
यत्र नाथ शिवरात्रिपदेऽस्मिन्
नित्यमर्चयति भक्तजनस्त्वाम् ॥१७॥

jyotirasti kathayāpi na kiṁcid-
viśvamapyati suṣuptamaśeṣam /
yatra nātha śivarātripade'smin
nityamarcayati bhaktajanastvām //17//

O Lord (*nātha*, O Lord), *yatra śivarātripade*, there is a place where Śivarātri is being functioned, Śivarātri is being celebrated.

Śivarātri means . . . Śivarātri, you know?

DENISE: Marriage of Lord Śiva and Pārvati.

SWAMIJI: Yes. When the marriage of Lord Śiva and Pārvatī took place, that is Śivarātri. The honeymoon of Lord Śiva with Pārvati, that night is called Śivarātri. And there is that Śiva*rātri*.

In that Śivarātri, in that night, *jyotirasti kathayāpi kiṁcid*, there is no light found in that night. In that night, there is no other light found; no light of the sun, no light of the moon, no light of the fire.

ALEXIS: *Atirahasyatvāt.*

SWAMIJI: *Atirahasyatvāt.*

Viśvamapi ati suṣuptaṁ aśeṣam, and the whole universe has absolutely fallen into sound sleep. The whole universe is asleep [on] that night. *Nityama*, and, [on] that night, during that period of night, only Your devotees are wakeful. Only Your devotees are wakeful and they celebrate Thy devotion wholeheartedly.

Chapter 15 (29:50)

सत्त्वं सत्यगुणे शिवे भगवति
स्फारीभवत्वर्चने
चूडायां विलसन्तु शङ्करपद-
प्रोद्यद्रजःसञ्चयाः ।
रागादिस्मृतिवासनामपि समु-
च्छेत्तुं तमो जृम्भतां
शम्भो मे भवतात्त्वदात्मविलये
त्रैगुण्यवर्गोऽथवा ॥१८॥

sattvaṁ satyaguṇe śive bhagavati
sphārībhavatvarcane
cūḍāyāṁ vilasantu śaṅkara pada-
prodyadrajaḥ sañcayāḥ /
rāgādismṛtivāsanāmapi samu-
cchettuṁ tamo jṛmbhatāṁ
śambho me bhavatāttvadātmavilaye
traiguṇya vargo'thavā //18//

O Lord Śiva, I don't want to get rid of *sattvaguṇa*, *rajoguṇa*, and *tamoguṇa*. I don't want to get rid of these three *guṇas*.[282]

Sattvaṁ satyaguṇe śive bhagavati. In Śiva, in the Lord, and in

282 See appendix 24 for a further explanation of the three *guṇas*.

satyaguṇe, in that Siva who is qualified with true qualifications (with real qualifications, *satyaguṇe*), let *sattvaguṇa* in me be utilized in worshiping Him. Let *sattvaguṇa* be utilized in worshiping my Lord.

Cūḍāyāṁ vilasantu śaṅkara pada prodyat rajaḥ sañcayāḥ, let *rājoguṇa* . . .

Rajoguṇa, in another [way], means . . . there are two meanings of "*rajoguṇa*". *Rajoguṇa* means when you are entangled with worldly pleasures. Those qualifications in man that get you entangled in worldly pleasures, that is called *rajoguṇa*. And, in other words, *rajoguṇa* is "dust"; *raja* is called dust also.

. . . let that dust of Thy, Your feet, *śaṅkara pada prodyat rajaḥ sañcayāḥ*, [let the] collection of that *raja* (that dust), which has come out from the feet of Lord Śiva, that dust, let that dust remain on my forehead. Let that dust live on my *cūḍā* (*cūḍā* means on my, this top of the forehead). I want that dust. I want that *rajoguṇa* for me.

I want that *sattvaguṇa* just to adore You. I want that *rajoguṇa* just to keep it on the top of my skull.

Rāgādismṛtivāsanāmapi samucchettuṁ tamo jṛmbhatāṁ. Let that *tamoguṇa* also shine in me. For which purpose? For what purpose? *Rāgādi smṛti vāsanāpi*, [so that] the impression of *kāma* (desire), *krodha* (anger), *lobha* (greed), *moha* (illusion), *mada* (lust), and *ahaṁkāra* (ego), that impression also will be vanished, will be removed by that darkness. When there will be darkness [of *tamoguṇa*, then] the impressions will also be dark, i.e., there will be no traces of any impression. All traces of impressions will be dark, absolutely washed off.

ALEXIS: So, he wants to convert all of these . . .

SWAMIJI: In divinity.

Śambho me bhavatātvadātmavilaye. O Lord Śiva, let, in this way, *traiguṇyavarga* (*traiguṇyavarga* is the class of the three *guṇas*), let these three *guṇas* govern in my mind just to get appeased in Your God consciousness, in Your supreme Self.

Chapter 15 (33:48)

संसाराध्वा सुदूरः खरतर-
विविधव्याधिदग्धाङ्गयष्टिः

भोगा नैवोपभुक्ता यदपि
सुखमभूज्जातु तन्नो चिराय ।

इत्थं व्यर्थोऽस्मि जातः शशिधर-
चरणाक्रान्तिकान्तोत्तमाङ्गस्-
त्वद्भक्तश्चेति तन्मे कुरु सपदि महा-
सम्पदो दीर्घदीर्घाः ॥१९॥

saṁsārādhvā sudūraḥ kharatara-
vividhavyādhi dagdhaṅgayaṣṭiḥ
bhogā naivopabhuktā yadapi
sukhamabhūjjātu tanno cirāya /

itthaṁ vyartho'smi jātaḥ śaśidhara-
caraṇākrāntikāntottamāṅgas-
tvadbhaktaśceti tanme kuru sapadi mahā-
sampado dīrghadīrghāḥ //19//

Really, this path of the universe is endless. There is no limit. It never ends. This path of the universe never ends. There is no end to it! And this path is not a clear path. At the same time, this path is not a clear path so that you could walk, tread on it, and travel without fear. All-round there is fear, step by step. On each step, there is fear of something to happen.

Kharatavividhavyādhi dagdhāṅgayaṣṭi. So, *aṅgayaṣṭi*, all of the limbs of your body, all of the limbs of ones body, are *dagdha*, almost burnt, almost *dagdha* (*dagdha* means "burnt") by *kharatara*, by those fearful and *vividha* (various) *vyādhi*, i.e., various pains, sadnesses, sorrows, tortures, and crisis.

So, [on] this pathway of this universe, first there is this problem that this pathway has no end. This is endless. There is no end. It is not an easy end. Easily, you won't end [traveling on] this pathway. And, at the same time, there are such fearful crises and tortures on the way.

"*Bhogā naivopabhuktā*" is incorrect. [It should read], "*bhogā-*

nevopabhuktvā[283] *yadapi sukhaṁ abhūjjātu tanno cirāya.*"

Bhogān evopabhuktvā. Now, I have enjoyed some pleasures in this universe. On the pathway, I have enjoyed some universal [pleasures], e.g., sex, some cheese, some fruit, some . . .

ALEXIS: Some cheese [laughter]

DEVOTEES: [laughter]

SWAMIJI: . . . *bhogān evopabhuktvā*, and after tasting these things, *yadapi sukhamabhūta*, whatever pleasure I have gained on this pathway, *tat no cirāya*, that too also didn't remain permanently. That also went away.

Ithaṁ vyartho'smijātaḥ. So, there is no fun in my living in this universe, in coming into this universe. There is no fun. I have come for nothing, *ithaṁ vyartho'smijātaḥ*, because this pathway I have not covered [completely because] this pathway is endless. And, at the same time, there is always torture, right and left, on the roadside. And sometimes I have enjoyed some worldly pleasures and those worldly pleasures too also faded away. *Yadapi sukhamabhūta*, whatever pleasure, whatever joy, I acquired in the enjoyment of worldly pleasures, that too didn't remain permanent. *Ithaṁ vyartho'smi jātaḥ*, so, I have been born in this universe for nothing. What is the purpose of my being here?

Śaśidhara caraṇa ākrānti kānta uttamāṅgaḥ tvad bhaktaśca. But, there is only one qualification in me. Although I have come uselessly here, but *śaśidhara caraṇa ākrānti*; *śaśidhara caraṇa* (*śaśidhara* means Lord Śiva who has kept on His forehead this crescent moon; the crescent moon, He has kept on His forehead), and His *caraṇa* (feet), I have *ākrānti*, I have caught His feet, His divine feet. I have held His divine feet.

Whose divine feet?

ERNIE: Lord Śiva's.

SWAMIJI: Lord Śiva's divine feet.

Krānti kānta uttamāṅgaḥ. And these divine feet, I have kept on my head. These divine feet, I have kept on my head. *Tvad bhaktaśca*, and I am Your devotee also. So, this is the only way

---

283 Swamiji corrected "*bhogānaivopabhuktā*" to read "*bhogān evopabhuktva*". The former reading translates as, "I have not enjoyed any enjoyment in this universe". As Swamiji explains, "It does not produce any sense because *yadapi sukhamabhūta*, where is that *sukha* (joy) then if he has not [actually] enjoyed any *bhoga* (enjoyment)?" *Śivastotrāvalī* (additional audio, USF archives).

out from this tortured path of the universe.

So, *tanme kuru*, so do that thing, but hurriedly. Otherwise, I will be ruined and what is the use of helping me afterwards when I am totally ruined and gone? So, You have to do it rapidly. You have to help me hurriedly.

Kuru sapadi mahāsampadaḥ dīrghadīrghā. And make me united with those eternal glories of Thee, [which] are everlasting with You, and I will be glorified with those glories.

Chapter Sixteen
Even Obstacles are a Path
Pāśānudbhedanāma ṣoḍaśaṁ stotram

न किञ्चिदेव लोकानां भवदावरणं प्रति ।
न किञ्चिदेव भक्तानां भवदावरणं प्रति ॥ १ ॥

na kiñcideva lokānāṁ bhavadāvaraṇaṁ prati /
na kiñcideva bhaktānāṁ bhavadāvaraṇaṁ prati //1//

There are two classes [of people] found in this universe. One class is of ordinary people (*lokas*) and another are those people who are Thy devotees (*bhaktas*).

Na kiñcideva bhavadāvaraṇaṁ prati. What is there, which is not *aurukaut* (an impediment) coming on their pathway? Everything is [an impediment] because those people who are away from Thy consciousness, their meditation also takes them away from You. And their being away is already away from You. But their meditation, their love for You, also becomes a means to take them away from Your God consciousness.

Who?

Those people who are worldly people.

Bhavat āvaraṇaṁ prati lokānāṁ na kiñcit eva. Everything is *na kiñcideva kākva*, an obstacle for them, even meditation!

ALEXIS: Is there anything which is not? It's a question, rhetorical question.

SWAMIJI: Yes.

And here it is not *kākvā*[284] for Thy devotees. *Bhavadāvaraṇaṁ prati*, there is no obstacle for Your [devotees]. Even those obstacles, which are obstacles already, those obstacles show them Your way.

Whom?

DENISE: Thy devotees.

---

284 A cry of lamentation.

SWAMIJI: Thy devotees.

So, Thy devotees have no obstacles and worldly people have no clearance at all.

ALEXIS: It is a wonderful verse.

SWAMIJI: Yes.

ALEXIS: It contains the entire Shaivism.

SWAMIJI: *Lokānāṁ bhavadāvaraṇaṁ prati na kiñcideva apitu sarvameva. Lokānāṁ bhavadāvaraṇaṁ prati na kiñcideva.*

ALEXIS: *Sarvameva.*

SWAMIJI: *Sarvameva.*

Bhaktānāṁ bhavat āvaraṇaṁ prati na kiñcit eva. Nothing is there, which gives [Your devotees] any hindrance in perceiving You. Even in hindrance also, hindrance itself is revealing to them Your nature.

Chapter 16 (02:20)

अप्युपायक्रमप्राप्यः सङ्कुलोऽपि विशेषणैः ।
भक्तिभाजां भवानात्मा सकृच्छुद्धोऽवभासते ॥२॥

apyupāyakramaprāpyaḥ saṅkulo'pi viśeṣaṇaiḥ /
bhaktibhājāṁ bhavānātmā sakṛcchuddho'vabhāsate //2//

Although Your *bhavānātmā*, Your Self, is attained by the successive way of Your means (i.e., *śāmbhavopāya*, *śāktopāya*, and *āṇavopāya*[285])–these successive means are meant for attaining You–and *saṅkulo'pi viśeṣaṇaiḥ*, and Your nature is dense, dense with Your qualifications (i.e., You are all-knowing, all-pervading, divine, omnipresent, etc.)–You have got so many qualifications–but, *bhaktibhājāṁ*, for Thy devotees, *bhavānātmā*, Your Self is revealed to them once and for all. It is not revealed to them in a successive way. They don't perceive Your nature in succession, in a limited way of understanding. They just . . . when they find You, they find You altogether. This is the greatness in Thy devotees.

285 See appendix 2 for an explanation of the *upāyas*.

Chapter 16 (03:49)

जयन्तोऽपि हसन्त्येते जिता अपि हसन्ति च ।
भवद्भक्तिसुधापानमत्ताः केऽप्येव ये प्रभो ॥३॥

jayanto'pi hasantyete jitā api hasanti ca /
bhavadbhaktisudhāpānāmattāḥ ke'pyeva ye prabho //3//

O Lord, really Your devotees have tasted the nectar of Your devotion (nectar means that liquor). They have tasted the liquor of Thy devotion and they have become mad, they have lost their senses. I will show You how they have lost their senses. I will put that [example] before You.

Jayanto'pi, whenever they conquer, they smile; when they conquer everybody, they smile. When they are conquered, they smile [laughter]. They smile in both ways, so they are mad! There is no distinctive feeling in them. When they conquer everybody, they smile. That is good. That was natural. When they are conquered by people, they smile [laughter]. At that time also, they smile. So, they are mad. Actually, they are mad.

Chapter 16 (05:09)

शुष्ककं मैव सिद्धेय मैव मुच्येय वापि तु ।
स्वादिष्ठपरकाष्ठाप्तत्वद्भक्तिरसनिर्भरः ॥४॥

śuṣkakaṁ maiva siddheya maiva mucyeya vāpi tu /
svādiṣṭhaparakāṣṭhāptatvadbhaktirasanirbharaḥ //4//

Śuṣkakaṁ maiva siddheya. I don't want to achieve those great *yogic* powers in a dry way, when there is dryness, i.e., when I am kept away from Your moistness of Thy devotion. If there is no moistness of Thy devotion, I don't want those *yogic* powers. *Śuṣkakaṁ maiva siddheya*, I don't want to achieve those powers in a dry way. If I am dry–internally I am dry–and I have achieved those *yogic* powers, what is there in those *yogic* powers if there is dryness in my heart? *Maiva mucyeya*, I don't want that liberation when I am dry inside. I don't want . . . let that liberation go to the dogs!

Svādiṣtha parakāṣṭhāpta tvad bhakti rasa nirbharaḥ. I want to get filled with that divine and tasteful, limitless attachment for You. *Bas*, I want that attachment for You. I don't want liberation, I don't want *yogic* powers, in that dry way. I want to become filled with that *svādiṣṭha*, with that tasteful devotion of Thee.

ALEXIS: Sweetest.

SWAMIJI: Sweetest.

Chapter 16 (06:55)

यथैवाज्ञातपूर्वोऽयं भवद्भक्तिरसो मम ।
घटितस्तद्वदीशान स एव परिपुष्यतु ॥५॥

yathaivājñātapurvo'yaṁ bhavadbhaktiraso mama /
ghaṭitastadvadīśāna sa eva paripuṣyatu //5//

Īśāna, O Lord Śiva, this taste of Your devotion I have achieved, but I have achieved [it and] I don't know how I have achieved it. You know that! This taste of Thy devotion, I have achieved. *Yathaiva*, in which way I have achieved this taste of Thy devotion, which was *ajñātapūrva*, I didn't know how to achieve it. I didn't know the ways and regulations of meditation by which I would achieve that devotion. And I have achieved that devotion of Thee.

How?

You know that. I don't know. I don't know how I have achieved that devotion. *Ajñātapūrva*, it was not known to me first; *ajñātapūrva*, at first, it was not known to me. And I have found that devotion. I have achieved that devotion. And that way of achieving that devotion, You already knew. And that devotion is now with me.

Tadvat, and, in the same way, I want one thing. *Īśāna*, O Lord Śiva, *sa eva paripuṣyatu*, the devotion must get dense, it must get strengthened. And that way also I don't know how it will be strengthened, how it will be developed. I don't know how to develop it.

This devotion I have achieved but how I have achieved it, I don't know that. You know how I achieved this devotion. And now I want that this devotion must be developed. And how it will be developed, only You know. I don't know. So, let You [develop] that also for me.

Chapter 16 (09:12)

सत्येन भगवन्नान्यः प्रार्थनाप्रसरोऽस्ति मे ।
केवलं स तथा कोऽपि भक्त्यावेशोऽस्तु मे सदा ॥६॥

satyena bhagavannānyaḥ prārthanāprasaro'sti me /
kevalaṁ sa tathā ko'pi bhaktyāveśo'stu me sadā //6//

Satyena, really, it is true, I tell You the truth, I am speaking the truth, I am not lying before You, *satyena bhagavan*, O Lord Śiva, *nānyaḥ prārthanā prasaro'sti me*, I have no other desire in me. I have no other desire! Only one desire is tickling in the background of my mind. That is, *tathā ko'pi bhaktyāveśa*, I want to get ruined, I want to get merged, in entering in the greatness of Thy devotion. That is my only desire.

Chapter 16 (10:11)

भक्तिक्षीवोऽपि कुप्येयं भवायानुशयीय च ।
तथा हसेयं रुयां च रटेयं च शिवेत्यलम् ॥७॥

bhaktikṣīvo'pi kupyeyaṁ bhavāyānuśayīya ca /
tathā haseyaṁ rūdyāṁ ca raṭeyaṁ ca śivetyalam //7//

Let me be, let me get intoxicated with that devotion (*bhaktīkṣīvo'pi*). When I am intoxicated by that devotion, *kupyeyaṁ bhavāyā*, let me get angry, let me show anger towards the universe [and yell at people saying], "What are you doing? What are you wasting your time in planting these things and earning this money for nothing?" I should get angry with them. *Anuśayīya ca*, and I must have pity on them [and say], "O, they are very poor; they are ruining their lives". *Bhaktikṣīvo'pi*, when I am intoxicated with Thy devotion, I will do this.

He wants to do this [laughter]. He wants to show anger to other people, other worldly people, and repent on their doings.

Tathā haseyaṁ, and, at the same time, I would laugh, *rudyāṁ ca*, I would weep, *raṭeyaṁ ca*, I would cry, "O Siva, O Siva, where are You?" *Bas.*

Chapter 16 (11:36)

विषमस्थोऽपि स्वस्थोऽपि रुदन्नपि हसन्नपि ।
गम्भीरोऽपि विचित्तोऽपि भवेयं भक्तितः प्रभो ॥८॥

viṣamastho'pi svastho'pi rudannapi hasannapi /
gambhīro'pi vicitto'pi bhaveyaṁ bhaktitaḥ prabho //8//

O Lord Śiva, O my Master, by the intensity of my devotion, *viṣamastho'pi*, let me remain in crisis altogether for my whole life. I don't mind. *Svastho'pi*, let me remain peaceful. I don't mind. If my life is peaceful, let it remain peaceful. If my life is miserable altogether from top to bottom, let it remain like that. *Rudannapi*, if I am bent upon weeping altogether day and night, let me remain like that. *Hasannapi*, if I am only laughing for my whole life, let it be like that. *Gambhīro'pi*, if I will be *gambhīra* (*bhīra* is grave), let me remain grave, reserved. *Vicitto'api . . .*

Vicitto'pi means that thing which is not to be revealed to people, that, too, you reveal. That is *vicitta*. When something [is a] secret, it is to be kept secret, but you don't keep it secret, you reveal it to people.

ALEXIS: A blabber mouth.

SWAMIJI: Yes, that is *vicitta*.

. . . and this position would come into me by the intensity of Thy devotion.

Chapter 16 (13:15)

भक्तानां नास्ति संवेद्यं त्वदन्तर्यदि वा बहिः ।
चिद्धर्मा यत्र न भवान्निर्विकल्पः स्थितः स्वयम् ॥९॥

bhaktānāṁ nāsti saṁvedyaṁ tvadantaryadi vā bahiḥ /
ciddharmā yatra na bhavānnirvikalpaḥ sthitaḥ svayam //9//
[beginning of verse missing in audio]

Really, for Thy devotees, nothing is known to them, [which is not] inside Your body or outside Your *svarūpa.*[286] Inside Your *svarūpa* or outside Your *svarūpa*, nothing else is known to them where *ciddharmā*, where Thyself, who is filled with consciousness and who is thoughtless, is not present. So, they feel Your presence everywhere, inside and outside the world.

Chapter 16 (14:09)

भक्ता निन्दानुकारेऽपि तवामृतकणैरिव ।
हृष्यन्त्येवान्तराविद्धास्तीक्ष्णरोमञ्चसूचिभिः ॥१०॥

bhaktā nindānukāre'pi tavāmṛtakaṇairiva /
hṛṣyantyevāntarāviddhāstīkṣṇaromañcasūcibhiḥ //10//

Thy devotees, when they are situated amongst those people who deny Your existence and who give You bad names–those people who are atheists, in the gathering of atheists, when they are seated amongst those atheists who give bad names to Lord Śiva–and [they] also, Your devotees also, agree with them. They don't deny [what the atheists say]. They say, "yes, Lord Śiva is treacherous. He is a very bad personality". And because the topic is Yours, by that topic, they are filled with joy because they deal with the topic of You. It may be against You but the topic is Yours because there is Your name.

So, by hearing Your name, [although] it may be against Your consciousness, but [still] they are filled with joy. But when they have to agree with their conclusion that, "God is not existing", "God is treacherous", "God is . . .", "He should be excluded from the scene", by that feeling, they get those, you know, *romāñca* (*romāñca* means those thrilling [sensations] in each and every pore of their hair, erected hair).

ALEXIS: It's called horripilation.

SWAMIJI: Horripilation.

They laugh in [the atheists'] company as if those devotees are also in their favor, but internally they are pricked; internally, they weep. Externally, they laugh with them. This is the position of Thy devotees.

---

286 Literally, *svarūpa* means "self-form or shape" but Swamiji generally translates *svarūpa* as "nature". [*Editor's note*]

Chapter 16 (16:48)

दुःखापि वेदना भक्तिमतां भोगाय कल्पते ।
येषां सुधार्द्रा सर्वैव संवित्त्वच्चन्द्रिकामयी ॥११॥

duḥkhāpi vedanā bhaktimatāṁ bhogāya kalpate /
yeṣāṁ sudhārdrā sarvaiva saṁvittvaccandrikāmayī //11//

Those devotees who possess the knowledge of Your Self, which is just enlightening knowledge (*candrīkāmayī*), and those devotees who possess the knowledge of Your light of consciousness everywhere, *duḥkhāpi vedanā bhaktimatām*, if they are tortured, if they have a crisis, if they have pain, that pain also carries them to that great enjoyment of God consciousness.

Chapter 16 (17:45)

यत्र तत्रोपरुद्धानां भक्तानां बहिरन्तरे ।
निर्व्याजं त्वद्वपुःस्पर्श रसास्वाद सुखं समम् ॥१२॥

yatra tatroparuddhānāṁ bhaktānāṁ bahirantare /
nirvyājaṁ tvadvapuḥsparśa rasāsvāda sukhaṁ samam //12

Yatra tatra uparuddhānāṁ bhaktānām. Thy devotees, wherever they are seated–wherever they are seated, internally or externally–but they [always] feel the nearness of Your divine touch and the joy, which comes from That divine touch. They feel That divine touch the same in Your absence as in Your presence, *nirvyājam*, without any obstruction (*nirvyājam* means "without obstruction").

Chapter 16 (18:56)

तवेश भक्तेरर्चायां दैन्यांशं द्वयसंश्रयम् ।
विलुप्यास्वादयन्त्येके वपुरच्छं सुधामयम् ॥१३॥

taveśa bhakterarcāyāṁ dainyāṁśaṁ dvayasaṁśrayam /
vilupyāsvādayantyeke vapuracchaṁ sudhāmayam //13//

O Lord (*Īśa* means "O Lord"), when Thy devotees worship You, in that worship, they remove away *dainyāṁśaṁ*, they remove away . . .

Dainyāṁśaṁ means *dīnatā*. You know *dinatā*? *Dainyāṁsaṁ* [means] "pitiable condition", the pitiable condition that comes out from dualistic, differentiated perception. That is a pitiable condition.

. . . that pitiable condition, they remove away while worshiping Your Self. And *āsvādayanti*, they enjoy *acchaṁ vapur sudhāmayam*, that pure and clean existence of Your presence, which is filled with nectar.

Chapter 16 (20:16)

भ्रान्तास्तीर्थदृशो भिन्ना भ्रान्तेरेव हि भिन्नता ।
निष्प्रतिद्वन्द्वि वस्त्वेकं भक्तानां त्वं तु राजसे ॥१४॥

bhrāntāstīrthadṛśo bhinnā bhrāntereva hi bhinnatā /
niṣpratidvandvi vastvekaṁ bhaktānāṁ tvaṁ tu rājase //14//

Tīrthadṛśa (*tīrthadṛśa* means *śāstradṛśa*), the viewpoints of various *śāstras* are different from each other, e.g., the viewpoint of Shaivism is one, the viewpoint of Vedānta is [something else]–*tirthadṛśa* (*tīrtha* means *śāstra*). They are *bhrāntāḥ* (*bhrāntāḥ* means "they are astray"), they are away from Your consciousness because *bhrāntereva hi bhinnatā*, to get separated from You is illusion. Separation is illusion. To be separated from You is illusion. But, for Your devotees, *niṣprati dvandvi*, everywhere they see the oneness of Your consciousness and That shines in them everywhere, always.

ALEXIS: So, they [i.e., *śastras*] are wrong because they have different positions.

SWAMIJI: Yes, different positions. Shaivism is not only Shaivism. Shaivism is every theory. Each and every theory is Shaivism.

ALEXIS: Even wrong theories.

SWAMIJI: Even the theory of atheists is also Shaivism from one point of view because the atheist is also God consciousness.

When you deny God, that is the existence of God. While denying God, you prove God.[287]

Chapter 16 (22:11)

मानावमानरागादिनिष्पाकविमलं मनः ।
यस्यासौ भक्तिमांल्लोकतुल्यशीलः कथं भवेत् ॥ १५ ॥

mānāvamānarāgādiniṣpākavimalaṁ manaḥ /
yasyāsau bhaktimāṁllokatulyaśīlaḥ kathaṁ bhavet //15//

That devotee of Thee whose mind is purified by the ripening of *māna*, *avamāna*, *rāga*, and *dveṣa* . . .

Māna, to be respected; to be disrespected (*avamāna* is to get disrespect); *rāga*, to be attached; *dveṣa*, to be detached.

. . . all of these, where they have been ripened ("ripened" means they have vanished), and by that vanishing of these two opposite things [in one] whose mind is *vimalaṁ* (purified), and that devotee of Thee, *loka tulya śīlaḥ katham*, how can you compare [him] with ordinary people, worldly people? He is beyond comparison. He is above the situation of ordinary people.

Chapter 16 (23:38)

रागद्वेषान्धकरोऽपि येषां भक्तित्विषा जितः ।
तेषां महीयसामग्रे कतमे ज्ञानशालिनः ॥ १६ ॥

rāgadveṣāndhakaro'pi yeṣāṁ bhaktitviṣā jitaḥ /
teṣāṁ mahīyasāmagre katame jñānaśālinaḥ //16//

Yeṣāṁ bhaktitviṣā rāgadveṣāndhakāro'pi jitaḥ. Those who have conquered the darkness of attachment and detachment (to be attached or to be detached is "darkness") and those who have removed this darkness from their minds by the light of devotion, by the light of being attached to You–they are attached to You and by that attachment they have conquered the darkness of being detached or being attached–*teṣāṁ mahīyasāṁ*, they are

287 See footnote 152.

kings, they are *mahīyasāṁ* (*mahīyasāṁ* means "they are honored kings").

ALEXIS: Truly great.

SWAMIJI: Very great!

And before them, *katamejñānaśālinaḥ*, who are *jñānaśālinaḥ*[288]? What [greater] possession is possessed by those who are informed in knowledge, who are filled with knowledge? They are nothing before them.[289]

Chapter 16 (25:11)

यस्य भक्तिसुधास्नानपानादिविधिसाधनम् ।
तस्य प्रारब्धमध्यान्तदशासूच्चैः सुखासिका ॥१७॥

yasya bhaktisudhāsnānapānādividhisādhanam /
tasya prārabdhamadhyāntadaśāsūccaiḥ sukhāsikā //17//

Those devotees who possess *bhakti sudhā snāna*, who possess, who know, the technique of bathing with the nectar of devotion, who have got the technique to bathe in the nectar of devotion, and who have got the technique to drink that nectar of devotion, who have got that technique, who possess that technique, *tasya prārabdhamadhyānta daśāsūccaiḥ sukhāsikā*, for [them], in the beginning, in the end, and in the center, everywhere the bliss of God consciousness shines.

Chapter 16 (26:15)

कीर्त्यश्चिन्तापदं मृग्यः पूज्यो येन त्वमेव तत् ।
भवद्भक्तिमतां श्लाघ्या लोकयात्रा भवन्मयी ॥१८॥

kīrtyaścintāpadaṁ mṛgyaḥ pūjyo yena tvameva tat /
bhavadbhaktimatāṁ ślāghyā lokayātrā bhavanmayī //18//

Bhavad bhaktimatāṁ, those who are Your devotees, they have got *kīrtyas cintāpadaṁ mṛgyaḥ pūjyaḥ tvameva*, You are the only

288 Those who are established in knowledge. [*Editor's note*]

289 That is, those who are informed in knowledge (*jñānaśālinaḥ*) are nothing in comparison to Thy devotees. [*Editor's note*]

being who is sung by them. You are sung by them, You are thought by them, You are searched for by them, You are worshiped by them; You are searched [for by them], You are sung [by them], You are thought of by those devotees.

Ślāghyā lokayātrā bhavanmayī. So, the journey of those devotees in this universe is *ślāghyā* (*ślāghyā* is respectable). It is a great journey, a divine journey. They possess this divine journey in this universe.

What is that divine journey?

Singing of the Lord, thinking of the Lord, searching for the Lord, and worshiping the Lord. This is their greatest journey in this universe.

Chapter 16 (27:52)

मुक्तिसंज्ञा विपक्वाया भक्तेरेव त्वयि प्रभो ।
तस्यामाद्यदशारूढा मुक्तकल्पा वयं ततः ॥१९॥

muktisaṁjñā vipakvāyā bhaktereva tvayi prabho /
tasyāmādyadaśārūḍhā muktakalpā vayaṁ tataḥ //19//

Prabho, O Lord, O my Master, this is a fact that *muktisaṁjñā vipakvāyā bhaktereva*, when Thy devotion is ripened, that is liberation. That is, in other words, to be liberated from this universe. *Tasyām ādya daśārūḍhā*, as we have stepped in that state of Your devotion, so we are liberated already. We have no worry for getting liberated. We are already liberated.

Chapter 16 (28:44)

दुःखागमोऽपि भूयान्मे त्वद्भक्तिभरितात्मनः ।
त्वत्पराची विभो मा भूदपि सौख्यपरम्परा ॥२०॥

duḥkhāgamo'pi bhūyānme tvadbhaktibharitātmanaḥ /
tvatparācī vibho mā bhūdapi saukhyaparamparā //20//

I welcome that continuity of pain in this world, continuity of sadness in this world. I welcome that sadness, that *duḥkha* (suffering). I welcome that suffering but only in [the] case of *tvad bhakti bharitātmanaḥ*, if I am filled with Your devotion. When I am filled with Your devotion, I welcome that pain. Let that pain destroy me! Let that pain shatter me into pieces, but there must be Thy devotion. *Tvat parācī*, when Your devotion is lost to me, when there is no devotion, I don't welcome that flood. If I am flooded with those pleasures and joys of the world, I don't accept that flood of joy and happiness.

When?

DENISE: When I am not filled with Thy devotion.

SWAMIJI: Yes.

Chapter 16 (30:00)

त्वं भक्त्या प्रीयसे भक्तिः प्रीते त्वयि च नाथ यत् ।
तदन्योन्याश्रयं युक्तं यथा वेत्थ त्वमेव तत् ॥२१॥

tvaṁ bhaktyā prīyase bhaktiḥ prīte tvayi ca nātha yat /
tadanyo'nyāśrayaṁ yuktaṁ yathā vettha tvameva tat //21

There is now one problem in this theory of devotion. *Tvaṁ bhaktyā prīyase*, it is a fact that You are pleased only when we are devoted to You. When we are devoted to You, You are pleased with us. But that devotion comes *prīte tvayi*, when You are pleased–then devotion will come.

DENISE: When You are pleased with us, then Your devotion comes.

SWAMIJI: When You are pleased with us, then devotion will come in our mind. But only with devotion are You pleased.

DENISE: But You are only pleased when we have devotion.

SWAMIJI: You are pleased when we have devotion [for You], but devotion cannot take place when You are not pleased. So, this is the theory, a mutually dependent circle (*anyo'nyāśraya*[290]).

This is not *cakradoṣa.*[291] It is *anyo'nyāśraya.*

There must be *bhakti*, then You will be pleased. You must be pleased, then there will be *bhakti*. So, only You can solve this mutually dependent theory of circle. *Tat anyo'nyāśrayam*, this

290 Mutual or reciprocal support or connection or dependance; mutually depending.

291 The defect of a circular argument.

anyo'nyāśraya, *yuktaṁ yathā vettha*, how You solve it, we don't know it. You must be knowing it [laughter].

GANJOO: Only You can solve this fallacy.

SWAMIJI: You can solve this defect in this logical theory. Because, it is a fact that when we are devoted to You, then You are pleased with us. And this is also a fact that when You are pleased [with us], then devotion will come. How can it be solved? You know that. We don't know it.

Chapter 16 (32:16)

साकारो वा निराकारो वान्तर्वा बहिरेव वा ।
भक्तिमत्तात्मनां नाथ सर्वथासि सुधामयः ॥२२॥

sākāro vā nirākāro vāntarvā bahireva vā /
bhaktimattātmanāṁ nātha sarvathāsi sudhāmayaḥ //22//

Nātha, O Master, You may be with form, You may appear with form, *nirākāro vā*, You may appear formless, *vāntarvā*, You may appear in our mind, *bahireva*, You may appear outside our mind, but for those who are mad with Your devotion, who are maddened by Your devotion, for them, *sarvathāsi sudhāmayaḥ*, You are sweet everywhere. You are sweet when You are with form, You are sweet to them when You are formless, You are sweet to them when You appear to them internally, and You are sweet to them when You appear to them externally. You are sweet every way for those who are devoted to Thee.

Chapter 16 (33:24)

अस्मिन्नेव जगत्यन्तर्भवद्भक्तिमतः प्रति ।
हर्षप्रकाशनफलमन्यदेव जगत्स्थितम् ॥२३॥

asminneva jagatyantarbhavadbhaktimataḥ prati /
harṣaprakāśanaphalamanyadeva jagatsthitam //23//

But, I have seen in this universe–in this very universe, in this tortured universe, in this universe which is filled with crisis, filled with sadness–in this universe, I have seen that in this universe also, *harṣa prakāśana phalam anyat eva jagatsthitam, bhavat bhaktim ataḥ prati*, those who are Your devotees, for Thy devotees, this whole universe appears as divine although it is filled with torture and filled with crisis and sadness. I have seen that.

Chapter 16 (34:17)

गुह्ये भक्तिः परे भक्तिर्भक्तिर्विश्वमहेश्वरे ।
त्वयि शम्भौ शिवे देव भक्तिर्नाम किमप्यहो ॥२४॥

guhye bhaktiḥ pare bhaktirbhaktirviśvamaheśvare /
tvayi śambhau śive deva bhaktirnāma kimapyaho //24//

I want Thy devotion secretly. I want Thy devotion secretly. *Pare bhaktiḥ*, I want devotion for the supreme Lord. I want devotion for the ruler of this universe. I want devotion for Thee. I want devotion for Śiva. I want devotion. I want devotion and nothing else. I want devotion.

Chapter 16 (35:04)

भक्तिर्भक्तिः परे भक्तिर्भक्तिर्नाम समुत्कटा ।
तारं विरौमि यत्तीव्रा भक्तिर्मेऽस्तु परं त्वयि ॥२५॥

bhaktirbhaktiḥ pare bhaktirbhaktirnāma samutkaṭā /
tāraṁ viraumi yattīvrā bhaktirme'stu paraṁ tvayi //25//

Only devotion. Thy devotion. Thy devotion. That supreme devotion. That intense devotion! I will weep, I will cry, loudly I will cry for that intense devotion [which] must be possessed by me.

Chapter 16 (35:40)

यतोऽसि सर्वशोभानां प्रसवानिरीश तत् ।
त्वयि लग्नमनर्घं स्याद्रत्नं वा यदि वा तृणम् ॥२६॥

yato'si sarvaśobhānāṁ prasavāvanirīśa tat /
tvayi lagnamanarghaṁ syādratnaṁ vā yadi vā tṛṇam //26//

This is a fact that, as *sarvaśobhānāṁ prasavāva avani*, O Lord, You are the abode of all glories in the universe, all glories are stored in Your Self, so, *tvayi lagnam*, when it is attached to You, when anything is attached to You, *ratnaṁ vā*, it may be a jewel, it may be just a blade of grass, it will become *anargham*, priceless. It has no price.

Chapter 16 (36:32)

आवेद्कादा च वेद्याद्येषां संवेद्नाध्वनि ।
भवता न वियोगोऽस्ति ते जयन्ति भवज्जुषः ॥२७॥

āvedakādā ca vedyādyeṣāṁ saṁvedanādhvani /
bhavatā na viyogo'sti te jayanti bhavajjuṣaḥ //27//

Those who are Thy devotees, they are glorified in this universe because *avedakāt ā ca vedyat*, just from, right from, subjective consciousness to the objective field, this *saṁvedanādhvani*, on the path of knowledge, they have no *bhavatā na viyogo'sti*, they are never separated from Thy consciousness. Right from subjective consciousness up to objective consciousness, they are never separated from Thee. *Te jayanti*, they are glorified in this universe.

Chapter 16 (37:36)

संसारसदसो बाह्ये कैश्चित्त्वं परिरभ्यसे ।
स्वामिन्परैस्तु तत्रैव ताम्यद्भिस्त्यक्तयन्त्रणैः ॥२८॥

saṁsārasadaso bāhye kaiścittvaṁ parirabhyase /
svāminparaistu tatraiva tāmyadbhistyaktayantraṇaiḥ //28//

O my Master, *saṁsāra sadaso*, there are some devotees of Yours who embrace You–embrace You where?–after leaving aside all of these worldly affairs. They enter in the caves of the Himalayas and then, there, they embrace You, they become one with You. There are such devotees.

But, there are some other devotees also who embrace You *in* the activity of this universe. They embrace You, *svāmin*, O Lord!

Paraistu, there are some, there are a few devotees of Thee, who *tatraiva parirabhyase*; *tatraiva*, in this world of activity, they *parirabhyase* (*parirabhyase* means "they embrace You"). *Tyaktayantraṇaiḥ*, and they have no rules and regulations for embracing You–without rules and regulations. They may embrace a [prostitute]. While embracing a [prostitute], they don't actually embrace the [prostitute], they embrace You![292] There are such devotees. There are such devotees because they feel Your presence everywhere.

Chapter 16 (39:17)

पानाशनप्रसाधन-
    सम्भुक्तसमस्तविश्वया शिवया ।
प्रलयोत्सवसरभसया
    दृढमुपगूढं शिवं वन्दे ॥२९॥

pānāśanaprasādhana-
    sambhuktasamastaviśvayā śivayā /
pralayotsavasarabhasayā
    dṛḍhamupagūḍhaṁ śivaṁ vande //29//

I bow to that Lord Śiva who is tightly embraced by Pārvati.

Pārvati. What is the position of Pārvati who embraces You?

Pāna aśana prasādhana sambhukta samasta viśvayā. She drinks (*pāna*); *aśana*, She eats sweet dishes; *prasādhana*, She adjusts fine make-up on Her body; *sambhukta samasta viśvayā*, and She enjoys all of the enjoyments of the senses; and *pralaya utsava sarabhasayā*, She enjoys the festival of universal destruction, and She tightly embraces You at that time. And, I bow to that Śiva who is embraced by Pārvati [who acts] in such a way.

---

292 "And prostitutes are to be worshiped. When you pass by the house of a prostitute, you should bow towards that house and go on with your work. You should not hate that [prostitute]. It was Lord Śiva's will that she has become a prostitute. All ladies are to be worshiped and respected." *Tantrāloka*, 15.296c (USF archives).

Chapter 16 (40:40)

परमेश्वरता जयत्यपूर्वा
तव विश्वेश यदीशितव्यशून्या
अपरापि तथैव ते ययेदं
जगदाभाति यथा तथा न भाति ॥३०॥

parameśvaratā jayatyapūrvā
tava viśveśa yadīśitavyaśūnyā /
aparāpi tathaiva te yayedaṁ
jagadābhāti yathā tathā na bhāti //30//

O Lord, there are two different glories of Thee existing in this universe. One *parameśvaratā*, one glory of Lord Śiva is that which is *īśitavyaśūnyā*, which is not governed by any other agent. That is grace, that is *anugraha*.[293]

Aparāpi, and there is another divinity of Thee who is also not goverened by any other agent and that it concealing your nature. Conceiling your nature is handled by You and revealing your nature is handled by You. And these two kinds of lordships they are glorified. And one is that Lordship where you feel revealing of your nature, revealing nature of God consciousness. Another lordship is when that nature is concealed totally.

293 "Your [i.e., the individual's] effort won't touch it." *Śivastotrāvalī* (additional audio, USF archives).

Chapter Seventeen
Festival of Divine Play
Divyakrīḍābahumānanāmākhyaṁ saptadaśaṁ stotram

अहो कोऽपि जयत्येष स्वादुः पूजामहोत्सवः ।
यतोऽमृतसास्वादमश्रूण्यपि ददत्यलम् ॥१॥

aho ko'pi jayatyeṣa svāduḥ pūjāmahotsavaḥ /
yato'mṛtarasāsvādamaśrūṇyapi dadatyalam //1//

This is a wonderful thing that the sweet [and unique] festival of Your devotion, the festival of Your worship, is glorified (*ko'pi* means "that unique festival of Thy devotion" and *svādu* means "the very sweet festival of Thy devotion"), is glorified all-round. By which festival, *amṛta rasāsvādana aśrūṇtyapi dadati*, even some drops of tears also carries you to that great joy of that festival.

Chapter 17 (01:01)

व्यापाराः सिद्धाः सर्वे ये त्वत् पूजापुरःसराः ।
भक्तानां त्वन्मयाः सर्वे स्वयं सिध्यय एव ते ॥२॥

vyāpārāḥ siddhidāḥ sarve ye tvat pūjāpuraḥsarāḥ /
bhaktānāṁ tvanmayāḥ sarve svayaṁ siddhaya eva te //2//

All of those activities, which are concerned with Thy devotion, all of those activities (*vyāpārāḥ sarve*, all of those activities), *ye tvat pūjā puraḥ saraḥ*, which are connected with Thy devotion, they bestow [upon] you those great powers, those great powers of great achievement.

But, for Thy devotees, all of those [devotional] activities in this universe become powers themselves. They are powers themselves. They are not the bestowers of powers, they are powers by themselves. For ordinary people, they bestow power. For Your devotees, they are powers themselves. They shine as powers.

Chapter 17 (02:14)

सर्वदा सर्वभावेषु युगपत्सर्वरूपिणम् ।
त्वामर्चयन्त्यविश्रान्तं ये ममैतेऽधिदेवताः ॥३॥

sarvadā sarvabhāveṣu yugapatsarvarūpiṇam /
tvāmarcayantyaviśrāntaṁ ye mamaite'dhidevatāḥ //3//

Those devotees of Thee who adore You simultaneously in each and every object, and always, and without a break (*aviśrānta*), those devotees who adore You that way, *te mama adhi devatā*, they are my presiding gods. They are my presiding . . . they have to rule on me. They have to take care of me. They are my gods. You are not my god. They are my gods who worship You like this.

Chapter 17 (03:09)

ध्यानायासतिरस्कारसिद्धस्त्वत्स्पर्शनोत्सवः ।
पूजाविधिरिति ख्यातो भक्तानां स सदास्तु मे ॥४॥

dhyānāyāsatiraskārasiddhastvatsparśanotsavaḥ /
pūjāvidhiriti khyāto bhaktānāṁ sa sadāstu me //4//

The festival of Your touch, the festival of Your touching [Your devotee], that is the great festival when You touch him. When You touch him, not by means–*dhyāna āyāsa tiraskāra ca*, you have not to meditate; you have not to meditate by the technique of *āṇavopāya* or *śāktopāya* or *śāmbhavopāya* or *anupāya*–without adoption of these techniques, those devotees of Thee who [experience] this festival of Your touch, without adoption of these means, *pūjā vidhir iti*, this is the real technique of worshiping You. And this is the technique, which is owned by Your devotees. And I want that technique to possess.

Chapter 17 (04:36)

भक्तानां समतासारविषुवत्समयः सदा ।
त्वद्भावरसपीयूषरसेनैषां सदार्चनम् ॥५॥

bhaktānāṁ samatāsāraviṣuvatsamayaḥ sadā /
tvadbhāvarasapīyūṣarasennaiṣāṁ sadārcanam //5//

Thy devotees have always this sacred time, [they] have possessed always this sacred moment of *viṣuvat* (*viṣuvat* means that sacred [time] when day and night are one).

ALEXIS: Equinox.

SWAMIJI: Equinox.

Tvat bhāva rasapīyūṣa rasena eṣāṁ sadārcanam. And they worship You by the nectar of [their] love for Thee.

Chapter 17 (05:33)

यस्यानारम्भपर्यन्तौ न च कालक्रमः प्रभो ।
पूजात्मासौ क्रिया तस्याः कर्तारस्त्वज्जुषः परम् ॥५॥

yasyānārambhaparyantau na ca kālakramaḥ prabho /
pūjātmāsau kriyā tasyāḥ kartārastvajjuṣaḥ param //6//

That devotee who has *anārambha paryantau na ca kālakramaḥ*, who has no time for Your worship, i.e., who has no restriction of time for Your worship, this is really the action of worship, this is really the act of worship. *Tasyāḥ kartāraḥ*, and worshipers [who worship] in such a way are really Your devotees.

ALEXIS: Because they devote every second of their life.

SWAMIJI: Every second. They don't keep a wristwatch for Your devotion.

ALEXIS: Now, it's time for meditation.

SWAMIJI: Everywhere, every time [is an occasion for Thy worship].

Chapter 17 (06:31)

ब्रह्मादीनामपीशास्ते ते च सौभाग्यभागिनः ।
येषां स्वप्नेऽपि मोहेऽपि स्थितस्त्वत्पूजनोत्सवः ॥७॥

brahmādīnāmapīśāste te ca saubhāgyabhāginaḥ /
yeṣāṁ svapne'pi mohe'pi sthitastvatpūjanotsavaḥ //7//

Those [devotees] are really the rulers of the great gods–Brahma, Viṣṇu, and Rūdra. They rule on those three great lords who are creators, protectors, and destroyers of this universe. They are actually rulers of those three lords.

Te ca saubhāgyabhāginaḥ. They are really *saubhāgya*, fortunate people.

Who?

For whom *svapne api mohe api sthita tvat pūjana utsavaḥ*, the festival of Your worship is existing in the dreaming state and illusion also.

Chapter 17 (07:36)

जपतां जुह्वतां स्नातां ध्यायतां न च केवलम्
भक्तानां भवदभ्यर्चामहो यावद्यदा तदा ॥८॥

japatāṁ juhvatāṁ snātāṁ dhyāyatāṁ na ca kevalam /
bhaktānāṁ bhavadabhyarcāmaho yāvadyadā tadā //8//

Thy devotees, no matter if they are reciting Your name, if they are doing Your *havan* (sacrificing), *snātam*, no matter if they are bathing, *dhyāyatām*, [or] if they are meditating on You–not only in these states, not only in the state of reciting Your name, not only in the state of [placing] offerings in fire, not only in the state of bathing, not only in states of meditation–those devotees have possessed the festival of Your devotion. *Yāvadyadā tadā*, they have everywhere, always . . . always they possess this festival, not only in these sacred states.

Chapter 17 (08:50)

भवत्पूजासुधास्वादसम्भोगसुखिनः सदा
इन्द्रादीनामथ ब्रह्ममुख्यानामस्ति कः समः ॥९॥

bhavatpūjāsudhāsvādasambhogasukhinaḥ sadā /
indrādīnāmatha brahmamukhyānāmasti kaḥ samaḥ //9//

Those devotees who have always possessed this joy, i.e., the enjoyment of the joy of tasting the nectar of Your devotion, who have possessed the joy of tasting the nectar of Your devotion, *indrādīnām*, [even among] those [gods], Indra, etcetera (Indra is the governor of the kingdom of heaven, and *brahma mukhyānām*, Brahma, Viṣṇu, and Īśvara, those who are creators, protectors, and destroyers of this universe), there is no comparison [of those gods with] that person who is always sentenced to this worship of Thee and who is enjoying that divine nectar of that worship. There is no comparison with those great lords of divinity.

Chapter 17 (10:23)

जगत्क्षोभैकजनके भवत्पूजामहोत्सवे ।
यत्प्राप्यं प्राप्यते किंचिद्भक्ता एव विदन्ति तत् ॥१०॥

jagatkṣobhaikajanake bhavatpūjāmahotsave /
yatprāpyaṁ prāpyate kiṁcidbhaktā eva vidanti tat //10//

The festival, the great festival of Your worship, the greatest festival of Your worship, is only that worship which destroys the agitation of the universe; which destroys *jagat kṣobhaikajanake*, which destroys the agitation of differentiated consciousness–it is destroyed by the great festival of Your worship. And, in that great festival of worship, *yat prāpyaṁ prāpyate*, that which is achieved in that great festival, that is not known to anybody. That is known to Your devotees only. Those devotees only know what is achieved in that festival. It is unknown to all other people.

Chapter 17 (11:35)

त्वद्धाम्नि चिन्मये स्थित्वा षट्त्रिंशत्तत्त्वकर्मभिः ।
कायवाक्चित्तचेष्टाद्यैरर्चये त्वां सदा विभो ॥११॥

tvaddhāmni cinmaye sthitvā ṣaṭtriṁśattattvakarmabhiḥ /
kāyavākcittaceṣṭādyairarcaye tvāṁ sadā vibho //11//

O Lord, there is one desire in me. I want to worship You always (*sadā tvāṁ arcaye*). I like to worship You always with body, with speech, with word, and with action. With body, with speech, with mind, and with action, I want to worship You always.

But I don't want to worship You from a distance! I want to worship You after entering in Your body [Swamiji weeps]. I want that [kind of worship]. Then, *tvad dhāmni cinmaye sthitvā*, I want to worship You after entering in Your body.

And I want to worship You, not only with flowers, but with all of the thirty-six elements of the universe, right from *pṛthvī* to *śiva*. I want to worship You.

I want to worship You after entering in Your body.

Chapter 17 (13:07)

भवत्पूजामयासङ्गसम्भोगसुखिनो मम ।
प्रयातु कालः सकलोऽप्यनन्तोऽपीयदर्थये ॥१२॥

bhavatpūjāmayāsaṅgasambhogasukhino mama /
prayātu kālaḥ sakalo'pyananto'pīyadarthaye //12//

I crave for only this point, this thing (*iyadarthaye*, I crave only for this thing), *bhavatpūjāmayāsaṅga saṁbhogasukhino mama*, because I am (*mama*), I am peaceful only when I am enjoying the nearness of Your worship. When I am enjoying the nearness of Your worship, [at] that moment, I become peaceful, I remain peaceful.

So, for me, this is the desire in me that *sakalo api ananto'pi*, [during] all of this time–and endless time–I don't want to die, I don't want to live, I don't want anything [except] I want that all of this time should pass in this act.

In which act?

Bas, in worshiping You, because I am only peaceful in Your worship and nothing else will give me any peace.

Chapter 17 (14:36)

भवत्पूजामृतरसाभोगलम्पटता विभो ।
विवर्धतामनुदिनं सदा च फलतां मम ॥१३॥

bhavatpūjāmṛtarasābhogalampaṭatā vibho /
vivardhatāmanudinaṁ sadā ca phalatāṁ mama //13//

Vibho, O Lord, *bhavat pūjāmṛta rasa ābhoga lampaṭatā*, I want *bhoga lampaṭatā*, passion for enjoyment, passion (*lampaṭatā* means passion), passion for enjoying the taste of the nectar of Thy devotion, of Thy worship. This passion of enjoying the taste of the devotion of Your worship, *vivardhatāṁ anudinaṁ*, let it rise each day; *vivardhatām anudinam*, let it grow each day.

And not only growing is the problem. The problem is *sadā ca phalatāṁ mama*, and it must bear fruit also [laughter]. That fruit is Your nearness.

Chapter 17 (15:42)

जगद्विलयसञ्जातसुधैकरसनिर्भरे ।
त्वदब्धौ त्वां महात्मानमरचन्नासीय सर्वदा ॥१४॥

jagadvilayasañjātasudhaikarasanirbhare /
tvadabdhau tvāṁ mahātmānamarcannāsīya sarvadā //14

Tvad abdhau, there is a great ocean of Thee–You are a great ocean, unlimited ocean–*jagat vilaya sañjāta sudhaika rasa nirbhare*, and that ocean is filled with the greatest nectar; *jagat vilaya eka sañjāta sudhā eka rasa nirbhare*, [it is] filled with that *sudhā*, filled with that nectar, which has appeared by the destruction of differentiated cognition, this differentiated knowledge of the universe. The destruction of the differentiated knowledge of the universe has created the taste of that nectar, and that nectar is filled in the ocean of Thy being. Your being is filled with . . . the nectar is filled in that being of Thee. And *tvāṁ mahātmanām*, You are a great being!

Arcannāsīya sarvadā, I wish I would devote all of my time in Your worship. That is my great . . . that is my only, craving.

Chapter 17 (17:24)

अशेषवासनाग्रन्थिविच्छेदसरलं सदा ।
मनो निवेद्यते भक्तैः स्वादु पूजाविधौ तव ॥ १५ ॥

aśeṣavāsanāgranthivicchedasaralaṁ sadā /
mano nivedyate bhaktaiḥ svādu pūjāvidhau tava / / 15 / /

There are devotees of Thee who offer their minds to Thee, and those minds, which are not distracted minds; [not] with those [minds that are] filled with worldly affairs. No. Sweet minds. They offer You their sweet minds, always. They offer You their sweet minds always, just to adore You. And the knots are always removed from their minds.

Knots of what?

Aśeṣavāsanā granthi, all of the impressions of worldly enjoyments, all cravings for worldly enjoyments. And they leave behind those impressions and those impressions are removed from their minds. And those minds are *sarala* (*sarala* means "straight", "straightforward", "unknotted"). And *svādu*, and those minds are very sweet minds, and they offer to You their sweet minds to Your being, always.

Chapter 17 (19:05)

अधिष्ठायैव विषयानिमाः करणवृत्तयः ।
भक्तानां प्रेषयन्ति त्वत्पूजार्थममृतासवम् ॥ १६ ॥

adhiṣṭhāyaiva viṣayānimāḥ karaṇavṛttayaḥ /
bhaktānāṁ preṣayanti tvatpūjārthamamṛtāsavam / / 16 / /

These very [organs] of cognition and these very [organs] of action, they carry the greatest and highest and priceless liquor of Thy worship to those devotees of Thee. They carry that liquor and they place that liquor before Thy devotees [without] depriving away, not keeping away, the enjoyment of the senses. In the very enjoyment of the senses, they carry this liquor to them for Thy worship.

Chapter 17 (20:11)

भक्तानां भक्तिसंवेगमहोष्मविवशात्मनाम् ।
कोऽन्यो निर्वाणहेतुः स्यात्त्वत्पूजामृतमज्जनात् ॥१७॥

bhaktānāṁ bhaktisaṁvegamahoṣmavivaśātmanām /
ko'nyo nirvāṇahetuḥ syāttvatpūjāmṛtamajjanāt //17//

Bhaktānām, there are devotees whose mind is *vivaśa*, whose mind has become beyond control, whose mind is beyond control, i.e., [they] can't control their minds. They are mad! They become mad.

By which? By what?

Bhakti saṁvega mahoṣma, by the fire of Thy attachment. This attachment for You is a kind of fire and that fire makes them mad for You. And that madness is *vivaśa* (beyond control), you can't stop that madness in them. Those are such devotees.

Ko'nyo nirvāṇa hetuḥ syāt. They are not freed, they are never freed from that madness, unless they are totally drowned in the nectar of Thy worship. If they are drowned in the nectar of That worship, then this madness is removed in them. Till then, . . .

ALEXIS: *Nirvāṇa hetu.*

SWAMIJI: . . . *nirvāṇa hetu*, you can't remove that madness from them. It is beyond control.

DENISE: You just have to drown them and then they'll be free.

SWAMIJI: Drown them in the *pūjā*, in the worship of Thee, then this [madness] will come under control.

ALEXIS: This is *śleṣa* (pun) here, isn't there?

SWAMIJI: Yes.

ALEXIS: *Nirvāṇa* and *nirvāṇa*.

SWAMIJI: Yes.

ALEXIS: "Putting out" and "enlightenment".[294]
SWAMIJI:

Chapter 17 (21:55)

सततं त्वत्पदाभ्यर्चासुधापानमहोत्सवः ।
त्वत्प्रसादैकसम्प्राप्तिहेतुर्मे नाथ कल्पताम् ॥१८॥

satataṁ tvatpadābhyarcāsudhāpānamahotsavaḥ /
tvatprasādaikasamprāptiheturme nātha kalpatām //18//

Tvat pada abhyarcā sudhāpāna mahotsavaḥ. This great festival of tasting the nectar of Thy devotion, of the devotion of Thy feet, tasting the nectar of the devotion of Thy feet, that festival is *tvat prasādaika samprāpti hetur*, this festival can be owned, not by our actions, not by our efforts, with our efforts, but only by Your grace (*tvat prasādaika samprāpti hetur*). *Nātha kalpatām*, let me have it [laughter]! Let me have that festival!

Chapter 17 (23:00)

अनुभूयासमीशान प्रतिकर्म क्षणात्क्षणम् ।
भवत्पूजामृतापानमदास्वादमहामुदम् ॥१९॥

anubhūyāsamīśāna pratikarma kṣaṇātkṣaṇam /
bhavatpūjāmṛtāpānamadāsvādamahāmudam //19//

Īśāna, O Lord, will that day come when I will experience in each and every action of [mine], in each and every action, *kṣaṇāt kṣaṇam*, and in *kṣaṇāt kṣaṇam*, . . .

ALEXIS: From moment to moment.

SWAMIJI: From moment to moment.

What I will experience?

Bhavat pūjāmṛta pāna mada āsvāda mahāmudam. The great taste, the great enjoyment, of becoming mad by tasting the nectar of Your worship. Will that day come ever?

---

294 That is, the word "*nirvāṇa*" appears to signify both the "extinguishing" or "putting out" of madness and the achievement of enlightement. [*Editor's note*]

Chapter 17 (24:02)

दृष्टार्थ एव भक्तानां भवत्पूजामहोद्यमः ।
तदैव यदसम्भाव्यं सुखमास्वादयन्ति ते ॥२०॥

dṛṣṭārtha eva bhaktānāṁ bhavatpūjāmahodyamaḥ /
tadaiva yadasambhāvyaṁ sukhamāsvādayanti te //20//

Now, You will say, "No, it is very difficult to achieve. It will come by-and-by. You will achieve this by-and-by." But, I have experienced that there are such people who have experienced this great enthusiasm of worshiping You. *Tadaiva yat yatna*, and they have only enthusiasm to worship You! And, by that enthusiasm, they are carried to Your God consciousness. They don't worship You at all [because] there is no time left for them [to do so]. Only enthusiasm [arises in them] and they are carried to God consciousness. I have seen with my own eyes [the existence of] such people. Why not me? Why I am deprived from this?

Chapter 17 (25:08)

यावन्न लब्धस्त्वत्पूजासुधास्वादमहोत्सवः ।
तावन्नास्वादितो मन्ये लवोऽपि सुखसम्पदः ॥२१॥

yāvanna labdhastvatpūjāsudhāsvādamahotsavaḥ /
tāvannāsvādito manye lavo'pi sukhasampadaḥ //21//

I believe–this is my belief, my Lord, this is my belief–*yāvat na labdhaḥ tvat pūjā sudhāsvāda*, until this great festival of tasting the nectar of Thy devotion is achieved, I have got such a belief, I have got this full belief, that he has not achieved anything! Although he [may have] achieved everything in this universe, he has achieved nothing. He is nil. So, this is the achievement to be achieved.

What?

Just tasting the nectar of Thy devotion. So, let me taste it!

Chapter 17 (25:56)

भक्तानां विषयान्वेषाभासायासाद्विनैव सा ।
अयत्नसिद्धं त्वद्धामस्थितिः पूजासु जायते ॥२२॥

bhaktānāṁ viṣayānveṣābhāsāyāsādvinaiva sā /
ayatnasiddhaṁ tvaddhāmasthitiḥ pūjāsu jāyate //22//
[beginning of verse missing in audio]

O Lord, there are such devotees who have not to collect the substances of adoration [for Your] worship. They don't collect those substances (for instance, *dhūpa*, *dīpa*, fruits, flowers, incense, *ghee*, etc.), which are used in worship. They don't collect those substances. Without collecting those substances, the celebration of their worship takes place automatically.

Chapter 17 (26:55)

न प्राप्यमस्ति भक्तानां नाप्येषामस्ति दुर्लभम् ।
केवलं विचरन्त्येते भवत्पूजामदोन्मदाः ॥२३॥

na prāpyamasti bhaktānāṁ nāpyeṣāmasti durlabham /
kevalaṁ vicarantyete bhavatpūjāmadonmadāḥ //23//

For Thy devotees, there is nothing to be achieved. And, for Thy devotees, there is nothing difficult to achieve. Only they roam and walk (*vicaranti*, they roam here and there[295]) and they are mad with the intoxication of Thy worship.

Chapter 17 (27:44)

अहो भक्तिभरोदारचेतसां वरद त्वयि ।
श्लाघ्यः पूजाविधिः कोऽपि यो न याञ्चाकलंकितः ॥२४

295 "They roam *peacefully* here and there." *Śivastotrāvalī* (additional audio, USF archives).

aho bhaktibharodāracetasāṁ varada tvayi /
ślāghyaḥ pūjāvidhiḥ ko'pi yo na yācñākalaṅkitaḥ //24//

Aho, it is wonderful, this is a great wonder to me, O giver of boons, O bestower of boons (*varada*)! *Bhakti bhara udāra cetaṣām*, those devotees who have an expanded and broad mind–they have got expanded and broad mind (*udāra cetasām*)–and the way of their worship is *ślāghyaḥ*, is supreme! And it is a very great way of their worship. *Yo na yācñākalaṅkitaḥ*, they don't ask anything from You; they just worship You, *bas*. They don't want anything from You. This is their greatness! *Yo na yācñā kalaṅkitāḥ*, they don't ask for boons from You. They just worship You.

Chapter 17 (29:14)

का न शोभा न को ह्लादः का समृद्धिर्न वापरा ।
को वा न मोक्षः कोऽप्येष महादेवो यदर्च्यते ॥२५॥

kā na śobhā na ko hlādaḥ kā samṛddhir na vāparā /
ko vā na mokṣaḥ ko'pyeṣa mahādevo yadarcyate //25//

Where the worship of Lord Śiva takes place, that is the glory, that is the ecstasy, that is the joy (the highest joy), that is the *samṛddhiḥ* (*samṛddhiḥ* means rise), that is the real liberation, and that is everything where Mahādeva is worshiped, [where] Lord Śiva is worshiped. Lord Śiva's worship is everything! That is the glory, that is the *ānanda* (supreme bliss), that is the rise, and that is the real liberation.

Chapter 17 (30:18)

अन्तरुल्लसदच्छाच्छभक्तिपीयूषपोषितम् ।
भवत्पूजोपयोगाय शरीरमिदमस्तु मे ॥२६॥

antarullasadacchācchabhaktipīyūṣapoṣitam /
bhavatpūjopayogāya śarīramidamastu me //26//

I have one request for You, O Lord. That is, I want my body [to be] meant only for Your worship. Let my body be worthy of worshiping You only, nothing else! Because, this body of mine is nourished by the nectar of devotion, which is very *accha*, very pure, and which rises from my internal heart. The *bhakti*, which has risen from the internal heart of mine, and by that nectar of devotion, it is nourished, this body of mine is nourished. So, I want this body to just be with the purpose of Thy devotion only, nothing else!

Chapter 17 (31:44)

त्वत्पादपूजासम्भोगपरतन्त्रः सदा विभो ।
भूयासं जगतामीश एकः स्वच्छन्दचेष्टितः ॥२७॥

tvatpādapūjāsambhogaparatantraḥ sadā vibho /
bhūyāsaṁ jagatāmīśa ekaḥ svacchandaceṣṭitaḥ //27//

Vibho, O Lord, O all-pervading Lord, *jagatāmīśa*, O ruler of all the three worlds, I would like to be dependent on tasting the nectar of Thy worship. *Tvatpāda pūjā sambhoga paratantraḥ*, I want to be dependent to that *sambhoga*, that enjoying the nectar of Thy worship. I want to be dependent to that. But, at the same time, side by side, on the side lines, *ekaḥ svacchanda ceṣṭitaḥ*, in the other outward world, I want to be absolutely independent.

You know what is that?

That is, in the outside world, I would like to be independent, not agreeing with [being dependent upon] any other thing in this world. But, where there is Your worship, I would like to be dependent to that worship; always dependent to that worship, and independent everywhere else.

Chapter 17 (33:27)

त्वद्ध्यानदर्शनस्पर्शतृषि केषामपि प्रभो ।
जायते शीतलस्वादु भवत्पूजामहासरः ॥२८॥

tvaddhyānadarśanasparśatṛṣi keṣāmapi prabho /
jāyate śītalasvādu bhavatpūjāmahāsaraḥ //28//

There are some devotees of Thee, O Lord, *tvad dhyāna darśana sparśa tṛṣi*, who have got *tṛṣi* (*tṛṣi* means "thirst"), the thirst for meditating on You and embracing You; meditating on You and embracing [You] at the same time (*dhyāna* and *sparśa*). And those unique devotees of Thee who have got this thirst, at the rise of this thirst, *jāyate śītala svādu bhavat pūjā mahāsaraḥ*, their thirst is quenched by adoration of Thee. Their thirst is quenched *mahāsaraḥ*, by adoration of Thee, and that adoration is just to dive in the great lake of Thy worship.

And that lake is *śītala* (*śītala* means very cool) and *svādu* (very sweet); the cool and sweet water of Thy devotion, Thy worship. And that is the lake, and when they dive in that lake, that thirst is quenched in them.

Chapter 17 (35:13)

यथा त्वमेव जगतः पूजासम्भोगभाजनम् ।
तथेश भक्तिमानेव पूजासम्भोगभाजनम् ॥२९॥

yathā tvameva jagataḥ pūjāsambhogabhājanam /
tatheśa bhaktimāneva pūjāsambhogabhājanam //29//

O Lord, just as You are the only *bhājana*, You are the only being worthy of enjoying the nectar of worship–You are worth enjoying the nectar of worship–just as You are worthy of enjoying the nectar, in the same way, Thy devotees also are worthy of enjoying the nectar of Thy worship.

So, there are only two beings, which have to enjoy the nectar of Thy devotion. That is, You have to enjoy, You are enjoying that nectar of Thy devotion of worship, and, in the same way, Your devotee also enjoys the nectar of Your worship.

Chapter 17 (36:26)

कोऽप्यसौ जयति स्वामिन्भवत्पूजामहोत्सवः ।
षट्त्रिंशतोऽपि तत्त्वानां क्षोभो यत्रोल्लसत्यलम् ॥३०॥

ko'pyasau jayati svāminbhavatpūjāmahotsavaḥ /
ṣaṭtriṁśato'pi tattvānāṁ kṣobho yatrollasatyalam //30//

Svāmin, O my master, that unique *mahotsavaḥ* (*mahotsavaḥ* means "great day"), . . .

ALEXIS: Festival.

SWAMIJI: Festival.

. . . the great festival of Thy devotion, great festival of Thy worship, that unique great festival of Thy worship, is glorified, always glorified, where *ṣaṭtriṁśato'pi tattvānāṁ yatra*, where *ṣaṭtriṁśato'pi tattvānāṁ*, all of these thirty-six elements are absorbed (*kṣobhaḥ* means *nāśaḥ*[296]).

All of these thirty-six elements absorb into nothingness then. Only Śiva remains.[297]

ALEXIS: It is not *bahi prasara*[298]?

SWAMIJI: *Antaḥ prasara*[299].

Chapter 17 (37:33)

नमस्तेभ्यो विभो येषां भक्तिपीयूषवारिणा ।
पूजान्येव भवन्ति त्वत्पूजोपकरणान्यपि ॥३१॥

namastebhyo vibho yeṣāṁ bhaktipīyūṣavāriṇā /
pūjānyeva bhavanti tvatpūjopakaraṇānyapi //31//

Vibho, O Lord, *namastebhyo*, I adore those devotees of Thee (*yeṣām*, those devotees) when they gather all of those substances for Thy devotion (flowers, fruits, and all of these things . . . incense, etc.) to offer on Your image. They gather [these substances but] they don't offer [them].

What do they do? Do you know?

Bas, they adore *those* substances because they feel that these substances are going to be offered to Lord Śiva, so these substances are worth worshiping. [They feel], "I must worship them first".

296 Destruction, or annihilation.

297 See appendix 25 for explanation of "nothingness".

298 External flow.

299 Internal flow.

Pūjānyeva yeṣāṁ bhaktipīyūṣavāriṇā. Those who worship by the *vāriṇā*, by the water of the nectar of devotion– who worship by the water of the nectar of devotion–these substances also [are worshiped by them] (*pūjā upakaraṇāni*; *upakaraṇāni* means *sāmagrī*[300]).

Chapter 17 (38:56)

पूजारम्भे विभो ध्यात्वा मन्त्राधेयां त्वदात्मताम् ।
स्वात्मन्येव परे भक्ता मान्ति हर्षेण न क्वचित् ॥३२॥

pūjārambhe vibho dhyātvā mantrādheyāṁ tvadātmatāṁ /
svātmanyeva pare bhaktā mānti harṣeṇa na kvacit //32//

Vibho, O Lord, *bhaktā*, those who are Thy devotees, at the beginning of worshiping You, at the beginning of Thy worship, they just meditate on Thy nature first, i.e., to whom worship is to be done.

When they meditate on You who are their *mantrādheyam* (*mantrādheyam* means by *ādheyam*, to be worshiped by all of these *mantras*), *svātmanyeva pare bhaktā*, *bhaktā mānti harṣeṇa na* [*kvacit*], then they know no bounds of joy by that, and they don't worship You at all. They just sink in that ecstasy [while] meditating on You and the rest of the worship does not take place [laughter].

Chapter 17 (40:28)

राज्यलाभादिवोत्फुल्लैः कैश्चित्पूजामहोत्सवे ।
सुधासवेन सकला जगती संविभज्यते ॥३३॥

rājyalābhādivotphullaiḥ kaiścitpūjāmahotsave /
sudhāsavena sakalā jagatī saṁvibhajyate //33//

When, to those devotees, this great festival of Thy worship takes place, they are bloomed, they get blossomed, just as one gets overjoyed by achieving the great honor of a kingdom, a great kingdom (*rājyalābhādiva utphullaiḥ*). They become blossomed by

300 *Sāmagrī* is a mixture of sanctified substances that are offered in a *havan*. [*Editor's note*]

that in celebrating Your worship.

Sudhāsavena sakalā jagatī saṁvibhajyate. And they are so overjoyed that they know no bounds of how to handle this joy of the nectar of Thy devotion. They distribute that nectar to each and every being in this world [laughter]! *Sudhāsavena sakalā jagatī saṁvibhajyate*, [they say], "Yes, you also take, you also take this liquor of that worship". So, this liquor of worship is being distributed by them everywhere.

DENISE: They want to share it with everyone.

SWAMIJI: They want to share it, yes.

Chapter 17 (42:05)

पूजामृतापानमयो येषां भोगः प्रतिक्षणम् ।
किं देवा उत मुक्तास्ते किं वा केऽप्येव ते जनाः ॥३४॥

pūjāmṛtāpānamayo yeṣāṁ bhogaḥ pratikṣaṇam /
kiṁ devā uta muktāste kiṁ vā ke'pyeva te janāḥ //34//

Those devotees who enjoy each and every second, who taste each and every second, the enjoyment of drinking the nectar of Thy devotion, drinking the nectar of Thy worship–who have got this enjoyment that takes place in them each and every moment–I can't understand who they are! *Kiṁ devā*, are they gods? *Uta muktā*, are they liberated? Are they some unique beings? I can't understand them. They are above my imagination. I can't understand those people. They are so great! I can't explain their greatness.

Who?

Those devotees who enjoy the nectar of Thy devotion, each and every moment in this world.

Chapter 17 (43:29)

पूजोपकरणीभूतविश्वावेशेन गौरवम् ।
अहो किमपि भक्तानां किमप्येव च लाघवम् ॥३५॥

pūjopakaraṇībhūtaviśvāveśena gauravam /
aho kimapi bhaktānāṁ kimapyeva ca lāghavam //35//

This is a wonder to me that those devotees of Thee, they have, on one side, they are reserved because they get entry, they get merged, in the substance of Your worship. They get merged in the substance of Your worship. When they handle flowers, they get merged in those flowers. They don't worship You. Worship has not taken place yet but they get merged in those substances.

Pūjā upakaraṇānī bhūta viśva āveśena. And this substance of Thy worship does not take place with flowers and all of these limited substances. No. This whole universe! They feel that the whole universe is meant for offering to Lord Śiva. You have to offer this whole universe to Lord Śiva. So, on one side, I feel–this is a wonder to me–that they are reserved [in this respect].

Aho kimapi bhaktānāṁ kimapyeva ca lāghavam. And they are very shallow inside.

You know what is that?

"Shallow"[301] [means that] they expose everything to everybody [laughter]. They expose all of the secrets of Thy worship to everybody. Nothing remains within them. They expose everything to everybody.

And they don't expose anything as long as they are merged in that substance of this universal Being. This universe seems to them [to be] meant for Thy worship, so they are reserved. This is their reservation. And they expose that secret to everybody. This is their shallowness. They are very light; nothing remains hidden in them.

Chapter 17 (46:03)

पूजामयाक्षविक्षेपक्षोभादेवामृतोद्गमः ।
भक्तानां क्षीरजलधिक्षोभादिव दिवौकसाम् ॥३६॥

pūjāmayākṣavikṣepakṣobhādevāmṛtodgamaḥ /
bhaktānāṁ kṣīrajaladhikṣobhādiva divaukasām //36//
[beginning of verse missing in audio]

Akṣa vikṣepa. *Bhaktānāṁ*, Thy devotees who have got *akṣa*

301 *Lāghava*: lightness of heart.

vikṣepa, who possess the *vikṣepa*, the agitation of all of their organs–*śabda*, *sparśa*, *rūpa*, *rasa*, and *gandha*, all of these organic functions–when they function this organic function, this function appears to them as Thy worship. When they see anything, when they have sex with a woman, it seems to them [as if] they are worshiping Lord Śiva. When they eat, it seems to them [as if] they are worshiping Lord Śiva. So, this *akṣa vikṣepa*, the agitation of this organic field, is just the worship of Thee for them.

DENISE: Is that *śāmbhavopāya*?

SWAMIJI: It is *śāmbhavopāya*.[302]

Pūjā maya akṣepa. So, *kṣobhāt eva*, by the *akṣa vikṣepa*, by the agitation of these organic sensations, the rise of nectar, supreme nectar, takes place in them. The rise of supreme nectar takes place in them [just] as supreme nectar rose from the agitation [of the milky ocean while] agitating that great snake, Vāsuki.

Because, [Vāsuki's] eyes would sometimes go this way, sometimes go that way. His eyes would go sometimes this way, sometimes that way, when [that ocean] was churned.[303] And so, his eyes were agitated by this press, and his eyes vomited blood at that time. That is *akṣa vikṣepa*.[304] By that, the rise of nectar took place afterwards from *kṣīrasāgara*, from the ocean of the milky ocean.

In the same way, when Thy devotees are agitated in their organic field, by the mere agitation of the organic field, the rise of nectar of God consciousness takes place in them.

Chapter 17 (48:52)

पूजां केचन मन्यन्ते धेनुं कामदुघामिव ।
सुधाधाराधिकरसां धयन्त्यन्तर्मुखाः परे ॥३७॥

pūjāṁ kecana manyante dhenuṁ kāmadughāmiva /
sudhādhārādhikarasāṁ dhayantyantarmukhāḥ pare //37

302 See appendix 2 for an explanation of the *upāyas*.

303 Vāsuki was used as the churning rope and *the* Mandāra mountain was used as the churning stick. [*Editor's note*]

304 The sensual agitation caused by the organic field. [*Editor's note*]

There are two sections of Thy devotees. One section are those who believe that Thy worship is just like *kāmadhenu*, just like that cow of heaven that gives boons to everybody–that is *kāmadhenu*–and that worship is just like that *kāmadhenu*. Thy worship bestows boons of every kind to everybody. Some devotees believe this.

But, there are some devotees who *sudhādhārādhikarasāṁ dhayantyantarmukhāḥ pare*, there are some devotees of Thee who drink the nectar of Thy worship. They taste that worship. They don't believe that this worship is doing such and such glory, i.e., that this worship is bestowing such and such glory [to them]. They just drink that worship in them[selves] and absorb it in their nature. They don't care for explaining and investigating Thy worship, e.g., what kind of worship is this, what is the quality of Thy worship. They just drink that worship! They don't care for explaining [laughter].

Chapter 17 (50:41)

भक्तानामक्षविक्षेपोऽप्येष संसारसंमतः ।
उपनीय किमप्यन्तः पुष्णात्यर्चामहोत्सवम् ॥३८॥

bhaktānāmakṣavikṣepo'pyeṣa saṁsārasaṁmataḥ /
upanīya kimapyantaḥ puṣṇātyarcāmahotsavam //38//

Akṣa vikṣepa, the agitation of the organic field, which is really admitted that this is the only cause of entangling oneself in the wheel of repeated births and deaths, . . .

When your mind, when your intellect, when your ego, and when your organs, are agitated, that is *saṁsāra*, that is that state of *saṁsāra*.

. . . but, for Thy devotees, it is not such a case. For Thy devotees, this *saṁsāra*–which is meant as *saṁsāra*, which is believed that it is *saṁsāra*, which is believed that it is the only cause of carrying you and entangling you in the wheel of repeated deaths and births–for [Thy] devotees, it is not like that.

This *akṣa vikṣepa*, this agitation of this organic field, *upanīya kimapyantaḥ puṣṇātyarcā mahotsavam*, this agitation of the organic field, for Thy devotees, internally carries and directs them and [makes] them enter in the great celebration, in the great festival of Thy devotion. So, this *akṣa vikṣepa*, the agitation of the organic field, is just Thy devotion for them.

Chapter 17 (52:42)

भक्तिक्षोभवशादीश स्वात्मभूतेऽर्चनं त्वयि ।
चित्रं दैन्याय नो यावद्दीनतायाः परं फलम् ॥३९॥

bhaktikṣobhavaśādīśa svātmabhūte'rcanaṁ tvayi /
citraṁ dainyāya no yāvaddīnatāyāḥ paraṁ phalam //39//

Īśa, O Lord, *tvayi svātma bhūte arcanaṁ bhakti kṣobha vaśāt*, by the flood of devotion, when Thy worship takes place, Thy worship takes place which is one's own worship; *svātma bhūte tvayi*, Thy worship is just the worship of [one's] own nature.

By the agitation, by the flood of Thy devotion, when that worship takes place, *citraṁ*, this is a wonder to me that, *dainyāya no*, it is not the state of *dīnatā*[305]. *Dīnatā* means, e.g., "O Lord, mine is the pitiable condition, . . . "

ALEXIS: Miserable condition.

SWAMIJI: ". . . miserable condition. Please forgive me!" It is not like that. *Dīnatāyāḥ paraṁ phalam*, it is just the establishment in God consciousness. It is that state, which establishes you in God consciousness. *Dainyāya no bhavati*, *yāvat dīnatāyāḥ paraḥ phalam*!

Chapter 17 (54:25)

उपचारपदं पूजा केषांचित्त्वत्पदाप्तये ।
भक्तानां भवदैकात्म्यनिर्वृत्तिप्रसरस्तु सः ॥४०॥

upacārapadaṁ pūjā keṣāṁcittvatpadāptaye /
bhaktānāṁ bhavadaikātmyanirvṛttiprasarastu saḥ //40//

There are some devotees for whom Thy worship is *upacāra-*

305 Scarcity, weakness.

padam (*upacārapadam* means Thy worship which takes place in *upacāra*; *upacāra* means in collecting those substances for Your worship), and that *pūjā* is meant to carry them to God consciousness. It is just a means; this worship is a means to carry them to God consciousness. They believe in that. Some devotees believe that this worship of Lord Śiva is the means to carry you to God consciousness. But, there are some devotees–amongst them, there are some devotees, some unique devotees–*bhavadaikātma nirvṛtti*, they feel that *this* is the God consciousness.

What is the God consciousness?

ALEXIS: *Pūjā*.

SWAMIJI: Just worshiping You. After worshiping, there is not a next step. This is the real existence of God consciousness.

DENISE: The act of worshiping.

SWAMIJI: Yes.

Chapter 17 (55:58)

अप्यसम्बद्धरूपार्चा भक्त्युन्मादनिरर्गलैः ।
वितन्यमाना लभते प्रतिष्ठां त्वयि कामपि ॥४१॥

apyasambaddharūpārcā bhakyunmādanirargalaiḥ /
vitanyamānā labhate pratiṣṭhāṁ tvayi kāmapi //41//

There are some devotees who have no bondages, no limitations, of Thy worship, because of their madness of [devotion for Thee]. They have achieved the madness of [devotion for Thee]. So, as they are mad, they don't know the rules and regulations of Your worship.

Rules and regulations of worship is just [the following]:

First, *āvāhana* (*āvāhana* is just calling Lord Śiva). Then, when Lord Śiva appears, then *sthāpana*, then [you] give Him a seat to sit [upon]. Then, *dhūpa* (incense), *dīpa* (light), [reciting] "*arghyaṁ samarpayāmi namaḥ*" and "*ācamanīyaṁ samarpayāmi namaḥ*"[306], all of these things take place afterwards. And then [reciting] "*puṣpaṁ samarpayāmi namaḥ*" and "*tāmbulaṁ samarpayāmi namaḥ*". All of these things take place afterwards, after

306 These are the *mantras* which accompany each of the offerings during worship. [*Editor's note*]

He is seated on the seat of being worshiped. Afterwards, when worship is over, then they say, "*visarjayāmi namaḥ*, You can go now".

ALEXIS: What kind of worship is that?

SWAMIJI: But this kind of worship does not take place in Thy devotees because it is *asambaddharūpārcā*, they will first send Him away [by saying], "*bas*, this is Your *visarjana* (dismissal)! Go!", and then [they] adopt worship.

DENISE: After He is gone [laughter].

SWAMIJI: After He is gone. Because they are mad! They do not know how to handle this system of Thy worship.

ALEXIS: So, that other system is humbug. How can you draw Lord Śiva to be in this point and then say, "go to another point"?

SWAMIJI: Yes. That is why those mad people [i.e., Thy devotees] think, those mad people, . . .

ALEXIS: They know.

SWAMIJI: . . . they know the reality of Lord Śiva, that Lord Śiva is all-pervading. Where will He go? [They say], "let Him go, then we will adopt His worship [because] He is already here!"

And *pratiṣṭhāṁ tvayi kāmapi*, so they achieve that great establishment in Thy nature by that devotion.

Chapter 17 (58:31)

स्वादुभक्तिरसास्वादस्तब्धीभूतमनश्च्युताम् ।
शम्भो त्वमेव ललितः पूजानां किल भाजनम् ॥४२॥

svādubhaktirasāsvādastabdhībhūtamanaścyutām /
śambho tvameva lalitaḥ pūjānāṁ kila bhājanam //42//

Śambho, O Lord Śiva, those ways of Thy worship, which are very sweet, which are filled with the nectar of Thy devotion, and by that fullness of Thy nectar of devotion, one's mind becomes un-minded, one-pointed. And, by that mind, this worship is produced (*cyutām*, is produced). This worshiping of Thee is produced by the mind, which is un-minded by tasting the nectar of Your devotion.

O Lord Śiva, those ways of worship are only absorbed and conceived by You–conceived by *You* only. You are the only worthy person for such worship.

And You are *lalitaḥ* (*lalita* means all-round sweet, all-round best, all-round tasty).

Chapter 17 (01:00:05)

परिपूर्णानि शुद्धानि भक्तिमन्ति स्थिराणि च ।
भवत्पूजाविधौ नाथ साधनानि भवन्तु मे ॥४३॥

paripūrṇāni śuddhāni bhaktimanti sthirāṇi ca /
bhavatpūjāvidhau nātha sādhanāni bhavantu me //43//

There is only one request. I want to place that request before You. I want this *bhavat sādhanāni*, these ways of Your worshipping, these ways of Your worship, must become fulfilled always. In me, whenever I worship You, it must be fulfilled. I must get its fruit there and then. And this worship must be pure, absolutely pure, without any fraud. *Bhaktimanti*, and this worship must be filled with the taste of Thy love. And this worship must be *sthirāṇi* (*sthirāṇi* means continuous and remaining). And such ways of worship, I want to have. Please bestow such ways of worship to me. This is my request before You.

Chapter 17 (01:01:31)

अशेषपूजासत्कोशे त्वत्पूजाकर्मणि प्रभो ।
अहो करणवृन्दस्य कापि लक्ष्मीर्विजृम्भते ॥४४॥

aśeṣapūjāsatkośe tvatpūjākarmaṇi prabho /
aho karaṇavṛndasya kāpi lakṣmīrvijṛmbhate //44//

O Lord Śiva, O my Master, when Thy adoration is done, when Thy adoration is functioned, and that adoration is *aśeṣa pūjā satkośe*, this is the treasure of all worship.

Aho, this is a wonder that *karaṇavṛndasya kāpi lakṣmī vijṛmbhate*, there, in that treasure, *karaṇavṛndasya*, my [entire] organic field is glorified with that great wealth of liberation, great wealth of devotion.

Chapter 17 (01:02:32)

एषा पेशलिमा नाथ तवैव किल दृश्यते ।
विश्वेश्वरोऽपि भृत्यैर्यदर्च्यसे यश्च लभ्यसे ॥४५॥

eṣā peśalimā nātha tavaiva kila dṛśyate /
viśveśvaro'pi bhṛtyairyadarcyase yaśca labhyase //45//

Nātha, O my Master, this *peśalimā*, this softness of Your hands is found only in You my Lord–this softness of Your hands–because nothing remains in Your hands! You bestow everything to Your devotees![307]

Viśveśvaro'pi, although You are always full, always You possess the kingdom of the whole wealth of spiritual wealth, *bhṛtyairyadarcyase*, at the moment when Your slaves [i.e., devotees] worship You, *yaśca labhayase*, they achieve, [at] that very moment, they achieve everything, whatever they desire.

This *peśalimā* is found, this softness is found, in only Your hands, not in any other hands, i.e., this softness. You give, You give; [You don't] take, [You] only give.

Chapter 17 (01:03:51)

सदा मूर्त्तादमूर्त्ताद्वा भावाद्यद्वाप्यभावतः ।
उत्थेयान्मे प्रशस्तस्य भवत्पूजामहोत्सवः ॥४६॥

sadā mūrttādamūrttādvā bhāvādyadvāpyabhāvataḥ /
uttheyānme praśastasya bhavatpūjāmahotsavaḥ //46//

This is my desire that the great festival of Thy worship should rise (should just rise, *uttheyāt*), should just rise, to me who is glorified. I am always glorified because I have got this intense desire to worship You. I am glorified. I am fortunate (*praśastasya*). So, this festival of Thy devotion, Thy worship, should rise always *mūrttāt*, from anything, from any solid thing; *amūrttāt*

307 "When you are a miser, money won't slip out from your hand. When you are generous, this [wealth] will slip out." *Śivastotrāvalī* (additional audio, USF archives).

vā, from any . . .

ALEXIS: Immaterial.

SWAMIJI: . . . from any subtle thing (immaterial), from any object, and from non-existent objects also. Everywhere this festival of Thy worship should rise for me because I am glorified with Thy devotion.

Chapter 17 (01:05:12)

कामक्रोधाभिमानैस्त्वामुपहारीकृतैः सदा ।
येऽर्चयन्ति नमस्तेभ्यस्तेषां तुष्टोऽसि तत्त्वतः ॥४७॥

kāmakrodhābhimānaistvāmupahārīkṛtaiḥ sadā /
ye'rcayanti namastebhyasteṣāṁ tuṣṭo'si tattvataḥ //47//

Those devotees of Thee who offer You their lust, their anger, and their ego–they offer You whatever lust they have, whatever anger they possess, and whatever ego they possess–*upahārīkṛtaiḥ*, they just offer You those things because they have earned only these three things in their whole lifetime. They have earned with great effort [these three things]: *kāma*, *krodha*, and *abhimāna*.[308] So, *upahārīkṛtaiḥ*, so they offer [these to] You, and those devotees who offer You these and adore You, *namastebhyaḥ*, I adore them, I adore those devotees. I don't adore You. *Namastebhyaḥ*, I want to bow before them. I don't want to bow before You. I want to bow before those people who adore You by offering their *kāma*, *krodha*, and ego, because *teṣāṁ tuṣṭo asi tattvataḥ*, in reality, You are pleased with them. You are really pleased with them. You are really happy with them.

Chapter 17 (01:06:57)

जयत्येष भवद्भक्तिभाजां पूजाविधिः परः ।
यस्तृणैः क्रियमाणोऽपि रत्नैरेवोपकल्पते ॥४८॥

jayatyeṣa bhavadbhaktibhājāṁ pūjāvidhiḥ paraḥ /
yastṛṇaiḥ kriyamāṇo'pi ratnairevopakalpate //48//

308 Lust, anger, and ego, respectively. [*Editor's note*]

Those devotees of Thee, they have got the supreme way of adoring You, they have possessed that supreme way of adoring You, which is always glorified; which is always glorified! Because–what is the supreme way?–*yastṛṇaiḥ kriyamāṇo api*, they adore You with blades of grass–with blades of grass, they adore You–and that adoration done with blades of grass, *pariṇāmas*, changes, . . .

ALEXIS: Becomes; is transformed into.

SWAMIJI: . . . becomes the producer of jewelry and diamonds.

Chapter Eighteen
Revealing Hymn
Āviṣkāranāma aṣṭādaśaṁ stotram

जगतोऽन्तरतो भवन्तमाप्त्वा
    पुनरेतद्भवतोऽन्तराल्लभन्ते ।
जगदीश तवैव भक्तिभाजो
    न हि तेषामिह दूरतोऽस्ति किञ्चित् ॥१॥

jagto'ntarato bhavantamāptvā
    punaretadbhavato'ntarāllabhante /
jagadīśa tavaiva bhaktibhājo
    na hi teṣāmīha dūrato'sti kiñcit //1//

Jagadīśa, O Lord of the universes, O Lord of one hundred and eighteen worlds, *tavaiva bhakti-bhājo*, those are Your real devotees who find You amidst the state of the universe, amidst the universal state. They find You, they achieve You, in the center of the universe–first. *Punaretat bhavato'ntarāt labhante*, then, when they find You, they find the universe in You. They find You in the universe, and afterwards, after finding You in the universe, they find the universe in Your body! *Tavaiva bhakti*, this is the way of the understanding of Your devotees. *Na hi teṣāṁ iha dūrato'sti*, there is nothing away from them; there is nothing far away for them, from their understanding. They understand the universe and You as one because they first experience You in the universe and then experience the universe in Your body. So, it is one and the same thing. It may be the universe, it may be You; this is one and the same thing.

Chapter 18 (01:41)

क्वचिदेव भवान् क्वचिद्भवानी
    सकलार्थक्रमगर्भिणी प्रधाना ।

परमार्थ पदे तु नैव देव्या
भवतो नापि जगत्त्रयस्य भेदः ॥२॥

kvacideva bhavān kvacidbhavānī
sakalārthakramagarbhiṇī pradhānā /
paramārtha pade tu naiva devyā
bhavato nāpi jagattrayasya bhedaḥ //2//

At some places, from one point of view, it seems that You are the only person existing in this universe. From another point of view, it seems that the universe is only existing.

ALEXIS: *Bhavānī*.

SWAMIJI: *Bhavānī* means the "universe" or "Pārvatī".

Paramārthapade, but, in the real sense of understanding, there is no differentiation between You or Pārvatī or this universe–this is one substance.

Chapter 18 (02:35)

नो जानते सुभगमप्यवलेपवन्तो
लोकाः प्रयत्नसुभगा निखिला हि भावाः
चेतः पुनर्यदिदमुद्यतमप्यवैति
नैवात्मरूपमिह हा तदहो हतोस्मि ॥३॥

no jānate subhagamapyavalepavanto
lokāḥ prayatnasubhagā nikhilā hi bhāvāḥ /
cetaḥ punaryadidamudyatamapyavaiti
naivātmarūpamiha hā tadaho hato'smi //3//

Avalepavantaḥ lokāḥ, those people who have got *avalepa*, who have got impurity in their minds, those persons who have got impurity in their minds, they don't understand, they don't experience *subhagamapi*; *subhagamapi rūpaṁ no jānanti*, they don't experience that sweet and wonderful nature of God because *prayatna subhagā hi nikhilā bhāvāḥ*, this whole collection of universal objects becomes refined and sweet only by meditation, by the effort of meditation.

When you meditate on [worldly objects], then they appear to you as divine. Otherwise, when you don't meditate on these worldly objects, they become deprived of divinity; they give you pain, they give you sadness, torture, everything–crisis. Otherwise, when you put effort, with effort, they appear to you as divine (*prayatna subhagā nikhilā hi bhāvāḥ*).

Cetaḥ–now, there is a problem in me–*cetaḥ punaryadidam udyatam api*, my mind is just bent upon finding the truth of this objective world, my mind is bent upon finding the truth of this objective world just to realize the divinity and the real nature of this objective world, but still then, it does not achieve [that realization]. Still then, if it does not achieve that, my mind does not achieve that, then really I am ruined. Where will I go? I am completely ruined. I am lost.

Did you understand this?

He says that this whole universe is divine. In the real sense, this [universe] is divine, but it does not seem divine to everybody. This divinity appears only when you put effort on it, i.e., meditate upon Lord Śiva and then this world becomes *jagadānanda*, it will be merged in *jagadānanda*.[309] Then it will be divine.

"But, in my case", this devotee [i.e., Utpaladeva] says, "in my case, I have put all of my effort to find it as divine, but, if I don't find it as divine, I am lost. I am ruined altogether. Where will I go? I have put all of my effort and still it does not happen".

DENISE: There's no answer?

SWAMIJI: No, it is just madness, just a cry [laughter].

Chapter 18 (06:26)

भवन्मयस्वात्मनिवासलब्ध-
सम्पद्भराभ्यर्चितयुष्मदङ्घ्रिः ।
न भोजनाच्छादनमप्यजस्रम्-
अपेक्षते यस्तमहं नतोऽस्मि ॥४॥

309 See appendix 16 for an explanation of *jagadānanda*.

bhavanmayasvātmanivāsalabdha-
sampadbharābhyarcitayuṣmadaṅghriḥ /
na bhojanācchādanamapyajasram-
apekṣate yastamahaṁ nato'smi //4//

There is such a devotee in this universe who *bhavanmaya svātmanivāsalabdha sampadbharābhyarcita yuṣmat aṅghriḥ*, who is residing in the nature of the Self, which is one with Your nature. [That devotee] who is residing in one's own nature–that is your own nature; that is the nature of Lord Śiva–*sampadbhara*, and who has achieved the glory, the highest glory, the greatest glory, there, by residing in Your nature–that person, that devotee of Thee who is residing in Your own nature and has achieved the fullness of glory (*sampat* means "glory")–and by that glory, [the devotee] who always adores You, *abhyarcita yuṣmadaṅghriḥ*, and who always adores Your feet, adores Your lotus-like feet, that person, *na bhojana ācchādanam api ajasram apekṣate*, he does not need to be fed with those eatable dishes afterwards; *ācchādana*, he does not need to be covered by shawls and coats and clothes. There is no need to cover his body or to eat anything. And that person who is like that, *tam ahaṁ nato'smi*, I bow to that person. I am really the slave of that person.

Chapter 18 (08:56)

सदा भवद्देहनिवासस्वस्थो-
ऽप्यन्तः परं दह्यत एष लोकः ।
तवेच्छया तत्कुरु मे यथात्र
त्वदर्चनानन्दमयो भवेयम् ॥५॥

sadā bhavaddehanivāsasvastho-
'pyantaḥ paraṁ dahyata eṣa lokaḥ /
tavecchayā tatkuru me yathātra
tvadarcanānandamayo bhaveyam //5//

Eṣa lokaḥ, this worldly group of people, worldly ignorant group of people, although those are *bhavat deha svasthopi*, they are residing, actually they are residing, in Your nature–everybody is residing in the nature of Lord Siva, in reality; in reality, everyone is there–although this worldly ignorant group resides in Your nature and has actually achieved a peaceful state by being in Your nature, but *antaḥ paraṁ dahyate*, but internally [they are] tortured and sentenced to crises and sadness, i.e., these worldly people. And this is Your desire; this is Your desire, by Your will. This does not take place according to their *karmas*. This takes place according to Your sweet will.

And I want Your sweet will in another way (*tavecchayā*). So, *tatkuru*, please act like that; act in such a way for me [so that] *yathātra tvadarcanānandamayo bhaveyam*, in this universe, I will be merged in worshiping You always. I want only this much in this universe. Because, already I am situated in You but it does not mean to me anything. And that too does not mean to me anything, i.e., if I am away from You, if I don't realize that I am residing in You. That is nothing, it has no weight for me. My only problem is that I want to worship You, everywhere.

Bas!

Chapter 18 (11:46)

स्वरसोदितयुष्मदङ्घ्रिपद्म-
द्वयपूजामृतपानसक्तचित्तः ।
सकलार्थचयेष्वहं भवेयं
सुखसंस्पर्शनमात्रलोकयात्रः ॥ ६ ॥

svarasoditayuṣmadaṅghripadma-
dvayapūjāmṛtapānasaktacittaḥ /
sakalārthacayeṣvahaṁ bhaveyaṁ
sukhasaṁsparśanamātralokayātraḥ //6//
[beginning of verse missing from audio]

My Lord, this is one desire in me: *svarasodita yuṣmat aṅghri padma dvaya pūjā amṛta pāna saktaḥ cittaḥ*, my mind should be directed towards tasting the nectar of worshiping Your lotus feet. And those lotus feet should appear to me without any effort, without [adopting] any means to have them. *Svarasodita yuṣmat aṅghri padma*[310], Your lotus feet should appear to me without [having to exert] any effort to achieve them, and I would like to worship those lotus feet of Yours and taste the nectar of that worship.

Sakalārtha caye, in this way, when I taste the nectar of that worship, worshiping Your lotus feet, in this way, I would like to possess the journey in this universe, the peaceful journey, in perceiving Thy worship in each and every action of the universe (*sakalārtha cayeṣu*); *sakalārtha cayeṣu* means, in each and every act of the universe, I must feel that this is only the worship of Your lotus feet. This is my desire in me.

Chapter 18 (14:03)

सकलव्यवहारगोचरे
स्फुटमन्तः स्फुरति त्वयि प्रभो ।
उपयान्त्यपयान्ति चानिशम्
मम वस्तूनि विभान्तु सर्वदा ॥७॥

sakalavyavahāragocare
sphuṭamantaḥ sphurati tvayi prabho /
upayāntyapayānti cāniśam
mama vastūni vibhāntu sarvadā //7//

O my Master, *prabho*, O my Master, there is another desire in me. That is, *sakala vyavahāragocare sphuṭamantaḥ sphurati tvayi prabho*, You must appear to me, I wish You appear to me, in each and every action of universality. In all universal actions, I want You to appear before me.

And then, *upayāntyapyānti cāniśam mama vastūni vibhāntu sarvadā*, and all of this objective world, let this objective world come to me or go to me.

ALEXIS: Go away from me.

SWAMIJI: Go away from me. I would like such a state of life.

ALEXIS: *Vibhāntu sarvadā*?

---

310 "*Aṅghri dvayam* means *jñāna* and *kriyā* from the Shaiva point of view. From the devotional point of view, *aṅghri dvayam* means *aṅghri dvayam*, i.e., [literally] two feet." *Śivastotrāvalī* (additional audio, USF archives).

SWAMIJI: *Vastūni vibhāntu.*

ALEXIS: *Upayānti?*

SWAMIJI: *Upayānti apayānti*, they[311] should come and go, they should come and go, and, in the same way, I must feel that their coming and going is exactly existing, taking place, in Your body, in Your body of that spiritual bliss.

Chapter 18 (15:32)

सततमेव तवैव पुरेऽथवा-
प्यरहितो विचरेयमहं त्वया ।
क्षणलवोऽप्यथमा स्म भवेत् स मे
न विजये ननु यत्र भवन्मयः ॥८॥

satatameva tavaiva pure'thavā-
pyarahito vicareyamahaṁ tvayā /
kṣaṇalavo'pyathamā sma bhavet sa me
na vijaye nanu yatra bhavanmayaḥ //8//

This is another desire knocking in the background of my heart. That is, *satatameva tavaiva pure'thavā pyarahito vicareyam ahaṁ tvayā*, I should always roam in Your kingdom. I want to roam and walk and rest and do all things in Your kingdom. *Tavaiva pure*, and I want to roam in Your kingdom along with You, *tvayā arahita*, and be attached to You. I must be attached to You and I would like to roam in this kingdom of Yours, in Your kingdom, and always! *Satatameva tavaiva pure*, in Your kingdom only, and always I want to roam in that kingdom along with You.

But, *kṣaṇalavo'pyathamā sma bhavet sa me na vijaye nanu yatra bhavanmayaḥ*, I don't want to have that slightest part of a moment where I would shine without Thee. I must die there and then! If I find sometimes in this world that I am away from You, I must die. I must not *vijaye*, *na vijaye yatra bhavanmayā*, I must not shine, I must just get myself destroyed at that very moment, I must not live at that moment, I prefer death at that moment, when You are not there.

311 Objects that appear in the universe.

Chapter 18 (17:54)

भवदङ्गपरिस्रवत्सुशीता-
मृतपूरैर्भरिते समन्ततोऽपि ।
भवदर्चनसम्पदेह भक्ता-
स्तव संसारसरोऽन्तरे चरन्ति ॥९॥

bhavadaṅgaparisravatsuśītā-
mṛtapūrairbharite samantato'pi /
bhavadarcanasampadeha bhaktā-
stava saṁsārasaro'ntare caranti //9//

Now, You will say that, "It is not possible to be attached to Me always. I have never been like that with any other devotee". To that, [Utpaladeva] says, "*bhaktāḥ, tava bhaktāḥ saṁsāra saro 'ntare caranti*, I have seen with my own eyes that Your devotees roam in the lake of this universe; they roam along with the glory of Thy worship. *Bhavad arcana sampadā*, having the glory of Your worship, they roam in the world. I have seen with my own eyes".

Bhavad aṅga parisravat suśīta amṛta pūrair bharite. Saṁsāra saro'ntare, this is the qualification of *saṁsāra saro'ntare*. This lake of the universe, which is filled with the nectar, with the *suśīta* nectar, cool nectar (*suśīta* means "very cooling"), that lake, which is flooded with the nectar which has come out from Your limbs of God consciousness, from Your limbs of consciousness, and that nectar is filled in that lake of the universe, and I have seen with my own eyes that there are such devotees who roam in that lake glorified with Thy worship.

Chapter 18 (20:03)

महामन्त्रतरुच्छायाशीतले त्वन्महावने ।
निजात्मनि सदा नाथ वसेयं तव पूजकः ॥१०॥

mahāmantrataruchāyāśītale tvanmahāvane /
nijātmani sadā nātha vaseyaṁ tava pūjakaḥ //10//

Nātha, O my Master, there is one desire in me. I want to remain in that great forest, in the grand forest, of Thee. The grand forest, he says, that dense forest is Your body. And, in that dense forest, which is *mahāmantratarucchāyā śītale*, which is everywhere cool, cooled by those trees, shady trees of I-consciousness, God consciousness (*mahāmantra* means *pūrṇāhantā*, "I-consciousness") . . .

I-consciousness is the shady trees in that dense [forest] and the dense [forest] is Your body.

DEVOTEE: *Mantra vīrya.*

SWAMIJI: *Mantra vīrya*, yes.[312]

. . . and in that dense forest, which is my own Self (*nijātmani*, which is my own Self, which is not other than my Self), I would like to reside there, always, just adoring You, and nothing else.

Chapter 18 (21:42)

प्रतिवस्तु समस्तजीवतः
प्रतिभासि प्रतिभामयो यथा ।
मम नाथ तथा पुरः प्रथां
व्रज नेत्रत्रयशूलशोभितः ॥ ११ ॥

prativastu samastajīvataḥ
pratibhāsi pratibhāmayo yathā /
mama nātha tathā puraḥ prathāṁ
vraja netratrayaśūlaśobhitaḥ //11//

It is a fact that in each and every object (*prativastū*, in each and every object), to each and every being (*samastajīvataḥ*), You appear in the form of *jñāna* (knowledge).

For instance, if you perceive these [spectacles], this perceiving,

312 *Mantra vīrya* is the power of all the letters of the Sanskrit alphabet beginning from the letter *a* and ending with the letter *kṣa*. Why? Because all sounds rise from those letters. That sound is called *Śabdarāśi*, the collective appearance of all letters. And the power and the essence of all those sounds is one sound, the soundless sound, the sound of I-being, *ahaṁ*, the supreme I, and that is *mantra vīrya*. *Shiva Sutras, The Supreme Awakening,* 1.22.68-69.

the way of perceiving, proves Your existence there. Whenever I feel that it is a lantern, "that is a lantern over there", this feeling is God consciousness. So, in each and every being, You appear to them like this, i.e., in the way of knowledge.

I don't want to have such knowledge. My desire is for something else. My desire is, *tathā puraḥ prathāṁ vraja netra* [*trayaśūlaśobhitaḥ*], I want You to appear before me with a physical body, taking hold of *trīśūla*, and with three eyes. I want You to appear to me in a physical body, with three eyes, and *triśūla* in Your hand. That is my desire.

I don't want to have this *jñāna* (knowledge). Knowledge must be possessed by those people who like that. I don't want knowledge. I want You to appear before me with three eyes on Your forehead and *triśūla* in Your hand.

Chapter 18 (23:45)

अभिमानचरूपहारतो
　　ममताभक्ति भरेण कल्पितात् ।
परितोषगतः कदा भवान्
　　मम सर्वत्र भवेद् दृशः पदम् ॥१२॥

abhimānacarūpahārato
　　mamatābhakti bhareṇa kalpitāt /
paritoṣagataḥ kadā bhavān
　　mama sarvatra bhaved dṛśaḥ padam //12//

I have acquired something, which I want to offer to You. This is my offering for You. That is, *caru* (sweet cake), the sweet cake which I have acquired in my whole life, that is the ego in me. I want to offer that ego at Your feet (*abhimāna carūpahārata*). And *mamatā bhakti bhareṇa*, and by the intensity of *mamatā* . . .

Mamatā means attachment regarding my-ness, e.g., "mine is God; God is mine". This is *mamatā*. "He is mine only; He is nobody else's."

. . . *mamatā bhaktibhareṇa kalpitāt–paritoṣagatāḥ*, in this way, *paritoṣagatāḥ*, You will be pleased with me. I want You to be pleased with me, *mama sarvatra bhaved dṛśaḥ padam*, and then

I would like You to appear to me in each and every act of the universe.

This ego would be offered to You first and then I would create *mamatā* for You (*mamatā*, attachment for You): "God is mine; I have possessed God!"

DENISE: Only mine.

SWAMIJI: Only mine, yes. That is *mamatā. Mamatā bhakti bhareṇa*, and that is devotional [attachment].

ALEXIS: That crude *mamatā* has disappeared.

SWAMIJI: Crude *mamatā,* no.

DENISE: What's crude *mamatā*?

SWAMIJI: Crude *mamatā* is . . .

ALEXIS: 'This is my book!"

SWAMIJI: . . . individual [attachment]. [Here], it is universal *mamatā*.

DENISE: *Māyīyamala*?

SWAMIJI: Yes, *māyīyamala* is crude.[313]

Chapter 18 (26:15)

निवसन्परमामृताब्धिमध्ये
भवदर्चाविधिमात्रमग्नचित्तः ।
सकलं जनवृत्तमाचरेयं
रसयन्सर्वत एव किञ्चनापि ॥ १३ ॥

nivasanparamāmṛtābdhimadhye
bhavadarcāvidhimātramagnacittaḥ /
sakalaṁ janavṛttamācareyaṁ
rasayansarvata eva kiñcanāpi //13//

There is another problem in me. I would like to reside in the ocean of supreme nectar, that supreme nectar (*nivasan parama* [*amṛta*], that supreme nectar). *Parama amṛta abdhimadhye*, I would like to reside in the center of the ocean of Thy nectar.

Bhavadarcā vidhi mātra magna cittaḥ. And my mind would be attached only in adoring You, in worshiping You. And then, in doing such worship, *sakalaṁ janavṛttamācareyam*, I would like

313 See appendix 15 for an explanation of the *malas*.

to do each and every worldly act–*śabda*, *sparśa*, *rūpa*, *rasa*, and *gandha*[314]–all of those worldly things I would function, I would do that, and *rasayan sarvataḥ*, I would not taste . . . I would hear sound but I would hear something else, *rasayan sarvataḥ kiñcanāpi*, I would hear something supreme.

ALEXIS: *Kimapi*.

SWAMIJI: *Kimapi apūrvam.*

Not [just] like ordinary people would I like to taste *śabda*, *sparśa*, *rūpa*, *rasa*, and *gandha*, these sensual pleasures, enjoyment of sensual pleasures. I would enjoy something else, something [like a] super-enjoyment.

Chapter 18 (27:56)

भवदीयमिहास्तु वस्तु तत्त्वं
विवरीतुं क इवात्र पात्रमर्थे ।
इदमेव हि नामरूपचेष्टा-
द्यसमं ते हरते हरोऽसि यस्मात् ॥ १४॥

bhavadīyamihāstu vastu tattvaṁ
vivarītuṁ ka ivātra pātramarthe /
idameva hi nāmarūpaceṣṭā-
dyasamaṁ te harate haro'si yasmāt //14//

Thy reality, let Thy reality reside where It is. *Bhavadīyamihāstu vastu tattvam*, let Thy reality reside where It is because *vivarītuṁ ka ivātra pātramarthe*, who can define That? Who can define Your reality? That is so great. It is so great that It can't be explained by anybody.

Idameva hi nāmarūpaceṣṭādi asamaṁ. This, Your name, Your formation, and Your act[ivity], is also not understood. Your name is Lord Śiva. Why is your name Lord Śiva? It can't be explained. What Śiva *bhāva* (state) is there? It cannot be explained. And *rūpa*, Your formation [cannot be explained].

Whenever He appears to His devotees, you know what they perceive? They perceive nothing! They cannot . . . if Lord Śiva appears to me–let Him appear to me tonight–when He appears

314 Sound, touch, form, taste, and smell, respectively. [*Editor's note*]

to me, then I won't see Him. At first, I won't see Him, I won't be able to see Him. I can't [perceive Him] because my circle of these senses is so limited that it can't calculate the [unlimited] formation of Lord Śiva. First, I will only perceive only light everywhere–nothing else, no form–and then, when I persist again and again, and still persist to be there to find [out] what It is, and then slowly and slowly That formation is developed [i.e., perceived] afterwards, i.e., the formation of Lord Śiva. It is so great, so joyous, i.e., His body, His shining body.

So, this also, Your *nāma* (name), *rūpa* (form), and *ceṣṭā* (Your action) is *asamam*, it is unparalleled, there is no parallel to it. Because, *haro asi yasmāt*, Your name is Hara.

"*Hara*" means that [which] takes away all distinctive and intellectual understanding from you. You can't understand Him.

So, let Your reality remain where It is. I don't want to define It. It can't be defined!

Chapter 18 (31:04)

शान्तये न सुखलिप्सुता मनाग्-
भक्तिसम्भृतमदेषु तैः प्रभोः ।
मोक्षमार्गणफलापि नार्थना
स्मर्यते हृदयहारिणः पुरः ॥१५॥

śāntaye na sukhalipsutā manāg-
bhaktisambhṛtamadeṣu taiḥ prabhoḥ /
mokṣamārgaṇaphalāpi nārthanā
smaryate hṛdayahāriṇaḥ puraḥ //15//

Bhakti sambhṛta madeṣu. Those devotees who are intoxicated with the alcohol of Thy attachment (*bhakti sambhṛta madeṣu*, those who are intoxicated with this wine of attachment, devotion), in those devotees, *śāntaye na sukhalipsutā manāk hṛdaya hāriṇaḥ puraḥ* (*hṛdaya hāriṇaḥ puraḥ* means "You who are *hṛdaya hāriṇaḥ*"), You just extract the hearts of people just by Your mere presence.

That is *hṛdaya hāriṇaḥ*. This is Lord Śiva's position. Whenever Lord Śiva is in front of you, your heart is gone. You can't think, you can't remember anything, you forget everything before Him. So, He is *hṛdaya hāri* (*hṛdaya hāri* means "He has extracted your heart"). You have no heart, you have no mind, no thinking, no thought, [before Him].

And before Him, in those people who are intoxicated with the alcohol of devotion, in the beginning, they determine that as soon as Lord Śiva will appear to them, they will [place] all of these demands before Him. The first demand is *śāntaye na sukhalipsutā*; *sukhalipsutā*, just for attaining peace, attaining joy, and peacefulness. The first demand is, "I want to attain joy and be peaceful". And the next demand is *mokṣa mārgaṇa phalāpi arthanā*, "just direct me towards the right path of *mokṣa* (liberation)". This was the second demand to put before Lord Śiva.

So, with this determination, they sit and think of Lord Śiva, but when Lord Śiva appears, their heart is gone. So, they don't demand *sukhalipsutā*, this attaining of that joy for peace, entire peace. They don't demand that. And *mokṣa mārgaṇa phalā arthanā*, and that *prārthana* (that means "craving for putting [their] feet on the path of *mokṣa*, on the path of liberation"), that also they don't remember [when they are] before You. What to speak of other things?[315]

That is the meaning of this *śloka*.

Śantaye na sukhalipsutā, not in the least [can] they think or [can] they demand anything from You! They just enjoy Your nearness. That is all.

Chapter 18 (35:08)

जागरेतरदशाथवा परा
यापि काचन मनागवस्थितेः ।
भक्तिभाजनजनस्य साखिला
त्वत्सनाथमनसो महोत्सवः ॥१६॥

jāgaretaradaśāthavā parā
yāpi kācana manāgavasthiteḥ /

315 "*Śāntaye na sukhalipsutā manāg bhakti saṁbhṛta madeṣu*. Because, that intoxication of that *bhakti* is so intense and so grown that they absolutely forget everything, i.e., what was to be asked to Him." *Śivastotrāvalī* (additional audio, USF archives).

bhaktibhājanajanasya sākhilā
tvatsanāthamanaso mahotsavaḥ //16//

These states of life, *jāgara* (*jāgara* means "wakefulness"), *itaradaśā* (*itaradaśā* means "the dreaming state"), and the dreamless state (*suṣupti*), *yāpi kācana manāg avasthiteḥ*, or other than these three states, which are existing in the cycle of daily life, all of those states become, to those who are *bhakti bhājana janasya* (*bhakti bhājana janasya* [means "those] who are just befitting, who are just capable of, becoming the containing pot of Thy devotion"; in brief words, "those who are Your devotees"), for those devotees, all of these states–wakefulness, the dreaming state, and the dreamless state, and all of the other states of daily life also–*tvatsanātha manasaḥ mahotsavaḥ* . . .

Tvat sanātha manasaḥ means . . . this is the adjective of *bhakti bhājana janasya*; *tvatsanātha manasaḥ bhakti bhājana janasya*. *Tvat sanātha manasaḥ* means "whose mind is just living because of You; whose mind is just existing or life-full because of Your nearness".

. . . for those devotees, all of these states are *mahotsavaḥ*, they are great festivals, they become great festivals. They are not to be avoided. Wakefulness [becomes] divine (wakefulness becomes divine for them), the dreaming state [becomes] divine, the dreamless state [becomes] divine, and all of the other states of life, they become divine for them.[316]

Chapter 18 (37:36)

आमनोऽक्षवलयस्य वृत्तयः
सर्वतः शिथिलवृत्तयोऽपि ताः ।
त्वामवाप्य दृढदीर्घसंविदो
नाथ भक्तिधनसोष्मणां कथम् ॥ १७ ॥

āmano'kṣavalayasya vṛttayaḥ
sarvataḥ śithilavṛttayo'pi tāḥ /

316 "Because they find Your existence in wakefulness, even in the dreaming state, and in the dreamless state. In the *turya* state, You are already there." *Śivastotrāvalī* (additional audio, USF archives). See appendix 3 for an explanation of *turya*.

tvāmavāpya dṛḍhadīrghasaṁvido
nātha bhaktidhanasoṣmaṇāṁ katham //17//

O my Master, this is a wonder to me. I can't understand the background of this: *āmano akṣavalayasya vṛttayaḥ sarvataḥ śithilavṛttayaḥ api tāḥ*, all of these actions of the senses including the mind (*āmanaḥ* means "including the mind", not up to mind; it is not *maryādā*[317]), which are everywhere seen as *śithila vṛttayaḥ*, not stable, always flickering, always going . . .

ALEXIS: *Cañcala* (fickle).

SWAMIJI: . . . *cañcala*, from here to this, from here [to that], they are always . . . they have no one fixed point.[318] And all of these flickering states of the senses, when You are achieved–this is a wonder to me–when You are achieved, these flickering states of all the senses become *dīrgha–dṛḍha dīrgha saṁvidaḥ*–they become established in the continuous flow of God consciousness. They become one with God consciousness. This is a wonder to me, how they become–these flickering states of the senses–how they take the formation of God consciousness in Thy devotees when You are achieved.

This is the cream of *Śivastotrāvalī*, i.e., these three [verses].[319]

Chapter 18 (39:32)

न च विभिन्नमसृज्यत किञ्चिदस्-
त्यथ सुखेतरदत्र न निर्मितम् ।
अथ च दुःखि च भेदि च सर्वथा-
प्यसमविस्मयधाम नमोऽस्तु ते ॥१८॥

na ca vibhinnamasṛjyata kiñcidas-
tyatha sukhetaradatra na nirmitam /

---

317 *Maryādā*: a frontier, limit, boundary; *āmanaḥ*: the mind along with the senses. [*Editor's note*]

318 "All of these *vṛttis* of the organs including the mind are *śithila vṛttayaḥ*, are just situated in the fickle state. They are never one-pointed; they never become one-pointed." *Śivastotrāvalī* (additional audio, USF archives).

319 Verse 15, 16 and 17.

atha ca duḥkhi ca bhedi ca sarvathā-
pyasamavismayadhāma namo'stu te //18//

This is a great sadness, this is a great torture in my mind. *Na ca vibhinnam asṛjyata kiñcid asti*, in this world, which You have created, You have not created this world away from Your God consciousness, away from Your spiritual state. You have created this universe as Your own nature. *Na ca vibhinnam aṣṛjyata na ca kiñcid asti*, nor is this universe existing away from You. *Sukhetarat atra na nīrmitam*, You have not created pain in this universe. You have created only God consciousness with super-joy and supreme bliss in this universe, i.e., when You have created this universe. You have created this universe as supreme God consciousness, as supreme joy, and supreme bliss.

But, for me, this is a great torture in me: I find in this universe everywhere pain! I don't find any joy in this universe! *Duḥkhi ca*, I find this universe always differentiated from Your nature, away from Your nature.

Sarvathāpyasama vismayadhāma. You are really . . . Your act of being is really uncontrollable [i.e., incomprehensible]. My head is at Your feet. I can't understand You.

Chapter 18 (41:38)

खरनिषेधखदामृतपूरणो-
च्छलितधौतविकल्पमलस्य मे ।
दलितदुर्जयसंशयवैरिणस्-
त्वदवलोकनमस्तु निरन्तरम् ॥१९॥

kharaniṣedhakhadāmṛtapūraṇo-
cchalitadhautavikalpamalasya me /
dalitadurjayasaṁśayavairiṇas-
tvadavalokanamastu nirantaram //19//

There is one desire in me. That desire is, I would like to clean the impurity of my mind, the impurity of my *vikalpa* (thoughts)–that is mind.

That impurity is *kharaniṣedha khadā* (*khadā* means "terrifying"; *niṣedha* means "being away from You"), and that being away from You is a terrifying ditch (*gahvara*). *Kharaniṣedha khadā*, and it cannot be filled with ordinary earth–it is such an abyss–and it must be filled with the water of the nectar of God consciousness. Otherwise, this abyss will remain as it is. It will always be torture for us. We'll fall in that abyss every now and then[320], in each and every point of this universe.

And *ucchalita dhauta vikalpa malasya me*, and then, when this flood of that nectar will be filling that abyss of the terrifying way of not knowing You–being away from You, that is the abyss–and that abyss will be filled with the nectar of God consciousness by the flood of that nectar of God consciousness, and I would also, at the same time, on the sidelines, I would wash my mind with that flood. I would wash the impurity of my mind with that flood of the nectar of God consciousness. And *dalita durjaya saṁśaya vairiṇaḥ*, and I would be away, I would be freed, from the enemy of doubt, i.e., doubting Your existence in this universe.

Because, we doubt, always we doubt, [God's presence] in the existence of the universe. The existence of God consciousness, we doubt in That. We say that, "God is only existing in Benares [or] in Haridwar. God is not here. He is absent here". We have got doubt in That.

And that doubt will also be vanished. That doubt will be removed in me and *tvad avalokanam astu nirantaram*, and I would like this, that I would perceive You in continuity always, everywhere, not only in a Varanasi temple.

Chapter 18 (45:05)

स्फुटमाविश मामथाविशेयं
सततं नाथ भवन्तमस्मि यस्मात् ।
रभसेन वपुस्तवैव साक्षात्-
परमासत्तिगतः समर्चयेयम् ॥२०॥

sphuṭamāviśa māmathāviśeyaṁ
satataṁ nātha bhavantamasmi yasmāt /

320 Swamiji uses the phrase "every now and then" in the sense of "continuously" or "repeatedly". [*Editor's note*]

rabhasena vapustavaiva sākṣāt-
paramāsattigataḥ samarcayeyam //20//

Nātha, O Lord, could You do one thing for me? That is, get entry in my body. You enter in my body, then, after Your entrance, after You enter in my body, I will enter in You. *Athā aviśeyaṁ satatam*, and this course must be functioned each day, each moment, each second.

"Why?" Now, You will say, "Why? What is the purpose of that? What is the fun in doing that, that you must get entry in My body and then I will enter in your body and visa versa, always?"

Satataṁ nātha bhavantamasmi yasmāt. Because I am Yours, I am one particle of Yours. Just as a ray is one with the sun, in the same way, I am one with You. I must be one with You. So, You get entry in my body and I will get entry in Your body, and visa versa. We will do only this much, always. We will this always [laughter].

Rabhasena vapuḥ tavaiva sākṣāt paramāsattigataḥ samarcayeyam. And in this functioning, in this functioning course, of getting [entry] in You and [You entering in me], this must be done with *rabhasa* (*rabhasa* means "with great zeal"), with great zeal and with great hurry. *Rabhasena vapustavaiva sākṣāt*, and while doing this function of both entries, I would like to worship You in doing this function. I would worship You when You get entry in my body and I will worship You when I will enter in Your body. I will worship You always. This is my desire.

DENISE: Is that like *spanda*?

SWAMIJI: Yes, it is *spanda*.[321]

ALEXIS: *Krama mudrā*?

SWAMIJI: This is *krama mudrā*, yes.[322]

Chapter 18 (47:41)

त्वयि न स्तुतिशक्तिरस्ति कस्या-
प्यथवास्त्येव यतोऽतिसुन्दरोऽसि ।

321 See appendix 26 for an explanation of *spanda*.

322 "*Krama mudrā* is the process to get entry in *jagadānanda* [lit., "rejoicing the world"]." See appendix 13.

सततं पुनरर्थितं ममैतद्-
यदविश्रान्ति विलोकयेयमीशम् ॥२१॥

tvayi na stutiśaktirasti kasyā-
pyathavāstyeva yato'tisundaro'si /
satataṁ punurarthitaṁ mamaitad-
yadaviśrānti vilokayeyamīśam //21//

Nobody has this power to sing the glory of You (*tvayi na stuti śaktiḥ asti kasyāpi*). Or, everybody can sing the glory of You. Nobody can sing the glory of You because You are absolutely away from this limited sphere of the universe, but everybody has the right to sing the glory of You.

Why?

Ati sundaro'si, You are very beautiful. You are the most beautiful person in this universe, in all of the one hundred and eighteen worlds. *Satataṁ punar arthitaṁ mamaitat*, this is not my problem. This is Your greatness that nobody can sing the glory of You because You are so great, but everybody sings Your glory because You are very beautiful, You are very attractive. Everybody is attracted towards You, so everybody sings Your glory from their sphere of thinking, from their level of thinking.

But, my problem is not that. My problem is that I want to look at You, I want to look at You *aviśrānti*, without pause, [while] I am living in this universe. *Bas*, I want to look at You. I don't want to eat, I don't want to drink, I don't want to go anywhere. Just to look at You.

Chapter Nineteen
Illuminating the Existence of Lord Shiva
Udyotanābhidhānaṁ ekonaviṁśaṁ stotram

SWAMIJI: *Udyotanābhidhānaṁ ekonaviṁśaṁ stotram*. This is *udyotan*, *udyotanābhidhānam*. This [*stotra*] is nominated as *udyotan*. *Udyotan* means . . .

ALEXIS: "Illumination" in English.

SWAMIJI: Illumination, yes. Illuminating the existence of Lord Śiva.

Chapter 19 (00:24)

प्रार्थनाभूमिकातीतविचित्रफलदायकः ।
जयत्यपूर्ववृत्तान्तः शिवः सत्कल्पपादपः ॥ १ ॥

prārthanābhūmikātītavicitraphaladāyakaḥ /
jayatyapūrvavṛttāntaḥ śivaḥ satkalpapādapaḥ //1//

Śiva is really [like] the *pārijāta* tree.

The *pārijāta* tree is found in heaven. You have heard about the *parijāta* tree? It gives you anything. It bestows all of your desires, [which] are fulfilled if you ask for anything, anything. It is called *kalpataru*[323], i.e., the *pārijāta* tree. It gives you everything, whatever you ask for.

And Śiva is really that tree. Glory be to Śiva who is that tree, like that tree, *satkalpa pādapaḥ* (*satkalpa pādapaḥ* means "supreme *kalpa pādapa*"; *pādapa* means "tree"). Glory be to That tree who is Lord Śiva!

He has made Lord Śiva as that tree.

It is *apūrva vṛttāntaḥ*, the history of This tree is unique. The history of that tree in heaven, it is already known to everybody. The history is that, [whatever] you ask for, you get. Whoever asks for anything, he gets that from that tree. But This tree of Lord Śiva is *prārthanā bhūmikātīta*–the story of This tree is some-

323 The wish-fulfilling tree.

thing else–*prārthanā bhūmikātīta*, you have not to ask [for anything]. Without asking, It will give you (*prārthanā bhūmi-kātīta*).

And *vicitra phala dāyakaḥ*, and It will give you not only one fruit, It will give you fruit from every respect. It will give you money, It will give you a wife, It will give you service, It will give you a motorcar, It will give you a house, It will give you liberation, It will give you everything! It will give you everything without [your] asking. There is no request. Without request, you get that; *vicitra phala dāyakaḥ*, you have not to request.

What can you request for? You don't know what everything is. You don't know what everything is. Everything is being bestowed from That tree and that everything you don't know because your vision of understanding is limited, always. It will remain . . . this vision will always remain in an individual as limited.

So, this tree of Lord Śiva is glorified (*jayati*). *Apūrva vṛttāntaḥ*, It has a unique history of Its being.

Chapter 19 (03:22)

सर्ववस्तुनिचयैकनिधानात्-
स्वात्मनस्त्वदखिलं किल लभ्यम् ।
अस्य मे पुनरसौ निज आत्मा
न त्वमेव घटसे परमास्ताम् ॥ २ ॥

sarvavastunicayaikanidhānāt-
svātmanastvadakhilaṁ kila labhyam /
asya me punarasau nijā ātmā
na tvameva ghaṭase paramāstām //2//

O Lord, this is a fact that because You are the treasure of everything, You are the treasure of all the universal things–all universal objects are found, are treasured, in You–and from That treasure, everything is achieved (*tvat svātmanastvad akhilaṁ kila labhyam*, everything is achieved). But, for me, it is not like that.

Asya me punarasau nijā ātmā na tvameva ghaṭase paramāstām. For me, nothing is achieved–this is Your greatness. My Lord, this is Your greatness that I have achieved nothing from

You. [Although] everything is achieved–this is written, this is propagated, this is everywhere expressed, that everything is achieved from Lord Śiva–but, for me, I find nothing is achieved from Lord Śiva.

Asya me punarasau nija ātmā na tvameva ghaṭase. You are not achieved; Your Self [is not achieved by] me. What should I say for other things? Other things are far away from my achievement. This is my position in Your kingdom.

Shame to You. Is it not a shame? It is shameful for You! You are the treasure of all the universal things, universal glories, and I have achieved not one glory, [not even] one-hundredth part of glory. I am still just like a beggar as I was before.

Chapter 19 (05:33)

ज्ञानकर्ममयचिद्वपुरात्मा
सर्वथैष परमेश्वर एव ।
स्याद्वपुस्तु निखिलेषु पदार्थे-
ष्वेषु नाम न भवेत्किमुतान्यत् ॥३॥

jñānakarmamayacidvapurātmā
sarvathaiṣa parameśvara eva /
syādvapustu nikhileṣu padārthe-
ṣveṣu nāma na bhavetkimutānyat //3//

In fact, Parameśvara is the Self, the conscious Self, always. [Parameśvara is] the conscious Self filled with knowledge and action. And that Parameśvara is found in each and every particle of the objective world. So, in these objective worlds, *nāma na bhavet*, you cannot nominate those objective worlds separatedly from that God consciousness. *Kimutānyat*, how can this objective world exist without Thee? You are everywhere!

Chapter 19 (06:34)

विषमार्तिमुषानेन फलेन त्वद्दगात्मना ।
अभिलीय पथा नाथ ममास्तु त्वन्मयी गतिः ॥४॥

viṣamārtimuṣānena phalena tvadṛgātmanā /
abhilīya pathā nātha mamāstu tvanmayī gatiḥ //4//

Nātha, O my Master, *tvat dṛgātmanā*, there is a path, there is one path, which is the path of understanding You, Your existence. The path of Thy understanding, this is a path, and on that path, *viṣamārtimuṣā*, and that path is *viṣamārtinuṣā*, it is that path where all ups and downs and crises and tortures are removed, finally removed. Tortures do not remain, sadness does not remain, nothing remains like that on that path. And *phalena tvat dṛgātmanā*, the fruit of that path is just to understand You.

Abhilīya pathā nātha. Let me be destroyed, let me be dissolved, on that path. You [should] make me dissolved on that path and I would like, at the time, at the moment of understanding You, I would like not to understand You at all. I would like, *bas*, only Your existence. I would be gone. My individuality would be shattered on this journey, this path.

For instance, any individual is travelling on that path, and all of his limbs, all of his facilities, all of his ego, everything is gone, and, in the end, where there is the residence of Lord Śiva, the residence of Lord Śiva only remains there–the residence of Lord Śiva.

I want it [to be] like that. I want to destroy, dissolve myself, dissolve my individuality on that path, so that I remain as nothing except You only.

Chapter 19 (09:08)

भवदमलचरणचिन्तारत्नलता-
लङ्कृता कदा सिद्धिः ।
सिद्धजनमानसानां विस्मयजननी
घटेत मम भवतः ॥५॥

bhavadamalacaraṇācintāratnalatā-
laṅkṛtā kadā siddhiḥ /
siddhajanamānasānāṁ vismayajananī
ghaṭeta mama bhavataḥ //5//

Your feet, Your lotus feet, are just so pure, and the memory of [Your] lotus feet, to remember those lotus feet of Thee, is just [like] a fine and beautiful creeper, a creeper of *cintāmaṇi* (*cintāmaṇi* jewels[324]). *Kadā siddhiḥ ghaṭeta*, when shall I achieve that great power from that creeper?

Cintāmaṇi latā is also, on the other side, existing in heavens– *cintāmaṇi latā*. That is also like *kalpa pārijāta vṛkṣa.*[325] It bestows, it fulfills, all of your desires, i.e., that *cintāmaṇi* creeper. That is *cintāmaṇi latā*. He does not want that creeper, which is existing in heaven. He wants the memory of Your lotus feet and *that* is *cintāmaṇi latā*.

This memory must . . . the memory in my mind must be continuous, i.e., memorizing Your lotus feet, always! And this *siddhi*, I want only this power, this achievement of power.

What achievement of power?

To remember You in continuity. When that power will come to me? When that power will be attained by me, which is *siddhajanamānasānām vismayajananī*, which produces wonder in those great masters, ancient masters? When that *siddhi*, when that power, will be achieved by me, not by my qualities, but by Your grace?

Bhavataḥ means "*bhavataḥ prabhāvāt*, by Your grace".

Not because it is due to me. It is not due to me. I am nothing. It must come to me by Your grace, not by my qualifications.

Chapter 19 (11:58)

कर्हि नाथ विमलं मुखबिम्बं
तावकं समवलोकयितास्मि ।
यत्स्रवत्यमृतपूरमपूर्वं
यो निमज्जयति विश्वमशेषम् ॥ ६ ॥

324 "*Cintāmaṇi* jewel is that kind of jewel, whatever you wish for, it will come true. It is the bestower of all your boons, all your desires. All your de-sires are fulfilled by that *cintāmaṇi*, that jewel." *Stava Cintāmaṇi* (USF archives).

325 The wish-fulfilling tree.

karhi nātha vimalaṁ mukhabimbaṁ
tāvakaṁ samavalokayitāsmi /
yatsravatyamṛtapūramapūrvaṁ
yo nimajjayati viśvamaśeṣam //6//

Nātha, O my Master, when that day will come when I will be perceiving or seeing Your pure face (*mukhabiṁbam*, I would perceive Your pure face)? And, by that perceiving–*yatsravatyamṛtapūramapūrvam*–and, by that perceiving, Your face would flow out . . .

ALEXIS: Release the flood of . . .

SWAMIJI: . . . release a flood of supreme nectar, unique nectar, and that flood would cover, would bury, all that differentiated perception of the universe.

DENISE: What's the difference between seeing Lord Śiva's lotus feet and His face? What does it mean? It's just poetic?

SWAMIJI: Yes.

Chapter 19 (13:19)

ध्यातमात्रमुदितं तव रूपं
कर्हि नाथ परमामृतपूरैः ।
पूरयेत्त्वदविभेदविमोक्षा-
ख्यातिदूरविवराणि सदा मे ॥७॥

dhyātamātramuditaṁ tava rūpaṁ
karhi nātha paramāmṛtapūraiḥ /
pūrayettvadavibhedavimokṣā-
khyātidūravivarāṇi sadā me //7//

O my Lord, I have created some trouble in my mind and that is due to *tvat avibheda vimokṣa akhyāti*; *tvat avibheda*, being deprived of Your oneness. When I am being deprived of Your oneness and I am away from God consciousness, I am kept away from God consciousness, and that has created a great disease in me. That is *vivarāṇi*; that is *nāsūra*.

Nāsūra is that deep hole, [which is produced] after [an infection], created in the body, and it is incurable afterwards–that *nāsūra*. When there is some wound and that wound will produce *nāsūra* by [an] abscess or by something. *Bas*, and afterwards it goes deeper and deeper, deeper and deeper, deeper and deeper, then it is a *nāsūra*. Then it is incurable; you can't cure it then. The cure is only by leaving this physical frame. It can't be cured. That is *vivara*; that is called *vivara*.

And it is *dūravivara* (*dūravivara* means "deep hole"), the deep hole of that wound of being away from Your God consciousness. I have been kept away from Your God consciousness and that has created this disease in my mind. And my mind has created this deep hole.

And this deep hole can be cured only by one medicine. And that is *tava rūpaṁ paramāmṛtapūraiḥ pūrayet*, Your state of being, Your state of God consciousness. That supreme divine nectar of God consciousness should be [poured] in that hole. And *pūrayet*, and It will fill it and it will be cleaned.

But, that God consciousness should not take place successively. *Dhyātamātra*, whenever I think of the Lord, I must get That, I must achieve That position. Not by doing practice always [in the] morning and evening and daytime and midnight–not by this kind of means. Just by remembering You and *bas*, entering in that God consciousness.

And, by that supreme nectar, [my *dūravivara*] will be filled and I would be relieved from this disease. When that cure will come to me, appear to me?

Chapter 19 (17:00)

त्वदीयानुत्तररसासङ्गसन्त्यक्तचापलम् ।
नाद्यापि मे मनो नाथ कर्हि स्यादस्तु शीघ्रतः ॥८॥

tvadīyānuttararasāsaṅgasantyaktacāpalam /
nādyāpi me mano nātha karhi syādastu śīghrataḥ //8//

Nātha, O Master, my mind has not yet become *tvadīya anuttara rasa āsaṅga santyakta cāpalam,* my mind has not removed the *cañcalatā*.

Cañcalatā means this . . .

ALEXIS: Instability.

SWAMIJI: Instability.

My mind has not removed that instability from its nature by *tvadīya anuttara rasa āsaṅga*, by being near to the taste of Your supreme nectar of God Consciousness. *Nādyāpi me*, even now it has not taken that state; my mind has not taken that state even now! *Karhi syāt*, when that will happen to me? Couldn't it happen to me now?

ALEXIS: Let it happen quickly.

SWAMIJI: Let it happen quickly. Let it happen now.

First he says, "when will it happen? Please tell me when it will come to me". Afterwards he says, "let it happen now, please" [laughter]. He is so fond of God consciousness!

Chapter 19 (18:38)

मा शुष्ककटुकान्येव परं सर्वाणि सर्वदा ।
तवोपहृत्य लब्धानि द्वन्द्वान्यप्यापतन्तु मे ॥१॥

mā śuṣkakaṭukānyeva paraṁ sarvāṇi sarvadā /
tavopahṛtya labdhāni dvandvānyapyāpatantu me //10//

All *dvandvas*, all opposite things in this universe . . .

For instance, cold and heat, pleasure and pain, sadness and joy, all of these are called *dvandvas*, opposite two things; *sukha* and *duḥkha*, pleasures and pains.

. . . all of these *dvandvas*, when they appear to me, I don't want to discard them. But, they must not appear to me dry, in dryness, nor in *kaṭu* (*kaṭu* means "in a bitter way") as everybody feels them. *Tavopahṛtya labdhāni dvandāni api āpatantu me*, I must feel God consciousness in them. Let these things happen to me. I welcome these opposite two things. Let pain and pleasure come to me, let joy and sadness come to me, let everything come to me . . .

ALEXIS: *Tavopahṛtya.*

SWAMIJI: . . . *tava upahṛtya*, but with You, along with You.

ALEXIS: Offering to You?

SWAMIJI: Yes. That is also true.[326]

Chapter 19 (20:13)

नाथ साम्मुख्यमायान्तु विशुद्धास्तव रश्मयः ।
यावत्कायमनस्तापतमोभिः परिलुप्यताम् ॥ १० ॥

nātha sāmmukhyamāyāntu viśuddhāstava raśmayaḥ /
yāvatkāyamanastāpatamobhiḥ parilupyatām //10//

O my Master, let Your rays shine and come near to me always, up to that moment when *kāyamanastāpa tamobhiḥ*, the darkness and sadness of my mind and body would be gone.

Chapter 19 (20:57)

देव प्रसीद यावन्मे त्वन्मार्गपरिपन्थिकाः ।
परमार्थमुषो वश्या भूयासुर्गुणतस्कराः ॥ ११ ॥

deva prasīda yāvanme tvanmārgaparipanthikāḥ /
paramārthamuṣo vaśyā bhūyāsurguṇataskarāḥ //11//

O Lord, I am looted by these thieves, the thieves of the senses of the organs. These senses of the organs are thieves because they are thieves and they have looted all of my wealth.

Which thieves?

The senses of the organs are thieves who have looted all of my wealth of spirituality. O Lord, *prasīḍa*, and there is one request from me to You. That request is, You remain on my side with a helping hand only up to that point when *tvan mārga paripanthikāḥ*, those who are *paripanthikāḥ*, . . .

Paripanthikā means . . .

JOACHIM: Highway robbers?

SWAMIJI: No. On the way, they divert you to the wrong way.

ALEXIS: Obstacles.

SWAMIJI: Obstacles. When you are treading on the right way, they will lead you to the wrong side–that is *paripathiṅkāḥ*. In

326 *Tava upahṛtya* can also mean "offering to You". [*Editor's note*]

Kashmiri, we call it "*rāhachok*". And those are these organs of the senses. They are [such] great thieves who take you away from the right side to the wrong side. And *paramārthamuṣā*–and they don't only do this thing–they *paramārthamuṣā*, they steal all of your wealth of God consciousness.

. . . and, until they are under me, they come under my control, You have to be there with a helping hand. Please [provide] that help to me. Otherwise, I will be no more; I will be gone.

Chapter 19 (23:12)

त्वद्भक्तिसुधसारैर्-
मानसमापूर्यतां ममाशु विभो ।
यावदिमा उह्यन्तां
निःशेषासारवासनाः प्लुत्वा ॥१२॥

tvadbhaktisudhasārair-
mānasamāpūryatāṁ mamāśu vibho /
yāvadimā uhyantāṁ
niḥśeṣāsāravāsanāḥ plutvā //12//

These limited desires, which are existing in individuals–e.g., I want a child, I want a wife, I want a car, I want a good job, all of these things, all of these are limited things, very limited things, and they are not stable, they always come and go–and these desires, they have a similarity with those *haṁsas* (swans). *Niḥśeṣāsāravāsanā*, these are *asāra vāsanā* (*vāsanā* means these "desires" and *asāra* [means] "with no substance in them, with no reality in them"), and they are [existing] in that mind, which is a lake without water. They are residing in that lake where there is no water. So, they are dry always. They are roaming uselessly there (i.e., these thoughts, these desires in you), and these are those *haṁsas*.

Haṁsas are . . .

ALEXIS: Swans.

SWAMIJI: Swans. So, these desires are similar to those *haṁsas*, which are roaming in that lake which is dry.

Let this lake be filled with the nectar of Thy devotion so that these swans will fly high in the sky and roam. Because, they will find this water [of Thy devotion and they] will get drowned in it and then they will fly (*uhyantām* means "they will fly").

Chapter 19 (25:24)

मोक्षदशायां भक्ति-
स्त्वयि कुत इव मर्त्यधर्मिणोऽपि न सा ।
राजति ततोऽनुरूपाम्-
आरोपय सिद्धिभूमिकामज माम् ॥ १३ ॥

mokṣadaśāyāṁ bhakti-
stvayi kuta iva martyadharmiṇo'pi na sā /
rājati tato'nurūpām-
āropaya siddhibhūmikāmaja mām //13//

Mokṣadaśāyāṁ–it is *naimittika saptamī*[327]–*mokṣadaśāyāṁ*, *mokṣadaśā prāptārthyāṁ*[328], *mokṣadaśā*, just to achieve the state of liberation, the means is Thy devotion.

How can that devotion be possessed by an individual? Thy devotion is so unlimited. The devotion of Lord Śiva is unlimited and the devotion of the individual is very limited. How that [unlimited] devotion will rise in a limited being (*kutaḥ iva*)? So, that devotion, I don't want such devotion, which is limited.

For instance, there are such devotees found in this universe, they devote only one hour of meditation and get entry in *samādhi*, and there are such devotees who devote their whole lives and never have entered in *samādhi*. That devotion is not devotion at all.

So, that devotion, *martyadharmiṇo'pi na sā rājati*, it does not suit that devotion, i.e., that supreme devotion does not suit that limited being. So, let me be an unlimited being; *tato anurūpāṁ siddhi bhūmikām āropaya*, let me ascend to the state of the supreme universal state of life . . .

ALEXIS: Raise me to that level (*āropaya*).

327 Locative case.
328 *Prāptārthya,* to obtain or achieve. [*Editor's note*]

SWAMIJI: Yes.

. . . and then I can devote my time with Your devotion. That devotion will shine.

You are so great and my devotion is so low. How can that devotion carry me to the state of Your being, [which] is so great? So, take me up to That level so that my devotion also becomes divine. This is my request.

Chapter 19 (28:11)

सिद्धिलवलाभलुब्धं
  मामवलेपेन मा विभो संस्थाः ।
क्षामस्त्वद्भक्तिमुखे
  प्रोल्लसदणिमादिपक्षतो मोक्षः ॥१४॥

siddhilavalābhalubdhaṁ
  māmavalepena mā vibho saṁsthāḥ /
kṣāmastvadbhaktimukhe
  prollasadaṇimādi pakṣato mokṣaḥ //*14*//

Vibho, O Lord Śiva, *siddhilavalābhalubdhaṁ māmavalepena mā vibho saṁsthāḥ*, let me not become attached to these limited powers, *yogic* powers. *Tvat bhakti mukhe*, taking in view Your devotion, this achievement of these *yogic* powers is very low. So, let me not be entangled, let me not become entangled, in those lower powers of *yoga*.

So, *prollasat aṇimādi pakṣato mokṣaḥ* is very low (*prollasad aṇimādi pakṣataḥ* means "the achievement of liberation through the achievement of *yogic* powers is very low"). It is a very mean achievement of liberation. The divine achievement of liberation is *just* liberation without touching the field of these *yogic* powers.

Chapter 19 (29:45)

दासस्य मे प्रसीदतु
  भगवानेतावदेव ननु याचे ।

दाता त्रिभुवननाथो
  यस्य न तन्मादृशां दृशो विषयः ॥ १५ ॥

dāsasya me prasīdatu
bhagavānetāvadeva nanu yāce /
dātā tribhuvananātho
yasya na tanmādṛśāṁ dṛśo viṣayaḥ //15//

Dāsasya me prasīdatu bhagavān. Let Thee become pleased with me who is Thy slave because You are *dātā*, You are the bestower of everything and You are the ruler of all the three worlds.

He is my bestower, He is the ruler of all the three worlds, and He is my master, and He is not seen by me. I have not seen Him. So far, I have not seen Him. It is a great wonder to me. I have got . . . He takes care of me, He is the giver of all the three worlds, the luxury of all the three worlds, and He is not perceived by me. This is a wonder.

I only crave for only this achievement: just be pleased with me. That is all.

Chapter 19 (31:14)

त्वद्वपुः स्मृतिसुधारसपूर्णे
  मानसे तव पदाम्बुजयुग्मम्
मामके विकसदस्तु सदैव
  प्रस्रवन्मधु किमप्यतिलोकम् ॥ १६ ॥

tvadvapuḥ smṛtisudhārasapūrṇe
mānase tava padāmbujayugmam /
māmake vikasadastu sadaiva
prasravanmadhu kimapyatilokam //16//

There is one desire in me. My mind is already filled with the nectar of remembering Your nature. My mind always remembers Your nature. So, my mind is always filled with the nectar of that memory of Thee. It is already . . . it has become divine; my mind has become divine already by Your remembrance, constant remembrance. But there is one problem in my mind. I want *tava padāmbujayugmam māmake vikasad astu sadaiva*, and in this mind, which is filled with the nectar of Your memory, there must be a lotus, one lotus, at least one lotus must grow in that. Because, in a lake, you find lotuses. There is not even one lotus in the lake of my mind.

My mind is a lake, which is filled with the nectar of Your memory. I remember, my mind always remembers, Your Self, and that memory is nectar, and that nectar is filled in [the lake of] my mind, and there is not even one lotus. Nothing is grown in that [lake of my mind]. At least it must grow at least two lotuses, i.e., Your two feet.

So, *māmake*, in that lake of my mind, *vikasadastu sadaiva*, let *tava padāmbujayugmam*, let Thy two lotus feet grow[329] in the lake of my mind. And *prasravanmadhu kimapi atilokam*, and let those lotuses drip, let them drip that supreme nectar of God consciousness on the water of my mind, the surface of my mind.

Chapter 19 (33:48)

अस्ति मे प्रभुरसौ जनकोऽथ
त्र्यम्बकोऽथ जननी च भवानी ।
न द्वितीय इह कोऽपि ममास्ती-
त्येव निर्वृततमो विचरेयम् ॥ १७॥

asti me prabhurasau janako'tha
tryambako'tha jananī ca bhavānī /
na dvitīya iha ko'pi mamāstī-
tyeva nirvṛtatamo vicareyam //17//

There is one desire in me and that is the last desire. I want to have one master and that master must be You. *Asti me prabhurasau*, and that master must be my father; my master and father [must be] You. And *tryambako'tha jananī ca bhavānī*, and

329 *Vikasat astu sadaiva*: let that always bloom.

Your Pārvatī as my mother; I want to have Your Pārvatī as my mother. I want to have You as my father. *Na dvitīya*, I have no one else; no one else is my father, no one else is my mother. My only father is Lord Śiva and my mother is Mother Pārvatī. *Ityeva nirvṛtatamo*, in this way, let me roam in this world filled with satisfaction, the highest satisfaction.

Chapter Twenty
Relishing the Real Taste Inside
Carvaṇābhidhānaṁ viṁśaṁ stotram

SWAMIJI: This [*stotra*] is nominated as "*carvaṇa*". *Caravaṇa* is just tasting the real taste inside.

Chapter 20 (00:12)

नाथं त्रिभुवननाथं भूतिसितं
त्रिनयनं त्रिशूलधरम् ।
उपवीतीकृतभोगिनम्-
इन्दुकलाशेखरं वन्दे ॥१॥

nāthaṁ tribhuvananāthaṁ bhūtisitaṁ
trinayanaṁ triśūladharam /
upavītīkṛtabhoginam-
indukalāśekharaṁ vande //1//

Nāthaṁ vande, I bow to my Master who is the Master of all the three worlds (*tribhuvana nātham*), *bhūtisitam*, whose body is white because of rubbing that *vibhūti* (*bhasma*).

ALEXIS: Ashes.

SWAMIJI: Ashes.

Trinayanaṁ, I bow to that Lord who has got three eyes, *triśūladharam*, who is holding *triśūla* in His hand, *upavītī kṛta bhoginam*, and who has blessed the great [snakes by] putting them around His neck.[330] And *indu kalā śekharam*, whose forehead is beautified with that crescent moon.

330 The eight great snakes which govern the universe are: Ananta, Vāsukī, Takṣakaḥ, Kārkoṭa, Saroja, Mahā-Padmaja-Nāgarāja, Saṁkha, and Kulikaḥ. *Tantrāloka*, 6.69 (USF archives). It is generally accepted that only Vāsukī adorns Lord Shiva's neck. [*Editor's note*]

Chapter 20 (01:25)

नौमि निजतनुविनिस्सरदंशुक-
परिवेषधवलपरिधानम् ।
विलसत्कपालमालाकल्पित-
नृत्तोत्सवाकल्पम् ॥२॥

naumi nijatanuvinissaradaṁśuka
pariveṣadhavalaparīdhānam /
vilasatkapālamālākalpita-
nṛttotsavākalpam //2//

Nija tanu vinissarat aṁśuka pariveṣa dhavala paridhānam. I bow to Lord Śiva, to that Lord Śiva, whose body is covered–just as our body is covered with our clothes–whose body is covered with the disk of His effulgent light of that effulgent halo; the halo of that disk of His effulgent light of His body. That has come out from His body, i.e., that effulgent light of the halo.

ALEXIS: *Aṁśuka pariveṣa*.

SWAMIJI: *Aṁśuka pariveṣa*.

And that is in place of clothes for Him. By His own *aṁśuka* (garment), He has covered His body by His own effulgent light of His glamour. I bow to that Lord Śiva.

And *vilasat kapāla mālā kalpita nṛttotsavākalpam*, and who is glorified, *vilasat kapāla mālā kalpita nṛtta utsavākalpam*, when He celebrates the dance, evening dance, evening *tāṇḍava*.

That dance takes place at the time of destruction. When He wants to destroy this whole universe, He dances, and by that dance, this whole [universe] is shattered to pieces, everything.

And, at that time, at the period when He dances, at the time of dusk, *vilasat kapālamālā kalpita nṛttot-savākalpam*, He is glorified with that *kapāla mālā*, by the garland of the skulls of all Brahmas. And His body is glorified with that garland at that time, at the time of dancing.

Chapter 20 (03:54)

वन्दे तान् दैवतं येषां हरश्चेष्टा हरोचिताः ।
हरैकप्रवणाः प्राणाः सदा सौभाग्यसद्मनाम् ॥३॥

vande tān daivataṁ yeṣāṁ haraśceṣṭā harocitāḥ /
haraikapravaṇāḥ prāṇāḥ sadā saubhāgyasadmanām //3

I bow to those devotees (*vande tān*), *sadā saubhāgya sadmanām tān vande*, those who are glorified, always glorified, with that spiritual fortune. *Yeṣāṁ daivataṁ haraḥ*, I bow to those whose *daivataṁ* (adorable deity) is Lord Śiva (*yeṣāṁ daivataṁ haraḥ*). I bow to those *yeṣāṁ ceṣṭāḥ harocitā*, whose actions are just for the sake of Lord Śiva. Any action, whatever they do, they do for Lord Śiva. There is nothing to be done except for Lord Śiva. I bow to those people. I bow to those devotees. And *haraika pravaṇāḥ prāṇāḥ*, I bow to those devotees whose life is bent upon searching for Lord Śiva. I bow to such devotees.

Chapter 20 (05:32)

क्रीडितं तव महेश्वरतायाः
पृष्ठतोऽन्यदिदमेव यथैतत् ।
इष्टमात्रघटितेष्ववदाने-
ष्वात्मना परमुपायमुपैमि ॥४॥

krīḍitaṁ tava maheśvaratāyāḥ
pṛṣṭhato'nyadidameva yathaitat /
iṣṭamātraghaṭiteṣvavadāne-
ṣvātmanā paramupāyamupaimi //4//
[beginning of verse missing in audio]

Tava maheśvaratāyāḥ pṛṣṭhataḥ anyat idam eva krīḍitaṁ. The one play, one divine play, first divine play, of Your glory is just the existence of Your kingdom. Your kingdom is one glory, i.e., Your kingdom of creating, protecting, destroying, concealing, and revealing. This is Your kingdom. [Your] kingdom is in these five great acts: creation, protection, destruction, concealing, and revealing (*sṛṣṭi*, *sthiti*, *saṁhāra*, *pidhāna*, and *anugraha*). This is the first kingdom, the main kingdom of Thee. This is Your kingdom. This is the blissful play of Your kingdom.

And there is another blissful play attached to this kingdom. And that kingdom is what he explains [now]. That is, *iṣṭa mātra ghaṭiteṣvavadāneṣu*, when I think of Your, these five acts, *iṣṭa mātra*, when I just desire, just think, just concentrate upon, these five acts of Yours in Your kingdom, *ātmanā paraṁ upāyaṁ upaimi*, I become also one with That kingdom. So, I begin to create, I begin to protect, I begin to destroy, I begin to conceal, and I begin to reveal. I become just like You. This is another divine play of Your kingdom.

One main play of Your kingdom is that You are established in Your kingdom. Another play of Your kingdom is that *we* are also possessing That kingdom; we also possess That kingdom. This is Your play.

So, this is just *śaktipāta* (grace). [There is] no difference between the individual and the universal Lord.

Chapter 20 (08:04)

त्वद्धाम्नि विश्ववन्द्येऽस्मिन्नियति क्रीडने सति ।
तव नाथ कियान् भूयान्नानन्दरससम्भवः ॥५॥

tvaddhāmni viśvavandye'sminniyati krīḍane sati /
tava nātha kiyān bhūyānnānandarasasambhavaḥ //5//

Nātha, O Master, *viśvavandye tvaddhāmni*, in Your kingdom, which is adored by each and every being–Your kingdom is adored and appreciated by each and every individual; Your kingdom is not denied–and in this *viśvavandye* (*viśvavandye* means "adored by *viśva*, adored by the whole universe"), and in Your kingdom, *iyati krīḍane sati*, this whole creation of this universe (e.g., beautiful flowers, beautiful ladies, beautiful people, beautiful birds, beautiful songs, beautiful music, etc.), this is only Your one particle of Your play! This is only one, just one, minute particle of Your play in Your kingdom.

If it is so, *tava nātha kiyān bhūyān*, I imagine to myself how great a joy would be possessed by You! If this whole universal joy, universal glory, is one particle of Your kingdom, what joy would be existing in Your kingdom? That is beyond our explanation; we can't compare that to anything else.

Can you understand?

Chapter 20 (09:57)

कथं स सुभगो मा भूद्यो गौर्या वल्लभो हरः ।
हरोऽपि मा भूदथ किं गौर्याः परमवल्लभः ॥६॥

kathaṁ sa subhago mā bhūdyo gauryā vallabho haraḥ /
haro'pi mā bhūdatha kiṁ gauryāḥ paramavallabhaḥ //6//

Now, there is one more thing to be explained by [Utpaladeva].

Kathaṁ sa subhago mā bhūt yo gauryāḥ vallabho haraḥ. Haraḥ, this Lord Śiva, is fortunate because He is embraced by Pārvatī. How can He not be fortunate because He is embraced by Pārvati? This Pārvatī is the embodiment of beauty, the embodiment of charm, the embodiment of every joy is Pārvatī, and Pārvatī has taken Him in Her arms. How could Lord Śiva not be glorified and fortunate? He is most fortunate because He is embraced by such a great lady.

Haro'pi mā bhūt atha kiṁ gauryāḥ parama vallabhaḥ. But who else could take Her in his arms except Lord Śiva? Lord Śiva was the only right person to take Her in His arms!

Chapter 20 (11:33)

ध्यानामृतमयं यस्य स्वात्ममूलमनश्वरम् ।
संविल्लतास्तथारूपास्तस्य कस्यापि सत्तरोः ॥७॥

dhyānāmṛtamayaṁ yasya svātmamūlamanaśvaram /
saṁvillatāstathārūpāstasya kasyāpi sattaroḥ //7//

Now, he explains here that a devotee of Lord Śiva is just like a beautiful tree–a beautiful, glorious tree–and that glorious tree, the roots of that glorious tree (that is, Your devotee), the roots of that glorious tree are soaked with Thy meditation, with the nectar of Thy meditation, because those devotees always meditate on Your form, on Your being. So, this nectar is always there at the root of that tree.

So, when the roots of that tree are soaked with that nectar of meditation (*dhyāna*), *saṁvit latāstatha rūpāstasya kasyāpi sattaroḥ*, and the branches and fruits and whatever that tree bears afterwards, those branches and fruits are also soaked with that nectar (*saṁvit latā*).

Latā means "the branches and creepers . . ."

ALEXIS: Of *saṁvit.*

SWAMIJI: Yes. *Saṁvit* is knowledge; knowledge concerning, pertaining to those devotees (*sattaru*[331]).

Tatha rūpa, [the tree's branches and fruits] are just like that *amṛta*, the supreme nectar of *dhyāna*.

Chapter 20 (13:30)

भक्तिकण्डूसमुल्लासावसरे परमेश्वर ।
महानिकषपाषाणस्थूणा पूजैव जायते ॥८॥

bhaktikaṇḍūsamullāsāvasare parameśvara /
mahānikaṣapāṣāṇasthūṇā pūjaiva jāyate //8//

O Lord Śiva, when a devotee of Thee has created this [itching] sensation of *bhakti* (devotion), and that itching won't be removed until You are there, You are present. Your main presence will remove that itching sensation.

Bhakti kaṇḍū samullāsāvasare. When the rise of *kaṇḍu* (*kaṇḍu* means that "itch") takes place, the itch of devotion, the rise of the itch of devotion takes place in devotees, then what happens? *Pūjaiva*, Thy devotion, worshiping You, worshiping Lord Śiva, becomes the pillar [*sthūṇa*] of wettingstone [*pāṣāṇa*] [and rubbing against] that is the only way to remove this itching sensation. The itching sensation will never be removed unless this worship takes place, the worship of Lord Śiva takes place.

331 Whose existence (*sat*) is like that of a tree (*taru*). [*Editor's note*]

Chapter 20 (15:00)

सदा सृष्टिविनोदाय सदा स्थितिसुखासिने ।
सदा त्रिभुवनाहारतृप्ताय स्वामिने नमः ॥९॥

sadā sṛṣṭivinodāya sadā sthitisukhāsine /
sadā tribhuvanāhāratṛptāya svāmine namaḥ //9//

I bow to my master who is always enjoying the act of creation (the act of creating this whole universe), who is always absorbed in protecting it, and who is always bent upon destroying it.

ALEXIS: He is blissful in these acts (*tṛptāya sukhāsine*).

SWAMIJI: Yes. Because, without destruction, freshness won't act. You see, when you are running in your thirties . . . I am running in my seventies, I feel weakness but internally I am not weak, I am just like Lord Śiva, filled with energy. So, that energy will be again charged when this body is destroyed. It will be recharged. I'll be just like Viresh[332] again, filled with energy [laughter]. So, energy is never lost.

So, *tribhuvanāhāra tṛptāya*, this is a great satisfaction to Lord Śiva that He creates, then He protects, then He destroys. Then He creates again–fresh!

So, destruction is most . . . it is a must!

Chapter 20 (16:50)

न क्वापि गत्वा हित्वापि
न किंचिदिदमेव ये ।
भव्यं त्वद्धाम पश्यन्ति
भव्यास्तेभ्यो नमो नमः ॥१०॥

na kvāpi gatvā hitvāpi
na kiṁcididameva ye /
bhavyaṁ tvaddhāma paśyanti
bhavyāstebhyo namo namaḥ //10//

332 The son of John and Denise Hughes. [*Editor's note*]

I bow to those fortunate souls who are Your devotees, Thy devotees–those are fortunate souls–I bow to those fortunate souls who *na kvāpi gatvā*, they don't go to maintain *tapasyā* (penance) in woods, forests, [nor] in seclusion. They don't go into seclusion. *Hitvāpi*, they don't abandon any pleasure or worldly enjoyments; they don't abandon that (*hitvāpi na kiṁcit*). *Idameva ye bhavyaṁ tvaddhāma paśyanti*, and those devotees feel and experience this very world filled with the great energy of that God consciousness. I bow to those devotees.

I don't bow to those devotees who go far away and are detached from worldly action, activities. I bow to those devotees who feel and experience [the great energy of God consciousness] in this very universe, in this universe filled with torture, [which is as it seems] for the time being [laughter]. But it is not torture, it is not crises, it is not sadness, it is not pain.

ALEXIS: It is also blissful.

SWAMIJI: It is filled with bliss; filled with actual bliss! And those who perceive like this, I bow to them.

Chapter 20 (18:42)

भक्तिलक्ष्मीसमृद्धानां किमन्यदुपयाचितम् ।
एतया वा दरिद्राणां किमन्यदुपयाचितम् ॥११॥

bhaktilakṣmīsamṛddhānāṁ kimanyadupayācitam /
etayā vā daridrāṇāṁ kimanyadupayācitam //11//

Those who are glorified with the wealth of Thy devotion (bhakti lakṣmī samṛddhānām, those who are glorified with the wealth of Your devotion), kim anyat upayācitam, what do they need? What else [do] they need? They have got everything.

Etayā vā daridrāṇām. And those persons who are deprived of this wealth of Thy devotion, who are deprived of this wealth of Your devotion, kim anyat upayācitam, what do they earn?

DENISE: They have nothing.

SWAMIJI: No,

If they earn a lot, if they earn a hundred million dollars, what then? They have not earned anything. They are paupers. They are always paupers. They remain always paupers, i.e., those who are deprived of having the wealth of Your devotion.

Those who have the wealth of Your devotion, if they have nothing in their purse–only one hundredth part of one cent; *bas*, nothing, half a *nayāpaisā*[333]–they are glorified with wealth, real wealth!

Chapter 20 (20:12)

दुःकान्यपि सुखायन्ते विषमप्यमृतायते ।
मोक्षायते च संसारो यत्र मार्गः स शांकरः ॥१२॥

duḥkānyapi sukhāyante viṣamapyamṛtāyate /
mokṣāyate ca saṁsāro yatra mārgaḥ sa śāṇkaraḥ //12//

On that path, on that pathway, where *duḥkhāni api sukhāyante*, pains, various pains, are transformed into various enjoyments, *viṣamapi*, and this poison becomes nectar on which path various pains are transformed into the shape of enjoyments, and on which path this poison takes the formation of nectar, and on which path, this universe, [which] is the only cause of getting you entangled in the wheel of repeated deaths and births, liberates you . . .*

Who liberates you?

It is the universe.

ALEXIS: It shines as *mokṣa*. It is *mokṣa*.

SWAMIJI: Yes, *mokṣāyate. Mokṣa vat ācarati*; "*āya*" *pratyaya* is "*vat*" for *vat prayoga*.[334]

Mokṣāyate ca saṁsāraḥ, it becomes *mokṣa*!

What?

DENISE: The universe?

SWAMIJI: The universe . . .

DENISE: Becomes the means to *mokṣa*.

SWAMIJI: . . . which was the means to entangle you in the wheel of repeated births and deaths, and it liberates you now.

*. . . on which path it happens, that is the path of Shaivism

---

333 A discontinued denomination of Indian currency equal to one-hundredth part of a rupee. [*Editor's note*]

334 That is, the *pratyaya* or affix "*āya*" in "*mokṣāyate*" denotes *vat prayoga*, the likeness of or causal connection between the universe and *mokṣa*. [*Editor's note*]

[laughter]! *Sa śāṅkaraḥ mārgaḥ*, that is the pathway of Siva.

ALEXIS: But not dualistic Shaivism; only monistic Shaivism.

SWAMIJI: Dualistic Shaivism is not Shaivism. That is "Pāśupāt-ism"[335]; this is something else.

Now, there is a problem. It is all fine, but there is again a problem [laughter]. That is my personal problem. He explains that.

Chapter 20 (22:33)

मूले मध्येऽवसाने च नास्ति दुःखं भवज्जुषाम् ।
तथापि वयमीशान सीदामः कथमुच्यताम् ॥१३॥

mūle madhye'vasāne ca nāsti duḥkhaṁ bhavajjuṣām /
tathāpi vayamīśāna sīdāmaḥ kathamucyatām //13//

Īśāna, O glorified Lord, there is one problem in me. It is alright that this is the reality of Your being. But there are Your devotees–*bhavat juṣām*, there are devotees–for those devotees, it is announced by You: "My devotees will never enjoy pain in the beginning, or in the center, or in the end. They are always blissful! They will remain always blissful." That is Your announcement. You have announced it: "*nāsti duḥkham bhavat juṣām.*" *Bhavat juṣām*, those who are Thy devotees, for those devotees in *mūla* (in the beginning), *madhye* (in the center), *avasāne* (in the end), *nāsti duḥkham*, there is no possibility of pain. But, the problem with me is something else.

Vayamīśāna, O Lord, *vayam sīdāmaḥ*, I have only experienced pain in my whole life and I am still experiencing pain. *Katham*, what is the cause of this? Please explain that cause. *Ucyatām*, please explain that, explain it to me, the cause. I am also Your devotee but I am always tortured by pain, continuous pain, in this world. It should not happen! But it happens. Why it should happen? Tell me the cause of this (*ucyatām*).

335 Referring to the dualistic Pāśupāta Shaiva school. [*Editor's note*]

Chapter 20 (24:34)

ज्ञानयोगादिनान्येषामप्यपेक्षितुमर्हति ।
प्रकाशः स्वैरिणामेव भवान् भक्तिमतां प्रभो ॥ १४ ॥

jñānayogādinānyeṣāmapyapekṣitumarhati /
prakāśaḥ svairiṇāmeva bhavān bhaktimatāṁ prabho / / 14

Prabho, O Lord, *jñānayogādina ānyeṣām apyapekṣitum arhati prakāśaḥ*, the experiencing of Your knowledge, experiencing Your state of blissful state, for other people, for other *sādhakas* (*yogīs*), they have to adopt *jñāna*, *yoga*, practice, meditation, discipline, *yama*, *niyama*, *āsana*, *prāṇāyāma*, *pratyāhāra*, *dhāraṇā*–all of these limbs of *yoga* they have to adopt–and then they will experience the *prakāśa*[336] of Thy nature. This is a fact.

But, there is one extraordinary thing and a unique thing that happens to Your devotees. *Svairiṇām*, without adjustment of *jñāna*, *yoga*, *dhāraṇā*, *dhyāna*, *samādhi* (i.e., the limbs of *yoga*), and all of these things–they don't adjust this–and without adjusting this, they are glorified in possessing that supreme *prakāśa* of Your consciousness. This is the difference between ordinary *sādhakas* (ordinary *yogīs*) and Thy devotees.

Chapter 20 (26:08)

भक्तानां नार्तयो नाप्यस्त्याध्यानं स्वात्मनस्तव ।
तथाप्यस्ति शिवेत्येतत्किमप्येषां बहिर्मुखे ॥ १५ ॥

bhaktānāṁ nārtayo nāpyastyādhyānaṁ svātmanastava /
tathāpyasti śivetyetatkimapyeṣāṁ bahirmukhe / / 15 / /

Bhaktānām, those who are Thy devotees, they have no *ārtaya* (*ārtaya* means *duḥkha*[337]). Thy devotees have no problems! *Nāpyasti ādhyānaṁ svātmanastava*, nor there is any desire in them [to go] in search of You. They don't desire to search/seek for You.

---

336 See appendix 5 for an explanation of *prakāśa*.
337 Pain, suffering.

ALEXIS: *Adhyāna*.
SWAMIJI: *Ādhyāna* means "searching".
They don't search for You. They are existing in Your consciousness, so there is no need, there is no fun, to search for You. You are always there!
So, neither, in Your devotees, are there problems nor are there any desires to achieve You. Although this is a fact [for Thy] devotees, still, "O Lord, O Lord, O Lord", this sound leaks from their mouths automatically. *Tathāpyasti śiva ityeṣāṁ kim-apyeṣāṁ bahirmukhe*, when they are moving here and there, "Śiva", this sound leaks out from their mouths automatically!
Otherwise, there is nothing, there is no problem in them. And they are always situated in Your consciousness. But still, this sound leaks out [from their mouths].

Chapter 20 (28:05)

सर्वाभासावभासो यो विमर्शवलितोखिलम्
अहमेतदिति स्तौमि तां क्रियाशक्तिमीश ते ॥ १६ ॥

sarvābhāsāvabhāso yo vimarśavalito'khilam /
ahametaditi staumi tāṁ kriyāśaktimīśa te //16//

Īśa, O Lord Śiva, that supreme I-consciousness, which is *sarvāvabhāsa*, which [illuminates] this whole universe, which is the cause of [illuminating] this whole universe (it is *sarva avabhāsa avabhāva*, [which is] *aham*, I-consciousness, I-God consciousness), *vimarśa valito*, although this is filled with *vimarśa*[338], . . .
ALEXIS: *Sarvāvabhāsa*, it illuminates all cognitions.
SWAMIJI: All cognitions.
. . . *vimarśavalito akhilam ahametat*, this *aham*, this I-consciousness, is really, in another sense, *kriyā śakti*, the energy of action. This is Your energy of action.
Because, there are five energies of action of Lord Śiva. One energy of action is the energy of creating, creating act. The second action is the protecting energy, the protecting act. The third energy is the act of destroying this whole universe. The fourth is

338 Self-awareness. See appendix 5 for an explanation of *vimarśa*.

concealing [His nature in] this universe. The fifth is revealing His own nature, when He reveals His own nature. [Utpaladeva] here touches that fifth energy. This *kriyā śakti* is *anugraha śakti*.[339] That is *ahaṁ*.

ALEXIS: So, this whole universe is grace from that point of view; act of grace, revelation.

SWAMIJI: Yes, act of grace. Because, in creation, He does not create this universe for [the sake of] creating; He creates this universe to bestow grace on it. He does not protect this universe just to protect it; He protects this universe just to reveal His nature to it. He destroys this universe just to reveal His nature to this. He conceals this universe just to reveal His nature to it. And, in the end, He reveals His nature. So, you must see in the commentary of Abhinavagupta of *Parātriṁśikā* [*Vivaraṇa*].

GANJOO: First line.

SWAMIJI: First line.[340] Although He is functioning the five acts, in the functioning of the five acts, He functions only the fifth act! It is *anugraha* that He does. He creates, He destroys, He punishes, etc., just to bestow grace on [someone]. He punishes . . . He does not punish for the [sake of] punishment. He punishes . . .

DENISE: For bestowing grace in the end.

SWAMIJI: Yes.

ALEXIS: But from the highest point of view, there is no recipi-

---

339 As Swamiji will explain, all five acts are acts of grace (*anugraha*). [*Editor's note*]

340 "Śiva conducts in the cycle of creation, in protection, in destruction, in concealing and in revealing. In all these five energies, the conducting process is handled by Śiva only, not Śakti. Śakti only pushes it out again, just for another trial. She gives another trial again to a human being, or anybody who is not capable of getting entrance in God consciousness in the cycle of the aspect of *anugraha* (grace), revealing, the fifth aspect.

"So, this creation is meant for *anugraha*, protection is meant for *anugraha*, destruction is meant for *anugraha*, and concealing is also meant for *anugraha*. It is meant for revealing your own nature. And you get a trial, again and again; again and again you get a trial. If you don't succeed once, you'll succeed next. If you don't succeed next, then the third time you'll succeed. This way we go in this world." *Parātriśikā Vivaraṇa* (USF archives).

ent of grace. It is only the expression of His own nature to Himself.

SWAMIJI: Yes, yes.

ALEXIS: *Svātmani svātmanaḥ.*

SWAMIJI: Yes, *svātmani vikṣepa vaisargiki sthitiḥ.*[341]

Chapter 20 (31:19)

वर्तन्ते जन्तवोऽशेषा अपि ब्रह्मेन्द्रविष्णवः
ग्रसमानास्ततो वन्दे देव विश्वं भवन्मयम् ॥१७॥

vartante jantavo'śeṣā api brahmendraviṣṇavaḥ /
grasamānāstato vande deva viśvaṁ bhavanmayam //17 [342]

In fact, this whole universe has not come out from Brahma. It is not like Brahma. Because, if it were like Brahma, then this whole universe ought to have [been] mixed, ought to have been entangled, only in sexual intercourse, only in sexual intercourses from one o'clock in the morning up to one o'clock in the [following] morning. Only the adoption of sex [would take place] if it was like Brahmā. But it's not like that.[343]

If it was like Viṣṇu, then it would be like that.[344]

It is like Śiva; this universe is like Śiva. Śiva is just eating. Always you are eating–sometimes drink, sometimes for taste, sometimes butter, sometimes tea, sometimes food, sometimes everything–[you are] always eating! So, *aśeṣā api brahmendra viṣṇavaḥ*, Brahmā, Indra, and Viṣṇu, all of these *devās* and all of those individual beings are just bent upon eating. So, this eating,

341 "The state of *visarga*, i.e., the creation, is not created anywhere. It is created from your own Self . . . and the Self is not created with any other element. The Self is created in the Self and from the Self. This is the reality of *visarga*, creation. Creation is from the Self, in the Self, and of the Self." *Tantrāloka*, 3.141 (USF archives).

342 In the first line, Swamiji corrected "*apa*", which appears in the text he was using, to read "*api*". [*Editor's note*]

343 That is, creation [viz., sex], which is the function of Brahmā, is not the only universal operation. [*Editor's note*]

344 Preservation, which is the function of Viṣṇu, is not the only universal operation. [*Editor's note*]

this is the sign of Lord Siva, i.e., eating, destroying, taking in.

ALEXIS: Absorbing.

SWAMIJI: Absorbing. So, the act of absorption takes place in this whole universe, day and night.

ALEXIS: In all the senses, all the time.

SWAMIJI: In all of the senses.

DENISE: The eyes are eating.

SWAMIJI: Yes.

Grasamānāstato vande deva viśvaṁ bhavanmayam. So, O Lord, it is why I bow to this whole universe, which is just one with You.

Birds are [always] finding [something] out, taking, drinking, etc.

ALEXIS: It's always flowing to that point.

SWAMIJI: Always flowing to that.

See Viresh, and whatever you give to him, he only eats [laughter]. This is the sign of Lord Śiva from the very start of birth. He has no choice [i.e., desire] for sex, but for eating, he has [laughter].

So, this is the sign of Lord Śiva![345]

Chapter 20 (34:28)

सतोविनाशसम्बन्धान्मत्परं निखिलं मृषा
एवमेवोद्यते नाथ त्वया संहारलीलया ॥ १८ ॥

satovināśasambandhānmatparaṁ nikhilaṁ mṛṣā /
evamevodyate nātha tvayā saṁhāralīlayā //18//

O my Master, when You destroy this whole universe, at the time of destroying this whole universe, You don't actually destroy this universe. You teach something to us. You give lectures there at that moment. This teaching comes out from Your being.

What?

Sato vināśa sambandhāt. Whatever is created will be destroyed in the end; whatever is created will be destroyed. This is [what] You teach [us] at the time, at the moment, when You

345 The all-consuming nature of Lord Śiva is also described in the *Śatapatha Brāhmaṇa*. [*Editor's note*]

destroy this whole universe. You teach us *sato vināśa*, whatever is existing, whatever has existed, will be destroyed.

So, *matparaṁ nikhilaṁ mṛṣā*, so, it is all a dream, except to Me. I only am the only [One who is] detached from this position because I am not born and I won't die. Whatever is born will die. *Evamevodyate nātha*, this is what You teach, *saṁhāra līlaya*, by the play of this destruction.

ALEXIS: But the mirror remains.

SWAMIJI: The mirror remains, yes.

Chapter 20 (36:05)

ध्यातमात्रमुपतिष्ठत एव
त्वद्वपुर्वरद भक्तिधनानाम्
अप्यचिन्त्यमखिलाद्भुतचिन्ता-
कर्तृतां प्रति च ते विजयन्ते ॥१९॥

dhyātamātramupatiṣṭhata eva
tvadvapurvarada bhaktidhanānām /
apyacintyamakhilādbhutacintā-
kartṛtāṁ prati ca te vijayante //19//

There are two classes of Your devotees. One class of Your devotees are Shaivite devotees. Shaivite devotees are real devotees. Vedāntic devotees, Vaiṣṇavite devotees, they are not real devotees of Thee. [Nevertheless], they are Your devotees because [one] who is devoted to Viṣṇu is devoted to Lord Śiva [and one] who is devoted to Brahmā is devoted to Lord Śiva because Lord Śiva is the glory existing in Brahmā and Lord Śiva is the glory existing in Viṣṇu. So, they have not personal glory there. Viṣṇu has not personal glory nor Brahmā has personal glory. Brahmā's glory has come out, it is borrowed, from Lord Śiva. Viṣṇu's glory is borrowed from Lord Śiva's glory.

ALEXIS: But the devotees contract That glory. They conceive Viṣṇu as *parāprakṛti* or . . .

SWAMIJI: *Parāprakṛti*, yes.

ALEXIS: . . . something low like that.

SWAMIJI: But that is the wrong way of experiencing.

Dhyāta mātram upatiṣṭhata eva tvat vapurvarada bhakti dhanānām. Varada, O bestower of boons (*varada* means "O bestower of boons")–You bestow boons to Your devotees, always–*varada*, O bestower of boons, O Lord Śiva, *dhyāta mātram upatiṣṭhata eva tvat vapur bhaktidhanānām*, those who possess the wealth of Thy devotion, those devotees who possess the wealth of Your devotion, for them, Your form, Your *svarūpa*, shines, not by [utilizing] the means of *yoga* (the *yoga* system), or *kriyā yoga*, or *jñāna yoga*, or *bhakti yoga*, or anything; *dhyāta mātram upatiṣṭhata*, they just begin to think of You and they get entry in Your God consciousness.

ALEXIS: Awareness is the means.

SWAMIJI: Awareness.

Dhyāta mātrameva upatiṣṭhata, at the time of meditating, He is there, He is appearing.

ALEXIS: No sooner they meditate and they are established.

SWAMIJI: No successive progress. This is for those devotees of Thee who are Shaivite devotees.

And for Vaiṣṇavite devotees and Brahma devotees, *acintyamapi*, if they devote their time, the whole period of their lives, in Thy meditation, still they cannot perceive You.

Akhila adbhuta cintā kartṛtāṁ prati te. So, it is why Shaivite devotees are glorified by the adoption of *adbhutacintā kartṛtā*; their thinking is divine, their action is divine, everything is divine to them.

Chapter 20 (39:32

तावकभक्तिरसासव-
सेकादिव सुखितमर्ममण्डलस्फुरितैः
नृत्यति वीरजनो निशि
वेतालकुलैः कृतोत्साहः ॥२०॥

tāvakabhaktirasāsava-
sekādiva sukhitamarmamaṇḍalasphuritaiḥ /
nṛtyati vīrajano niśi
vetālakulaiḥ kṛtotsāhaḥ //20//

Niśi means "in this universe, in the darkness of this universe". This is *māyā*.

[In this universe], *vīrajana*, there are *vīras* (heroes).

Because, in darkness, nobody goes. You will have to hold a torch with you, otherwise you can't walk. And in a graveyard, you will never walk without a torch. But there are *vīrajana*; *vīrajana* means those devotees, that Shaivite devotee, he is called a hero (*vīrajana*). [Among] *sādhus*[346], there are *aghorīs*. They reside in graveyards always, i.e., *aghora panthis*. Like that, like *aghora panthis*, this Shaivite *yogi* is. He also resides in graveyards. He not only resides, he dances in graveyards.

What is the graveyard?

The graveyard is your body. The graveyard is your body! Your own body is a graveyard because in a graveyard you will find bones, flesh, blood, pus, all of that substance, it is there. So, this is a graveyard, this body is a graveyard. In this graveyard, that hero, that Shaivite hero, dances in this graveyard.

He does not dance alone in this graveyard of the body. *Vīrajana*, this hero, dances in this graveyard, *niśi*, during the night, *vetāla kulaiḥ kṛtotsāhaḥ*, and he is already *utsāha* (*utsāha* means "encouraged"), he is encouraged by *vetālas* (*vetālas* means "ghosts").

There are so many ghosts in graveyards [that are] seen during the night and those ghosts are the eyes (these two eyes, these are two ghosts), the nostrils are two ghosts, the mouth is one ghost, [the ears are] two ghosts, and the skin [is a] ghost, and this sexual organ [is a] ghost, and the organ of that excretion, that is also a ghost. All of these ghosts, the class of ghosts, are there in this graveyard. And, with these ghosts, these ghosts are encouraging him, they encourage him.

ALEXIS: *Marmamaṇḍala sphuritaiḥ vetāla kulaiḥ.*

SWAMIJI: That is *maṇḍala*, *marma maṇḍala*. *Marma maṇḍala* is *maṇḍala*.[347]

ALEXIS: And they are blissfully vibrating.

SWAMIJI: Yes. Blissfully vibrated by what? They drink alcohol. And what is that alcohol? *Tāvaka bhakti rasāsava*, the

346 Spiritual aspirants.

347 *Marman*: mortal spot, vulnerable point, any open or exposed or weak or sensitive part of the body.

alcohol of Thy devotion. Those *yogīs* who are heroes, they drink the alcohol of Thy devotion and they dance in this graveyard.

ALEXIS: Like *vīravrata.*

SWAMIJI: Like *vīravrata*, encouraged by those *vetālas*, encouraged by those ghosts, nine ghosts.[348]

Chapter 20 (43:26)

आरब्धा भवदभिनुतिर्-
अमुना येनाङ्गकेन मम शम्भो
तेनापर्यन्तमिमं कालं
दृढमखिलमेव भविषीष्ट ॥२१

ārabdhā bhavadabhinutir-
amunā yenāṅgakena mama śambho /
tenārpayantamimaṁ kālaṁ
dṛḍhamakhilameva bhaviṣīṣṭa //21//

In the end, there is one request to You. I have placed this request before You, O Lord. This is the request:

Arabdha bhavad abhinutir amunā yenāṅgakena mama śambho. I have composed this, I have composed these glorious songs of Thee, this *Śivastotrāvalī.* I have composed this. With what purpose I have composed this? That is not the thing to be known. I have composed this, this *stotra*. With what ambition? Which ambition was there in me to compose it?

And by that ambition, with that ambition, *arpayantam imaṁ kālaṁ dṛḍhamakhilam*, I [have] only one request for You that You should bestow [upon] me this sensation that I would always sing Your glory for my whole lifetime, remaining lifetime. I would like to sing Your glory. That is all. That is my request.

|| Here ends Śivastotrāvalī ||

Jai Guru Dev

348 That is, the nine openings (*randras*) of the body.

Appendix

1. ***Utpaladeva***

Śivastotrāvalī of Utpaladevācaryā with the Sanskrit commentary of Kṣemarāja, edited with Hindi commentary by Rājānaka Lakṣmaṇa (Swami Lakshmanjoo), (Chowkhamba Sanskrit Series 15. Varanasi, 1964).

2. ***Upāyas***

The meaning of the Sanskrit word "*upāya*" is "means". The word "*upāya*" in Kashmir Śaivism is used to indicate the means to enter into Universal God Consciousness from individual consciousness. Our Śaivism proclaims that there are three means for entering into Universal God Consciousness: *śāmbhavopāya* (the supreme means), *śāktopāya* (the medium means), and *āṇavopāya* (the inferior means).

Āṇavopāya is the means found in the world of duality and is known as *bhedopāya*. The means which exists in the world of mono-duality, in the world where duality and nonduality exist together, is *śāktopāya* and is called *bhedābhedopāya*. That means which exists in the world of pure monism (*abheda*) is *śāmbhavopāya* and is called *abhedopāya*.

Śāmbhavopāya is also called *icchopāya*, as it is the means which exists in *icchā śakti*. The means which exists in *jñāna śakti* is *śāktopāya* and is called *jñānopāya*. *Āṇavopāya* is called *kriyopāya* because it is the means which is found in *kriyā śakti*.

Kashmir Shaivism–The Secret Supreme, 5.33-40.

[Lord Śiva's] energies are the means; [His] energies have become the *upāyas*. The energy of His will is explained as *śāmbhavopāya*, the energy of knowledge is *śāktopāya*, and the energy of action is *āṇavopāya*. The energy of action is breathing exercises, reciting *mantras*, reciting *ślokas* (hymns), and *pūjā* (worship). All these are in action, in the world of action. So, all these things are included in *āṇavopāya*. And they will carry you to the state of Lord Śiva. And [the energy of] knowledge, this is *śāktopāya*.

Perceiving, middle-ing, centering, all these are in the world of *śāktopāya*. They will also carry you to the state of Lord Śiva. And [the energy of] will is the first start of each and every action. That is *śāmbhavopāya*. That will carry you to Śiva's state.

Swami Lakshman Joo, *Tantrāloka* 1:70, USF archive.

The difference between *āṇavopāya*, *śāktopāya*, and *śāmbhavopāya* is this: In *āṇavopāya*, the strength of your awareness is such that you have to take the support of everything as an aid to maintain and strengthen your awareness. In *śāktopāya*, your awareness is strengthened to the extent that only one point is needed as a support for your concentration and that point is the center. In *śāmbhavopya*, the strength of your awareness is such that no support is needed. You are already residing in the meant (*upeya*). There is nowhere to go, just reside at your own point. The rest is automatic.

It is important to realize that though there are different *upāyas*, all lead you to the state of one transcendental consciousness. The difference in these *upāyas* is that *āṇavopāya* will carry you in a long way, *śāktopāya* in a shorter way, and *śāmbhavopāya* in the shortest way. Although the ways are different, the point to be achieved is one.

Kashmir Shaivism–The Secret Supreme, 5.33-40.

3. ***Turya* and *Turyātītā***

When, by the grace of a master, this subjective body enters into subjective consciousness with full awareness, and maintaining unbroken awareness becomes fully illumined in its own Self, this is called the fourth state, *turya*.

From the Trika Shaivite point of view, predominance is given to the three energies of Śiva: *parā śakti*, the supreme energy; *parāparā śakti*, medium energy; and *aparā śakti*, inferior energy. The kingdom of *aparā śakti*, the lowest energy, is found in wakefulness and dreaming. The kingdom of *parāparā śakti*, the medium energy, is established in the state of sound sleep. And lastly, the kingdom of *parā śakti*, the supreme energy, is found in the state of *turya*.

The state of *turya* is said to be the penetration of all energies simultaneously, not in succession. All of the energies are residing there but are not in manifestation. They are all together without distinction. *Turya* is called "*savyāpārā*" because all of the energies get their power to function in that state. At the same time, this state is known as "*anāmayā*" because it remains unagitated by all of these energies.

Three names are attributed to this state–by worldly people, by *yogins*, and by illuminated humans (*jñānīs*). Worldly people call it "*turya*", which means "the fourth". They use this name because they have no descriptive name for this state. They are unaware of this state and, not having experienced it, simply call it "the fourth state". *Yogins* have attributed the name "*rūpātītā*" to this condition because this state has surpassed the touch of one's self and is the establishment of one's Self. The touch of one's self was found in sound sleep, however, the establishment of one's Self takes place in *turya*. For illuminated humans, *jñānīs*, the entire universal existence is found in this state of *turya*, collectively, as undifferentiated, in the state of totality. There is no succession here. *Jñānīs,* therefore, call this state "*pracaya*", the undifferentiated totality of universal existence.

Turyātītā is that state which is the absolute fullness of Self. It is filled with all-consciousness and bliss. It is really the last and the supreme state of the Self. You not only find this state of *turyātītā* in *samādhi*, you also find it in each and every activity of the world. In this state, there is no possibility for the practice of *yoga*. If you can practice *yoga*, then you are not in *turyātītā*. In practicing *yoga*, there is the intention of going somewhere. Here, there is nowhere to go, nothing to achieve. As concentration does not exist here, the existence of the helping hand of *yoga* is not possible.

There are only two names actually attributed to this state of *turyātītā*–one given by worldly people and one by *jñānīs*. Worldly people, because they know nothing about the state, call it "*turyātītā*", which means "that state which is beyond the fourth". *Jñānīs*, on the other hand, also have a name for it. They call it "*mahāpracaya*", which means "the unlimited and unexplainable supreme totality". *Yogins* do not actually attribute any name to this state because they have no knowledge of it. It is completely outside of their experience. *Yogins* have though, through the use of their imagination and guesswork, imagined one name which might be apropriate for this state: "*satatoditam*", which means

"that state which has no pause, no break". It is a breakless and unitary state. In *samādhi*, It is there. When *samādhi* is absent, It is there. In the worldly state, It is there. In the dreaming state, It is there. And in the state of deep sleep, It is there. In each and every state of the individual subjective body, It is there.
Kashmir Shaivism–The Secret Supreme, 11.72-84

The difference between *turya* and *turyātītā* is, in *turya*, you find in *samādhi* that this whole universe is existing there in the seed form, germ. The strength, the energy, of universal existence is existing there . . . but here, he has [yet] to come out [into activity]. In *turyātītā*, he comes out in action and feels universal consciousness. This is the difference between *turya* and *turyātītā*.
Tantrāloka (USF archives) 10.288.

4. ***Kuṇḍalinī***

Kuṇḍalinī śakti is the revealing and the concealing energy of Lord Śiva. On the one hand, it is the revealing energy and on the other hand, it is the concealing energy. It reveals and it conceals. This *kuṇḍalinī śakti* is not different from the existence of Lord Śiva, just as the energy of light and the energy of heat are not separate from the fire itself. *Kuṇḍalinī*, therefore, in the true sense, is the existence of Śiva. It is the life and glory of Śiva. It is Śiva Himself.

In our Trika Shaivism, *kuṇḍalinī*, which is that internal serpent power existing in the shape of a coil, is divided in three ways.

a) *Parā kuṇḍalinī–kuṇḍalinī* functioned by Lord Śiva.
b) *Cit kuṇḍalinī–kuṇḍalinī* functioned in consciousness.
c) *Prāṇa kuṇḍalinī–kuṇḍalinī* functioned in breath.

The supreme *kuṇḍalinī* is called *parā kuṇḍalinī*. This *kuṇḍalinī* is not known or experienced by *yogins*. It is so vast and universal that the body cannot exist in its presence. It is only experienced at the time of death. It is the heart of Śiva. This whole universe is created by *parā kuṇḍalinī*, exists in *parā kuṇḍalinī*, gets its life from *parā kuṇḍalinī*, and is consumed in *parā kuṇḍalinī*. When this *kuṇḍalinī* creates the universe, Śiva conceals His real nature and is thrown into the universe. When the universe is created, He becomes the universe. There is no Śiva left which is separate from the universe.* This is His creative energy. And when *kuṇḍalinī* destroys the universe, Śiva's nature is revealed. So, the creative energy for the universe is the destructive energy for Śiva, i.e., it is the revealing energy for the universe and the concealing energy for Lord Śiva. And the destructive energy for the universe is the creative energy for Śiva, i.e., it is the concealing energy for the universe and the revealing energy for Lord Śiva.

Parā kuṇḍalinī is the supreme *visarga* of Śiva. As you know from studying the theory of *mātṛkācakra*, *visarga* (:) comprises two points. These points are said to be Śiva and Śakti. In the real sense, however, these points are not Śiva and Śakti, they are the revealing point and the concealing point.

Cit kuṇḍalinī is experienced by *yogins* by means of concentrating on the center between any two breaths, thoughts, or actions; between the destruction and creation of any two things. The happiness and bliss that you experience here [in *cit kuṇḍalinī*] cannot be described. It is ecstasy beyond ecstasy, just like sexual bliss. In comparing sexual happiness with the happiness experienced in *cit kuṇḍalinī*, however, you will find that sexual happiness is one millionth part of the happiness experienced in *cit kuṇḍalinī*. In addition, simultaneously with the experience of ecstasy, you also realize the reality of Self. You recognize your real nature and you know, "I am only bliss (*ānanda*) and consciousness (*cit*)." In the actual rise of *cit kuṇḍalinī*, you will only get a glimpse of it and then come out. The full rise of *cit kuṇḍalinī* takes place only by the grace of your master and by the grace of your own strength of awareness.

Prāṇa kuṇḍalinī also comes about through the process of centering. *Prāṇa kuṇḍalinī*, however, is only experienced by those *yogins* who, along with their attachment to spirituality, also have attachments to worldly pleasures. If your desire and attachment is only for spirituality, then *cit kuṇḍalinī* takes place. Whether you experience the rise of *kuṇḍalinī* as *cit kuṇḍalinī* or as *prāṇa kuṇḍalinī* depends on your attachments. If you have attachment for spirituality and also for worldly pleasures, then the rise of *kuṇḍalinī* takes place in the form of *prāṇa kuṇḍalinī*. If you do not have attachments for worldly pleasures and are only attached to spirituality, then the rise of *kuṇḍalinī* takes place in the form of *cit kuṇḍalinī*. There is nothing you can do to determine how the rise of *kuṇḍalinī* will take place. It rises in its own way, depending on your attachments.

Kashmir Shaivism–The Secret Supreme, 17.117-121.

*Unlike a pantheism, however, the pan-entheistic philosophy of Kashmir Shaivism declares that Lord Śiva simultaneously occupies the position of transcendence and immanence. [*Editor's note*]

5. ***Prakāśa* and *Vimarśa***

In the world of Shaivite philosophy, Lord Śiva is seen as being filled with light. But more than this, Lord Śiva is the embodiment of light and this light is different than the light of the sun, of the moon, or of fire.

It is light (*prakāśa*) with consciousness (*vimarśa*), and this light with consciousness is the nature of that supreme consciousness, Lord Śiva.

What is consciousness? The light of consciousness is not only pure consciousness. It is filled with the understanding that, "I am the creator, I am the protector, and I am the destroyer of everything". Just to know that, "I am the creator, I am the protector, and I am the destroyer", is consciousness. If consciousness was not attached to the light of consciousness, we would have to admit that the light of the sun or the light of the moon or the light of a fire is also Lord Śiva. But this is not the case.

The light of consciousness (*vimarśa*) is given various names. It is called *cit-caitanya*, which means the strength of consciousness; *parā vāk*, the supreme word; *svātantrya*, perfect independence; *aiśvarya*, the predominant glory of supreme Śiva; *kartṛtva*, the power of acting; *sphurattā*, the power of existing; *sāra*, the complete essence of everything; *hṛdaya*, the universal heart; and *spanda*, universal movement. All these are names in the Tantras, which are attributed to this consciousness.

This I-consciousness, which is the reality of Lord Śiva, is a natural (*akṛtrima*), not a contrived, "I". It is not adjusted I-consciousness. Limited human beings have adjusted I-consciousness. Lord Śiva has natural or pure I-consciousness. There is a difference between adjusted consciousness and natural consciousness. Adjusted or artificial consciousness exists when this I-consciousness is attributed to your body, to your mind, to your intellect, and to your ego. Natural consciousness is that consciousness that is attributed to the reality of the Self, which is all-consciousness.

This universe, which is created in His consciousness, is dependent on That consciousness. It is always dependent on That consciousness. It cannot move outside of That consciousness. It exists only when it is residing in His consciousness. This is the way the creation of His universe takes place.

Self Realization in Kashmir Shaivism, 3.56-57.

There are two positions of Śiva. One is *prakāśa* and another is *vimarśa*. . . . When He feels this blissful state as His own nature, that is *prakāśa*. When He feels, "That blissful state is My glory", that is *vimarśa*. When He feels that, "This blissful state is My being", that is Śiva. When He believes that, "This is My glory", that is *śakti*. The cycle of glory is residing in *śakti* and the cycle of *prakāśa* is residing in Śiva. Both are in one. That is indicated by *visarga* in Śiva, [the vowel] '*aḥ*' or ':'. So, *vimarśa śakti* is supreme *parā parameśvarī* attributed to *svātantrya śakti*. It is the intensity of the independence, of the *svātantrya*, of Bhairava.

Parātriśikā Vivaraṇa, USF archives.

6. **Kula system**

The Kula system teaches you how you can live in *caitanya* (universal consciousness), the real nature of yourself, in both the ascending and the descending act. While you rise from the lowest to the highest state, you realize your nature, and while you descend from the highest to the lowest state, you also realize your nature. In the Kula system, there is no break in the realization of your own nature either in the highest or in the lowest circle. This system, therefore, teaches you how you can live in totality. In fact, the word "*kula*" means "totality".

In the practice of the Kula system, you have to realize the totality of the universe in one particle. Take one particle of anything which exists in this world. In that one particle is to be realized the totality of the whole universe. The totality of energy is found in one particle. Everything is full of one thing and one thing is full of all things. . . . the Kula system teaches you how you can rise from the lowest degree to the highest degree, and all the while experience the nature of your Self on the same level and state. Śiva, which is realized in *pṛthvī tattva* (earth element), is the same level, the same reality of Siva which is realized in *śiva tattva*. Here, there is complete realization in every act of the world.

Kashmir Shaivism–The Secret Supreme, 19.131-132.

7. **Right and wrong**

mahābodha-samāveśāt-puṇyapāpāsaṁbandhaḥ //12//

When the entry in supreme God consciousness takes place, *mahābodha samāveśāt*, by entering in supreme God consciousness, *puṇyapāpa asaṁbandha*, you feel nothing is right and nothing is wrong.

[But] at the stage when you are unaware of God consciousness [and] you feel nothing is right, nothing is wrong–that is the reality [that you may experience] when you are in just an ignorant state of being–you feel that good and bad is the same, that feeling is incorrect. By that feeling, you will fall. This feeling must come through that God consciousness, then that feeling is quite right.

Vātūlanātha Sūtras of Anantaśaktipāda, translation and commentary by Swami Lakshmanjoo, original audio recordings, USF archives, Los Angeles, 1979.

To the question that, "There are some texts, for instance, in the Kula system, that advocate the taking of forbidden substances as a part of spiritual practice because they give rise to bliss (*ānanda*)", Swamiji gave the following answer:

"They give rise to *ānanda* only when there is the possibility of the rise of *kuṇḍalinī* there. When, during your sexual act, the rise of *kuṇḍalinī* takes place, then that *vīrya* (vital energy) is not lost. Although [semen] has gone in the other organ, that strength is not lost. That strength is again maintained by the rise of *kuṇḍalinī* at that moment."

Tantraloka, 3.230-231 (USF archive).

8. ***Parameṣṭhi guru***

Utpaladeva was Kṣemarāja's *parameṣṭhi guru*, his great grand-master. Utpaladeva's disciple, Lakṣmanagupta, was Abhinavagupta's master in the Pratyabhijñā system and Abhinavagupta, in turn, was Kṣemarāja's master.

Kashmir Shaivism–The Secret Supreme, 19.131.

9. ***Nirvikalpa***

In reality, everything, whatever exists, it is in the *nirvikalpa* state [where] you can't define anything . . . you can define only in the *vikalpa* state, in the cycle of *vikalpa*, e.g., when you say, "This is a specks cover". But it is not a specks cover in the real sense, in the state of God consciousness. It is just *nirvikalpa*. You can't say what it is, but it is! *Saṁketādi smaraṇam*, when you understand, "This is mine", "O, this was in my house and this is mine", this memory takes place in the *vikalpa* state, not the *nirvikalpa* state. And that *vikalpa* state cannot exist without *anubhavam*, the *nirvikalpa* state.

Nirvikalpa is the cause of all *vikalpas*; the undifferentiated state is the cause of all *vikalpas*. . . . It is not something foreign [to *vikalpas*]. It is their life. It is the life of all *vikalpas*.

Parātrīśikā Vivaraṇa (USF archives).

10. ***Parā visarga***

In the kingdom of *mātṛkācakra*, there exists three kinds of *visargas*, three kinds of flow. These three *visargas* are known as *śāmbhava visarga*, *śākta visarga*, and *āṇava visarga*.

The first *visarga* exists at the stage of *ānanda śakti*, and is represented by the letter '*ā*'. This *visarga* is known as *śāmbhava visarga*. The mode of this *visarga* is said to be *cittapralaya*. The word "*cittapralaya*" indicates that state where your mind does not function, where only thoughtlessness exists. Here, the mind does not work at all. This is the thoughtless flow. This *śāmbhava visarga* is also known as *parā visarga*, the supreme *visarga*. This supreme *visarga* is concerned with Śiva.

The second *visarga* is known as *śākta visarga*. It is also known as *parāparā visarga*, the highest-cum-lowest or medium *visarga*. This *visarga* is represented by the last letter of the vowels, the letter '*aḥ*', which in grammar is also designated as *visarga*. The mode of this *visarga* is called *cittasaṁbodhah*. *Cittasaṁbodha* indicates that state where awareness is maintained in one-pointedness.

The third and last *visarga* is called *āṇava visarga*. It is also known as *aparā visarga*, the lower or inferior *visarga*. It is the

visarga of the individual (*nara*). This *visarga* is attributed to the letter '*ha*', the last letter of the Sanskrit alphabet. The mode of this *visarga* is called *cittaviśrānti*. The word "*cittaviśrānti*" indicates that state where the mind rests in concentration, where the mind takes a permanent seat in concentration.
Kashmir Shaivism–The Secret Supreme, 3.26-27.

11. ***Svātantrya***
This *svatantratā*, this being independent, the state of independence, is attributed only to Lord Śiva.
Swami Lakshman Joo, *Tantrāloka* 9:9a, audio commentary, USF archive.

Svātantrya śakti is the germ of all His five energies. He has got five energies: *cit śakti* (energy of consciousness), *ānanda śakti* (energy of bliss), [*icchā śakti*], energy of will, [*jñāna śakti*], energy of knowledge, and [*kriyā śakti*], energy of action. All these five energies of God consciousness are produced by His *svātantrya śakti* of freedom, His free power.
Swami Lakshman Joo, *Special Verses on Practice*, USF archive.

That essence of *svātantrya* is *anavacchinna* (beyond limitation), all-round beyond limitation. There is no such limit found in that state. *Vicchinna camatkāra maya viśrāntyā*, and this limited state of being is also found there. [Lord Śiva] is unlimited, but the limited cycle of God consciousness is also found there. So It is both limited and unlimited. That being who is limited only, he is not true. That being who is unlimited only, he is not true. Why? Because he is limited. The being who is unlimited is not true because he is unlimited only [and] not limited. That fullness of God consciousness is found [in one] who is limited and at the same time unlimited also. That is the fullness of God consciousness. The fullness of God consciousness is where nothing is excluded. Whatever is excluded, it is also one with That. That is fullness of God consciousness.
Swami Lakshman Joo, *Parātrīśikā Vivaraṇa*, audio commentary, USF archive.

Lord Śiva creates this external universe for the sake of realizing His own nature. That is why this external universe is called "*śakti*", because it is the means to realize one's own nature. Therefore, in order to recognize His nature, He must first become ignorant of His nature. Only then can He recognize it.

Why should He want to recognize His nature in the first place? It is because of His freedom, His *svātantrya* (independence). This is the play of the universe. This universe was created solely for the fun and joy of this realization. It happens that when His fullness overflows, He wants to remain incomplete. He wants to appear as being incomplete just so He can achieve completion. This is the play of His *svātantrya*–to depart from His own nature in order to enjoy it again. It is this *svātantrya* that has created this whole universe. This is the play of Śiva's *svātantrya*.

This kind of action cannot be accomplished by any power in this universe other than Lord Śiva. Only Lord Śiva can do this. Only Lord Śiva, by His own *svātantrya*, can totally ignore and mask His own nature. This is His *svātantrya*, His glory, His intelligence. Intelligence does not mean that in this super-drama called creation you will only play the part of a lady or a man. With this kind of intelligence, you will also play the part of rocks, of trees, of all things. This kind of intelligence is found only in the state of Lord Śiva and nowhere else.

Self Realization in Kashmir Shaivism–Fifteen Verses of Wisdom, chapter 1, Verses 5, 6 and 7, pp.23-26.

12. The *mantra* "*sauḥ*"

To begin with, you must understand that in the field of *mantras*, in the field of sacred words, the *mantra* that digests these thirty-six elements in its body is "*sauḥ*". It is the supreme *mantra*. It is not a creative *mantra*, it is a destructive *mantra*. Why? Because it winds up the complete cycle of the thirty-six elements. This *mantra* shows you the trick of how to wind up . . . these thirty-six elements and, in the end, rest in the element of Śiva. So it is not expansion, it is winding up. And this winding up is not actually destruction, it is contraction, just as a giant tree is contracted in a seed.

In this way, the entire universe consisting of thirty-six elements resides in the *mantra* "*sauḥ*". This *mantra* is called "the heart*mantra*" because it is the essence of all *mantras*. How is this so? In the same way that a clay bowl or a clay plate are only produced by changing earthen clay, the essence of this bowl or plate continues to be clay. Or, just as ice and vapor, which are produced by watery substances, are actually water.

So, in the realm of the supreme *mantra* "*sauḥ*", if you go into the depth of the thirty-one elements from *pṛthivī* (earth) to *māyā*, you will find that existence (*sat*) is the reality of these elements. All these elements are all existing externally.

After this, you must ascertain that, residing in the second part of the *mantra* "*sauḥ*" is the letter '*au*', which is superior to '*sa*', and which contains the elements *śuddhavidyā*, *īśvara*, and *sadāśiva*. These three elements are the essence of knowledge (*jñāna*) and action (*kriyā*). They are the embodiment of *śakti*.

Greater than the letter '*au*', and residing in the third part of the *mantra* "*sauḥ*", is the letter '*aḥ*', a creative energy which is twofold. This twofold creative energy is comprised of a higher creative energy and a lower creative energy. The higher creative energy is of Śiva and the lower creative energy is of Śakti. This two-part creative energy, above and below, are the two points of the Sanskrit *visarga* (:).

The first part of the *mantra* "*sauḥ*", '*sa*', is in the cycle of *nara*, the second part of the *mantra* "*sauḥ*", '*au*', is in the cycle of *śakti*, and the third part of the *mantra* "*sauḥ*", '*aḥ*', combining both of the creative energies, is in the cycle of Śiva. So, the Trika system of Kashmir Shaivism is the combination of *nara*, Śakti, and Śiva.

In this way, this seed *mantra* "*sauḥ*" is the supreme *mantra*. It is above all other *mantras* including the blessed *mantras* "*ahaṁ*", "*oṁ*", and "*so'ham*". This supreme *mantra*, which is both universal (*viśvamaya*) and transcendent (*viśvottīrṇa*), is the essence of Trika.

Self Realization in Kashmir Shaivism, 3.67-69.

13. ***Krama mudrā***

In the *Krama Sūtra*, it says that a *yogi* first enters *krama mudrā* in the introverted state. Then, owing to the intensity of *krama mudrā*, he emerges from the introverted state and enters into the outer, external cycle of consciousness.

First, from outside, he goes inside, and then from inside he goes outside. This movement of going in and coming out and then again going in and coming out takes place by the force of the absorption (*samāveśa*) of *krama mudrā*, not by the effort of the *yogi*.

Where the *yogi* travels from outside to inside and then from inside to outside, just to come to the understanding that outside and inside are not different aspects but one, that is *krama mudrā*.

There is one more thing for you to understand. The one who experiences this state of the absorption (*samāveśa*) of *krama mudrā* experiences this whole universe melting into nothingness in the great sky of God Consciousness (*cid-gagana*). Although he opens his eyes and perceives that everything is melting into that state, yet, when he strives to come out of that state, it becomes very difficult for him. As it is very difficult for us to enter into that state, in the same way, it is very difficult for that *yogi* to come out of it.

But why does he want to come out? He wants to come out for the fun of it, but he cannot come out. The intensity of God Consciousness does not let him come out. Yet he struggles to come out. Then for a moment he rises up, and after that he again, filled with intoxication, rests inside. Then, again, he strives to come out. He continues trying to come out and he gets out briefly but then again he is united inside. This happens again and again and this called "*krama mudrā*".

Self Realization in Kashmir Shaivism, 5.114.

This is an automatic process. It does not come by functioning it. You can't function it . . . *Krama mudrā* is no *mudrā*; *krama mudrā* is automatic . . . [*Krama mudrā* is] just to observe that state of *samādhi* in [the external world] also. When it is not so clearly found outside, go again in *samādhi* and pull it out with that *samādhi* and see in external world again. And again and again, again and again, you have to [experience] this way of *krama mudrā* until [you gain] entry in *jagadānanda*. When *jagadānanda* takes place, then everthing is divine, no [more] *krama mudrā*.

Tantrāloka 3.263-264 (USF archives).

When you are established in the process of *krama mudrā*, then you experience that ecstasy in action. When you eat, you are in that bliss. When you talk, you are in that bliss. When you walk, you are in that bliss. Whatever you do, you remain in that Universal state. This is the state of "*jīvanmukti*", liberated in life. This state is experienced, not by ordinary *yogins*, but only by great *yogins*. This is the real state of *cit kuṇḍalinī*.

In the actual rise of *cit kuṇḍalinī*, you will only get a glimpse of it and then come out. The full rise of *cit kuṇḍalinī* takes place only by the grace of your master and by the grace of your own strength of awareness. The experience of establishing the full rise of *cit kuṇḍalinī* through the process of *krama mudrā* can take place in one day, one life, or one hundred lifetimes.

Kashmir Shaivism–The Secret Supreme, 17.120.

The establishment of *krama mudrā* is called *jagadānanda*, which means "universal bliss" This is the seventh and last state of *turya*. In this state, the experience of the universal transcendental Being is never lost and the whole of the universe is experienced as one with your own transcendental I-consciousness.

Kashmir Shaivism–The Secret Supreme, 16.114.

14. **The Seven Perceivers**

The first state is called *sakala*. The *sakala* state is that state where perception takes place in the objective world and not in the subjective world. In other words, I would call this state the state of *prameya*, the state of the object of perception. It is realized by its *pramātṛ*, the observer who resides in this state, in the field of objectivity and its world.

The second state is called *pralayākala*. This is the state of negation, where the whole world is negated. And the one who resides in this world of negation is called *pralayākala pramātṛ*, the observer of the *pralayākala* state. And this *pramātṛ*, this perceiver, does not experience the state of this voidness because it is actually the state of unawareness. This state would be observed at the time of *mūrcchā*, when one becomes comatose, which is like unnatural and heavy sleep, like deep sleep devoid of dreams. And the observer, *pralayākala pramātṛ*, resides in that void of unawareness.

These two states function in the state of individuality, not in the state of your real nature. These are states of worldly people, not spiritual aspirants.

The third state is called *vijñānākala pramātṛ*. This state is experienced by those who are on the path of *yoga*. Here, the *yogi* experiences awareness at times but this awareness is not active awareness, and at other times his awareness is active but he is not aware of that active awareness. This *vijñānākala pramātṛ*, therefore, takes place in two ways: sometimes it is full of action (*svātantrya*) without awareness and sometimes it is full of awareness without action.

The fourth state of the observer is called *śuddhavidyā* and its observer is called *mantra pramātṛ*. In this state, the observer is always aware with *svātantrya*.

The next state is called *īśvara* and its observer is called *mantreśvara pramātṛ*. The word *mantreśvara* means "the one who has sovereignty on *mantra* (*ahaṁ*–I)". This state is like that of *mantra pramātṛ*, full of consciousness, full of bliss, full of will, full of knowledge, and full of action, however, this is a more stable state. The aspirant finds more stability here. The *mantra* for this state is "*idaṁ-ahaṁ*". The meaning of this *mantra* is that the aspirant feels that this whole universe is not false. On the contrary, he feels that this whole universe is the expansion of his own nature. In the state of *mantra pramātṛ*, he felt that the universe was false, that he was the [only] truth of this reality. Now he unites the state of the universe with the state of his own consciousness. This is actually the unification of *jīva*, the individual, with Śiva, the universal.

The next state is the state of *sadāśiva*. The observer of this state is called *mantra maheśvara*. In this state, the observer finds himself to be absolutely one with the universal transcendental Being. He experiences this state to be more valid, more solid, and deserving of confidence. Once he enters into this state, there is no question at all of falling from it. This is the established state of his Self, his own Real nature. The *mantra* of this state is "*ahaṁ-idaṁ*". The meaning of this *mantra* is, "I am this universe". Here, he finds his Self in the universe, while in the previous state of *mantreśvara*, he found the universe in his Self. This is the difference.

The seventh and last state is the state of Śiva and the observer of this state is no other than Śiva Himself. In the other six, the state is one thing and the observer is something else. In this final state, the state is Śiva and the observer is also Śiva. There is nothing outside Śiva. The *mantra* in this state is "*ahaṁ*", universal-I. This-ness is gone, melted in His I-ness. This state is completely filled with consciousness, bliss, will, knowledge, and action.

Kashmir Shaivism–The Secret Supreme, 8.51-54.

15. ***Malas***

In our Shaiva system, there are three *malas* or impurities. These *malas* reside in *māyā*, they do not reside in *svātantrya śakti*. Even though *svātantrya śakti* and *māyā* are one, yet they are different in the sense that *svātantrya śakti* is that state of energy which can produce the power of going down and coming up again, both at will, whereas *māyā* will only give you the strength of going down and not the ability of rising up again. Once you have come down, you can not move up again. This is the reality of the state of *māyā*. It binds you.

Māyā śakti is that universal energy which is owned by the individual being, the individual soul. And when that same universal energy is owned by the universal Being, it is called *svātantrya śakti*. *Svātantrya śakti* is pure universal energy. Impure universal energy is *māyā*. It is only the formation that changes through a difference of vision. When you experience *svātantrya śakti* in a crooked way, it becomes *māyā śakti* for you. And when you realize that same *māyā śakti* in Reality, then that *māyā śakti* becomes *svātantrya śakti* for you. Therefore, *svātantrya śakti* and *māyā śakti* are actually only one and the three impurities (*malas*), which are to be explained here, reside in *māyā śakti*, not in *svātantrya śakti*.

Kashmir Shaivism–The Secret Supreme, 7.47.

The three impurities (*malas*) are gross (*sthūla*), subtle (*sūkṣma*), and subtlest (*para*). The gross impurity is called *kārmamala*. It is connected with actions. It is that impurity which inserts impressions such as those which are expressed in the statements, "I am happy", "I am not well", "I have pain", "I am a great man", I am really lucky", in the consciousness of the individual being.

The next impurity is called *māyīyamala*. This impurity creates differentiation in one's own consciousness. It is the impurity of ignorance (*avidyā*), the subtle impurity. The thoughts, "This house is mine, that house is not mine", "This man is my friend, that man is my enemy", "She is my wife, she is not my wife", are all created by *māyīyamala*. *Māyīyamala* creates duality.

The third impurity is called *āṇavamala*. It is the subtlest impurity. *Āṇavamala* is the internal impurity of the individual. Although he reaches the nearest state of the consciousness of Śiva, he has no ability to catch hold of that state. That inability is the creation of *āṇavamala*. For example, if you are conscious of your own nature and then that consciousness fades away and fades away quickly, this fading is caused by *āṇavamala*.

Āṇavamala is *apūrṇatā*, non-fullness. It is the feeling of being incomplete. Due to this impurity, you feel incomplete in every way . . . Though you feel incomplete, knowing that there is some lack in you, yet you do not know what this lack really is. You want to hold everything, and yet no matter what you hold, you do not fill your sense of lacking, your gap. You cannot fill this lacking unless the master points it out to you and then carries you to that point.

Of these three impurities, *āṇavamala* and *māyīyamala* are not in action, they are only in perception, in experience. It is *kārmamala* which is in action.

Kashmir Shaivism–The Secret Supreme, 7.47-49.

This whole universal existence, which is admitted by other thinkers that it is ignorance, that it is *māyā* (illusion), that is pain, it is torture–they explain it like that–but we Shaivites don't explain like that. We Shaivites explain that this [universe] is the expansion of your own nature. *Mala* is nothing, *mala* is only your free will of expanding your own nature.

So we have come to this conclusion that *mala* is not a real impurity. It is your own choice, it is the choice of Lord Śiva. The existence of impurity is just the choice of Lord Śiva, it is not some "thing". It is *svarūpa svātantrya māṭraṁ*, it is just your will, just your independent glory.

If you realize that it is *svarūpa svātantrya māṭraṁ*, [that] it is your own play, then what will an impure thing do? An impure thing will only infuse purity in you . . . if you realize that the impurity is not existing at all, it is just your own play, just your own independent expansion.

Mala is neither formless nor with form. It is just ignorance. It doesn't allow knowledge to function–knowledge is stopped. *Mala* is the absence of knowledge. *Mala* is not something substan-

tial. . . . So, this absence of knowledge takes place only by ignorance. . . . Otherwise, there is no *mala*. In the real sense, *mala* does not exist, impurity does not exist.
Tantrāloka, 9.79-83 (USF archives).

16. ***Jagadānanda***
This is the seventh and last state of *turya*. In this state, the experience of universal transcendental Being is never lost, and the whole of the universe is experienced as one with your own transcendental I-consciousness.
Kashmir Shaivism–The Secret Supreme, 16.114.

17. ***Unmīlanā samādhi* and *nimīlanā samādhi***
Nimīlanā samādhi is internal subjective *samādhi*. In your moving through these six states of *turya*, this *samādhi* becomes ever more firm. With the occurrence of *krama mudrā*, *nimīlanā samādhi* is transformed into *unmīlanā samādhi*, which then becomes predominant. This is that state of extraverted *samādhi* where you experience the state of *samādhi* at the same time you are experiencing the objective world. And when *unmīlanā samādhi* becomes fixed and permanent, this is the state of *jagadānanda*.
Kashmir Shaivism–The Secret Supreme, 16.114.

18. **Yogic Powers**
The eight worldly powers are: *aṇimā* (the power to make one's body extremely small), *mahima* (the power to make one's body infinitely large), *garima* (the power to become infinitely heavy), *laghima* (the power to become weightless), *prāpti* (the power to be anywhere), *prākāmya* (the power to achieve any desire), *īśtva* (the power to possess absolute sovereignty), and *vaśitva* (the power to subjugate). [*Editor's note*]

4. *garbhe cittavikaso'viśiṣṭa vidyāsvapnaḥ*

When a yogi's mind is satisfied with the expansive body of illusion, then he falls in the world of differentiated perceptions and his knowledge of Being is just like that of ordinary living beings.

Here, the Sanskrit word "*garbha*" means, that expansive body of the energy of illusion. That is *mahāmāyā*, the great illusive energy of Lord Śiva. The body of illusion that is being referred to are the limited *yogic* powers (e.g., creating divine incense or the materialization of sacred ash to give to disciples, walking on water, flying in air, etc.). All these powers are existing in the sphere of *māyā*. When the *yogi* exhibits the world of limited powers and his mind becomes satisfied and does not move ahead, then for him, his knowledge of being is like the world of dreams–it is not knowledge at all. His knowledge is just the same as the knowledge held by ordinary worldly people. And so, like ordinary living beings, he falls and is established in the world of differentiation with various perceptions and thoughts.

> Those lights in the center of the eyebrows and divine sounds in the center of heart are obstacles for *samādhi*.
> (Pātañjali's *Yoga Sūtra*, 3.37)

Shiva Sutras–The Supreme Awakening, 2.4.87.

The achievement of the state of *yoga* is not the question. The point is achieving the nearness of God. When you are carried near to God, that is enough, that is all. What more do you need? There may not be *yoga* at all, only oneness with God consciousness. That is enough.

So, *māmeva*, he is focused towards Me only. *Nānyat-bhajate*, he does not think of any other things which are concerned with *yoga*, e.g., *aṣṭa siddhi*, the eight great powers of *yoga*. He does not worry for them. He worries only to achieve Me, achieve My personality. He is the greatest *yogi*, *parameśvara saṁāviṣṭaḥ*, because he has got full entry in God consciousness.

So, the *jñāna* (knowledge) of *yoga* with faith and attachment for Lord is the highest knowledge. The knowledge of *yoga* with powers of *yoga* is not the highest. The knowledge of *yoga* with this faith that, "I will be one with Lord Śiva, God consciousness", that is the real *yoga*.

Bhagavad Gītā, 6.49 (USF archives).

19. **Efficacy of *mantra***

"*Oṁ padmani oṁ*", "*Oṁ namaḥ śivāya*", "*Svacchanda*

bhairavāya namaḥ", these sentences are collections of sacred words. Collections of sacred words are not *mantras*, but just a waste of time for the aspirant.

> Those *mantras* which are recited with the lips and with the mind are not really *mantras*. *Devatās* and *Gandharvas*, all these great souls, have deluded themselves in thinking that these are actually *mantras*. And additionally, they are filled with tremendous pride thinking that they are verbally reciting the name of God. (*Sarvajñānottara*, 16–17)

> The life of all *mantras* is solely the energy of God consciousness. When that energy is absent, all those collections of words are useless just like a mass of clouds in the rainless autumn sky. (*Tantra Sadbhāva*)

Shiva Sutra–The Supreme Awakening, 2.1.76.

3. vidyāśarīrasattā mantrarahasyam / /

The secret essence of mantra is the establishment in the body of the knowledge of oneness.

Here, "knowledge" means, the supreme knowledge of oneness. It is, in the real sense, the supreme God who is the formation of the collection of all sounds. It is from this point that all sounds are created and stored. So, in another sense, it is the state of God consciousness that is one with the universe and filled with supreme I-consciousness.

This is the essence of all *mantras*. By the words "essence of all *mantras*" is not meant the *mantras* such as "*Oṁ namaḥ śivāya*", "*Oṁ namo bhagavate vāsudevāya*", etc. These *mantras* are not *mantras* in the real sense. *Mantra*, in the real sense, is that supreme I-consciousness. This is the secret about *mantras*.

Shiva Sutra–The Supreme Awakening, 2.3.80.

20. **Eternal and non-eternal**

In fact, these aspects of Lord Śiva, three aspects (all-pervading, being eternal, and consisting of universal forms, i.e., universality), these three aspects also are not occupied by Lord

Siva because He is [also] not universal, He is [also] not all-pervading, He is [also] not eternal. If He were only all-pervading and not [not-]all-pervading, then not-all-pervadingness would be excluded. . . . So, you can't say that He is all-pervading only. You can't say that He is eternal only. You can't say that He is universal only. He is the negation of the universe also, He is the negation of all-pervadingness also, and He is the negation of universality.

Tantrāloka, 1.66 (USF archives).

21. **Perceiving everything in everything**

Sarvasarvātmakata, take anything–it is full with everything. Take just a particle of just a germ, a small particle of a germ, a minute particle of a germ, which cannot be experienced by your own eyes, but [only] with that [microscope], that small germ, in that small germ, in the body of that small germ, you will find one hundred and eighteen worlds. This is the teaching of *Mālinī*. . . . each and everything existing in this world is filled with everything–nothing is ignored, nothing is outside.

Parātrīśikā Vivaraṇa (USF archives).

22. **No qualifications for receiving Grace**

You never think while showering grace (You never think, *karhicit*). *Prāpta*, but You ought to have thought, You ought to have thought. This "ought" and "never", these two words declare, indicate, *anapekṣitvamūcivān*, this *śaktipāta* . . . is *anapekṣitva*, it does not recognize your qualifications. Qualifications are not recognized there, nor fitness, nor capacity, nor ability–it is not recognized before Him. . . . *Bas*, He [just] showers grace.

Tantrāloka, 13.291 (USF archives).

23. ***Saptadāśī kalā***

[*Saptadāśī kalā*] is the seventeenth *kalā* because this seventeenth *kalā* is above *prameya bhava*, [the field of objectivity]. That sixteenth *kalā* [i.e., *amākalā*] is in *prameya bhāva*. *Kalā saptadaśī tasmāt amṛtākāra rūpiṇī*, [the seventeenth *kalā*] is filled with the formation of nectar.

Tantrāloka, 3.138 (USF archives).

So, when this cognitive world and subjective world is found resting in the objective world, that sixteenfold-ness of the objective world becomes seventeen-fold. It becomes *saptadaśī kalā*, this seventeenth movement. . . . Seventeenth movement is above all. . . . That, in the real sense, is the supreme Goddess, and *yājyā*, [She] is to be adored, to be owned, is to be possessed in oneness.

Parātrīśikā Laghvṛtti, verse 32 with commentary (USF archives).

24. **Three *guṇas***

That individual you can't find in this world–or, right from heaven to this mortal world–you won't find such an individual existing who has not come in the grip of the three *guṇas*. So, everybody, whoever is existing in this world or in the heavens, are entangled in the cycle of three *guṇas*, the three *guṇas* [which are] borne from *prakṛti*.

These three tides of three *guṇas* are, in the real sense, one with God consciousness.

Swami Lakshmanjoo, *Bhagavad Gītā* audio, USF archive.

25. **Nothingness**

"Nothingness" is Lord Śiva because Lord Śiva is not this thing, not that thing. What is Lord Śiva? No thing. No thing is something, something which is not thinkable, inexpressible; which is not felt, which can't be felt; which can't be imagined; which can't be known; which can't be thought. That is "nothing".

Vijñāna Bhairava (USF archives).

When there is no thing, it is full. When there is some thing, it is not full, it is incomplete. This is the way of understanding completion and incompletion. When you are incomplete, you are some thing. When you are complete, you are no thing. No thing is complete, some thing is incomplete.

Tantrāloka, 3.97 (USF archives).

26. **Spanda system**

The fourth system which comprises the Trika philosophy is called the Spanda system. The word "*spanda*" means "movement". The Spanda school recognizes that nothing can exist without movement. Where there is movement, there is life, and where there is no movement, that is lifelessness. They realize that there is movement in wakefulness, dreaming, deep sleep, and *turya*. Though some thinkers argue that there is no movement in deep sleep, the philosophers of the Spanda system realize that nothing can exist without movement.

The teachings of the Spanda system, which is an important practical system, are found embodied in the *Vijñāna Bhairava Tantra*, the *Svacchanda Tantra*, and in the 6th chapter of the *Tantrāloka*.

Kashmir Shaivism–The Secret Supreme, 19.134.

Spanda is nominated as *sphurattā* (vigor, life, life-giver, power of existence), *ūrmiḥ* (tide), *balam* (strength), *udyoga* (force), *hṛdayam* (heart), *sāram* (essence), and *mālinī* (supreme energy). These are nominations which are attributed to this *spanda* in the *śāstras*.

Spanda Saṁdoha of Kṣemarāja, translation and commentary by Swami Lakshmanjoo (original audio recording, USF archives, Los Angeles, 1981).

> The one who is always completely aware to apprehend the essence of *spanda* in each and every movement of life quickly gains entry in God consciousness in the very state of wakefulness.
>
> *Spanda Kārikā*, 1.21

> This universe, which is a world of consciousness, is filled with and is one with the supreme state of God consciousness. God consciousness is *spanda*, a unique reality of supreme movement filled with nectar and an outpouring of the supreme bliss of independence.
>
> *Shiva Sutra–The Supreme Awakening*, 1.9

The element of *spanda* is that Being of God consciousness in which this whole universe exists and from which this whole universe comes out. . . . And [God consciousness] is not only the resting place of the universe, This is the *prasara sthana* also, the flowing energy. This universe comes out from That . . . It *has* to exist in God consciousness and it is coming out from God consciousness *in* God consciousness, because there is no other space for the universe to exist.

Parātrīśikā Vivaraṇa (USF archives).

Bibliography

Swami Lakshmanjoo - Published text

Bhagavad Gita–In the Light of Kashmir Shaivism (with original video), Swami Lakshmanjoo, ed. John Hughes (Universal Shaiva Fellowship, Los Angeles, 2013), xxi, 683.

Kashmir Shaivis– The Secret Supreme, Swami Lakshmanjoo, ed. John Hughes (Universal Shaiva Fellowship, Los Angeles, 1985-2003).

Self Realization in Kashmir Shaivism–The Oral Teachings of Swami Lakshmanjoo, ed. John Hughes (State University of New York Press, Albany, 1995).

Śivastotrāvalī of Utpaladevācaryā With the Sanskrit commentary of Kṣemarāja, edited with Hindi commentary by Rājānaka Lakṣmaṇa (Swami Lakshmanjoo) (Chowkhamba Sanskrit Series 15. Varanasi, 1964).

Shiva Sutras–The Supreme Awakening, Swami Lakshmanjoo, ed. John Hughes (Universal Shaiva Fellowship, Los Angeles, 2002).

Vijñāna Bhairava–The Manual for Self Realization, Swami Lakshmanjoo, ed. John Hughes (Universal Shaiva Fellowship, Los Angeles, 2007).

Swami Lakshmanjoo - Unpublished texts (USF archives)

Bhagavad Gitartha Samgraha of Abhinavagupta, translation and commentary by Swami Lakshmanjoo (original audio recording, USF archives, Los Angeles, 1978).

Interview on Kashmir Shaivism, Swami Lakshmanjoo with Alexis Sanderson and John Hughes (original audio recordings, USF archives, Los Angeles 1980).

Janmamaraṇavicāragranthaḥ, Janma Maraṇa Vicāra of Bhaṭṭa Vāmadeva, Swami Lakshmanjoo (original audio recording, USF archives, Los Angeles, 1980).

Kashmir Shaivism, The Secret Supreme, Swami Lakshmanjoo (original audio recording, USF archives, Los Angeles, 1972).

Paramārthasāra of Abhinavagupta, with the commentary of Yogarāja, translation and commentary by Swami Lakshmanjoo (original video recording, USF archives, Los Angeles, 1990).

Parātriśikā Laghuvṛtti with the commentary of Abhinavagupta, translation and commentary by Swami Lakshmanjoo (original audio recording, USF archives, Los Angeles, 1982).

Parātriśikā Vivaraṇa with the commentary of Abhinavagupta, translation and commentary by Swami Lakshmanjoo (original audio recording, USF archives, Los Angeles, 1982-85).

Śivastotrāvalī of Utpaladeva, translation and commentary by Swami Lakshmanjoo (additional audio recording, USF archives, Los Angeles, 1975-80).

Spanda Kārikā of Vasugupta with the Nirṇaya (commentary) of Kṣemarāja, translation and commentary by Swami Lakshmanjoo (original audio recording, USF archives, Los Angeles, 1975).

Spanda Saṁdoha of Kṣemarāja, translation and commentary by Swami Lakshmanjoo (original audio recording, USF archives, Los Angeles, 1981).

Stava Cintāmaṇi of Bhaṭṭanārāyaṇa, translation and commentary by Swami Lakshmanjoo (original audio recording, USF archives, Los Angeles, 1980-81).

The Tantrāloka of Abhinavagupta, Chapters 1 to 18, translation and commentary by Swami Lakshmanjoo (original audio recording, USF archives, Los Angeles, 1972-1981).

Vātūlanātha Sūtras of Anantaśaktipāda, translation and commentary by Swami Lakshmanjoo (original audio recordings, USF archives, Los Angeles, 1979).

Additional sources – Books

Pratyabhijñāhṛdayam, *The Secret of Self-Recognition*, Sanskrit Text with English Translation, Notes and Introduction by Jaideva Singh (Motilal Banarsidass, Delhi, 1963-2011).

History of Kashmir Shaivism, Dr. B.N. Pandit (Utpala Publications, Srinagar, Kashmir, 1990).

Index

Also by Swami Lakshmanjoo published by The Lakshmanjoo Academy

Bhagavad Gita, In the Light of Kashmir Shaivism

Essence of the Supreme Reality,
Abhinavagupta's Paramarthasara

Vijñāna Bhairava, The Manual for Self Realization

Revelations on Grace and Spiritual Practice

Shiva Sutras, The Supreme Awakening

Kashmir Shaivism, The Secret Supreme

Self Realization in Kashmir Shaivism,
The Oral Teachings of Swami Lakshmanjoo

The teachings of Swami Lakshmanjoo are a response to the urgent need of our time: the transformation of consciousness and the evolution of a more enlightened humanity.

The Universal Shaiva Fellowship and its educational branch, The Lakshmanjoo Academy, a fully accredited non-profit organization, was established under Swamij's direct inspiration, for the purpose of realizing Swamiji's vision of making Kashmir Shaivism available to the whole world. It was Swamiji's wish that his teachings be made available without the restriction of caste, creed or color. The Universal Shaiva Fellowship and the Lakshmanjoo Academy have preserved Swamiji's original teachings and are progressively making these teachings available in book, audio and video formats.

This knowledge is extremely valuable and uplifting for all of humankind. It offers humanity a clear and certain vision in a time of uncertainty. It shows us the way home and gives us the means for its attainment.

For information on Kashmir Shaivism or to support the work of The Universal Shaiva Fellowship and the Lakshmanjoo Academy and its profound consciousness work,

visit the Lakshmanjoo Academy website or

email us at info@LakshmanjooAcademy.org.

www.LakshmanjooAcademy.org

Instructions to download audio files

1. Open this link to download the free audio . . .
   https://www.universalshaivafellowship.org/HymnsToShiva

   It will **direct** you to "**Hymns to Shiva - Audio**".

2. Select "**Add to basket** " which will send you to the next page.

3. Copy "**Hymns**" into the "**Add Gift Certificate or Coupon"** box

4. Click "**Checkout**" and fill in your details to process the free downloads.

If you have any difficulties please contact us at:
www.LakshmanjooAcademy.org/contact

www.ingramcontent.com/pod-product-compliance
Ingram Content Group UK Ltd.
Pitfield, Milton Keynes, MK11 3LW, UK
UKHW021037270726
13967UKWH00013B/2825

9 780981 622835